Critical Dialogues in Southeast Asian Studies

Charles Keyes, *Vicente Rafael*, and *Laurie J. Sears*, Series Editors

Critical Dialogues in Southeast Asian Studies

This series offers perspectives in Southeast Asian Studies that stem from reconsideration of the relationships among scholars, texts, archives, field sites, and subject matter. Volumes in the series feature inquiries into historiography, critical ethnography, colonialism and postcolonialism, nationalism and ethnicity, gender and sexuality, science and technology, politics and society, and literature, drama, and film. A common vision of the series is a belief that area studies scholarship sheds light on shifting contexts and contests over forms of knowing and modes of action that inform cultural politics and shape histories of modernity.

Imagined Ancestries of Vietnamese Communism: Ton Duc Thang and the Politics of History and Memory
by Christoph Giebel

Beginning to Remember: The Past in the Indonesian Present
edited by Mary S. Zurbuchen

Seditious Histories: Contesting Thai and Southeast Asian Pasts
by Craig J. Reynolds

Knowing Southeast Asian Subjects
edited by Laurie J. Sears

Making Fields of Merit: Buddhist Female Ascetics and Gendered Orders in Thailand
by Monica Lindberg Falk

Love, Passion and Patriotism: Sexuality and the Philippine Propaganda Movement, 1882–1892
by Raquel A. G. Reyes

Gathering Leaves and Lifting Words: Histories of Buddhist Monastic Education in Laos and Thailand
by Justin Thomas McDaniel

Justin Thomas McDaniel

Gathering Leaves & Lifting Words

Histories of Buddhist Monastic Education in Laos and Thailand

University of Washington Press *Seattle & London*

This book is published with the assistance of a grant from the Charles and Jane Keyes Endowment for Books on Southeast Asia, established through the generosity of Charles and Jane Keyes.

Printed in the United States of America
Designed by Thomas Eykemans
13 12 11 10 09 08 5 4 3 2 1

UNIVERSITY OF WASHINGTON PRESS
PO Box 50096, Seattle, WA 98145
www.washington.edu/uwpress

The paper used in this publication is acid-free and 90 percent recycled from at least 50 percent post-consumer waste. It meets the minimum requirements of American National Standard for Information Sciences—Permanence of Paper for Printed Library Materials, ANSI Z39.48–1984.

LIBRARY OF CONGRESS
CATALOGING-IN-PUBLICATION DATA

McDaniel, Justin.
Gathering leaves and lifting words : histories of Buddhist Monastic education in Laos and Thailand / Justin McDaniel.
p. cm. — (Critical dialogues in Southeast Asian studies)
Includes bibliographical references and index.
ISBN 978-0-295-98848-1 (hardback : alk. paper)—ISBN 978-0-295-98849-8 (pbk. : alk. paper)
1. Buddhism—Study and teaching—Laos—History. 2. Buddhism—Study and teaching—Thailand—History. 3. Buddhist monks—Education—Laos—History. 4. Buddhist monks—Education—Thailand—History. I. Title.
BQ162.L28M33 2008
294.3'7509593—dc22

2008006065

For Christine, Henry, and Jane

We hibernate among the bricks
and live across the window panes . . .
indifferent to what the wind does
indifferent to sudden rains
softening last year's garden plots
and apathetic, with cigars
careless
while down the street the spring goes
inspiring mouldy flowerpots
and broken flutes at garret windows.

T. S. Eliot (1911)

Contents

Acknowledgments *ix*

Note on Transcription *xii*

Introduction 3

PART I STRUCTURAL MECHANISMS
The Institutional History of Monastic Education

1 From the Sala Vat to the Institut Bouddhique 25

2 Wandering Librarians 69

3 Kings and Universities 92

PART II PROXIMATE MECHANISMS
Toward a Curricular History of Monastic Education

4 Genres, Modes, and Idiosyncratic Articulations 119

5 The Culture of Translation 161

6 Canons and Curricula 191

PART III VERNACULAR LANDSCAPES
Teaching Buddhism in Laos and Thailand

7 From Manuscript to Television 207

8 Philosophical Embryology 228

Conclusion 247

Notes 259

Note on Manuscripts, Archives, Monastic Libraries, and Catalogs 313

Bibliography 317

Index 347

Acknowledgments

In his diaries, Christopher Isherwood sums up his adopted home of Southern California by stating simply that "the architecture is dominated by vegetation." If this book is the architecture, then my colleagues and mentors are the vegetation. Their insight and guidance have enlivened and enveloped each sentence, paragraph, and chapter. My ideas are intertwined with their criticisms and questions. They pulled the ideas up. They softened and shaped the prose.

Specifically, I was encouraged early in my research by Damrongsak and Anong Suksuksiang, Prapod Assavavirulhakarn, Suchitra Chongstitvatana, Carol Petillo, Malai Prachathorn, Dhida Saraya, Suwanna Satha-Anand, Michael Collins, and Bualy Paphaphanh. Studying with them in Philadelphia, Boston, Laos, and Thailand led me to undertake this project. Prapod and Suchitra, in particular, were always available to answer questions and correct my readings of texts. I have continually sought out their advice, borrowed their books, stayed in their homes, and eaten their food.

Dissertation research started with the inspiration of Oskar von Hinüber and Charles Hallisey, who encouraged me to undertake a study of *nissaya* manuscripts in Northern Thailand. I already had experience as a teacher in monasteries in the region; they showed me how to combine ethnographic experience with philological investigation. The former read my 2003 dissertation closely and clarified my argument and corrected my mistakes. For their time and patience in discussing my dissertation, I also thank my teachers at Harvard University, especially Stephanie Jamison, Leonard van der Kuijp, James Russell, and Robert Gimello.

I received generous research funding from the Fulbright program, the Social Science Research Council, the Department of State, Chulalongkorn

University, Harvard University, Ohio University, and the University of California, Riverside.

In archives and monastic libraries in Europe and Southeast Asia, I was supported and often taken to lunches by Monique Cohen, Balee Buddharaksa, Thong Xeuy, Kongdeuane Nettavong, Harald Hundius, and dozens of helpful novices and monks at Vat Mai, Vat Xainyaphum, Vat Naxai, Vat Nom Lam Chan, Vat Ong Teu, Vat Inpeng, Vat Xiangthong, Wat Lai Hin, Wat Sung Men, Wat Nong Bua, Wat Phra That Lampang Luang, Wat Rampoeng, Wat Phra Singh, and Wat Suan Dok, among many others. Without their help in finding, cleaning, and reading manuscripts, this project would have never emerged.

As the dissertation grew into a book, I realized that I still had much to learn about the way *nissaya* manuscripts structured and sustained the oral and textual modes of expression in Buddhist Laos and Thailand. I was guided here by Bounteum Sibounheuang, Louis Gabaude, Michel Lorrillard, Harald Hundius, Phra Prasoet, François Lagirarde, and Renoo Wichasin. I benefited greatly from conversations with Phra Sugandha and Arthid Sheravanichkul and often found myself rewriting entire chapters in my head while listening to their views all and sundry. Phra Sompong Mudito guided me through some difficult Pali passages and helped me to understand modern changes in monastic education. In particular, Peter Skilling tirelessly tolerated my persistent questions, my poor grammar, and my constant requests to borrow a book or steal an idea. He always had a plate of mangos and a joke to lighten the mood.

In the editing stage I was helped by the close reading and criticisms of Peter Skilling, Grant Evans, Thomas Bugos, Jacques Leider, Anne Blackburn, Thomas Borchert, Michael Jerryson, Edward Miller, Jeffrey Samuels, Daniel Veidlinger, and my closest friend and toughest critic, Matthew Wheeler. David Chandler and Anne Hansen must be credited with helping me structure the entire book. Other scholars who I pestered with questions and always received great help from include Ruang Sasithorn, Pattaratorn Chirapravati, Rujaya Abhakorn, Michael Montesano, Bernard Faure, Robert Sharf, Mark Allon, Chalong Soontravanich, Filemon Gemil, David Wharton, Maria Heim, Kannikar Satraproong, Henk Maier, Michael Feener, David Biggs, Andrew Jacobs, José Cabezón, Christian Lammerts,

Sunait Chutintaranont, Penny Edwards, Richard Gombrich, Gregory Miller, Charles Genuardi, Vesna Wallace, Avery Wright, Erik Braun, Jeffrey Shane, George Weckman, Elizabeth Collins, Maitrii Aung-Twin, James McHugh, Rita Langer, Rupert Gethin, Thongchai Winitchakul, Alexander von Rospatt, Patrice Ladwig, Eric Beverley, Alexander Keefe, Michael Keogh, Robert Briscoe, Firmin and Yara Debrabander, Carol Compton, Peter Koret, Chonlada Reuangruglikit, Kate Crosby, John Hartmann, Caverlee Cary, Tamara Loos, Phi Somneuk, and many others. Craig Reynolds and William Pruitt greatly improved the style of the book. I value their friendship and honest criticism. The entire manuscript was read closely by Steven Collins, whose acerbic wit and eye for detail made me stop and rethink the entire project at several important junctures. Simply, Luang Pho Sombun is my preceptor, and Donald Swearer is my *achan*.

I value the comments of the external readers. The editors at the University of Washington Press, Michael Duckworth, Charles Keyes, Laurie Sears, Vicente Rafael, Mary Ribesky, and Jane Lichty, were supportive at every stage of the publishing process. My colleagues at Ohio University and the University of California, Riverside, put up with my hermit-like ways while I was writing. The questions and comments of my students have humbled and delighted me. They make me love my job and the creeping vegetation of my adopted home of Southern California.

Finally, this book could not have been written without the warmth of my brother, Garvan; my sister-in-law, Monica; my in-laws, Wendy and Thomas; and my extended family in Ireland and North America. My dear parents, Adelene and Thomas, taught me how to read and, most important, laugh. Readers concerned with the play-dough and juice stains on any pages of this book can blame my son, Henry, who has grown up among manuscripts and his father's exhaustion and has reminded me that neither matters much during playtime. As this book entered press, Jane was just starting to open her bright eyes. Christine has wasted a perfectly good life on me. I owe her much more than words and ink.

Note on Transcription

Anyone in the field of Lao and Thai studies knows that transcription and transliteration is a complicated and contested issue. I have geared the transcription system to a general audience without advanced skills in Khoen, Lao, Leu, Pali, Thai, Sanskrit, or Yuan. Experts will disagree over the importance of phonetic accuracy versus international conformity. I have attempted to be simple and consistent, but the texts I translate are often inconsistent. Unpredictable phonetic and morphological changes abound. Orthographic inconsistency reigns especially in manuscripts (see chapter 4). Practically, there is no generally accepted system of transcribing Lao. However, I follow the advice of Grant Evans and follow the American National Standards Institute in its *System for the Romanization of Lao, Khmer, and Pali*, published in 1979. This system avoids, as much as possible, the use of special diacritical marks and is useful because it is the one used by international library catalogs. Alongside a few other minor changes for proper names, like Evans, I use the French transcription "X" for most renderings of the letter s, since many foreign readers are familiar with French maps, signs, colonial documents, and secondary sources. For Thai, I follow with minor exceptions the Royal Institute's *Romanization Guide for Thai Script* (Bangkok, April 1968), which also elides most diacritical marks for easy reading. This closely follows international library standards. Pali transcription is now relatively consistent internationally. This book includes the many hybrid Sanskrit-Thai and Pali-Thai words in Thai and Lao (although there are considerably fewer in Lao and the Lao script has gone through some major re-standardizations over the past century to remove or simplify Sanskrit and Pali spellings). This often accords with Lao and Thai spellings, but not pronunciation. This system is not useful for Lao and Thai linguists and philologists; however, they are trained in the various local scripts.

I avoid the International Phonetic Alphabet and the Thai "graphic" system, so phonetically and phonemically it is not completely accurate, but it is clear and "unornamented" for the general reader. I follow the standard *Critical Pali Dictionary* (*CPD*) (Helmer Smith, *Critical Pali Dictionary, Epilogomena to Vol. 1* [Copenhagen, 1948]) used by the Pali Text Society. For Yuan, Leu, Shan, and other Thai scripts used in manuscripts cited in this book, I follow the Kasem Siriratphiriya's comprehensive *Tua Muang* (Sukhothai, Thailand, 2549 [2006]), which is consistent in its transliteration from these various scripts to Central Thai script. There are too many script guides to list. I refer to some intertextuality. For Tham script in Laos I follow the transcription system for Tham into Lao first developed by Phay Luang Maha Sena Phouy, *Méthode d'enseignment élémentaire du Laotien pour apprendre a lire les caractères Tham dans les textes Palis* (Vientiane, Laos: Institut bouddhique, 1934). Most of the manuscripts I use in this study are bi- or trilingual, but the scribe often renders these different languages in a single script; I follow the manuscript and transcribe the two to three languages in one manuscript according to the *CPD* system. When there are letters not found in Pali, I follow François Lagirarde and François Bizot's system developed in 1996 (see bibliography) and generally followed by École française d'Extrême-Orient publications today with minor adaptations. I provide a script chart for this system in McDaniel, "Invoking the Source: Nissaya Manuscripts, Pedagogy, and Sermon-Making in Northern Thailand and Laos" (2003). This allows the reader a chance to see, as much as can be done in roman script, the way a scribe saw and heard these languages. Since the scribe often did not distinguish, in script or other markers, when he was switching between Pali and Lao or Pali and Tai Yuan, and so forth, I do not distinguish them in citations. In this way, readers of the vernaculars and Pali will better be able to see how Pali was rendered and how authors created cognates in the various vernaculars. Certain Pali terms and Lao and Thai names for places and people, like Buddha, Supaphan na Bangchang, Lampang, dhamma, sangha, Chiang Mai, Luang Pho, nibbana, Mahathat, Vientiane, and Chulalongkorn, have become well known without diacritical marks and are even included in some dictionaries in English and French. I follow Standard English spellings for them throughout. Unless otherwise noted, all translations are mine.

Gathering Leaves & Lifting Words

Introduction

A few years ago, at a monastery in Laos, I spent some time looking for a key. The monastery, Vat Xainyaphum, sits on the banks of the Mekong River, and on its grounds is the largest monastic school in Laos.[1] I wanted the key to open an old wooden cabinet in a small office on the upper floor of the main classroom building, where, I imagined, the textbooks used at the school would be kept. The key was not easy to find. Several of the monks I spoke with claimed they had never seen it. A lay administrator and part-time math teacher swore she had seen it the week before and begged me to wait while she sent a young novice monk to find another teacher, who was in his monastic cell resting and who, she claimed, probably had it. An hour later the novice appeared. No luck. Another young novice suggested we use a knife. A heavy-set monk named Suman suggested I come back another day. When I politely told him that I would wait, he responded, "Well, why not come to my class?" The key, he asserted, "would surely turn up."

I stuck out in the class, as I was the only person not wearing saffron-colored robes and my head was not freshly shaven. I was also much older than the students, most of who were in their late teens. However, I could follow the lecture well since it was on the life of the Buddha and seemed to be drawing from the *Jātaka-nidāna*, a biography of the Buddha that introduces a collection of stories describing the Buddha's past lives. The text was originally composed in the classical Pali language, but the lecture was in vernacular Lao and based on a Lao summary of the Buddha's life called the *Buddhabavat*.

The teacher used the common practice of *yok sab*, or "lifting [Pali] words" from the story and then explaining the words in Lao. He often went off on tangents and compared the Buddha's life to that of famous heroes from Lao folktales or to previous Buddhas. He mentioned a *jātaka* tale about the importance of leaving one's family to ordain and compared it to the Buddha leaving his wife to become an ascetic. (I assume this was the story of Revata.) He also discussed the importance of being aware of one's desires as the Buddha was aware of the armies of Māra, the tempter. He skipped long sections of the Buddha's life from the *nidāna*, but the outline of the story was intact.

The choice of Pali words "to lift" seemed idiosyncratic. For example, he explained the word *carati* (he walks) in Lao, but not *viharati* (he resides), and gave a Lao rendering of dhamma (*Phra Tham*), which surely every novice monk understood, but not of the lesser-known word *miga* (wild animal). Many students took notes vigorously, trying to copy every word. Sometimes two students would share one notebook. Many doodled; one student whispered to me to borrow a pen. One student was hiding a biology textbook underneath his notebook and studying for another class. After the short lesson the teacher asked students to come up front and recite their notes from the previous class. After each class, he told me, they had to memorize their notes and then recite them to the others. He listened and made corrections as they spoke. After each student recited his notes, usually while fidgeting and constantly readjusting his robe, the teacher sought volunteers to ask the presenter a question. At first the questions were relatively basic—"Where was the Buddha born?" and "Who did the Buddha first teach?"—but as easy questions were exhausted others asked, "How do you say *kāma* (desire) in Lao?" "What was the name of the Buddha before Gotama?" and "How do you say *anatta* (no-self) in Lao?" The teacher helped answer a couple questions, joked that the bad students were embarrassing themselves in front of the *falang* (foreigner), and then closed his own notebook.

After class, I asked to look at this notebook and found that it was a series of Pali words and notes about their meaning in Lao, along with some side notes. He told me that the source of the information came partly from a previous teacher named Sompon, who had died ten years previously, and partly from "ancient" (*bolān*) Lao manuscripts of the *jātaka*. I looked quickly but had to give the notebook back because it was to be used by another teacher in another class for younger students. It was very important and could not be lost, as it was the only copy. That is why students had to listen closely and take good notes.

I went back to the office to wait for the key, which finally turned up. It had been at the home of a former administrator who had stopped coming to work a few months previously. I was told that he had gotten a job as a merchant of some sort and now spent a lot of time across the river in Thailand trading in the market. So after three hours of waiting I unlocked the cabinet to find that all it contained was several copies of the first volume of a textbook on Pali grammar originally composed by Mahasila Viravong in 1960 and printed by the Lao Ministry of Education in 1998 with the help of French scholars. It seemed never to have been assigned for a class or consulted by a teacher at the school, indeed never to have been used at all, since the binding was not cracked.

There were no canonical texts in Pali or vernacular translations at the school. The Buddhist curriculum for the school was based solely on handwritten notebooks such as those used by Venerable Suman. After talking with some other teachers and students and attending a sermon at the main monastery next to the school, I went back to my hotel on the river, lamenting a wasted day in search of a key to nothing. The books in the cabinet, it seems, were much the same as the cabinet that held them: unused pieces of furniture inside a larger piece of furniture that was rarely unlocked. By now, perhaps, the key I disturbed from its slumber has slipped behind a desk onto the floor or has been taken home by a well-intentioned monk and placed in a chest or in a jar on a table, never to be found again. It will not be missed.

As a scholar of Buddhism in Laos and Thailand I have been trained to read Pali palm-leaf manuscripts inscribed in a wide variety of scripts and languages. I have spent the past several years in monastic libraries, in Lao and Thai government and university archives, and in French, British, and American manuscript collections, translating and describing hundreds of Pali, Lao, Thai, Leu, Khoen, and Shan palm leaves. As a graduate student I was trained in Indic philology and grammar—in reading Sanskrit and Pali canonical and commentarial texts to supplement my vernacular skills. However, sitting in that class at Vat Xainyaphum, I realized that my study of texts was only partially useful in understanding Buddhist education in Laos and Thailand. In studying Pali and Sanskrit I had been studying "language" and not "languaging." The difference is great. As Alton Becker writes, "A *language* is a system of rules or structures, which . . . relates meanings and sounds, both of which are outside of it. A language is essentially a dictionary and a grammar. *Languaging*, on the other hand, is context shaping. Languaging both shapes and is shaped by context. It is a kind of attunement between a person and a context. Languaging can be understood as taking old texts from memory and reshaping them into present contexts. . . . It is done at the level of particularity."[2] This is what the students and the teachers were doing; they were languaging Pali. They were not learning the Pali language.

I had set out to study the manuscripts, generally called *nissaya* (support), used by monastic teachers in the premodern period (the sixteenth to the nineteenth centuries), hoping to be the first scholar to define the Buddhist monastic curriculum of the region through these texts. What I found was much more. It has helped me to redefine my idea not only of "language" and "languaging" but also of the larger context in which languaging happens—"curriculum." Curricula are intertextual. Curricula put texts into different contexts. They bring together texts and oral performance in a dynamic context of teaching and learning, a developing process of negotiation between teachers and students, canon and commentaries, classical and vernacular, oral and written, physical and intellectual, aesthetic and ethical, secular and religious. The manuscripts I read, just like the notebook used by the teacher at Vat Xainyaphum, existed in a network of relationships between local Lao monks and manuscripts in Pali and Lao. The monastic students of the sixteenth century developed these traditions through copying, adapting, memorizing, reciting, questioning, and answering, just as students of the third millennium continue to do.

In retrospect, I should not have been surprised by the lack of "official" textbooks at the monastic school or by the importance of an old, tattered notebook. Eight years previously, after I had been living in Thailand for two years, I ordained as a monk at a small monastery on the border of Thailand and Laos near the Mekong. My abbot was a Lao speaker, and my fellow monks were young men from northern Cambodia, Laos, and Northeastern Thailand. There was an ascetic *maechi* (nun) who lived at the far end of the monastery. Like most, our monastery did not have an official school, but we received sermons from our abbot and were asked to memorize hundreds of pages of prayers and incantations to use in chanting and in performing weddings, funerals, and protective rites. A full set of the Pali canon, printed in Bangkok, had been donated to the monastery three years earlier, but it had not been removed from its plastic wrap. Most reading material at the monastery was in the form of prayer manuals, anthologies of sermons by famous monks, a few Pali grammar textbooks, several copies of the *Nithan Thammabot* (sermons based on some stories drawn from the commentarial *Dhammapada-atthakathā*), the *Abhidhamma chet kamphi*, and many works on the advantages (*ānisaṃsa*, "blessings") to be derived from doing various things. There was also a notebook used by my abbot to prepare sermons. Instruction, besides meditation and memorization of important liturgical and magical texts, was based largely on our abbot teaching us the meaning of important Pali terms and telling us the history of the righteous acts of previous teachers. On Sundays, I would paddle a canoe downriver to teach English in a similar way to novices at another local monastery. Since I did not have any materials, I wrote English words on the portable blackboard in the open-air classroom and explained them in Lao. Students were asked to conduct English conversations in front of the class using these new vocabulary words. More time was spent laughing and asking, "How do you say that again?" than in actual learning of English. All the better, I suppose.

As monastic teachers, Suman at Vat Xainyaphum, my abbot and I had more in common than just our robes. We all taught by "lifting words," the primary pedagogical method of Buddhist monks and a practice ubiquitous in Thailand and Laos. It is seen in premodern palm-leaf manuscripts and in modern lecture notes, mass-produced teachers' guides, and in sermons. Pali words are lifted from texts, both canonical and noncanonical, and then creatively engaged with and explained by teachers based on their own experiences. This method, and the texts and teachers who employ it over time, has never been studied, but to understand the history and teachings of Buddhism in Southeast Asia one must start with how Buddhists teach Buddhists to be Buddhists, and it is only by understanding this method and the texts that reveal it that one can begin to do so. Discovering which words are lifted from which texts will illuminate the interpretative communities, reading cultures, action-oriented pedagogies, and practical canons of Laos and Northern Thailand between the sixteenth century and the present.

The study of lifting words as a Buddhist pedagogical method, as a means of seeing texts in their living context, is a first step toward the most general aim of this book, which is to establish "curriculum" as an interpretative category for the history of religions and for Southeast Asian studies. Instead of studying the books of canonical, pan-Asian, Buddhism, I examine how local teachers gathered palm-leaf manuscripts to create their own curricula. A close look at a local curriculum reveals the contours of local meaning-making and religious memory. Particular communities at particular times have gathered local stories, an idiosyncratic collection of "ancient" texts (which themselves are evolving repositories of a whole range of other local and translocal texts), and memories of their teachers' words. These sources have created curricula that attempt to preserve both this memory and these texts according to contemporary needs. Instead of describing "Buddhism" in the region, I am interested in how knowledge locally referred to as "Buddhist" has been formed and transmitted. How has this living episteme been transmitted from teacher to student? To explore the curriculum of a particular religious community at a particular time and place is to look at its pedagogical methods, textual resources, physical practices, and educational structures, as well as at the relationship between the ideal religious authorities of the past and the constantly evolving lives of exegetes, pedagogues, and novice consumers. By tracking changes over time the sociohistorical forces that affect the way religious groups educate themselves and their society are apparent. In addition, I look at differences between official religious canons of scripture and actual curricula and at the uses of classical and vernacular languages in education, attempting to trace changes between premodern and modern educational developments. The category of curriculum in fact allows one to study religious communities and their literature beyond dichotomies such as classical-vernacular, canonical-commentarial, liturgical-analytical, and past-present. It allows one to move beyond the recording of descriptive taxonomies and nomenclature. Texts, whether palm-leaf manuscripts or printed textbooks, are polyvalent parts of a curriculum, rather than simply parts of a canon, liturgy, library, or reference collection, and they exist in a context of relationships between orality and textuality, temporality and timeless authority, lay life and monastic life, the local and the translocal. A curriculum both constitutes and reacts to the cultural and historical forces of a particular time. It changes according to the needs of the students and teachers, as a space where normative ethics, authority, and interpretations are challenged and new forms created. One cannot study the vicissitudes in a religious community unless one studies its forms of education, and any study of education must begin with a mapping and analysis of curriculum.

To this end, this book looks at the *nissaya*, *vohāra*, and *nāmasadda* genres of manuscripts. These genres are uniquely useful because they reveal the source texts that were deemed important for instruction in a monastic context in a particular place at a particular time. They enable one to define the interpretative communities of Northern Thailand and Laos across time and space better than do less accurate designations like "canon," "sect," "Pali," "Theravada," "Northern Thai," or "Lao." They are genres that demand and bring about a certain way of reading, writing, teaching, and learning. Here I adopt William Johnson's term "reading culture," derived from his study of Roman practices of reading and writing. What, he asks, is the "sociocultural context in which reading takes place"? What are the "communicative practices" of a particular textual community? What are the traditions of reading and writing? He looks at the reader's "stance towards . . . material informed by scholastic traditions, some peculiar to the institution [in the present case a Buddhist monastery] . . . informed by a set of inherited, that is, trained dispositions (such as attention to inter-textual references, or appreciation for certain aesthetic characteristics)." Reading, he emphasizes, is a

> highly complex socio-cultural system that involves a great many considerations beyond the decoding by the reader of the words of a text. Critical is the observation that reading is not simply the cognitive process by the individual of the "technology" of the writing, but rather the negotiated construction of meaning. . . . [T]his has far less to do with cognition than with the construction of a particular reading community, one which validates itself through texts deemed important to a shared sense of culture and cultural attainment.[3]

The study of reading cultures and interpretative communities can be seen as similar to David Biggs's and J. B. Jackson's studies of "vernacular landscapes."[4] Although they refer to the experience of people living in a community in environmental history, I use this term to signify a study of the everyday schooling experience versus the study of the politico-administrative accoutrement of education. Vernacular landscapes are messier and more idiosyncratic. They change because of local need, not national and transnational efforts to control. In order to understand the vernacular landscape of Northern Thailand and Laos in this period, one must first look at the manuscripts in detail to see how they were composed, in what context, for what purpose, with what technology, by whom and for whom, and then move on to see the larger practices of reading, writing, teaching, and learning through historical investigation of monasteries, economies, politics, and libraries. From there one can look at the methods and the changing media that were used to convey the information in these texts. This approach makes clear how a study of *nissaya*, *vohāra*, and *nāmasadda* manuscripts and the methods used to teach them can provide information on educational history, as well as on curriculum development, pedagogical methods, and homiletics. Moreover, the study of these pedagogical manuscripts reveals the relationship between the vernacular and classical, such that the study of educational history becomes a study of rhetoric, pedagogy, creative expression, and epistemology and not a history of institutions, a litany of sects, and a catalog of canonical and noncanonical texts. Therefore, this is a study not of texts but of interpretative communities, both diachronically and synchronically.

Michel de Certeau and Roger Chartier explore the relationships created between the text, the reader, and the audience over time. I believe that this relationship is congruent with the relationships formed between the reader and the text when teaching. I approach Buddhist texts following de Certeau by taking into consideration both the *espaces lisibles* (discursive and material forms of texts) and their *effectuation* (procedures of interpretation in changing contexts). He writes that, "whether it is a question of newspapers or Proust, the text has meaning only through its readers; it changes along with them; it is ordered in accord with codes of perception that it does not control. It becomes a text only in relation to the exteriority of the reader, by an interplay of implications and ruses between two sorts of 'expectation' in combination."[5] To this Chartier adds: "The dialectic [when reading and I would argue teaching] between imposition and appropriation, between constraints transgressed and freedoms bridled, is not the same in all places or all times or for all people. Recognizing its diverse modalities and multiple variations is the first aim of a history of reading that strives to grasp—in all their differences—communities of readers and their 'arts of reading.'"[6] A community's curriculum incorporates not only what its members read but also how they read and convey it. The art of reading is part of the larger art of teaching. This textual-oral interaction is the work of an interpretative community.

The common division between secular and religious literature is unhelpful when reading these texts and tracing these communities.[7] Even though the modern period has seen a greater departmentalization of monastic education, partly due to influences from Japan, the West, and Central Thailand, today as in the premodern period education is not divided along what outsiders might call religious-secular lines. Formal courses, specifically in mathematics, biology, foreign languages, and communications, are part of the monastic university curriculum in Northern Thailand, but they are taken alongside religious courses, and in monastic high schools the division is even less pronounced. Buddhist courses on Abhidhamma, which emphasize philosophical and psychological analysis, also include biological material, because that analysis intimately connects mind and body. Pali and Sanskrit language courses often concentrate on the use of Pali words for sermon giving, ritual use, and chanting, but they are also designed to teach grammar. Ethics courses discuss government policy, and lessons from the *jātaka* are part of communications courses. The English grammar textbooks at monastic colleges in Vientiane and Chiang Mai instruct young students how to teach Buddhist concepts in English, and they use examples like "The Buddha taught the Dhamma" instead of "See Spot run." In the premodern period manuscripts on medicine, myth (romances and adventures), astronomy, magic, history, grammar, and animal husbandry are found in the same collections (and occasionally bound together in one manuscript) with those on religious subjects such as monastic discipline (how to wear robes, eat, address a senior monk, etc.), moralistic narrative, meditation instruction, and protective ritual. Furthermore, it is debatable whether specific subject areas like astronomy, protective magic, monastic discipline, Pali grammar, and mythological stories are easily called either "religious" or "secular." These subjects have always been central to monastic education, which was and is an organic education that teaches the whole person a number of secular and religious skills combined.

The vernacular landscapes constructed by interpretative communities and reading cultures, whether they are called secular or religious, are not simply cerebral expressions and intellectual groupings. Education is not simply reading texts. There are physical, economic, social, and aesthetic dimensions to monastic education. Economically and socially monkhood offers access to prestige and free education. It exposes young, highly localized men to a world where monks travel and often become involved in translocal, mobile intellectual communities. Moreover, monks do not just study and converse with teachers about texts. Monks sweep, clean, eat, chant, prostrate, shave, meditate, dress, and walk in restrictive and formal ways. A central aspect of a monk's education is to learn to imitate the "look" of a monk. Physical and aesthetic awareness and discipline are complimentary to textual study, memorization, ritual specificity, and concentration. Jeffrey Samuels's observations of Sri Lankan Theravadin monastic students emphasize that monks often learn more from doing and memorizing than from reading. He calls this "action-oriented pedagogy." Through these repetitive actions and mimicry of more senior monks, these students become "ritualized" agents. He writes that "despite the fact that novices memorized texts and verses, their learning about what it means to be a monastic and how a monastic should act did not necessarily come from learning the content of the texts; instead . . . [a]ction, in short, functioned to mold the bodies and minds of the novices."[8] Evidence from *nissaya* and other texts, as well as observational evidence, demonstrates that the content of many canonical and non-canonical texts is important for more than memorization in the Lao and Northern Thai contexts for novices, laity, nuns, and monks. Samuels nonetheless makes an important contribution. This approach could also be expanded to include the physical practice of copying texts and delivering sermons.

The importance of the visual, the kinesthetic, and the affective sides of text-based education is often ignored. Texts are delivered, in parts or wholes, orally. Murals, images, incense, and candles flank the lecturer/preacher, who shifts his feet and occasionally coughs. Texts are not just read but are heard in a cacophonous sensory atmosphere. For example, Bounteum Sibounheuang, a professor at the Monastic College in Vientiane, told me that many monks learn from performances of Buddhist and "secular" narratives like the *Vessantara jātaka* (*Phra Vet*) and from stories told through music and dance. Thong Xeuy of the National Library of Laos told me that in the 1960s he studied for many years in monasteries in Savannakhet and Vientiane and that it was the "example" of his teacher—the way he spoke, wore his robe, kept his room, and spoke with the laity—that taught him how to be a good monk. In Thailand, Thamrongsak Suksuksiang, a former monk from Ayutthaya and now a high school physics teacher, said that he did not learn much Buddhist history or Pali language as a monk, but even years after disrobing he could remember how to perform protective rituals, draw protective diagrams (*phra yan*), and chant at a wide range of rituals. Temple murals, which most often depict local interpretations of *jātaka* and local historical events, are often used by monks to teach. The different images of the Buddha, monks, and deities in different poses and holding different symbols can also be "visual aids" for creative teachers. Even decomposing corpses or photographs of these corpses are implements used to teach impermanence and compassion. In Phrae (Northern Thailand), a young monk named Athit jokingly told me that he learned how to be a good monk from his mother. It is funny, he said, she knew more about the proper life of a monk by watching her sons and other local monks and novices than they seemed to know. She could spot when they had trouble chanting, when they did not know how to wear their robes properly, and when they were sleeping instead of meditating. These extended textual morphologies inform students and are, in a sense, curricular.

Texts are central to monastic education, but texts are not stable objects. Instead they reveal relationships between author and reader, reciter and audience, and teacher and student. They also reveal changing patterns of interpretation, trends in rhetorical style, and pedagogical methodology. The source texts of a curriculum also reveal, in part, what constitute the values of a good Buddhist in the region. They convey what a good Buddhist ideally should know in a particular community. Since the most common texts in the curriculum are protective rituals, ethical tales with a good bit of romantic liaisons and adventurous escapades, and monastic rule books, one can surmise that teachers, students, and lay audiences valued, quite naturally, protection from sickness, poverty, and disaster, as well as order and predictability. Moreover, the narratives reveal that entertainment and ethical stories set on quotidian themes (e.g., family drama, romance, and travel) were popular. The values of altruism and etiquette are emphasized as ways of accruing merit for favorable rebirths instead of nirvana. Most of my students in Buddhism courses in the United States are interested in meditation and enlightenment. Many scholars of Buddhist studies are concerned with textual history, textual integrity, provenance, and dating, as well as philosophical and ethical coherence. However, these do not seem to be the primary concerns of educators in premodern and modern Laos and Thailand. Order was valued over tradition, safety and wealth over emptiness and asceticism, and ritual technology over meditational achievement. Looking at the source texts of monastic education forces one to consider what local Buddhist communities valued, instead of assuming that every community, East and West, premodern and modern, saw the teachings of the Buddha as valuable for the same reasons.

The incongruity in notions of what makes a good Buddhist can be partly blamed on the fact that the history of Buddhist interpretative communities and reading cultures in Southeast Asia has been written through the "canon." The texts contained in the *Three Baskets* (Tipiṭaka / Pali canon) were listed in their present form at least as long ago as the fifth century by the great scholar-commentator Buddhaghosa. In the nineteenth and early twentieth centuries European and Asian scholars mistakenly took this bibliographical categorization to be a sociohistorical fact. It was assumed that the canon represented the oldest and hence, it was generally assumed, truest teachings of the Buddha. This Western, modernist reification of the canon and the Pali language in which it was composed has had ramifications for educational practices and textual sources used in monastic instruction in Southeast Asia. Recently, however, there has been a paradigm shift in this understanding of the canon, because many have observed that the ideal canon is rarely taught, read, or even known by the vast majority of Buddhists in the region. In 1917 Louis Finot noticed that no Lao monasteries possessed an entire set of the canon and most texts were ritual guides and vernacular stories.[9]

Scholars have responded to Finot's observation in various ways. In order to add to this discussion, I want to emphasize the use of the term *curriculum*, hoping to provide a new way to define "canonicity" and to expand the idea of a "practical canon" by focusing on which Pali texts were most commonly translated and used in educational settings and how they were used. The pedagogical purpose of texts in Laos and Northern Thailand is revealed by the choice of the texts the authors chose to translate and comment on and by the semantic content of the stories and ritual instructions themselves. While certain Tipiṭaka texts written in Pali are found, sometimes in large numbers and widespread across a region, the specific texts that were translated, copied, and taught, and which were the subjects of sermons at rituals and other community events, formed a practical vernacular canon as part of a larger curriculum that dominated language instruction. Such a focus can help one break away from the scholarly tendency to study Pali texts rather than their often quite different vernacular translations. The texts of the curriculum were not well copied and beautifully illustrated for royalty and wealthy patrons; they did not remain unread and neglected in the royal libraries or large monastic libraries of Thailand and Laos. Nor were they simply collections of Pali liturgical prayers, protective chants, or blessings. Instead, they were individually fashioned lenses through which individual scholars read, translated, and commented on Pali texts in the vernacular, and they were individually forged means by which scholars taught. Scribes were creatively engaged and constantly altered manuscripts. Mimetic fidelity was not an ideal. These teachers and students were not merely amanuenses. They willingly and frequently changed the content and structure of Buddhist texts in the process of teaching and translating them. As Bernard Faure, inspired by Michel Foucault, writes, "A tradition and the canon that represents it are the result of a process of limitation, of a rarefaction of discourse. It represents the ascent of an ideology."[10] In other words, in looking for a canon or an orthodoxy, the supposed divergences and heresies are created and, in turn, become marginalized. In this book, I am concerned with what is left out in the process of canonization, either by local reformers or by foreign scholars, and the historicizing and emplotting of a "tradition," with the messy things that do not quite fit in a packaged tradition.

One of the most common facts in Southeast Asian studies is that Indic, Arabic, and Sinic classical and/or canonical literature, art, liturgies, and rituals change, often radically, when they are introduced into the Burmese, Malay, Vietnamese, Khmer, Lao, and other intellectual communities. Pioneer scholars, colonial officials, museum collectors, and translators such as C. O. Blagden, D. G. E. Hall, H. G. Quaritch Wales, J. A. Stewart, G. E. Luce, C. Hookyaas, and George Coedès, among others, impressed upon subsequent generations of scholars and students that this "Indianization," "Sinicization," and "Arabization" characterized the cultural expression of the region. Later scholars like Judith Jacob, Hla Pe, H. L. Shorto, M. C. Ricklefs, Manas Chitakasem, and others seriously questioned this classical-centric approach of essentializing the region as derivative of Indic and other civilizations. More recent trends in scholarship closely attend to Southeast Asian cultural expressions without seeking out their possible Sinic, Arabic, or Indic origins. Southeast Asian history and society are now seen by many as important places to study the impact of transnational flows of various global cultural, economic, and political ideologies. Rarely have scholars, using these approaches, seriously questioned why things change and specifically how they change. For example, it is often repeated that classical texts like the *Mahābharata*, the *San kuo chi* (Three Kingdoms), Ibn `Arabi's so-called *Wahdat al-Wujud*, and the *Vessantara jātaka* are radically different in their Southeast Asian content, ritual context, and performance style. However, why are they so different? Simply stating that change happened without tracing how, by whom, and why suggests, on the negative side, that Southeast Asia was full of poorly trained scribes, forgetful students, and bad artists. On the positive side, it simply suggests that Southeast Asian literati and religious specialists either did not care about the integrity of the classical tradition or were creative simply for the sake of being creative. Historically, scholars often still remain at the level of description.

When the reasons for change are offered, they are most commonly linked to Marxist or Foucauldian analyses of power, liberation, and/or oppression. While it is true that royal scribes and Marxist revolutionaries reframed Indic or Sinic myths, images, and rituals to justify their own power, why would teachers at rural monasteries or village schools change Confucian classics or Buddhist *jātaka*? Were they nothing more than political opportunists who manipulated classical tropes to garner prestige or oppress the populace? Why would magicians in present-day Laos change the meaning of Pali grammatical texts to draw protective tattoos? Are they simply trying to impress and fool their patrons for financial gain? Then why change these texts and not others? Have analyses removed agency from local teachers and artists?

In order to move beyond a purely functional interpretation of ideological, aesthetic, and ritual change in Southeast Asia one needs to listen to conversation and trace interpretative processes "on the ground." There are many types of ground. In this book I look at the national ground to demonstrate how a certain ideal of an educated Buddhist has been displayed. I also look at the institutional ground to see how sects, schools, examinations, and curricula have been designed and implemented. In contrast to previous studies, I also walk around other grounds: the classrooms, the sermon halls, the monastic cells, and the libraries. In these spaces, the struggle over defining Buddhism is most clearly seen. These are contested and intertextual spaces where the everyday needs of learning how to read and write, of gaining prestige for one's family, or of healing one's mother's illness are articulated alongside aspirations for moral integrity and psychological enlightenment. Scholars often attribute change in religious traditions to elite reform or government interference. However, evidence shows that changes in educational methods, textual interpretations, and ritual expressions often are initiated by "ordinary" teachers and students in rural schools. Elite power is never total.

Approaching the study of literature through a study of pedagogical methods, performance prescriptions, gender and class restrictions, and curricular needs allows one to trace individual texts through different interpretative communities. Teachers, students, and source texts are not subject bodies, but works in progress.[11] In seeing the monastic school space as a series of changing relationships, one can see in close detail how, when, by whom, and even why texts changed locally when introduced into communities with their own ritual needs, ethical conundrums, and social concerns.

Who made these changes? Who were they, and why did they put together materials from Laos and Northern Thailand? Reading manuscripts, learning from teachers, in both areas, I realized that these two regions, despite their national borders, were intimately intellectually and aesthetically connected. Indeed, the national border is a relatively recent phenomenon. These regions shared texts, images, trade, kings, queens, cognoscenti, and disease. Ideas and methods link them as easily as rivers and mountain passes do. Although the history of people, money, and war has divided this region politically and institutionally, there is still much overlap in the ways Buddhists educate themselves. Manuscripts confirm what is easily observable on the ground at monasteries in the region today. Monastic students and teachers move frequently. Many monks travel long distances every year to study with different teachers, visit their families, share relics and stories, deliver messages, perform in state and private rituals (especially funerals), and offer guest sermons. Young monks travel to receive higher Buddhist degrees in the major monastic high schools, colleges, and universities in the cities of Luang Phrabang, Vientiane, Savannakhet, Chiang Mai, Lampang, and Nan. Monasteries and monastic schools exist in a network rather than each occupying a separate space. There is great similarity in the general curriculum, but this should not suggest that pedagogical practices at regional schools are a mere simulacrum of a central educational ideal. Since teachers and students have always traveled often, the physical institutions and geographical locations of monasteries are secondary to the flow of information among them. The study of Buddhist education should be dislodged from a physical institution, a central library, and a standard curriculum. In fact, because of a general preference for Pali texts and/or Foucauldian institutional studies of Buddhism, Lao and Northern Thai Buddhism is often ignored.[12] In de Certeau's terms, historians of Thailand have paid attention only to the "strategies" of those in power, rather than to the everyday "tactics" of individual Buddhist students and teachers who are attempting to design their own practices, beliefs, and ways of knowing. Monastic educators are not simply pawns of secular government forces but are active agents who often operate outside and in direct opposition to ideological nation-building coercion.

Besides establishing curriculum as a category in the study of religion, a secondary aim of this book is to contest the scholarship that perceives a sharp difference between premodern and modern religious education in Northern Thailand and Laos based on the advent of the modern state. Scholars who hold this view see the trend as starting with the modernizing and Westernizing reforms of King Rama IV and King Rama V in Siam and with French colonial influence followed by the Communist reaction to the United States in Laos. This historiography of "break" and "loss" sees a strong discontinuity between the premodern and the modern. Using this approach, scholars often elide the continuities that exist, in religious education and monastic training, through curricula, textual practices, pedagogical methods, and local rituals. In contrast, by tracing the consistent reinforcing of a certain, particularly local, vocabulary and the consistent deployment of a particular rhetorical style, one sees a fundamental continuity from the sixteenth century to the present—trajectories of Buddhist pedagogical history that do not begin or end with the advent of modernity.

Although the premodern/modern division is often a convenient heuristic tool, this very dichotomy is questioned throughout the study. This dichotomy tends to depict Lao and Thai Buddhists as "impacted" by globalization or "rampant" modernization. It sees the "traditional Buddhist worldview" challenged by technology and the global market with "dramatic consequences." I warn that this type of approach, which has been taken by most Buddhist studies scholars over the past century, establishes a dichotomy of victim/victimizer among the Lao and Thai Buddhist communities. It suggests that Lao and Thai Buddhism was a static entity that existed in a pristine state before modernization (i.e., the West) assaulted it. Instead, I map how Lao and Thai Buddhists have been dynamic arbiters and sponsors of ideology and innovation. As Lorand Matory has shown in his study of Black Atlantic (West African–Brazilian) religious communities, I see the vernacular landscape of Lao and Thai Buddhist ways of knowing as being in constant dialogue with histories, memories, and ideations of "multiple other locales" and times. Furthermore, like Matory, I want to avoid the use of vague terms like *deep-seated drives* and *underlying patterns*, and, I would add, even more ambiguous terms like *syncretism* and *foreign influence*. The vagary is sustained by a study of structural mechanisms—reforms, edicts, laws, standardized texts, and canons. Instead, I closely examine the "proximate mechanisms" of knowledge change and continuity.[13] The study of pedagogy, reading cultures, and curricular development is the study of proximate mechanisms. In this way, Lao and Thai Buddhist teachers are not simply the supine receivers of modernization who choose to profit from it or be overrun. Instead, changes and continuities are mediated through a particular epistemological approach—the *nissaya* method.

This book can in many ways be seen as a concerted effort to cross several boundaries. A broad view of curriculum allows one to cross barriers such as those between classical and vernacular, oral and written, canonical and noncanonical, physical and cerebral, monastic and lay. The nature of the spatial and the temporal locations requires that one cross contemporary political borders and the temporal boundaries between modernity and premodernity. The key that enables one to do so is found in the hands of the teachers and students. Lao and Northern Thai thinkers can be thought of as scholars and practitioners who are constantly looking for Buddhism rather than possessing it—constantly reinterpreting and re-creating their own religion and not merely learning and transferring a packaged form. They are not waiting for modernity to crush them or developing firewalls to stop foreign influences or new ideas generated locally. They are not being dragged into modernity by the West. On the contrary, they are reviewing, innovating, reforming, and negotiating with their religion. The speed with which new ideas are circulated and the level of interaction with non-Lao and non–Northern Thai speakers have both increased manyfold over the past century, but the manner in which new ideas are negotiated, incorporated, and taught has changed in much subtler ways. For most Buddhist educators, scholars, and practitioners change is neither feared nor overwhelmingly embraced. They have remained relatively outward looking and willing to combine multiple concepts and practices. The new is discussed in relation to the old. Others have associated Lao and Northern Thai Buddhism with stagnancy, tradition, orthodoxy, purity, and isolation. I believe that local flexibility, openness, and negotiated innovation are the hallmarks of their curricula.

This book is organized into three parts: "Structural Mechanisms" (chapters 1–3), "Proximate Mechanisms" (chapters 4–6), and "Vernacular Landscapes" (chapters 7–8). The first part has four objectives: (1) although abbreviated, to provide the first, in any language, institutional history of monastic education in Northern Thailand and Laos based on known sources; (2) to bridge the divide between the premodern and the modern; (3) to show the limitations of an institutional history and the need for a curricular approach to the study of Buddhist monastic education; and (4) to emphasize the fundamental connections between monastic education in Laos and Northern Thailand and to encourage scholars to see this region as a whole. Despite these limitations there is much that can be learned from the institutional history, including the dynamic ways monastic schools survived through political change and the way they created temporal and spatial authenticity through an invocation of axiomatic moments in translocal Buddhist history. The second part investigates curricular history. Little is known about what actually went on in the classroom. What texts were used, in what language were they composed, how were they taught, and what type of student was the monastic school interested in producing? The first section was about limitations; this section is about possibilities. A study of curricula can help one understand the ways Lao and Thai Buddhist teachers made meaning, treated knowledge, and understood their place in the larger Buddhist world. The sources for the curricular history of the region are plentiful but heretofore have not been examined, or even been considered important for the historical record.[14] Furthermore, the massive influences of these premodern sources, namely, *nissaya*, *vohāra*, and *nāmasadda* manuscripts, on the modern period have not been acknowledged. In the third part there are two case studies that are models for ways in which the study of curriculum can be applied. These case studies explore the possibilities for the category of "curriculum" in enhancing religious studies, anthropology, philology, and history. Therefore, this will help show that any curriculum is not simply a list of texts but a way of seeing texts and how they are used as "movable bridges" that link orality, textuality, canon, commentary, lecture, sermon, and vernacular and classical texts.[15] Texts are not static entities that provide content for examinations but are open sources that can be divided, invoked, glossed, and constantly reinterpreted by lay and monastic interpreters. The integrity, grammar, authenticity, and age of the source texts are rendered secondary to the idea of the Buddha's word as invaluable and powerful. The idealized position of the teacher is often as a protector of bodies and places. Monastic education creates teachers. They are the progenitors of local tradition and arbitrators of translocal prestige.

PART I

Structural Mechanisms

The Institutional History of Monastic Education

1 From the Sala Vat to the Institut Bouddhique

*In 1895, Emile Lefèvre, a French traveler, provided one of the only known pre-*twentieth-century descriptions of a Buddhist monastic school in Laos (Vat Mai in Luang Phrabang):

> [At] Wat Mai there are four or five big houses standing perpendicular to the pagoda and some feet above the ground. *This is the monastery of Wat Mai where young monks study*. They are dressed like their teachers, in sort of a saffron yellow gown fastened at the hips and which leaves the right shoulder free, in the fashion of a Roman toga. At the end of these houses, the one that is closest to the pagoda, is situated the residence of the Sathouk, the head of the monks and in a way the pope of Luang Phrabang. One enters his lodgings by the way of a ladder of a few steps and then one is in a room approximately three meters square, which is a *real junkroom, so little affinity do the objects have with each other. The sacred books, the Buddha themselves rub shoulders with an empty bottle of absinthe and a pair of clogs*. On two music boxes, gifts from Mr. Pavie [an earlier French explorer], one sees plates of enameled iron, the Sathouk's latest passion . . . on the wall are attached some of these vulgar colored posters . . . these together with two canvas chairs, are the strange items of the Sathouk's furniture. It is in these lodgings, worthy of the ancient alchemists, that seated on a mat, he passes his days in contemplation or absorbed in reading sacred books. Sathouk almost never puts a foot out-

> side. Suffering for some time, he does not seem to be able to come outside without being struck by a sort of light sunstroke.[1]

The impression that Lefèvre leaves is not that of a group of monastic students and teachers hard at study, but that of an enfeebled, mischievous, and lazy teacher who keeps his manuscripts next to bottles of absinthe, pipes, and a tasteless menagerie of European wares for which he has grown greedy. He distains the sun and human contact, and his shiftless students, who are said to "study" at Vat (Wat) Mai, are neither engaged nor engaging.

This account is similar to those by members of the Mission Pavie, James McCarthy, Marthe Bassenne, and others, who describe the "canary-yellow robes," "completely shaven heads," and "vacant eyes" of the monks, who are "set free from the worries of having to earn a living." They also criticize the monks for allowing young Lao men and women to sexually frolic on the grounds of the monastery and Burmese traders to set up shop next to their serene idols.[2]

Early French officials and travelers had a generally condescending attitude toward the Lao. They were called "naturally lazy, morally as well as physically slothful, working only when constrained and forced to do so. . . . The ignorance and insolent apathy of the Lao nation in general are the reason why they leave unexploited the natural riches and products of which they do not even suspect the existence."[3] Many French colonists saw it as their duty to inform the Lao of these natural riches so that they could provide the labor to remove them for the French. In 1901, eight years after France officially annexed most of the territory that makes up modern-day Laos, the résident supérieur, Marie Auguste Armand Tournier, stated that "the central idea of the organization [of the administration of Laos] has been as follows: to administer this country with the least possible expense [to France]."[4] French officials were intent on making Laos profitable and hence increasing their chances of being transferred out of Laos to the salons and chateaux of Saigon and Phnom Penh, to the beaches of French Polynesia, or to promotions and offices back in Paris. Indeed, Laos was seen as a place where the morals were similar to what one would "ascribe to Scotland" (as one French official remarked) and the people uncivilized and dangerously alluring.[5]

This hopelessness in the face of "civilizing" and educating the Lao meant that the French spent more time setting up coffee plantations, mining tin, and cutting trees and less time building schools, hospitals, and roads. For this reason, little is known about the state of monastic education in Laos at the end of the nineteenth century. French explorers, ethnographers, entrepreneurs, and administrators paid little attention to it. Even less is known about how Lao monks interpreted French concepts of education and schooling. Generally, the French separation of secular schooling from ritual, festival, and community religious life made little impact on monastic approaches to education.[6]

If one were to go only by these accounts to paint a picture of monastic education in the precolonial and colonial periods, then there would seem to be no reason to study Lao monastic education at all or even believe that monks and novices in Laos had any intellectual life of which to speak. Moreover, the descriptions of the "lack of morality" by Lefèvre, Bassenne, and others suggest that Lao monastic education had no effect on the daily lives of the Lao lay population. Monks, it seems, were not the moral exemplars the French had expected. However, these descriptions are part of the colonial project and are similar to colonial narratives seen in British India or the American Philippines in which local education was disparaged in part to justify colonial control and, in some cases, its Christian values.[7] At first it seemed that the French and other foreigners saw themselves as saving Laos and its Buddhist monks from ignorance, illiteracy, and disorganization. The French nominated themselves, beginning in the 1890s, as the new stewards of Lao Buddhism. As I demonstrate, however, the early French colonial scholars were not simplistic orientalists. They often worked closely with Lao royalty and monks. Yet colonial representatives did very little to ameliorate or corrupt monastic education. There is a difference between the rhetoric of modernity and the ideology of reform and the initiation and implementation of reform on the ground.

This book attempts a history of Buddhist monastic education in Laos and Northern Thailand, one that goes beyond a mere history of elite (royal and colonial) institutions and ideologies. However, it is useful to review briefly the histories of these institutions before and after the French arrived. This overview is not meant to be a comprehensive history. It provides a sociohistorical context before moving on to a deeper study of the epistemological and pedagogical history of Buddhist monastic education in the region. More important, it demonstrates why a new approach to the history of Lao and Northern Thai Buddhist education is needed.

Precolonial Buddhist Monastic Institutions in Laos

To date there has been no study of Buddhist schools or teaching methods in what is now called Laos.[8] By monastic "schools" I mean any place where there are teachers and students who gather to discuss texts and learn how to conduct rituals. A village can have several monasteries (*vat*), but usually only one serves as a central place for students to gather for textual instruction. Informal instruction on etiquette, ritual performance, discipline, and meditation takes place at every monastery. Places of instruction range from informal rural monasteries with three to four students and one teacher to large urban schools with classroom buildings and dozens of teachers and students. Education is also offered to laity in sermons, through art and image, and in ritual performance. In Lao historical sources, whether in the *Tamnan Phra Bang* or the *Phongsavadan Muang Luang Phrabang* (or Thai and Chinese historical sources that mention Laos), generally there is information only about the large urban schools, but there is no description of the daily life of students and teachers. There is little evidence describing the institutional administration of monastic schools; the founding dates; teacher qualifications; "graduation" or completion rates; how students were tested, or if they were tested; whether they studied in the *vihāra* (Lao: *vihan*, sermon hall), *sala vat* (monastic open-air pavilions), or outside; or whether they studied one-on-one or in groups. Manuscript colophons reveal a little about the movement of students between monasteries. In subsequent chapters I look closely at pedagogical manuscripts to help uncover the ways classes were held at premodern monasteries and to show the regional curriculum.

Although, sadly, Lefèvre's passing quibbles are some of the only eyewitness reports available on monastic education in Laos before the twentieth century, they are supported by a few other Lao and French sources. Vat Mai, where the eccentric and effete monk Sathouk was abbot, was indeed the central monastery where military and royal ceremonies took place. It was also the center of royally sponsored Buddhist monastic education in the kingdom before the French begin establishing official colonial control in 1893. Although Vat Mai was most likely the largest monastic school in the precolonial period, it was not the first.

Vat Vixun in Luang Phrabang is the earliest known formal Buddhist monastic school. It was built under the supervision of King Vixun in 1503.[9] It housed the ritually powerful Buddha image—the Phra Bang Chao. The king, his scribes, and senior monks believed that the Buddha himself had predicted that a great king would sit on the stone throne on the very grounds where King Vixun had the monastery established. The monastery sits near the base of Phu Si Hill in the center of Luang Phrabang. The Lao see Phu Si as the axis mundi (Mount Sumeru) of the Buddhist/Hindu world and is directly opposite the Grand Palace of Luang Phrabang on the other side of the hill. This strategic placing and the legitimizing chronicle that attends the monastery and its main image were part of King Vixun's efforts to make Luang Phrabang an attractive center of Theravada Buddhist ritual, scholarship, and art, and they remind one of similar efforts that were being made in Chiang Mai and Ayutthaya at this time.[10] Famous monks attracted wealthy patrons and brought increased trade, manpower, artists, devotees, and pilgrims. Kings certainly saw it as advantageous and prestigious to keep the best-educated, most regionally connected, most influential (and, therefore, most dangerous) teachers and students close. The monastic schools profited from this arrangement as well since they received royal gifts, protection, patronage, and good food. There probably were dozens of smaller, more rural monastic schools, but because they left no record only the ones the royal family supported are known about.

At Vat Vixun ordained, shaven-headed, saffron-robe-clad, male novice students (Pali: *samanen*) would have studied most likely outside under the shade of a wooden *sala* on hot days or in the *vihāra*.[11] Informal lessons in front of the *kuṭi* (monastic cell) would have also been the norm and are common in monasteries today. Male monk teachers (Pali: *ācāriya*) would read from palm-leaf manuscripts, and students would repeat the text verbatim, practice writing, and learn how to use Pali terms and passages for rituals, chanting, and meditative mantras and as triggers to vernacular lessons on history, ethics, medicine, magic, cosmology, and grammar. Examinations were most likely oral expositions of memorized passages and questions about the meanings of Pali terms and Buddhist ethical teachings. A solid knowledge (memorization) of the *Paṭimokkha* (monastic disciplinary code) would have been an essential part of this training.

The students at Vat Vixun would have been particularly well trained, because when the monastery was dedicated in 1506 the king invited several high-ranking monks and donated several large rice fields and a large quantity of silver to help support the students and teachers.[12] One of these teachers was Phra Maha Dep Luang Chao (also known as Dhamma Sena Chao), who composed one section of the famous Lao history, the *Nithan Khun Borom* (composed in the Lao vernacular). He had originally lived at Vat Manoram, where the Phra Bang Chao image was kept and moved with it to Vat Vixun. One can imagine that some of his students moved as well or lived at Vat Manoram and studied with him at Vat Vixun as these monasteries are very close to each other. The movement of teachers and students was quite common, as it still is. The king was so impressed with Phra Dep Luang Chao that he promoted him to the leadership of the entire Sangha (community of monks), thus making Vat Vixun the ceremonial, symbolic, and educational center of the emerging regional power. King Vixun himself ordained for a short time at this monastery and sponsored manuscript production there and at other monasteries.[13] Clearly, monastic education was of central concern to the king, and it benefited the monks to stay close to the royal family in the city, although there is one report in which the king sent a monk to study at a rural *ho tai* (library; literally "Tipiṭaka hall"), whose location is unknown.

Vat Vixun's school was the center for a number of literate monks. After King Vixun's death, his son, King Phothisarat, increased the prestige of Vat Vixun by inviting the scholar monk Maha Sichantho to be the supreme patriarch and to be the abbot of Vat Vixun. This monk was personally responsible for the king's Buddhist instruction.[14] He also invited many scholar monks from Chiang Mai to bring copies of the Buddhist Tipiṭaka (Buddhist "canon") and "other texts" to the monastery. It is not known exactly which of these texts were used in King Phothisarat's training, but the monastic manuscript library holds many and varied texts. Very few date back to the time of the king's training in 1523 (when the shipment from Chiang Mai came), but, undoubtedly, many of these texts formed the basis of the monastery's curriculum.[15] I discuss the problems with the term Tipiṭaka later, but for now it is important to note that, like Lao monastic archives in general, the vast majority of manuscripts held in the library of Vat Vixun are noncanonical. In fact, only 12 of the 101 manuscripts found at the monastery in 1912 were composed in Pali. Many are mixed Lao and Pali pedagogical manuscripts—*nissaya* type. Only five of the twelve are canonical (the *Mahāvagga*, the *Buddhamant*, the *Cakkanibāt*, the *Dhammachak*, and the *Dighanikāya*). The *Dighanikāya* in this instance is only a brief Pali summary of the contents of the canonical *Dighanikāya*, and the *Mahāvagga* is an incomplete section of the Vinaya. The *Cakkanibāt* is the fourth section of the *jātaka*; the *Dhammachak* is the *Dhammacakkapaṭṭhāna sutta*; and the *Buddhamant* is an extracanonical collection of canonical *paritta* (or protective) texts. The other seven Pali manuscripts are commentarial or known only locally. These texts do not constitute even a small part of nor are they even included in the Buddhist Tipiṭaka, but they certainly are considered "other texts."

Even if little is known about the institutional administration or educational policies of Vat Mai, Vat Manoram, or Vat Vixun, the library at Vat Mai in Luang Phrabang provides insight into the contours of the Lao Buddhist curriculum during and after King Phothisarat's reign. Vat Mai holds one of the largest collections of manuscripts in all of Laos. Of the more than eleven hundred total manuscripts, more than 80 percent are in Lao. Although most of these manuscripts were composed in the eighteenth and nineteenth centuries, one can still be fairly sure that the king's, as well as most other students', education was one centered on the vernacular exposition of both Pali and Lao religious and secular texts. While a full discussion of this issue must wait for now, if the libraries' holdings are any indication of the institutional objectives of this and other monasteries, then the teachers saw as their primary goal the dissemination of Buddhist narratives, Buddhist histories, ritual texts, and sermons drawn from the Abhidhamma. King Phothisarat must have studied some of these other texts with Maha Sichantho at Vat Vixun.

Two of these monasteries in Vientiane, Vat Inpeng and Vat Ong Teu, were, and still are, centers of scholarly activity and education. The exact dates of the construction of Vat Inpeng are not known because of the massive destruction of it and almost every other monastery in Vientiane at the hands of Siamese armies in 1827. Vat Inpeng was burned that year, but the basic layout of the monastery was rebuilt, modeled on the original (in fact, its reconstruction is still under way in present-day Vientiane, and monks still study through the sounds of hammering, drilling, and sanding). Its *vihāra*, next to the library, has a large covered veranda and would be a convenient and cool place to study. The unique feature of Vat Inpeng is its manuscript library. Tham Xayasithsena relates a story, for which he does not provide a source, in which the famous Lao king Fa Ngum installed the Phra Bang Chao image at Vat Inpeng.[16] The image, the story goes, was carried with the Buddhist Tipiṭaka (again it does not say which actual texts or whether they were Pali or Lao or Khmer) on a boat up the Mekong River from Cambodia. A Cambodian monk, Maha Pasmanta Thera, carried the image and performed a ceremony marking its installation on Done Can Island near Vientiane (then called Vieng Kham). When the statue was being moved from the island to the city it sank under the weight of its gold and magically reappeared on the grounds of Vat Inpeng. Later the Phra Bang Chao was moved to Luang Phrabang (first to Vat Vixun and later to the National Museum). When the Phra Bang Chao was moved north, the hall built to house it was renamed the library. Here one sees the connection between the kingdom's palladium, its king, and a major monastic school. Perhaps the Buddhist texts placed in this library were seen as an adequate replacement for the image. Chronicles suggest that the ritual and educational centers for the kingdom were closely related. While many of the story's details are most likely conflated from a mixture of legends, political agendas, and actual events, it forms the basis of legitimacy for the existence of the monastery and attracts many patrons, teachers, and students.

This Khmer-style library, which still stands, is one of the best examples in the country. Manuscript surveys revealed a large collection of texts, again mostly extra-canonical vernacular texts (two out of fifty-eight are in Pali, and the two Pali texts are extra-canonical ritual manuals). These manuscripts are mostly pedagogical *nissaya* used in daily monastic instruction and confirm the fact that Vat Inpeng was a major learning center in premodern Laos.[17] At present Vat Inpeng is a center for Buddhist students who study there and at Vat Ong Teu, fewer than fifty meters away on the same street.

Ong Teu means "Very Heavy (Buddha) Statue." The monastery was named after a large Buddha image that King Sethathirat ordered cast in 1569. Originally the statue was to be housed in Vat Inpeng. However, according to legend, the Burmese army was poised to attack Vientiane, and the Queen Chirapapha suggested that the king ask the Burmese to delay their attack until the statue was complete. Using this added time, the queen planned to trick the Burmese. She had magicians cast a spell on the Burmese soldiers as they slept on the opposite side of the Mekong River from Vientiane. The spell allowed Lao soldiers to sneak into their camp and paint their throats with white powder. When the Burmese soldiers woke up they could not figure out why their necks were painted white. Lao spies hiding among them told them that the Lao king himself sneaked into their camp and painted their necks white to demonstrate that he could have slit their throats while they slept, but he was merciful. Therefore, the Burmese respected the Lao king and his power and decided to make a peace treaty instead of burning the city. The king and queen invited the Burmese to partake in the merit accrued through casting the giant Buddha image. This image was considered so magnificent that an entire new monastery was built to house it—Vat Ong Teu. No matter the veracity of the story, the monastery, especially its monastic school, quickly rose to prominence in the city.[18]

Vat Ong Teu's school grew during the reign of King Surinyavong (1638–95). Although King Surinyavong, like the various noblemen of Chiang Mai, Lampang, and Nan, was paying tribute to the Burmese, he ruled over a fifty-seven-year period of relative peace and prosperity. He used this time to invest a great amount of royal funds in Buddhist education. By the end of his reign Vientiane had become the premier center of Buddhist education in the region, attracting monks, according to manuscript colophons, from Northern Thailand (Lan Na), as well as from Shan, Khoen, and Leu territories. Hundreds of manuscripts were brought into the region, and new monasteries were built and well patronized.

Although there is not much direct evidence of the education system at Vat Ong Teu before the twentieth century, there are descriptions by traveling European missionaries and traders. Gerrit van Wuysthoff, a Dutch merchant, traveled from Batavia (modern Jakarta, Indonesia) to forge a trading relationship with King Surinyavong. Although he was not very interested in Buddhism, he wrote that monks in the city were "as numerous as the soldiers of the Emperor of Germany." He also noted that many of the monks in the city were from Cambodia and Siam and were studying in the monasteries of Vientiane.[19] If his observations are correct, they may have been attracted by the patronage of the king and by the teachers and texts available.

A rather different picture of monastic education comes from an Italian Catholic missionary, Father Giovanni-Marie Leria (as transmitted by his colleague Father Giovani Filippo de Marini). Father Leria was viscerally opposed to the lives and work of Lao monks. Although he clearly does not approve of the manner of their education, like van Wuysthoff, he does admit that monks from Siam went to Laos in great numbers to study. However, he attributes these foreign monks' desire to study in Laos to his observations that Lao monks have no morality and do not strictly study what he understood as normative Buddhism. In his words, the education in Lao monasteries possesses "a greater reputation" since it does not "entirely conform to the old tradition." Leria's missionary perspective is obvious. A selection of titles of his short descriptions compiled during his stay in Laos from 1642 to 1648 is a veritable litany of Christian bigotry: "The Doctors [Who Include Monks] among the Laotians Are Not Wise"; "Their [the Monks'] Writings Are Full of Contradictions"; "The Delusions of the Laotians"; "The Blindness of These People"; "They Insult the Sacred Mysteries of Our [Christian] Religion"; "They Have Had Some of the Devil's Sins"; "Their Blasphemies against God"; "Against Jesus Christ"; "The Superstitions of the Laotians"; "Their Debaucheries in Their Temples"; "The Monks Are Deeply Involved in Magic"; "The Respect before the Idols"; "Their Abominations"; "A Monk Stabs Two Sisters"; and "Their Sordid and Criminal Greed." In fact, Father Leria's first entry describing the daily life of monks, titled "On the Institutions of Priests," sets the tone of the rest of the work: "This kind of people [Buddhist monks] is the most treacherous of the whole kingdom, the scum and dregs of society, the most horrible and lazy and the greatest enemies of work. Their monasteries are like so many universities of very vicious men, affiliates of tramps and mercenaries and schools of all kinds for bad deeds and abominations . . . they have hearts of bronze and are merciless and cruel like wild beasts."[20]

Despite this derisive attitude, Father Leria gives the only explicit description there is of monastic education before Lefèvre. He visited monastic schools and attended sermons and rituals. He speaks of examinations that monks had to pass at the age of twenty-three and in which the monks had to summarize their knowledge of Buddhist teachings and rituals. There is no other supporting record indicating that these exams took place, how they were conducted or judged, or their specific content. Leria disparagingly comments only that "most of this [examination] is only posturing and an ostentation rather than a demonstration of their scholarship and abilities" (52). He makes his assessment of monastic schools in one paragraph:

> The schools of those who are educated to become masters and chiefs of the religion consist in three principle classes which are filled with those who profess the religion, be it as monks or as laymen. In the first, the origins of the world, of man and of the gods, under a thousand fabulous appearances, are taught, and this doctrine is for them the old law. In the second, they teach the doctrine of *Xaca* [Buddha] which passes for the new law. In the third, they apply themselves to the reconciliation of conflicting passages, to resolving the doubts and opinions and to align the old and the new law, i.e., to become more blurred and confused, and to constructing legendary monsters. (35)

In describing the monks' daily activities Leria briefly mentions that the novices "study the ceremonies, learning to read and write in two systems one of which is indigenous to the country and the other suited and specific to monks, as the local language and Latin would be studied at home [most likely Tham script and Lao vernacular script]" (35). Besides studying to prepare for ceremonies and public chanting, Leria reports that the monks use their studies to practice protective magic to produce holy water and medicinal "potions" and to protect themselves against wild animals. He also reports only on the monks' teachings on vernacular texts that describe heavens and hells, the origin of the kingdom, the life story of the Buddha, the importance of giving alms, the nature and reasons for rebirth, and the rewards one would receive in the next life for meritorious actions in this life. One learns nothing more of what or how the monks studied in seventeenth-century Vientiane. As for teaching, Leria provides two passages that criticize the way Lao monks preached. In one passage they are criticized for enticing the crowds at the New Year's festival to donate money to the monks. In another he describes their preaching method: "A preacher climbs the pulpit where he, after having made a short recapitulation of all that was said by the others on the subject in their sermons during the month, adds a beautiful speech. The method of preaching . . . is to appear standing up like an immobile statue arms crossed over one's breast, with great humility and without ever moving them" (73).

These descriptions, for several reasons, do not reveal much about monastic teaching and learning and are obviously the product of a frustrated and isolated missionary justifying to his Italian audience why he did not gain many converts in his six-year stay in Laos.[21] First, he does not mention the study of Pali, but he does discuss the fact that monks studied two scripts. Second, he notes how "academic" study was focused on the craft of preaching and the performance of public and private rituals. He consistently shows that monks did not separate their study of texts from their ritual practices. Third, even though he does not mention the texts the monks were drawing from, he does indicate that most Buddhist teachings were orally taught rather than solely gleaned from texts. The teachings he describes were clearly drawn from *jātaka* stories of the previous lives of the Buddha that describe the benefits of meritorious acts "of man and of the gods, under a thousand fabulous appearances." From the content of manuscript libraries one can speculate that other stories were probably drawn from the *Dhammapada-atthakathā* and apocryphal *jātaka* and from vernacular narratives in which charity (*dāna*) and other acts of merit are the main themes but heavens and hells are also described. In addition to these, vernacular texts like the *Nithan Khun Borom*, *Xin Sai*, *Siang Miang*, and other Lao folktales and legends about "the origins of the world" and "legendary monsters" could have been included in their sermons and studies. This is confirmed by the content of texts from the period. Ritual texts like the *kammavācā*, *paritta*, and *ānisaṃsa* that guided ordinations, house blessings, new robe offerings, and healing and protective rites must have also been included since "magic" and "holy water," in Leria's words, were the chief "superstitions" of the Lao "talapoins" (monks). Fourth, he consistently emphasizes the "great pomp" and visual display that accompanied sermons, confirming the importance of etiquette, physical deportment, and ritual beauty in monastic education. Finally, Leria's distinction between the "new law" and the "old law" taught in monastic schools reflects the contents of Lao pedagogical and other texts in which indigenous Lao and translocal Buddhist narratives, rituals, ethical teachings, and histories are intimately intertwined. Moreover, his description of classes that aim at the "reconciliation of conflicting passages, to resolving the doubts and opinions and to align the old and the new law" is most likely of vernacular and Pali commentaries that are found in large numbers in Lao archives (particularly *nissaya*, *nāmasadda*, and *vohāra*).[22] Leria is certainly correct that these "new" and "old laws" have been "blurred and confused" in manuscripts and are certainly mixed in texts and sermons in present-day Laos. However, unlike Leria, the present study considers this aspect of Lao (and indeed Southeast Asian Buddhism in general) a hallmark of local creative engagement with Buddhist teachings, not as a mark of Lao "laziness" and "superstition." The unique way the new and the old, the local and the translocal, the Pali and the vernacular have been negotiated and blurred in Laos has much to teach about Buddhist epistemology and education.

Father Leria became frustrated with the "laziness" and "idolatry" of monks in Vientiane, from an assessment of Vat Ong Teu, Vat Naxai, Vat Mixai, Vat Inpeng, and other libraries. However, records show that during Father Leria's time in Vientiane, there was great manuscript production and the monasteries were full of students. Like other centers of learning, the vernacular pedagogical texts (*nissaya* and *nāmasadda*) formed the basis of the curriculum. These instructional manuals used in oral performance were drawn from the Abhidhamma, *Paññāsa jātaka* (Lao: *Ha sip chat*), and *Vessantara jātaka* and from romantic local epics like the *Siao Savat*, *Xin Sai*, *Phra Lak Phra Ram* (Lao version of the *Rāmayāna*), and *Thao Hung Thao Chuang*. This mixing of romantic/secular epic poems and Buddhist canonical and non-canonical texts is common in Lao education and entertainment.[23] Vat Ong Teu in particular possesses a large collection of *chalong* (ceremony or celebration; sometimes transcribed as *xalǫng*) manuscripts. These texts, like the *Chalong dok mai* (Flower [Offering] Ceremony), *Chalong Buddharup* (Buddha Image [Offering] Ceremony), *Chalong kathin* (Monastic Robes [Offering] Ceremony), attest to the major role Vat Ong Teu has played in the ritual, as well as the educational, life of the city. One in particular, the *Chalong Pidok* (Buddhist Tipiṭaka Text [Offering] Ceremony) is particularly important since Vat Ong Teu has been one of the major centers of textual study and religious instruction since its inception.[24]

So what is known about monastic education in Laos before the arrival of the French? Not much. There are texts but no eyewitness descriptions of how those texts were actually taught. I take up this subject in chapters 3–8. There I expand the history of education outside of a limited concept of institutionalized "schooling" using the Buddhist canon as its textual foundation. For now, I summarize the Lao collection in a few sentences. Texts (palm-leaf and mulberry-leaf manuscripts, stone and metal inscriptions, travelers' reports, and printed texts) are the primary sources for the history of Buddhist education in Laos. These sources provide information on Lao Buddhism only from the fourteenth century, and many remain unexposed to scholarly scrutiny in monastic, governmental, and royal archives. A survey of the information gleaned from these sources reveals a fragmented and contested history of royal patronage and governmental reform, as well as a creative engagement between local, indigenous beliefs and a translocal religion.

Buddhist Monastic Education in Indochine

By the time Lefèvre arrived in Luang Phrabang, the monastic schools of Laos had over four hundred years of development. Besides pedagogical manuscripts there is little one can know about this history. The French did not base their secular and Catholic educational institutions on local monastic models, nor did they invest in the maintenance of monastic schooling. In fact, "Western" influence, in practice and theory, seems to have bypassed monastic educational practices. Where the French influence is seen is at the elite institutional level and in attempts for French scholars to "renew" Buddhist education. Early on the French mistook their own conceptions of ideal Buddhist education for what was the "original" local conception.

The French based their primary administrative offices for Indochine in Vietnam. Ideally in each French-designated town there was one public *école cantonale* (primary school) and in the major French administrative regions there were *écoles d'arrondissement* (district schools), which were supposed to be directed by a French-born teacher and over time assisted by native teachers. In Vientiane, Savannakhet, Luang Phrabang, and Paksé there were eventually Catholic schools, and major urban centers had one *école cantonale*.[25] These schools were primarily run by Vietnamese hired by the French.

The French established a ministry of education with a French administrator. His primary goal was to open French language schools and train young Laos to help in the organization and administration of the country. French-speaking Laos were permitted to be primary school teachers in new schools built with limited colonial funds. In 1896 the first French language school opened in Luang Phrabang. This school served only the elite Lao in the city, while monastery schools operated without French involvement in most of the city and in rural areas. Soon other *écoles primaire* opened in Champasak, Vientiane, and Xiang Khoang. Secondary education was limited to a two-year institution in the capital. In order to complete a secondary school degree, Lao students had to study in Hanoi or Saigon, Vietnam. By "1940 only 7,000 students attended state-run schools. By 1945 only ten Lao had gained tertiary qualifications."[26] A small percentage of the students at these schools were women. Under the French, school even for men was not an important option for Lao families. A few elite Lao, like King Sisavangvong and the well-known Lao scholar Somchine Pierre Nginn, studied in Paris, but most common Lao women and men had little commerce with French schools.

The vast majority of lay and ordained students still studied at monastic schools without influence from the French language or curriculum. The French did not oppress or discourage monastic education. Quite the opposite, the French encouraged monks to study at these schools as well, but there was neither funding given to monastic schools nor any significant effort to change the curriculum.[27]

It is difficult to determine whether the French even saw informal instruction at rural monasteries as "education."[28] The French needed a certain number of French-speaking administrators, and these were supplied by the Vietnamese, who the French largely saw as culturally and ethically superior to the Laos. This staff was adequately produced at the small number of primary and secondary schools in urban Laos. It is unclear whether monastic education was seen as secondary to secular education or whether "graduates" from monastic schools were seen as "educated" citizens. In short, French records reveal little about the schedules, duties, examinations, pedagogical methods, curricular content, and so forth of monastic students and teachers. However, although the French did not actively support countrywide monastic education, they invested in the study of Buddhism, Lao history, linguistics, epigraphy, archaeology, and art history.

The École française l'Extrême-Orient (EFEO), which was founded in Saigon in 1898, sent French scholars to Laos in the early part of the twentieth century to research in the vast manuscript archives and to analyze the Buddhist and other monuments there.[29] Louis Finot, the first great French scholar of Laos, composed the first major catalog of Lao palm-leaf manuscripts.[30] In the first half of the twentieth century, unlike EFEO scholars in Indonesia and Vietnam, the focus was less on ethnography and contemporary history and more on Buddhist texts, architecture, and images. It seems that palm leaf and stone were more important to foreign Buddhologists than were the actual lives and education of Buddhist monks. How Lao monks used these texts in practice was of no interest.[31] The focus on Buddhist texts and learning in general led the EFEO not only to catalog manuscripts but also to promote the composition and preservation especially of Pali texts. To this end, in 1922 under the influence of Finot, the Cambodian king Sisovath and the résident supérieur of Laos agreed to establish the École supérieure de Pâli under the patronage of the EFEO. This focus on a Pali school was due to the general attitude that Pali was the "original" and thus superior Buddhist language of learning. Even though Finot's own survey concluded that Pali composition and commentary were not a primary part of the Lao Buddhist intellectual heritage, the EFEO saw Pali instruction as its priority. The Pali language was seen as tying together the regions populated by Sri Lankan– and Mon-influenced "Theravada" Buddhism (Sri Lanka, Siam, Burma, the Shan States, Sipsongpanna, Northern Thailand, Laos, and Cambodia). Moreover, the general attitude among Western Buddhologists in the early twentieth century was that contemporary Lao Buddhism had unfortunately been cut from its Indic roots and had become corrupted with animist and other local beliefs. This focus on Pali also viewed Laos as derivative to other Theravada kingdoms in Sri Lanka, Burma, Cambodia, and Siam.

It seems that the French sought to renew Lao Buddhist education to a state that never actually existed. This attitude is reflected in the 1910 Catholic encyclopedia, which reported the following: "Its [Buddhism's] philosophy, scarcely understood by a few bonzes and educated laity, is a mystery to the mass of the population. The Laotine of the present day is a nature-worshipper and a fatalist."[32] According to the EFEO, Pali helped develop "the study of Buddhist theology by the rational teaching of ancient, sacred languages, Pali and Sanskrit, and the knowledge indispensable for the comprehension and explanation of religious texts."[33] To further support the "rediscovery" of Pali (and Sanskrit) by the Lao bonzes/monks, Suzanne Karpelès, a well-known French Indologist, was brought from Cambodia. The first Pali schools were established (before she arrived there) in 1909 and 1914. Her hope for the Cambodians, with French governmental support, was that they, "[les Cambodgiens,] élaborent l'édition d'un Canon bouddhique complet, établissant le texte en pâli (notamment à partir des textes de la Pali Text Society, basée à Londres)."[34]

One of the growing criticisms of colonial-era orientalist scholars was that they privileged classical over vernacular languages and the ancient over the modern; in the case of Southeast Asia, it was the Indic over the indigenous. This attitude and approach to research were replete with a messianic rhetoric—the colonizers were not exploiters, but restorers and preservers. They were there to discover the Lao past and its glorious Indic roots for the Lao. Based on this generalization, the orientalist rubric can be applied to early EFEO scholars in Laos, especially since most of them were trained Indologists and their initial projects were centered not only on collecting manuscripts and investing in renewing Pali education but also on restoring monuments.[35] However, this description is much too simplistic. To be fair, even the earliest EFEO scholars did not see Laos as merely a passive receptor of other Buddhist cultures. Their work was never explicitly derisive or dismissive. These were not ordinary colonizers, travelers, or missionaries. First, the budget and expertise of the EFEO was limited in Laos. Most French ethnographers, economists, botanists, archaeologists, and so forth worked in Vietnam or Cambodia. There is a rich tradition of French musicology, anthropology, secular literature, and even ethnobotany in Vietnam. Second, although Finot and Karpelès favored Pali texts and education, Finot did make a great effort to document vernacular and non-Buddhist literature.[36]

It is difficult to define the colonial "influence" on the study of Lao Buddhism or on Lao intellectual and literary life in general. There was not one model of a good colonist, just as there was not one model of what made a good monastic student. There certainly seems to be little direct colonial influence on Lao monastic education. The wide variety of classical and vernacular texts and the dynamic integration of textual and ritual practices seen in Lao monasteries past and present have generally been reflected in the scholarship. In Laos, the convenient division between the premodern and the modern or the pre- and postcolonial is of limited use.

The Lao case presents a new perspective on the nature of colonialism and orientalism. There was not an overwhelming and internally consistent colonial ideological machine that attempted to change all modes of Lao intellectual and religious expression. The motivation of many EFEO scholars was not simply "orientalist"; that is, they were not trying to discount the local and the present in favor of the ancient and the pan-Asian. Their concerns were highly local. Although Finot and Karpelès saw the Pali Text Society's idea of the Pali canon as ideal and original, Karpelès herself stated that the establishment of a Pali school in Laos would be useful as a way of keeping Lao monastic students from moving to study in Siam, while it would simultaneously connect Lao students to their supposed "Theravada" comrades in Cambodia. Although Siam (especially the regions of Northeastern and Northern Thailand) and Laos are much more closely related in language, curricula, and ritual than are Cambodia and Laos, the French needed to bind Indochine together and encourage the Lao to travel down rather than across the Mekong to study.[37] The investment in Pali education and the entire Institut bouddhique, a group of colonial scholars focused on the study of Buddhism, was largely practical and institutional, not ideological or epistemological.

In 1931, Suzanne Karpelès, M. l'Administrateur Mantovani (representing the résident supérieur of Cambodia), S. E. Tiao Phetsarath (the first president of the Institut bouddhique in Laos), Prince Sisaleum, Jules Georges Théodore Bosc (representing the résident supérieur of Laos), and Prince Sutharoth of Cambodia's representative (because the prince could not travel such a long distance from Phnom Penh) met in Vientiane to inaugurate the official opening of the Institut bouddhique.[38] Monks were invited to chant at the ceremony, and books "de morale écrits" in Lao "caractères" (which I assume means that they were short Pali prayers, *beum suat mon* in Pali written in Lao script) were distributed to the crowd.[39] Later that afternoon, in conjunction with this ceremony, was the opening of the newly rebuilt manuscript library at Vat Sisaket, which had been looted and burned by Siamese armies in 1827. This certainly was a symbolic act to establish the French as the defenders of the Lao against the Siamese. The simple fact that the French established their primary colonial offices in Vientiane and largely rebuilt the city was a sign of renewal after the Siamese had depopulated and almost completely destroyed the city a century earlier. It was also economically better connected to Cambodian-centered trade. The head of the Lao Sangha is reported to have thanked the French for preserving Lao Buddhism and conserving "des monuments religieux du pays et de la sollicitude dont elle entourait la pratique du culte bouddhique."[40]

At this ceremony it was also announced that a new Pali school (École élémentaire de Pâli à Bassac) was being opened in Bassac (known today as Champasak, Paksé Province, in the deep south of Laos, about fifty miles from the Cambodian border). Bassac was to draw Lao students closer to their fellow monks in Cambodia. Karpelès stated that Bassac was an area "très fertile, très peuplée, se développe rapidement au point de vue économique."[41] The Pali school was one small part of the hopes of the French of linking Cambodia and Laos culturally, as well as economically and politically.[42]

Karpelès's expertise was in Cambodia, where she had worked for a lengthy period before being assigned to Laos.[43] In speeches, she continually attempted to connect Cambodia to Laos. For example, she invited Cambodian officials to Laos for the opening of the Institut bouddhique.[44] She brought together Lao monks from all over the country and introduced them to Cambodian monks. Twelve of these Lao monks actually traveled with her to Phnom Penh. In Phnom Penh the Lao monks were questioned on their knowledge of the Vinaya and trained on opening a Pali school in Laos.[45] Karpelès stated directly that this would help Lao monastic students study Pali without going to the monastic schools in Bangkok. The bulletin of the EFEO for 1931 states that these students "inévitablement l'attrait de Bangkok et, chaque année, des bonzes laotiens vont dans la capitale du Siam *pour leurs études religieuses*. La création d'une Ecole de Pâli à Bassac, serait de nature à *remédier à cette fâcheuse situation et à retenir chez nous les jeunes gens désireux de se livrer à l'étude de la langue sacrée*."[46] The establishment of the Pali school by the French not only showed their support of Lao Buddhism but also "remedied a sad situation and helped retain the young men" who would otherwise seek to "read and study the sacred [Pali] language" in uncolonized/non-French Bangkok (335). The résident supérieur of French Laos echoed Karpelès's pan-Indochine mission for the EFEO. At the inauguration of the Institut bouddhique, he stated,

> The mission [or scope of work] of this new [intellectual] body extends not only over all of Cambodia and Laos, but also covers a large part of the provinces of Southwest Cochinchina, where more than 200,000 souls effectively remain Cambodian and deeply attached to their native land. They continue, despite the numerous trials that they have undergone, to practice with rigor the precepts of the Buddha. In order to help them preserve intact the pious heritage of their ancestors, the institute has provided a much-needed moral foundation by establishing a constant relationship between them [Southern Lao] and their Cambodian brothers. For Laos and the Khmer kingdom, the institute is striving to renew the common intellectual heritage that formerly existed between these two countries. (337)

At this ceremony, high-ranking monks from the sangha in Cambodia and Laos gave speeches. However, the differences between their speeches are telling and may reflect some subtle tensions in the management of Buddhist scholarship and education under colonial control. Venerable Nath of Cambodia, the director of the Pali school in Phnom Penh and the head of the "Tipiṭaka Commission," like his new French leaders discussed the links between the Buddhism(s) of Cambodia and Laos. In fact, Venerable Nath of Cambodia even stated that the Buddhist monks of Vietnam were "equally" students of the Buddha and therefore the differences between the Hinayana and Mahayana sects were less significant than was their status as Buddhists. He made this connection between the three major Indochinese groups by emphasizing the importance of studying the Tipiṭaka (although it is not known which texts, and the importance of the texts being in Pali was not emphasized). Indeed, the Vietnamese never had a tradition of studying Pali texts. Venerable Nath of Cambodia did mention a story from the canonical *Aṅguttara-nikāya* in which the Buddha emphasized the importance of monks studying the Dhamma and keeping their monastic rules. However, he emphasized more the importance of the king and the government protecting the Tipiṭaka than he did the actual contents of the teachings. The emphasis on the power of the king as well as the government may indicate an attempt to remind the French that the monks still paid allegiance to their own ceremonial and political leader.

The speech from the unnamed head of the Lao Sangha is strikingly different. Perhaps emboldened by the fact that the ceremony was taking place at one of the most sacred Lao monasteries, Vat Chan, or because he resented speaking after his Cambodian equivalent, the Lao monk did not mention Cambodia, Vietnam, Indochine, or brotherhood, whereas they were mentioned several times by the others. He concentrated his remarks only on the heritage of Lao Buddhism and the Lao people. He thanked the governor-general, but only because he was helping the Lao people protect their texts by building a library that would hold "Tham" manuscripts. By using the word "Tham" instead of "Pali" or "Buddhist" or "Hinayana" or "Theravada," he was indicating that the newly restored manuscript library at Vat Sisaket and the new Institut bouddhique were important because they protected Lao texts written in the Tham script, a script that is unique to Laos (341). Lao monastic education was for the Lao and by the Lao. The French merely supplied a building.

Notwithstanding the remarks of the head of the Lao Sangha, Karpelès and her colonial bosses aimed to steer Lao monks toward Cambodia and the Pali schools at Bassac and Phnom Penh. This was part of a larger vision of binding together the peoples of Indochine culturally, educationally, and religiously. It was particularly important for the French to create a history in which Vietnam, Cambodia, and Laos were "naturally" "brothers," to defend against Siam's claims to Cambodia and Laos. Siamese armies had occupied large swaths of the two countries intermittently between the fifteenth and nineteenth centuries. The French had to create an Indochine culture at the expense of Siam. In this situation, Karpelès can be seen more as a practical colonialist than as a condescending orientalist. Although she worked "with" Lao and Cambodian scholars and monks instead of "above" them, she cannot be labeled solely one or the other. In this regard though, EFEO scholars and the résident supérieur for the French colonial government remained practical and administrative in their relationship with Lao monastics.

The Lao Sangha was placed under official French authority on September 5, 1927. Article 1 of the religious code referred to education and stated that the French were to assure that the Lao monks maintained their rituals and preserved their monasteries. Furthermore, the French were supposed "to develop, in light of an intellectual and moral recovery of the people, the monastery school where the children receive the first parts of their education." It is clear that this colonial rhetoric of "recovery" and "moral improvement" links Leria, Lefèvre, Bassenne, and the French colonial government. Besides these administrative rules, there is very little mention of monastic education except for four articles in the general French colonial "resolution on religious affairs." Articles 13–15 of the colonial religious code briefly mention monastic education. According to the articles monks are supposed to "observe Buddhist discipline and law" and "to study the teachings of the Buddha." The articles state specifically that "two years after one's admission into the Buddhist clergy, each novice must know how to read and write Lao, and each monk must know how to read tham [script]. Each religious [aspirant] who does not give proof of possessing these intellectual skills will be removed from the order. The abbot is to maintain himself . . . a monastery school where children from the surrounding villages come to study Lao writing and mathematics."[47]

Article 31 states that there are certain texts with which novices and monks should be familiar: "the *Thatou pattivek*, *Patticoula*, *Tangtianika*, *Atita* (for novices) [Pali: *Dhātupaccavekkhanaṃ*, *Paṭikkūlapaccavekkhanaṃ*, *Tankhaṇikapaccavekkhanaṃ*, *Atītapaccavekkhanaṃ*] and the *Paṭimokhala sangvaiasine*, *Indrigna*, *Asiva palisukasine*, *Pattiaya sinenesittasine* [Pali: *Paṭimokkhasaṃvarasīlaṃ*, *Indriyasaṃvarasīlaṃ*, *Ājīvaparisuddhasīlaṃ*, *Paccayasannissitasīlaṃ*] (for fully ordained monks)."[48]

This was not a stringent set of rules (and there is no evidence that they were actually enforced). Lay children were expected to learn basic mathematics and Lao vernacular reading and writing. Novices were expected to learn how to read and write in the Lao vernacular, and monks were expected to know Lao and the old Buddhist script—Tham. Knowledge of Pali grammar or the ability to translate and compose Pali texts was not required. Moreover, the minimal curricular requirements (of which, again, there is no evidence that they were enforced) were not more than or any different from standard precolonial texts. The texts for the novices listed above are no more than parts of the basic monastic precepts and chanting that are necessary to know (or memorize) to perform the ordination ceremonies and for morning and evening ceremonies (*tham vat xao* and *tham vat yen*). The texts required specifically for monks are little more than four short chapters from the noncanonical Visuddhimagga. The French were not directing the study of particular canonical Pali texts but were simply following what Lao novices were actually studying and memorizing in the precolonial period. In fact, the novice's requirements are fewer than five pages of Pali text (memorized for basic prayers). Handbooks that guide novices' and monks' chanting are still commonly available in Laos, and these short Pali texts were common in manuscript form as well. The first chapter of the Visuddhimagga, from which the texts for the monks derive, is common in *nissaya* form in Laos. The common criticism that colonial and/or Western Buddhologists discounted and devalued local Buddhist practice and learning cannot be universally applied to the scholars of the EFEO, members of the Institut bouddhique, or officials of the French colonial government.

Although Karpelès did promote the study of Pali and seems to have had a genuine desire to enhance Lao education far and above the needs of French colonial security, very few monks ever actually studied at the Pali schools in Cambodia. In practical terms, these schools were far away from the traditional seats of Lao monastic education in Luang Phrabang and Vientiane. Few monasteries had the funds to send monks to Cambodia, and few Lao monks could speak Khmer or French. Where a Lao person could learn Thai in a few weeks, Khmer and Lao are two different language families with entirely different syntactic, morphological, and phonological foundations and rules. Simply put, the impact of French reform on Cambodian monastic education, as discussed extensively by François Bizot, Penny Edwards, and Anne Hansen, was not seen in Laos.[49]

Still, there is evidence that Lao monks did see Cambodian Pali schools as desirable seats of learning. Edwards provided me with several letters and telegrams from the résident supérieur du Cambodge collection of the National Archives of Cambodia in which Lao novices and monks were given permission to study in Phnom Penh. For example, a twenty-four-year-old Lao monk named Thong Di (Phra Thammapanya) was one of the first Lao monks sent, in July 1923. His letter of introduction states that he had studied Pali at Vat Phra Chinalong in Luang Phrabang for six to seven years and was being sponsored for further study by the Lao Ministre des cultes. This suggests that Lao scholar monks were not being forced to study in Cambodia, and that the Pali school in Phnom Penh was actually considered as capable of providing instruction to the best and brightest young monks in Lao.[50]

Other letters (in Khmer and translated into French) support this interpretation. On April 25, 1929, eight Lao monks were given permission to travel to study at the Pali school in Phnom Penh because of their "grand interest" and for the sake of improving their previous studies in Laos. A letter written two days later states that these Lao monks were accepted and provided with housing at Vat Unnalom (a major monastery in Phnom Penh) and that they would be greeted by Prea Nhien Bovar Vichea, the director of the Pali school himself. In a letter dated May 27, 1929, the Cambodian minister of public education, Ponn, provides the names of other Lao monks who moved from Laos to Phnom Penh for the primary purpose of studying Pali: Sathou-Bonthon, Kho-Keo, Sathou-Pheng, Kho Thūng, Sathou-Somchin, Am, Ung, Souk, and the novices Neo, Tho, Phoumy, and Uon. This relatively large contingent of monks and novices, who probably had the ability to speak some French and some Khmer and who had proved some previous study in Pali, suggests that the Pali school in Cambodia was more than an ambitious colonial project that only existed on paper, but not much more.

I have not been able to discover the impact that these Lao monks had on their Khmer classmates or that their studies (methods and texts) had on Lao monastic education after they returned (if they indeed all returned) to Laos.[51] The exchange encouraged by the French and by the royal families in both countries seemed to have little lasting effect (in terms of long-term intellectual exchanges, shifts in pedagogical methods, or printed texts) on monastic education in general. One letter speaks to the lofty ambitions of these leaders as much as to their quiet failures. On April 28, 1937, the secretary-general of the royal family sent a letter to the colonial authorities stating that monks at the monastic school at Vat Mai in Luang Phrabang were sending Phra Chan Souk and a novice to Phnom Penh to make Lao translations of the "tipiṭaka" (it does not specify which texts). I believe that this is most likely the Lao monk Souk who is mentioned in the above letter as moving to Cambodia to study in 1929. "Phra Chan Souk" is most likely a French mistake—it should read Phra-a-chan Souk (Phra Āchān Souk / Phra Ācāriya Sukha), or "Venerable Teacher Souk." The senior-ranking monks of Laos would probably entrust a project of this importance to a monk trained in Pali who spoke Khmer and who had lived in Cambodia. The letter states that Karpelès herself arranged this trip and its funds (of the Institut bouddhique) in April 1935. Phra Chan Souk and his accompanying novice were given three hundred piastres as an annual stipend to cover their room and board and other needs in Phnom Penh. Although Karpelès made the arrangements, the king of Laos himself seemed to be the instigator of this trip since he ordered fifteen hundred copies of the "tipiṭaka" (Sanskrit: Tripiṭaka), of which half would be distributed to local Lao monasteries and the rest would be sold. This is a considerable project, given that any copy of the Tipiṭaka would comprise at least thirty-five volumes (often over forty, depending on the number of pages in each volume).[52] It is unclear still what was considered the "tripiṭaka," and since the Tripiṭaka edition in Cambodia was not completed in 1937, it is unclear what would have been available for Lao translation. The king of Laos sent Phra Chan Souk to translate the Khmer version of the Tripiṭaka into Lao, but there is no evidence that this project was even partially completed.

I have serious doubts that this project produced any texts or that the Lao received a new edition of the Tipiṭaka from their Khmer colleagues. French records reveal that a "book bus" was sent from Cambodia to Laos, but so far I have been unable to determine what was actually in that transport. It certainly was not fifteen hundred copies of the Tipiṭaka or even fifteen hundred single volumes. There has never been a "complete" Tipiṭaka translated into Lao (the nature of the term Tipiṭaka in Southeast Asia is the subject of chapter 6). This project, by all accounts, was never completed, and there is no evidence that any Lao translations of Khmer Pali texts were ever distributed to Lao monasteries. I have never seen Tipiṭaka texts from Cambodia in any Lao monastery or archive. This is not simply the result of unskilled monks, intellectual debate, a lack of royal and French funding, a lack of materials, or clerical bungling. World War II and the Japanese occupation of the capitals of Southeast Asia certainly must have inhibited this work, as did the Khmer independence movement of the late 1940s and early 1950s.

Whether Phra Chan Souk indeed did go to Phnom Penh first in 1929 and whether Karpelès sent a letter in 1935 for him to work on the Tripiṭaka project, one can see that these projects were long-term endeavors hampered by distance, available experts, language, and funding. Regardless, these contacts certainly must have produced valuable personal relationships between the two sangha.[53]

In sum, over the entire colonial period, the Institut bouddhique and the royal family of Laos never completed a major publication project in Laos. The French cannot be classified simply as brutal oppressors or orientalist preservers in Laos. French scholars were simply more invested in Cambodian texts and practices. For example, the first Khmer dictionary "commission" was initiated by the institute in 1914; the project was started in 1929 (completed in 1938).[54] In 1931 in Cambodia, a "full" translation of the Tipiṭaka (from Cambodian manuscripts) was started (completed in 1969). Scholars working for the Institut bouddhique and the EFEO completed nothing comparable in Laos. In fact, a project to produce an edition of the Tipiṭaka in Tham script in Vientiane was started in 1957 and never completed. The three volumes produced are no more than an unedited copy of the Yuan script version from Northern Thailand. It was not until the postcolonial period in the 1960s that any serious textual work was undertaken by French scholars in Laos, and then it was mostly work on vernacular, not Pali, texts. In fact, it was a Lao scholar named Maha Sila Viravong who as the Pali professor at Vat Ong Teu's Sangha College (Vithyalai Song) promoted the study (especially the grammar) of canonical Pali in Laos in the 1930s. He was trained in Bangkok and had little commerce with French scholars.[55] However, even Sila Viravong edited and promoted Lao vernacular literature more than he did Pali canonical or extra-canonical material. The colonial period did not signal the return of classical and canonical texts to monastic education, nor did the French or their Lao scholarly interlocutors suppress local Buddhist customs in favor of Catholicism or an ideal, translocal, ancient form of Theravada Buddhism.[56] The great Lao-Khmer monastic exchange envisioned by Karpelès and members of the colonial government and the EFEO never came to fruition and ended in the waning years of Indochine in the 1950s.

However, Lao scholar monks were never entirely dependent on French funding or intellectual vision. Work in the realm of Buddhist education and textual production grew after Indochine. Certainly, monks like Phra Chan Souk and Thong Di mentioned above did not request Pali texts from Cambodia or seek to study in Cambodia because they were forced by the French. They were motivated to learn more, gain new experiences, look for more textual material to improve their practice, and answer important ethical, epistemological, and ritual questions. However, their motivations and the fruits of their intellectual labors did not fundamentally change the way Lao monastics approached Buddhist learning. This does not mean there were no tangible intellectual achievements in twentieth-century Lao Buddhist scholarship and education. It just did not come from direct colonial assistance. For example, an event on June 1, 1975, at Vat Mai, the monastery school that Lefèvre described in 1895, proved that intellectual activity was still alive and quite organized. On that day the first Lao edition of the Tipiṭaka in Lao script and the Lao vernacular language (*Phra Tripidok sabap Lao*) was initiated. The first volume contained the first four stories in the first book, the *Dīghanikāya*, of the Suttanta piṭaka. Somdet Phra Buddhachinorot Sakonmahasanghapamokkha of Vat Mai in Luang Phrabang wrote the introduction and headed the project, which a staff of fifty-six had begun in 1972. This staff of monks, scholars, and novices studied and taught at Vat Mai and other monasteries in the old royal capital. They drew from the Thai script edition of the Tipiṭaka printed at the end of the nineteenth century. Somdet Phra Buddhachinorot Sakonmahasanghapamokkha stated that he consulted unnamed Thai history texts printed as late as 1974. To my knowledge, a "complete" set was never printed because of the fall of the American-supported royalist government on December 2, 1975. By June 1, 1975, the new Marxist government was already usurping formal power throughout the country. Luang Phrabang was occupied by communist troops on August 23. Most monastic publishing and printing was discontinued for over fifteen years, until a revival after 1990.

The first volume of the Tipiṭaka reflected the tenuous relationships between the royalty and the new Marxist government. In the introduction there is a dedication to both the anticommunist Prince Suvannabhuma (Souvanna Phouma) and the communist supporter Prince Suphanuvong (Souphanouvong). Prince Suvannabhuma was stripped of power soon after 1975. The Tipiṭaka project has yet to be restarted. However, some Lao summaries of Pali canonical texts have been published by pro-royalist Lao-Americans, especially in California. Laos is the only majority Buddhist "nation" in the world without its own printed/published edition of the Buddhist canon.

The Opiate of the People: Monastic Education in Modern Laos

In March 1979 Kupa Thammayano, an eighty-seven-year-old monk, quietly floated on a raft made of inflated rubber tires across the Mekong from Laos to Thailand.[57] He was no ordinary monk. As the head of the entire Lao Sangha, the Sangharāja, his escape from Laos reflected the degree to which the Lao Patriotic Front / Communist Party (Neo Lao Hak Xat) had inhibited his ability to run the Buddhist ecclesia and its educational institutions in the fledgling communist polity. He was not alone; almost 10 percent of the Lao population fled the rule of the Lao Patriotic Front, or Pathet Lao, between 1975 and 1980.[58] Laos gained independence from the French in 1954. French scholars remained in Laos, but central administrative control of monasteries ceased to be enforced, and it was not until the Marxist takeover by the Pathet Lao party in 1975 that Buddhist educational institutions were monitored and administered by the state. The latter half of the twentieth century saw a significant decline in the population and patronage of Lao monastic schools.

In brief, for the period between 1954 and 1975, despite the rise in printing in Laos and the growth in anthropological and economic interest in Laos by foreign, especially American, scholars, there remain very few descriptions of the day-to-day pedagogical practices among Buddhists in Laos.[59] Several older Lao scholars who had been monks in Laos in the 1960s (and some still are) told me that education was relatively informal.[60] Interviews with them over the past eight years (1998–2006) have greatly improved my understanding of the period. I also interviewed a number of Lao monks who now reside in Thailand (in Ubon Ratchathani, Nong Khai, Mukdahan, Roi Et, Udon Thani, Nan, and other places) and in the United States (especially in Providence, Rhode Island; Columbus, Ohio; and Riverside, California). Generally, I was told, the abbot or senior teacher would give sermons on general subjects, and novices, lay students, and young monks were expected to learn how to memorize Pali and Lao prayers and to learn how to read and write the Tham and Lao scripts. Evidence shows that there was not a formal curriculum for Lao Buddhist students until very recently and that curriculum operates only at large urban monasteries.

Although monastic education in Laos after 1954 can be called informal at best, there are some basic institutional facts that are available. Between 1959 and 1975 American "advisors" were ubiquitous in Laos. They saw the monastery as one place where the "hearts and minds" of the Lao populace could be "won" and turned against the Red menace. Buddhism had been made the "state religion" by the royal government after independence from the French. An American scholar, Joel Halpern, observed that the royal government used "suppressive measures" to control Buddhist teachers who were opposed to the government.[61] In May 1959 a royal ordinance stated that all "correspondence between administrative levels of the Sangha had to pass through government channels. Even the appointment of the Phra Sangharāja while made by the monarch, was subject to procedures involving the Ministry of Religious Affairs."[62] Geoffrey Gunn notes that the Americans had encouraged these actions and had also actively recruited monks in their fight against communist insurgents.[63]

These efforts to modernize and internationalize the Lao Sangha were not merely the results of American anticommunist machinations. In fact, they can be seen as connected to indigenous Lao nationalism and the growth of nationalism and so-called development monks across the river in Thailand. The most significant Lao monastic national movement linked to changes in monastic education was that of the Buddhavong Association (Samakhom Buddhavong) and the Buddhist Youth School of Laos (Honghian Oplom Sinsilatham Buddhayaovason Lao), founded by Phra Mahapan Anantho (lay name: Pan Kaeochumphu) on May 22, 1959. A popular monk, especially in Vientiane, Phra Mahapan was born into a rice-farming family in rural Savannakhet in 1911. As a young man he did just what Karpelès was trying to prevent—he traveled to Bangkok to study Buddhism. His efforts to reform Lao monastic education and to spread Buddhist teachings to Lao youth were certainly influenced by his schooling in Thailand. Phra Mahapan Anantho studied material at Mahachulalongkorn Monastic University in Bangkok and received the rank of Udombarinya (one the highest ranks in Thailand). I have found no record that states he passed the ecclesiastical examinations in Thailand, but it is said that he studied up to the eighth level (*prayok baet*) at Vat Chanthabuli in Vientiane; however, since there were not regular examinations there, I am not sure how his level was determined.[64] From his writings, of which there are several short books clearly drawn from Thai textbooks for youth (see chapters 3 and 5 herein), a book on Lao customs, and dozens of collected sermons, he certainly was interested more in spreading meditation practice and teaching social responsibility than he was in teaching the Pali language or Buddhist history.[65] This is confirmed in the newspaper account of his funeral, which states that he studied nine years of *vipassanā* meditation, a practice that had experienced a popular revival in Thailand at that time. In 1961, it is reported that he traveled to India to participate in a worldwide Buddhist ecumenical meeting, and in 1963 he visited Cambodia.

In 1967 Phra Mahapan summarized the objectives of the Buddhavong Association and the Buddhist Youth School of Laos.[66] They read as follows:

> To support Buddhism and to maintain the good tradition and culture of the nation; to study, research, plan, and propagate Dhamma to all organizations in the nation; to coordinate with other organizations with the same aims; to study the ways on how to construct and restore the temples and public places; to look for funds . . . ; to assist and promote the youth to be able to study Dhamma, culture, and the traditions of the nation; to help poor children . . . ; to extend the activities at home and abroad and to cooperate with all Buddhist organizations all over the world.[67]

To these ends the school and the association published fifty-eight short volumes of a Buddhavong magazine, ran a weekly radio program, organized three hundred public lectures, and opened five branches of an Abhidhamma school, a library with "about 3,000 books," an orphanage, dozens of *vipassanā* mediation centers (ten in Vientiane alone), and fifteen schools for lay and ordained youth with approximately 3,690 students (very similar to Mahanikaya projects sponsored by monks at Wat Mahathat and Wat Rakhang Khositaram in Bangkok in the 1950s). In addition to students, they also claimed to have 687 adult members of the association spread out over ten provinces (370 of who lived in Vientiane). While these numbers are certainly exaggerated and the Buddhavong magazine was never a substantial publication, they show the extent of this project, which was the brainchild of neither the Americans nor the French.[68]

Turning specifically to the schools connected with the association, the first was founded on August 9, 1959, at Vat Paluang under the direction of Phra Mahapan himself. He claimed inspiration for the school from the Buddhist Youth School of Sri Lanka, which he had visited in 1958. Subsequent branches were opened by Phra Maha Khampui Sirimangalo, Phra Maha Inpeng Busaba, Phra Maha Thong Khun Tuthathammo, Phra Maha Khampui Sisavat, Phra Maha Khamlek, and many others between 1966 and 1971. Lay scholars like Kaeo Viphakon and Bualy Chandara were also involved in school management. These schools started a school newspaper; opened "Sunday schools" (another Sri Lankan influence); composed nationalistic Buddhist songs; put on Buddhist "plays" and dances; started *vipassanā* meditation classes (similar to those growing in popularity in Cambodia, Thailand, Burma, and Sri Lanka at the time); performed charitable "social welfare"; and sponsored debates. These activities were completely foreign to traditional Lao monastic education.[69] A Lao-language poster distributed in Vientiane on March 5, 1972, summarized their activities. The poster advertised the Buddhavong Association and the Buddhist Youth School's support of the Lao nation and parliament. It calls Buddhism the "national religion" (*Sasana phacham chat Lao*). In honor of their allegiance to the state and the nation's youth they organized a festival of traditional dance, music, Buddhist chanting, and sports, and a procession from the famous stupa of That Luang to the Parliament building, linking the future of the nation with the future of Buddhist education.

During this period, many members of the Lao Sangha traveled abroad to study or to meet with high-ranking government and religious figures in India, Sri Lanka, Thailand, and Cambodia. For example, Mahapan himself wrote a book on his travels to Sri Lanka—*Sing thi dai phop hen nai Langka thavip*.[70] This book includes one of the only photographic records of Mahapan's travels. It contains a photograph of the prime minister of Sri Lanka offering Mahapan a gift and descriptions of his meetings with different Sri Lankan monks. A few Lao translations of Thai Buddhist texts emerged in this period as well, like Leuam Thamxot's translation of Phra Sutthithamrangsi Khamphiramethachan's *Dhammabanyai bang suan.*[71] This is a Lao summary of some of Phra Sutthithamrangsi's progressive sermons on the importance of a monk's social engagement. Leuam claims to have been close friends with Phra Sutthithamrangsi since 1959 and to have sought to bring the latter's teaching to the people of Laos. The Buddhavong magazine, besides providing a good source of texts and teachings common in the capital at the time, also published numerous editorials about "khao nok prathet" (international news), which reported on, for example, religion and government policy in the United States, Buddhism in Korea, and religious sites in India. These volumes are a rare font of information about the many and varied views of leading intellectual monks and religiously devout laypeople in Laos in the postcolonial / pre-Marxist period. Furthermore, one of the only known pre-1980 textbooks for Lao monastic students, *Banha Vinai phak 1* (Problems in the Vinaya, vol. 1; as far as I know no other volume was printed) was composed by a Lao monk, Phra Maha Sikham Vorachit, who, it is proudly stated on the cover, received his bachelor's degree from India. The cover also displays a hand-drawn depiction of a formal classroom, with a monk seated at a desk, rows of students in front of him also seated at desks, a map of Laos on the wall, and a flag and globe in the front of the classroom. This book uses the short "question and answer" format similar to the notebook described in my introduction.[72]

This Buddhist youth education movement, the growing international visibility of Lao monks, and the American "clandestine" operations, as well as the efforts of the royal government, had little long-term or widespread effect however on the lives of students and teachers in monasteries. The Abhidhamma schools are gone, the youth school branches have been closed or transformed into traditional monastic secondary schools, and only the remnants of the Buddhavong Association are seen at Vat Paluang on the outskirts of Vientiane. *Vipassanā* classes (and herbal saunas) have grown in popularity in the tourist areas, and at certain "progressive" monasteries like Vat Nakon Noi and Vat Paluang in the Vientiane province, but they are associated more with informal lay education than with institutionalized monastic education.[73] During these years Laos, especially in its rural areas, had a deeply depressed economy. Rural and urban monastic schools operated largely undisturbed until American bombs began falling by the thousands in the late 1960s and early 1970s. Many of my Lao teachers attended monastic schools in the 1960s and 1970s, before the Marxist takeover. However, the rise of secular education under the French and later royal interwar government and the "cave" schools run by the communists during American bombing raids did draw students away from monastery schools. Christian Taillard and Georges Condominas, working in Laos in the early 1970s, noted that the rural monastery was the major center of education in villages, but its universal hold on education in Laos was slowly being replaced.[74] Secular education grew under the French between 1893 and 1949 and had grown under the royal and communist governments between 1947 and the present, reducing the educational role of the monastery.[75]

In 1975, Laos, like Cambodia and Vietnam, was "liberated" by or "fell" to Marxist rebels—the Pathet Lao. The Pathet Lao was the Lao equivalent of the Vietminh/Vietcong in Vietnam and the Khmer Rouge in Cambodia. However, its interpretation of social reform and Marxism differed from that of its Indochinese comrades. Looking specifically at its policies regarding Buddhist education, the Pathet Lao (later the Satharana Pasason Pathet Lao, or Lao People's Democratic Republic) subsumed the Sangha under the Ministry of Education, Sports, and Religious Affairs headed by Phoumi Vongvichit, while the party was in the jungle fighting royalist and American forces. In December 1975, when the party was on the verge of defeating the American-backed royalist government, the Pathet Lao held the National Congress of People's Representatives. The president of the new government, Kaysone Phomvihan, spoke to the congress, six of whom were monks themselves, and urged them "to contribute actively to reviving the spirit of patriotic union, encourage the population to increase production and to economize, help in educating people so as to raise their cultural standard, contribute to persuading, educating and correcting those who do not live virtuously or misbehave, so that [they can] become good citizens."[76] This veiled warning to the Sangha was quickly followed by a series of restrictive reforms. First, the populace was banned from offering food to monks and novices in the morning, eliminating the primary way for the laity to make merit. Second, the teaching of Buddhism was banned in all schools. Third, members of the Sangha were told to till the soil and be self-sufficient, ostensibly removing their ritual, ethical, and social significance since the mere act of tilling soil involved breaking the very precepts that made a person a monk. Proactively, the government forced members of the Sangha to attend monthly indoctrination seminars (about seven days long with close to thirty-five senior monks from the capital), where monks were told that they should "actively contribute in transmitting the policies of the Party and the State, educating young people and providing medical care for the population." They were also encouraged to "study politics to consolidate their political background and make it conform to progressive revolutionary politics. This will enable them to more easily integrate themselves into the revolutionary ranks."[77] Martin Stuart-Fox notes that many of these monks did "integrate" themselves. For example, Phra Khamtam Depbuali announced to a delegation of visiting Vietnamese monks at the annual That Luang festival that "the Buddhist monk has the capacity to become a revolutionary, sharing the tasks of the nation and people" (103).

Being a revolutionary did not preclude the monks from their role as teachers or from their own study, but it did transform it. Phoumi Vongvichit declared in October 1976 that

> Buddhist monks assigned to teach the people in rural areas must understand the people who attend their sermons. They must select an appropriate sermon to give the people in order to change their line of thinking . . . they should mix the themes of current politics and Buddhist politics in giving sermons and using present examples . . . the policy of the Party and the government is . . . to request Buddhist monks to give sermons to teach the people and encourage them to understand that all policies and lines of the Party and the government are in line with teachings of the Lord Buddha so that the people will be willing to follow them. Thus there will be no lazy people, thieves, or liars in our country. (103)

This standard fear of "ancient times," the condescending attitude toward the general populace's ability to understand the "present reality," and the call to "work hard" as seen in all revolutionary literature are too transparent to warrant commentary; however, it is important to note that the Lao Communist Party, unlike its contemporaries in Cambodia, did not completely eliminate Buddhist education but did attempt to revolutionize it. Monks were constantly informed that Buddhism and socialism were congruent and complementary since both promoted equality, communal sharing, and the objective of ending suffering. The Buddha himself sacrificed his own wealth by leaving his family and palace for the sake of all sentient/socialist beings; therefore, monks and novices should walk in the Buddha's footprints and work for the people. The teaching of Buddhism, even with a Marxist veneer, was formalized and closely monitored. The Sangha was reorganized under the "Lao Union of Buddhists." Monks were enlisted by the government to teach the youth and adults how to read and write as part of its "campaign for the elimination of illiteracy."[78] They also were told to head public seminars in order to encourage the people to trust the government and wholeheartedly incorporate its new policies into their daily lives.

To ensure adherence to these policies, the government initiated a two-step program to educate the monks and novices and dismantle their power base and structure. There was no overall organization for Lao Buddhist education. Each monastery largely educated its monks and novices in its own way based on available texts, ritual and homiletic demands, and the particular lineage of teachers and teachings passed down from generation to generation. While there are certain similarities that bind Lao Buddhist teachings and teachers, there was no formal institutional unity, curriculum, or educational governance. Therefore, the party decided to formalize Buddhist schooling while infusing it with socialist teachings. What the party failed to realize was that Buddhist education had never been formalized even in the precolonial period.

Vat Ong Teu, being a traditional center of Buddhist education, was particularly seen as a place that needed reform. It was the single largest monastic school, with 341 students in 1979. First, monks were commanded to submit their books to the party for censorship. Manuscripts were largely ignored since most monks and certainly most party officials could not read them in the "ancient" (Tham) script. The texts had to be in line with what Pierre-Bernard Lafont calls the "three principles—not to sin [i.e., the five precepts against lying, stealing, sexual misconduct, inebriation, and killing]; to increase one's excellence; and to purify one's own heart—all of which are compatible with Marxism-Leninism."[79] Monks were banned from teaching the concept of karma or merit to ensure that the people did not waste their resources on giving food to monks or to the upkeep of statues and temples. Furthermore, they were banned from teaching about heavens, hells, or *phi* (ghosts or spirits). The Buddhist cosmology based on thirty-three heavens and eight hells occupied by gods, goddesses, and munificent and nefarious ethereal spirits was criticized, and the teaching based on temple murals that often depicted these worlds and their various fantastic denizens was forbidden. All monastic schools, including Vat Ong Teu, were "given directives" according to the revolutionary congress, "whereby they will function in conformity with the orientation of national education."[80]

One can understand why Kupa Thammayano would subject his eighty-seven-year-old frame to the currents of the Mekong to escape this radical overhaul of the Sangha and the removal of his power. Rumors that twenty monks had been executed by the party in Champasak Province in Southern Laos in May 1978 and that two other monks critical of the party had "disappeared" may have also contributed to his fear. Not only did monks like Thammayano flee, but many gave up the robes or entering the monkhood altogether. After 1975 there was a significant decrease in the numbers of monks in Laos. Martin Stuart-Fox notes that

> pagodas left with no monks were taken over as [secular] schools. Some were even reported to have been used on occasion as barracks and storage barns. Buddha images and other ritual objects from these monasteries were consigned to museums. . . . An important overall effect of government measures was to break down the key relationship between monks and the lay community that had sustained the position of the Sangha in traditional lay society. . . . Refugees claimed that monks complied out of fear: even if there was no known PL [Pathet Lao / Communist Party] official present, it was taken for granted that there would be some informer in the audience. The traditional Pali formula of homage to the Buddha, *Dharma* and Sangha was all but replaced by repetition of the five ideals of the Lao People's Democratic Republic.[81]

The most recent governmental guidelines for religion in Laos are summarized by the Lao Front for National Construction (LFNC), a branch of the

Lao communist government that manages the relatively new Department of Religious Affairs. In 2003 it published, oddly enough in English rather than Lao, its new guidelines for Lao religious institutions, written by Maha Khampheuy Vannasopha. These policies are based on Article 9 of the Constitution approved on August 15, 1991 (updated in 1995). This English publication most likely reflects the need to convince the World Trade Organization and the United Nations of its promotion of civil rights and religious freedom. Indeed the second half of the sixty-five-page document has letters of support from Evangelical Christian, Baha'i, Cambodian Buddhist, and Catholic churches operating in Laos. They are explicit attempts to prove that the Lao government does not oppress religion. As the publication states, religion is seen as a useful part of the LFNC's efforts to "enhance the tradition of patriotism, loving the regime [*sic*], make people be proud of the nation, create a spirit of self-reliance, self-autonomy, enhance unity among the entire Lao people including the Lao expatriates."[82] Although this document discusses Islamic, Christian, Taoist, and other religious institutions in Laos, its main focus is on Buddhism. It states that Buddhist education is important because "temples used to play a partial role for teaching; it was a place to educate the public to behave themselves in dharma, to be kind, hospitable towards each other and avoid bad behavior. . . . Under the light of the revolution, the Monks and Buddhists have strictly behaved by the dharma principle of Buddha; have joined in the nationalism procession, contended with the imperialism and colonialism for national liberation" (9). Institutionally the LFNC instituted a new policy to issue identity cards to all monks, novices, and nuns (as well as Christian and Islamic clergy) and to register all "movable and immovable properties" at places of religious practice (16). Speaking of the Lao government's role in protecting Buddhism and all religious groups, the text continues, "the Central Party Committee and Lao Front for National Construction are assigned to cooperate to lay down the contents and education methods to enable a suitable system to advise all sectors" (12). Article 14 specifically states that "the printing of books, documents for dissemination, signs and various plates related to religion shall be authorized by the Ministry of Information and Culture with the approval of the Central Committee" of the LFNC. Furthermore, "it is forbidden for believers in the Lao PDR [People's Democratic Republic] to publish or possess books, documents, photographs, signs, videocassettes, VCDs [video compact discs], films or other media having characteristics of superstitions, pornography, distortions of truth, slandering or obstructing the progress of the nation" (19). In addition to these restrictions, all monastic building, communication with foreigners, study tours, and so on must be approved by the LFNC. These institutional changes are reminiscent, although more ecumenical and with different rhetoric, of the policies of King Phothisarat and the résident supérieur of France. However, just like the institutional changes brought on by their predecessors, the LFNC's policies have not changed seriously the way that Buddhism is taught or the choice of texts and methods on the ground.

Today, the government will not allow the Sangha institutional freedom, and monks are not freely allowed to enter the monkhood without permission (nunhood, *buat maechi* or *buat maesin*, has all but disappeared in Laos); however, more monks are entering monastic schools in Vientiane, Savannakhet, and Luang Phrabang, and even rural monasteries are frequented more often. The active sermon tradition of the pre-communist era has been curtailed, and education in many rural areas has been replaced by ritual occasions like funerals, weddings, and house blessings and calendrical rituals like the *Bun ban fai* and *Bun Phra Vet* (which certainly have educational content as well, as I discuss below), but there are signs of greater activity in the educational practices of monks. Government policy recently has remained strict in presentation but weak in actual implementation. For example, recently monks in Vientiane, as well as Savannakhet and Paksé, have published printed copies of their sermons (Pali: *desanā*) alongside the more common ritual liturgical handbooks. Monks at these monasteries tell me that there has been no government interference or crackdown. As I discuss in the introduction, personal notebooks are used in teaching monastic students. These are not subject to review, restriction, or approval by the government. Many monks and lay scholars have been involved in the collecting, cataloging, cleaning, copying, preserving, and storing of palm-leaf manuscripts, funded by German, French, and Japanese research organizations and corporations. I sat with the minister of information and culture recently at a Lao Buddhist ceremony to honor the preservation of manuscripts at Vat Na

Son, near Vientiane. He participated in the rituals and gave a speech thanking the monks and scholars for their efforts. There was no explicit oppression, and the minister himself, like most lay participants, could not read the Tham script of the manuscripts or understand the Pali chanting. Several monks and former monks (in private) have told me that they feel no restrictions on their teachings, although they did in the 1970s and 1980s.

A mood that they should not question the legitimacy of the party persists. Although there were both efforts to politicize Lao monks by the ruling elite and efforts by monks like Mahapan Anantho and others to offer their "Buddhist" voice to politicians, there never has been a major sustained Lao "liberation" Buddhist movement, as seen in Islam and Catholicism in other historical contexts or among Theravadan monks at different periods in Sri Lanka, Cambodia, Burma, and Thailand. This does not mean that Buddhism is by nature apolitical in Laos or other places; indeed it is often highly political and revolutionary in many Buddhist countries and cultures. However, in Laos, aside from some isolated local rebellions led by lay "holy men" (*phu mi bun*) in the late nineteenth and early twentieth centuries in Northeast Thailand near the present-day Lao border, there is simply no evidence that links Buddhism to rebellion in Laos. These holy men were not teachers or students in monasteries.[83] In short, Lao monastic educators have never fostered large-scale or consistent rebellion against king, colonialist, or communist.[84]

Still, despite institutional organization and governmental requirements and oversight, many Buddhist pedagogical methods and texts have been little affected by Marxist institutional reform. The Lao Sangha has had a long history of overcoming reform, oppression, economic and demographic declines, and government interference. In fact, one wonders if the workings of the Lao Revolutionary Party are much different or any more damaging to religious freedom than were periodic royal reforms and French colonial restrictions since the sixteenth century. In order to understand the lives of monastic teachers and students in post-1975 Laos, one has to listen to them and examine their curriculum. Below I give a brief description of the curriculum at the only postsecondary Sangha college in Laos, as well as some notes on the institutional structure of monastic high schools. In subsequent chapters

I engage in a deeper investigation into the nature of various Lao monastic curricula.

Monastic Education Today

Vat Ong Teu is the headquarters of the National Monastic College of Laos and a good place to witness institutional changes in Buddhist education. I had the opportunity of attending classes there with some several hundred novices and fully ordained male students. Institutionally, Vat Ong Teu is the most prestigious center for higher Buddhist learning in the country. The curriculum is striking in its simplicity.

The students take the following courses: on Monday, Tipiṭaka Studies (Lao: *Traipidok vichan*), Mathematics (*Kanitsat*), and English (*Phasa Anggit*); on Tuesday, Writing and Translating Pali (*Taeng-pae Pali*), Abhidhamma Studies (*Phra Apitham*), *Pattana sum son* (National Development), and *Borihan kan seuksa* (Educational Administration); on Wednesday, Writing and Translating Pali, Sanskrit (*Phasa Sansakit*), Lao Culture (*Vattanatham Lao*), and (Current Events from) Newspapers (*Kan kao nang seu phim*); on Thursday, English, Lao Culture, and extra classes in English, Sanskrit, and Pali; and on Friday, Mathematics and Pali.[85]

This schedule changes week by week, and other classes may be taken, like Suttanta Piṭaka Studies (*Phra Suttanta pidok vichan*), Vinaya Studies (*Vinai pidok vichan*), Ethics (*Thamma vichan*), Pali Literature (*Vannakhadi Pali*), Lao (*Phasa Lao*), Rhetoric (*Vadasat*), Logic (*Takkasat*), History of Buddhism in Laos (*Pavat Buddhasasana nai Pathet Lao*), Lao Buddhist Art (*Buddhasilapa nai Pathet Lao*), Introduction to Law (*Kotmai dua bai*), Pali Grammar (*Vaiyakon Pali*), Religious Ritual (*Phithikam thang Sasana*), Editing (*Pannalaksat*), World Religions (*Sasana dua bai*), Lao Archaeology (*Buhankhadi Lao*), Ancient Lao Script (*Akson Lao buhan*), Monastic Administration (*Kanpokgong Song Lao*), and Pali Translation (*Pae Pali*). Examinations are given every Friday afternoon, and there are "free" (*vang*) periods for group and individual study.[86]

Most of these classes are taught by senior monks, but lay teachers teach English, Sanskrit, educational administration, Lao culture, mathematics, and Lao. Surprisingly, lay teachers also teach Pali Writing and Translation, Pali

Translation, and Pali Literature courses. I even gave an impromptu lecture on Pali grammar one afternoon and often tutored students in English and Buddhist history. This curriculum is a major change from the curriculum of the premodern period. First, of course, English is a new subject. However, there is no evidence that Sanskrit, law, Lao Buddhist art, religious studies, or archaeology was never taught before the modern period. Since mathematics was part of the first curriculum sanctioned by the French, there is good reason to believe some form of mathematics was taught in the premodern period since the French did little to change the curriculum. Courses on Lao culture, current events ("drawn from newspapers"), national development, educational administration, and law are all part of the Lao national government's efforts to make monks productive members of the proletariat when and if they decide to disrobe (which most do at the age of twenty). As for Pali, it was a major subject in premodern monastic education in Laos, but there is no evidence that Pali Literature was taught as a general subject.[87] Literature as a separate subject of inquiry is certainly modern. In fact, organizing learning under these curricular subject headings is a product of modernity in the region. Secular subjects such as law and mathematics, religious studies, and Sanskrit courses in this curriculum closely follow developments in Siamese/Thai monastic educational reform after 1902. Certainly Lao monks and the Lao government were heavily influenced by these Thai developments. Many Lao scholars traveled and studied in Bangkok. During the late nineteenth century many Lao were forcibly moved into central Siam.[88] The famous Lao scholar Sila Viravong spent years studying in Bangkok and researching at the National Library of Thailand.[89] Bualy Paphaphanh, a professor of Lao history and literature who lived and worked in Thailand, and many monks at Vat Ong Teu have traveled to their neighboring country (Bualy Paphaphanh also received his master's degree in Moscow and his doctorate in Hanoi). One of Prince Wachirayan's books on the role of Buddhism in government was translated from English into Lao by a Lao monk under royal patronage in 1967 (the monk does not give his name and only signs his translation "luksit phu neung" [a student]).[90] The *Khu meu samlap phu bolihan vithayalai song* (Handbook for the Administrators of the Monastic College), published in-house in 1999 and written by "dean" (phu amnuaikan) (Phra Achan Maha) Puakham Saliput, follows closely the format of the official curriculum of Mahachulalongkorn Monastic University in Bangkok. Courses on current events and national development are not found in Thailand, but the curricular format is largely the same. The major difference between modern Thai and modern Lao monastic higher learning is the access and use of textbooks. Lao monastic schools at all levels simply do not have or use many books. More subtle pedagogical differences are discussed in subsequent chapters.

There are some books at the Vat Ong Teu Monastic College, however. The library, which was once the library of the Institut bouddhique, has hundreds of dusty copies of Thai editions of canonical and commentarial Pali texts in Thai and Pali. These sit next to a number of Sanskrit handbooks donated by the Indian embassy and some copies of the Pali grammar written by Sila Viravong (published by the EFEO in 1996). There are also small collections of Lao sermons and Buddhist maxims and even some Russian science textbooks that were donated in the 1980s.[91] Strangely, none of the Institut bouddhique's publications like the *Thavat Buddhasāsanā latthi Hinayan* (The Foundations of Hinayana Buddhism) by Sombon Baengratnawong and Kham Champakaeomani or the quatri-lingual (Pali, Lao, French, and English) Dhammapada published by the American-supported Young Buddhist Association in 1975 are found in the library. The texts that are there remain dusty and unopened. Handwritten notebooks, glossaries, dictionaries, anthologies, and oral commentary are still the basis of instruction, as they were in a sense, as I discuss, at the time of Leria, Lefèvre, and King Phothisarat.

These institutional modernizations felt indirectly at Vat Ong Teu are certainly not influential outside Vientiane (few other monasteries in, for example, Luang Phrabang, Muang Singh, and Savannakhet, follow the official Vat Ong Teu curriculum). They certainly are not influential in rural monastic education. For example, Vat Nom Lam Chan in rural Savannakhet Province (south-central Laos), despite having one of the largest palm-leaf manuscript libraries in the country, has no formal classes; the abbot merely gives sermons to the three students at the monastery. I attended "classes" with nine novices (ages eight to sixteen) at Vat Don Khong in Champasak Province in the far south of the country. The students simply gathered together in the late afternoon to listen to a sermon and then had secular Lao writing practice books, which were hardly used. They were never tested. Pali is not taught except through the gloss and explanation of Pali words in sermons. In fact, two of the students of Vat Nom Lam Chan could not read Lao or Pali. The state of Buddhist education in rural Laos is poor if judged in comparison to Vat Ong Teu's formality, organization, and range of courses. Furthermore, rural Laos has very few well-trained teachers (in terms of being able to read and write and having taken classes at an urban or regional secular or monastic school). Many do not even have classrooms with reliable electricity or textbooks, pencils, and blackboards. Three to four students often study with their abbot on the porch of his monastic cell or in the open-air *sala*. Sometimes, education takes the form of one-to-one teaching between older and younger monks and novices. It is informal, based on the explanation of Pali terms, and deeply connected to quotidian disciplinary and ritual duties, and progress is rarely marked. However, in terms of the subject matter, this should not suggest that there is a great divide in terms of method or sources between Vat Ong Teu and less prominent monastic schools. Despite these modernizations, the manner in which monks and novices are taught at Vat Ong Teu and other Lao monastic schools is reminiscent of the pedagogical methods and textual sources used between the sixteenth and nineteenth centuries. One needs to do more than merely look at the titles of the courses taught at Vat Ong Teu and at the amount of electric power in its classrooms to see the connections between the past and the present and to trace the history and define the state of Lao Buddhist education.

Despite decades of French, American, Russian, and Thai "influence," Lao monastic education has developed and maintained its own, unique curriculum.[92] Lao monastic students have had to be creative in the ways they become "educated." For example, on August 1, 2006, I interviewed two first-year novice (*samāṇera*) students at Vat Ong Teu. Both Bunthavi Mongphasi, from Saravan Province, and Phonthavixo Inthilat, from Savannakhet Province, were eighteen years old. The former is studying according to the standard Vat Ong Teu curriculum, but he has also crossed the river to study in Thailand. He has also been told that the curriculum might change to match

"Bangkok's," which he fears. If this is the case, he might disrobe and become a lay student. The latter studied at Vat Xainyaphum and then moved to Vientiane, where he studies at Vat Ong Teu, but he also studies English on the Internet and math with a lay friend. Both agree that they might have to go to Thailand to advance as monks or become lay students at the National University of Laos. Their movement and insatiable search for books and teachers are not particularly new phenomena. Manuscripts and teachers have moved throughout the region for centuries.

2 Wandering Librarians

*In 1886 King Chulalongkorn (Rama V) of Siam ordered a survey of monas*tic libraries in the vassal state of Northeast Thailand. After reading the report he concluded that the teaching of Buddhism in that rural region on the edge of Siam was "lew lew lai lai" (full of nonsense) because it involved the teaching of fantastic stories of the Buddha's past lives when he was a frog or a servant or a maiden.[1] King Chulalongkorn was a powerful voice in the Siamese royal reform of monastic education in the late nineteenth and early twentieth centuries. The Sangha Act of 1902 was the institutional culmination of this reform, and a number of scholars have seen it as the historical fulcrum between the premodern and modern periods of Buddhist education in Siam and its vassal states. By examining the institutional history of monastic education in Northern Thailand, this chapter questions the significance of this 1902 Sangha Act, which establishes an artificial break between the premodern and the modern.

Monastic Education in Chiang Mai

Chiang Mai, known in tourist magazines as the "Rose of the North" or the ancient capital of Thailand's Northern kingdom, Lan Na (the Kingdom of One Million Fields), slowly became the regional center for state-monitored formal religious education in the twentieth century.[2] This is not without historical precedent. Chiang Mai was the largest city in the region, and many of its large monasteries had attracted the best monastic students and teachers for centuries. Wat Suan Dok, Wat Chedi Luang, Wat Chiang Man, and

Wat Phra Singh had run large monastic schools since the fourteenth century, and all had large libraries of palm-leaf manuscripts. Many Sri Lankan, Burmese, Shan, Khoen, Leu, Lao, Siamese, Mon, and Yuan monks had studied or taught in the city and then returned to their places of origin with texts.

Before the Burmese takeover in the 1550s, Chiang Mai was the center of Buddhist education in the region. Phra Sumana, a famous monk of the Sri Lankan and Mon tradition, brought texts, images, and students from Sukhothai, about two hundred kilometers south of Chiang Mai, to the city of Haripunchai (present-day Lamphun). His brand of Buddhist practice distinguished Chiang Mai from other Burmese, Lao, Khmer, and Siamese regional expressions. Many monks and serious laypeople traveled to study with Phra Sumana. The region around Chiang Mai became a major educational and ritual center.[3] This is reflected in the Pali and vernacular histories. Commentaries composed by local scholar monks, as well as the calling of the council of learned monks to organize and revise the canon by King Tilokarat in 1477 in Chiang Mai, were products of this intellectual activity. These scholarly endeavors helped attract manpower to the region to build monasteries and populate schools.

Buddhist education continued under the Burmese, who militarily occupied and culturally influenced the region, between the 1550s and 1770s.[4] The Burmese takeover of Chiang Mai in the mid-sixteenth century did not destroy Buddhist education in the region, but it did lead to many changes. First, the monks who came with Burmese armies brought new genres of religious texts like *nissayas*. Second, Pali grammatica and narratives common in Burma were copied and glossed in Northern Thailand. Third, the Burmese occupation and growth of the Lao economy led in part to increased contact among Lao, Shan, Khoen, Leu, and Northern Thai monks and lay scholars.

The monasteries of Chiang Mai continued to grow and attract students. Wat Chedi Luang has been the crown jewel of Chiang Mai monasteries for almost seven hundred years. It lies in the center of the city, and the spire atop its main stupa, even after it partially collapsed following an earthquake, was the highest point in the city until very recently, when high-rise hotels were built along the river. The stupa/*chedi* was built under the sponsorship of King Saen Meuang Ma in 1391. King Sam Fang Kaen deposited a relic of the Buddha brought from Sri Lanka in 1423. The *chedi* was enlarged in 1481. This was the year that the most honored Buddha image in the Tai world, the Emerald Buddha, was installed there. In 1511 the *chedi* was covered in gold leaf. The "city pillar" of Chiang Mai is also on the grounds of the monastery, making Wat Chedi Luang the ritual and cosmic center of the city. This cosmic center is reinforced by a local belief that the god Indra had two mythical god-man creatures bring the pillar from the thirty-third heaven to Chiang Mai. Every May tens of thousands of people turn out for a seven-day celebration held at the monastery in honor of the pillar and the *chedi.* All of these aesthetic, ritual, and royal accouterments effectively made Wat Chedi Luang the center of at least the Yuan-speaking world, if not the entire Tai-speaking religious world that in the early sixteenth century covered present-day Northern Thailand, eastern Burma, and Laos.[5] In 1546 the king of Lan Xang (centered in Luang Phrabang) was invited to rule the city of Chiang Mai and its tributaries.[6] His first order of business when he entered the city was to bring his retinue, which included many newly ordained monks, to Wat Chedi Luang. Like Burmese, Shan, Siamese, Khoen, and Yuan monks, these Lao monks studied at the monastery. Famous scholar monks studied and taught at Wat Chedi Luang as well since there was a regular exchange of monks between different monasteries in the region. Moreover, these scholar monks would have been compelled to visit the Emerald Buddha and the relic held in the great *chedi* to pay obeisance. Still, despite this activity, there is little record of activities at Wat Chedi Luang until 1823, when a golden preaching chair was donated by the king of Chiang Mai. At this time there were 101 monks in residence at the monastery. Since a new ordination hall was also consecrated at this time, the monastery had certainly planned to attract more students.[7] Unfortunately, these generalities must suffice for now because, as with most other monasteries, historical records reveal virtually nothing of the day-to-day activities of students and teachers at Wat Chedi Luang before the modern period, when it became the regional campus of the Mahamakut Monastic University of Bangkok.

Wat Suan Dok is home to the other great secondary school and monastic university of the North. One of the oldest monasteries in Chiang Mai, Wat Suan Dok was built in 1371 under the direction of Phaya Keu Anasong as a place where the aforementioned Phra Sumana could rest during the rainy season. Within five years, Phaya Keu Anasong added a reliquary (*chedi*) and a protective surrounding wall and brought relics from Sri Sachanalai. Phra Sumana was so impressed that he spent the last sixteen rainy seasons of his life at Wat Suan Dok. Because of Phra Sumana's presence at the monastery, students came to study with him and the Lankawong (Pali: Lankavaṃsa, Buddhavaṃsa also known as the Nikāya Ramaṇa) school/lineage/*nikāya* he represented. The report of Phra Sumana's auspicious dream of deities visiting the region and bringing relics only increased the fame of the monastery. In fact, Phra Sumana's school became so synonymous with Wat Suan Dok that locally it was known as the Wat Suan Dok school of Buddhism (Nikāya Wat Suan Dok).[8] This sect came from Sri Lanka via the teachings of Swami Udumbara of Martaban in the Mon region of present-day Burma. For years monks from Wat Suan Dok traveled to Burma to study, and monks trained in the Mon tradition worked at Wat Suan Dok.[9] Saraswati Ongsakun argues that this simple move of Phra Sumana's going to Wat Suan Dok made Chiang Mai the new center of Buddhism and made monks who had studied with Phra Sumana at Wat Suan Dok sought after by monasteries elsewhere in the region.[10] Long after Phra Sumana's demise, the monastery held this status as a center of Buddhist education.

Phaya Kaeo, who ruled Chiang Mai from 1495 to 1525, was perhaps the greatest supporter of Wat Suan Dok. Despite constantly raising armies to attack Ayutthaya and Chiang Tung, he built several new structures at the monastery. He also promoted the study of Pali at Wat Suan Dok and in other monasteries in the city and sponsored another copy of the Pali canon (Tipiṭaka) based on King Tilokarat's 1477 "edition." Neither sets' content is actually known, nor is it known even whether they were completely in Pali. Phaya Kaeo wanted not merely to renew King Tilokarat's efforts but to surpass them, and so he sponsored several commentaries and had them sent to royal courts in Luang Phrabang and Ava (Burma).[11] Three of the greatest Pali writers of this era, Phra Sirimaṅgala, Phra Ratanapañña, and Phra Ñāṇakitti, were probably descendents of the Sri Lankan lineage that came to Chiang Mai in 1369 under the aegis of the monk Sumana and influenced monastic education at Wat Suan Dok. Pali education seemed to decline in the twenty years before the Burmese armies entered and conquered (relatively bloodlessly in three days) Chiang Mai in 1558. Intellectual monks, artisans, and scribes had long been moving to Luang Phrabang before the military arrived.

Little information is available about education at Wat Suan Dok under Burmese rule (starting in the 1550s). There is no evidence that its school closed, but certainly it was not thriving as it had during the time of Phra Sumana.[12] Pupapha Kunyosaying asserts that for this two hundred–year period the monastery was in a state of decline (*sut som*).[13] No account exists of the names of the abbots of the monastery, and very few buildings were constructed at the monastery during this period. One reason that education may have declined at Wat Suan Dok is that the area around the monastery was used as a military base. Wat Suan Dok is situated about two kilometers west of the Suan Dok Gate of the Chiang Mai city walls. It is in a good position from which to prepare troops for a northern assault on the city. The Chiang Mai Chronicle mentions an occasion in which the area was used as a military garrison in 1545 and was burned.[14]

However, Wat Suan Dok was not completely ignored by the Burmese. After the Burmese military took over Chiang Mai in 1558, Burmese monks studied at Wat Suan Dok during this period and received patronage from Burmese rulers. For example, King Sudodhamma (Burmese: Bayinnaung) gave gifts to Wat Suan Dok and invited monks from the Wat Suan Dok training and ordination lineage to give sermons.[15] Bayinnaung also invested in the improvement of education at the monastery. He gave funding and also expelled from many monasteries monks who failed examinations. Unfortunately, it is not known what these examinations entailed. Most likely they involved taking oral tests, listening to monks chant in Pali, or even undergoing written examinations. In any case, failing these examinations carried with it the threat of being disrobed. Therefore, results were used as a way to gain more direct control over religious affairs in the city.[16]

Architecturally, the *vihāra* (central ceremonial hall) at Wat Suan Dok is the largest in the city and one of the largest in the Buddhist world. It is well known as a popular place to deliver sermons to crowds of hundreds. Pupapha writes that Wat Suan Dok "is the center of education and scholarship thanks to the incredibly large *vihāra* which is wide and long so that members of the Sangha in Chiang Mai use it as lecture hall for students and for sermons. This has been a custom in Chiang Mai since its founding and every year since it was built the sangha in the city has met here."[17] In fact, on the grounds of Wat Suan Dok, which was in particular so associated with the center of learning in the North that the famous monk Krupa Sri Wichai gave sermons there in the late nineteenth and early twentieth centuries, is where the Northern head of the entire Thai Sangha has resided since the 1960s and where the major monastic university of Bangkok, Mahachulalongkorn Monastic University, opened up its Northern branch in 1997. The popularity of Krupa Sri Wichai's sermons and ascetic powers, as well as the desire to pass state-sponsored Buddhist examinations, has continually drawn students to Wat Suan Dok. However, little is known of the monastery's curriculum before the 1950s.

Although little is known about Wat Chedi Luang and Wat Suan Dok, it is much more than is known of other monastic schools in the region. The only other school that can be identified as a significant education center is Wat Phra Singh. It was founded in 1454 and became a center of pilgrimage throughout Southeast Asia because of the Buddha image, Phra Buddha Sihing, housed there and made popular by texts such as the *Jinakālamālīpakaraṇam*, *Tamnan mūlasāsanā*, and *Tamnan Phra Buddha Sihing*. Sacred relics and images were the main form of advertisement for monastic schools. A common theme in canonical and extra-canonical texts from all schools of Buddhism is that studying or even sitting in the presence of the Buddha can lead to enlightenment through little self-effort. The myths attached to the region's images and relics—for example, the Phra Buddha Sihing, the Emerald Buddha, and the relics in Lampang, Haripunchai (Lamphun), Chiang Mai, Nan, and Phrae (e.g., the Phra Bang Chao and Phra Ong Teu in Laos)—emphasize that being in the presence of the relic or image is like being in the presence of the Buddha. These incentives drew famous teachers and students much as the promise of research funding, library resources, and high-tech laboratories draw famous professors to universities today. It can be said that virtually all regional monasteries first become ritual centers through their possession of certain images, relics, or royal seals. These ritually powerful objects enabled these monastic schools to attract charismatic teachers and skilled scholars and draw large audiences to sermons and students to lectures. This ritual legitimacy allows them texts and funding needed to become educational centers. The chronicles describing the origins of these relics and images offered a monastery (and the monarch who patronized it) temporal and spatial authenticity and can be seen as having a similar function to the brochures and pamphlets published by modern schools.[18] This image and the Buddhist school at Wat Phra Singh drew the famous teacher Phra Maha Agyachulathera and ten of his students to the monastery from Haripunchai, further making Chiang Mai the center of Buddhist education in the fifteenth and sixteenth centuries. The abbot at Wat Phra Singh was one of the first to pay homage to the Burmese king Bayinnaung, and it was there that Burmese monks took up residence.[19] Little information is available on the activities, educational or otherwise, at Wat Phra Singh during the Burmese period. However, after this period, as evidence shows, there was much activity at the monastery. In 1806 the supreme patriarch of the North, Phra Chao Nantha, was consecrated at Wat Phra Singh along with the two other highest-ranking monks of the region, Phra Chao Kamphira and Phra Phan Tao.[20] King Kawila, the new monarch of post-Burmese Chiang Mai, acknowledged Wat Phra Singh as the center of Buddhism in the North and built the main *uposatha* hall there. In 1821 the main *vihāra* was given a new Buddha image. Later the monarch made his residence next to the monastery, and in 1827 the main *vihāra* was repaired and consecrated by the king.

Like Wat Suan Dok, Wat Phra Singh was known as a center of education. In fact these monasteries are so close to each other that students must have walked between them quite often (as they do today; many students who study at one monastery actually reside at another and commute to class every day). Sometimes this commute was quite taxing. In 1833 Krupa Kañcana of Phrae walked from Wat Sung Men, some two hundred kilometers away from Chiang Mai, to request that the abbot of Wat Suan Dok produce a new copy of the Tipiṭaka and then led a ceremony to mark the occasion at Wat Phra Singh. Krupa Kañcana went to Wat Suan Dok first because the supreme patriarch was residing there at the time. An inscription on the back wall of the library at Wat Phra Singh tells of his visit. It was because of this library that Krupa Kañcana wanted to have the work on the Tipiṭaka done at Wat Phra Singh. The library, the finest example of its kind in the North, was built in 1811, replacing the former library built in 1488.[21] Krupa Kañcana had reason to see Wat Phra Singh as the appropriate place for Buddhist textual scholarship since the library had been further renovated in 1826 and the Siamese king Rama III had visited the library in 1829. Rama III was so impressed that he had royal scholars from Bangkok move to Wat Phra Singh to study its manuscripts.[22] These manuscripts influenced curricula and canon formation in Siam.

Chiang Mai was and is a city where Buddhist monastic education has thrived. So many students crisscrossed the city to attend different schools and work with different teachers that the whole city can be seen as a large campus. This becomes even more apparent later in the discussion on some of the pedagogical manuscripts composed and used there. Chiang Mai is a place to which monks and scholars traveled and where royal power and monastic scholarship were intertwined. The schools and the scholars in the periphery looked to their respective cities for prestige, guidance, and opportunity. However, this should not suggest that the monastic scholars in the periphery willingly abdicated their right to define their own Buddhism. In fact, monks like Krupa Kañcana did most of their work in the rural areas and taught and studied far from the control and curriculum of the urban monastery. Today scholars of Buddhist history must look to the rural monastery to find texts and traditions that often escaped urban conflagrations, theft, and haphazard distribution. This does not mean that the urban and rural religious transcripts were completely different; rather, it means that before the advent of the state-sponsored/urban-centered curriculum of 1902 and its subsequent spread to the provinces the rural areas enjoyed a great degree of intellectual and educational independence.

Monastic Schools outside of Chiang Mai

There were dozens of monastic schools in Northern Thailand, each with a different curriculum, different degrees of organization, and different numbers of teachers and students. However, unlike Chiang Mai monastic schools, rural monasteries rarely appear in royal, image, or relic chronicles or in votive inscriptions. Because of their distance from military camps, major markets, and royal historians, only the premodern activity of these schools is known, from manuscript colophons and local legends passed down orally. While colophons have been the subject of scholarly analysis in Thai, German, and English, local legends popular at these monasteries have been ignored. The value of these legends, I argue, is not in their possible truth-value, but in how they have worked to attract and retain students, teachers, and patrons. They are a legitimate part of the historical record, because they are often treated as actual history locally. They help construct the local episteme and are part of a monastic school's institutional memory. Although they are disorganized and eclectic, these colophons and legends lead one to believe that there was great intellectual activity in rural Northern Thai monastic institutions before 1902. I offer two local legends below to highlight the reason certain monasteries became centers for education and manuscript production.

Wat Sung Men and Krupa Kañcana

In 1537 a student of Michelangelo, Jacopo Sansovino, was commissioned to build an ornate library on the Piazza San Marco in Venice. This library was lauded as the "most magnificent and ornate structure built since ancient times."[23] The library was dedicated to Bessarion, the former Vatican librarian, who had collected 746 manuscripts. John Addington Symonds offers these words of warning to historians examining Bessarion's manuscript collections: "At first glance . . . the student recoils as from a chaos of inscrutable confusion . . . to treat of them collectively is almost impossible."[24] Sixteenth-century Italy was in many ways similar to Krupa Kañcana's nineteenth-century Northern Thailand and Laos. Italy was a fragmented world marked by a great mixing of peoples, intermittent warfare, and demographic movement. Manuscript collections were diverse linguistically and topically. Krupa Kañcana, like Bessarion, was one of the greatest manuscript collectors of his time. A manuscript library was also built in honor of his work. The manuscript library, which has been rebuilt several times, is a small building, surrounded by a narrow moat, with a sloping, ornate roof and tall but narrow wooden doors. The moat is intended to keep away fire and deter insects that might chew on the sweet palm of the texts. The thick doors and the absence of windows were designed, as they were in manuscript libraries throughout Laos and Thailand, to let in very little sunlight to further protect the texts. The libraries both on the Piazza San Marco and in Sung Men village speak to the life's work of the men who filled the libraries' shelves and to the students who praised their endeavors.

Sources for monastic education in this region reflect a world of "chaos of inscrutable confusion." With all these scattered monastic schools and different collections of texts, how can one know anything about premodern Buddhist education in the region? Treating the monasteries in Phrae, Savannakhet, Chiang Mai, Chiang Saen, Kengtung, Luang Phrabang, Nan, Lampang, and other towns "collectively is almost impossible." The only possible way to understand the institutional history of monastic schools is to keep the focus narrow and take it one monastery at a time.

Recently, the history of Wat Sung Men was compiled from oral legends by Luang Pho Krupa Kamphirasan of Phrae Province. This monastic history begins with the story of a young mother who went to the forest to give birth. After her son was born, a tiger carried him away. When her husband returned from a long day working in the paddy fields, he called out for his wife. After receiving no response and seeing the tiger tracks, he deduced her fate. He sent his other two sons to the village of Sung Men to report the tragic news. The community refused to accept that his wife was lost and formed a search party, carrying torches and following the tiger's tracks. After a night of searching, they came to a brook south of the present-day city of Den Chai, about fifteen kilometers south of Sung Men. They found the tiger gently caressing the mother and her newborn, who were both unharmed and sleeping. The tigress had washed the newborn with her tongue. They thanked the tigress and returned to Sung Men, where they built a new home.

This story was related by a student of a student of this newborn over 150 years later. The story is important because the newborn in the story went on to become the abbot of Wat Sung Men. Wat Sung Men is no longer in a forest near a brook. It now sits on a newly built highway in the remote province of Phrae. It is flanked by rice paddies, auto repair shops, tailors, rattan furniture stands, and noodle shops. Driving by at 70 mph, most people would hardly notice it. Still, it is known to scholars and devotees alike because of the work of an abbot whose first breaths touched the fur of a tiger.

Krupa Kañcana Araññavāsi Mahāthera (locally known as Krupa Kañcana or Krupa Mahathen), born in 1789, traveled throughout the region (including Laos) in the early nineteenth century collecting manuscripts and bringing them to Wat Sung Men. There he supervised what was perhaps the greatest manuscript production center of premodern Northern Thailand.

Although there are few historical records, his work can be assessed from manuscript colophons and three inscriptions. The first inscription, as noted above, was on the library at Wat Phra Singh in Chiang Mai. The second and third are from Nan Province and date from 1833 and 1839, respectively. The first states that Krupa Kañcana came to Nan to collect manuscripts and order copies. Later he went to Luang Phrabang to collect manuscripts. The second inscription regards his persuasion of the governor of Nan, on June 18, 1837, to order the composition/copying of 1,103 manuscript fascicles. Two years later these manuscripts were moved to Wat Sung Men. This movement of manuscripts between the regions of Laos and Northern Thailand was frequent, and Krupa Kañcana was carrying on a long tradition that had begun in the 1520s.[25] He was also part of a royal project that had started three years previously. In 1830 the king of Chiang Mai gave manuscripts and Buddha images to monks from the city of Xiang Khoang near Luang Nam Tha in (present-day) northwest Laos.[26] Early-nineteenth-century sources reveal the direct movement of manuscripts from Laos to Northern Thailand.[27] The records of Reverend Schmitt of the Mission Pavie state that in 1836 the king of Luang Phrabang, along with the royal leader of Phrae, and lay followers donated a large amount of silver, as well as gold, needed for gilding the edges of the leaves for the project. Krupa Kañcana was well supported by Lao royalty and farmed out work to monasteries in both Laos and Northern Thailand. Like Phra Sumana before him, he attracted students, patrons, and teachers to his school. Krupa Kañcana died in southwest Tak Province on the Thai-Burmese border. This ended a long and productive career, which produced over fifteen thousand bundles (*phuk*), the largest collection in Northern Thailand.[28]

Although Krupa Kañcana is not well known nationally, he is a local hero to many people in the village of Sung Men and to the monks of Phrae.[29] His statue and his *chedi* at Wat Sung Men are given offerings every day. Krupa Kañcana is honored for his support of local vernacular literature, not for his Pali scholarship. Indeed, he may not have known Pali grammar well, and there is no evidence that he ever composed a Pali text. Still, every monk I talked with in Phrae knew of Wat Sung Men, its large number of manuscripts, and its *chedi* for Krupa Kañcana. Phra Suwat of Wat Sri Chum told me that Phrae monks held Krupa Kañcana in esteem because he could write the local vernacular beautifully. His skills in Pali, if he did have them, were not mentioned. Being famous locally for promoting vernacular Northern Thai texts is perhaps one of the reasons he is not known nationally. Little effort has been made to investigate the period after the rise of Burmese power in 1558 and before the full Siamese administrative takeover in the early twentieth century, perhaps because of Nationalist Thai policy or because of the scholarly inertia of focusing on pre-sixteenth-century history. Historians are not asking why there are no substantial sources for this long and recent period. Finally, Lao, Khoen, Burmese, Northern Thai, and Western sources have not been incorporated in any comprehensive study to date; there has not been a historiographical comparison of the different modes of discourse in the available sources as to what groups, interests, and ideas of time and space they represent. This is particularly striking considering the large numbers of manuscripts composed in the region; however, it is telling because it demonstrates the general emphasis on the study of Pali manuscripts versus vernacular manuscripts. Most of the holdings of Wat Sung Men (and the surrounding monasteries) are in the local language, not Pali. Therefore, they have much to teach about local religion, local social and intellectual history, and local pedagogical methods. Once the center of Buddhism, history, and education moved to Bangkok in Central Thailand, the individuality and the contributions of the periphery were considered less important.

Krupa Kañcana is essential to any history of monastic education because many of the manuscripts that he commissioned, composed, or copied (by his own hand or by the scribes at his scriptorium) are *nissaya*, *nāmasadda*, and *vohāra* that were used in the everyday education of nuns, monks, novices, and serious lay students. These bilingual vernacular and Pali manuscripts have been overlooked because they are rough, notebook-style texts; however, these manuscripts are only further evidence of how education was actually conducted at Wat Sung Men and the surrounding rural monastic schools. I discuss these texts in due course.

Wat Lai Hin and Mahāthera Kesarapañño

Second only to Wat Sung Men's collection is that of Wat Lai Hin Kaeo Chang Yeun (Monastery of the Elephant Who Stands on a Crystalline Hill; Pali:

Selāratanapabbatārāma). Thanks to the surveying of Singkhla Wannasai of Chiang Mai University, beginning in 1961 hundreds of Pali, vernacular, and bilingual manuscripts have been cataloged at this monastery. However, the monastery's own history and its present abbot do not emphasize the importance of the manuscripts; in fact, when I first visited Wat Lai Hin, the abbot gave me a tour of the *chedi* and showed me a few Buddha images and a collection of amulets, glass beads, and ritual implements kept in the monastery's small museum/storehouse. In addition, he related the story of the origin of the monastery, which is also recorded in local legends.[30]

The monastery was founded on this particular spot in rural Lampang, far from the river and any urban center, because of the idiosyncrasies of an elephant. The story begins with two famous Buddhist envoys in Pataliputra (northern India), Kumārakassapa and Meghiya, who were told by the first Buddhist king, Asoka, to build stupas holding the bodily relics (*sārīkadhātu*) of the Buddha to be spread throughout the known world. The two monks put one relic on the back of an elephant and let the elephant lead them to the place where the relic wanted to rest. The elephant wandered from India to Northern Thailand and after bypassing many seemingly suitable places decided to stop and stand still at the very spot where the present-day Wat Lai Hin stands on a small, forested hill in rural Lampang Province. The elephant would not move, and eventually it was decided to build a stupa for the relic and a monastery to house the monks who would honor it. A competing version of the story states that the elephant merely rested at the place where Wat Lai Hin was built and actually stopped permanently at Wat Phra That Lampang Luang, about four kilometers away.[31] Both monasteries claim a connection to the elephant and the relic. Stories of fickle elephants are very common in the region.

This small monastery attracted many students, and from the differences in vocabulary and orthographic style of the manuscripts, one can assume that they came from long distances. They most likely stayed at Wat Lai Hin and the larger Wat Phra That down the road. The monastery's chronicle reports that some students from Wat Luang Pa Chang Haripunchai, about fifty kilometers away, also studied there. Since Haripunchai was a well-known center of Phra Sumana's school, this might have given Wat Lai Hin some local fame. One student in particular was a young novice who wore a very dark colored robe, and his oddly shaped head is said to have looked like a "nest full of animal feces."[32] The other monks and novices supposedly stayed away from him, seeing him as diseased. This strange novice was also exceptionally lazy and did not memorize texts, write, or read according to his teacher's orders. One day the abbot, most probably the monk Phra Kudī, gave this strange novice the task of memorizing the *Vessantara jātaka* so he would be able to chant it for the laity at the celebration for the beginning of the rains retreat (*khao pansa*). However, when the day of the celebration came, the abbot was terribly nervous and feared that the people would not believe his sermons if they did not trust his student's ability to chant. Since he had not seen the strange novice study, he feared the worst. However, in front of the crowd, the strange novice prostrated three times to the Buddha, the Dhamma, and the Sangha and sat down on the preaching throne (*dhammāsana*). He did not pick up the manuscript containing the *Vessantara jātaka* that his teacher tried to hand him. Instead he chanted the entire story (which is quite long) without one mistake. The abbot was so doubtful of his ability that he had to pick up the manuscript and read along as the strange novice chanted. He confirmed the novice's perfect memory. After the celebration the teacher still wondered about the novice's skills and decided to test him again. He took every manuscript in the monastery and removed the strings that bound the palm-leaf pages together. He removed the wooden covers and scattered the leaves. He picked up the leaves at random and mixed them up. He took this well-shuffled collection of palm leaves and placed them in a large box (*hip*). He then asked the student to put all the manuscripts back in proper order. The strange novice did what many researchers today cannot—he reassembled, perfectly, all the texts in less than an hour. The abbot was convinced of his ability, and soon the novice was ordained as a monk, with the name "Mahāthera Kesarapañño Bhikkhu." Soon he rose to the rank of abbot and, as the story goes, made Wat Lai Hin a famous school. Mahāthera Kesarapañño was particularly famous for being able to tirelessly inscribe (*chan*) dozens of pages of palm leaf a day. It is said that he inscribed the local script (*akson beun meuang* / Yuan) beautifully with a stylus made out of a coconut shell and often meditated in a distant cave.

One day Mahāthera Kesarapañño decided to travel in the forest a long distance in order to find a quiet place to meditate. He came to the area of

Kengtung (Chiang Tung) (in modern-day eastern Burma, about 350 kilometers north of Lampang), an area populated by the Khoen people, whose monastic practice and knowledge of the Dhamma had waned. Mahāthera Kesarapañño, it is said, soon fixed that problem with his great ability to teach. The local populace asked him, "Which monastery are you staying at while in our region?" To which he answered in a riddle: "At a monastery with a shell that cannot be bitten through."[33] After seven months of their wondering what this peculiar answer meant and after a couple of foiled royal tricks, Kesarapañño revealed that since he used a coconut shell as the handle for his stylus, the "monastery with a shell that cannot be bitten through" was his stylus. The knowledge of the Dhamma and the ability to transmit it was the only monastery of true value. Despite this teaching, the prince of Kengtung wanted to build a proper monastery for this clever teacher, and he ordered his slaves to come south from Kengtung and build a spectacular monastery in 1683.

This monastery is one of the smallest but most ornate and best preserved in the region. Its walls measure only thirty-two meters by twenty meters, and this small space holds a *vihāra*, a *chedi*, and a small shrine. Inside the gate is a stone sculpture of a coconut. That many students could have studied inside the walls is doubtful, but today, as there must have been in the seventeenth century, there are three buildings outside the walls, one of which is a library, built in 1919 by Phaya Saen Tao of Chiang Mai. The students most likely studied under the wooden roofs of the *sala* and performed rituals inside the walls. In the main *vihāra* is a statue of Mahāthera Kesarapañño placed on a preaching throne next to a Buddha image. From the hand of the statue is a white string that leads to a manuscript box, thus magically protecting its contents.

Monastic Education and Manuscript Production

Besides this local legend, the half coconut, and the statue, little information is available about the manner in which Mahāthera Kesarapañño or any of the other teachers at Wat Lai Hin taught. There is simply no known information about daily life in monastic educational institutions in rural Northern Thailand. In short, there are no eyewitness reports, no royal edicts, and no photographs that can provide a snapshot of the day in the life of a Northern Thai teacher or student before the twentieth century.

So before the twentieth century there are little more than legends and manuscripts, but if one reads closely, manuscripts and legends can reveal a lot. The stories of Krupa Kañcana and Mahāthera Kesarapañño indicate some important characteristics of premodern monastic schools. First, they were occupied by students, patrons, and teachers who traveled from distant towns and cities (including those in present-day Laos and Burma) and were attracted to the schools because of their important relics and famous teachers, known not only for their Pali scholarship but also for their ability to chant and teach the local vernacular. Frequent mobility is a virtue in Buddhist monastic life as it promotes nonattachment. The lack of family obligations also helps students and teachers move relatively freely outside of periods of the rains retreat (three months or more when monks and novices are required to stay in one monastery). Teachers and students also are personally motivated to travel to monasteries that are well patronized and have texts, images, medicine, prestige, and food. Many monks want to be ordained at well-patronized monasteries so that they can forge contacts (i.e., form a "network") and secure favorable royal appointments of mercantile positions when and if they decide to disrobe. These legends say little about the training of students at these monastic schools and manuscript production centers, but they do reveal that monastic schools were not isolated from one another. Colophons show that students and scribes (both lay and ordained) traveled between monasteries. This is quite common today, and it is not strange to find students from many different towns and cities studying together. Lao, Khoen, Leu, and Northern Thai texts as well as teachers like Kañcana and Kesarapañño frequently moved between these areas.[34] Even today students from Sipsongpanna in southern China, Kengtung in Burma, and several regions of Laos come to study in Northern Thailand.[35] Second, it is known that in Northern Thailand, like Laos, vernacular texts were produced in much greater numbers than were Pali manuscripts.[36] Vernacular texts were not considered secondary to Pali texts for teaching, and teachers could become famous for their ability to write the vernacular and teach eloquently in the vernacular. Third, local leaders saw supporting textual production (and thus, one assumes, monastic education) as important alongside the forging of images, construction of *chedi*, and building of monasteries.[37] Although the teachers themselves sponsored the copying and composition of many manuscripts, wealthy patrons, including, royalty, were active in the support of textual production. Finally, there was no overarching standard curriculum at these or other monastic schools. These teachers and others did not systematically copy, translate, or comment on texts that fall into any discernable chronological, regional, or thematic order.[38]

In looking at the manuscript collections broadly, one sees that, as with education in Laos, both urban and rural monasteries in Northern Thailand based their curriculum mostly on vernacular or bilingual commentaries and glosses worked on by students from a variety of locales. No two collections are the same, and the orthography and the colophons confirm a lack of a regional unified approach to the study of Buddhism.[39] For example, in 1855 the local ruler of Nan had monasteries repaired and ordered the copying of Buddhist scriptures, that is, of the "Pali and nipāta and nikāya and niyāya."[40] This large collection includes a variety of canonical and extra-canonical, vernacular and Pali texts.

The manuscript libraries throughout Northern Thailand and Laos not only contain many more vernacular and bilingual manuscripts, but they also contain "secular" works like medical (*tamra ya*) and astrological (*horasat*) texts and romances and adventures (*nithan*), and these secular texts are often bound with Pali and vernacular "religious" texts. These genres are so mixed (as I discuss below) that dividing them along secular/religious lines is untenable. For example, I was surprised when one manuscript I opened in Lampang contained a *suat mon* (Pali ritual chanting book), a *waiyakon/vyākaraṇa* (a vernacular text explaining some minor grammatical points), and a vernacular medical text.[41] Wat Sri Mongkon in Nan has a collection almost completely dominated by medical texts, protective incantations (*yan/saiyasat*), protective mantras (*paritta*), and non-Vinaya ritual guides. Most of these texts are written in a mixture of vernacular and Pali, and often medical texts, mantras, and protective texts are bound together, which suggests the social history of these manuscripts and the way traditional medicine and protective magic incorporate Pali *mant(r)a* (Pali: *manta*; Sanskrit: mantra; English: incantation). Many manuscript collections of the Buddhist monasteries of Northern Thailand and Laos contain secular and vernacular texts that may seem out of place at a place of religious training. The training at these monasteries was nonstandardized. The orthography, colophon styles, votive declarations, choice of what texts to copy or sponsor, and vocabulary in manuscripts all point to highly independent teachers and students whose training was more organic than systematic. No standard seems to have been established as to when a novice or monk was considered "trained." No standard examination system seems to have been in place, and no evidence is found of social events like "graduation."[42] Indeed, Kesarapañño was seen as a lazy student and was given two idiosyncratic tests by his teacher.

There seem to have been a number of novice, monk, and lay scribes at monasteries in the region.[43] A patron provided the funding for the copying of a particular manuscript, most often narratives or ritual texts, in no discernible order, and a scribe, whether a novice, young monk, or lay devotee, under the supervision of the abbot or another senior monk, copied the manuscript. Some monasteries, like Wat Sung Men and Wat Lai Hin, as well as Vat Mai, Vat Ong Teu, or Vat Vixun in Laos, attracted a number of patrons; however, a monastery was only as successful as the skill of its teachers (e.g., Wat Sung Men and Wat Lai Hin both ceased to be active producers of texts after the deaths of Kañcana and Kesarapañño, respectively) and of the generosity of its patrons. Like many present-day professors who need to win private and public grants and fellowships, scholar monks had to market their skills and service. Monks had the advantage of promising karmic "merit" (*puñña*) and a good rebirth versus the more amorphous value, depending on how one looks at it, of a modern academic's need for "verifiable research results."

Evidence suggests strongly that scribes usually aurally copied the work; that is, a monk read one manuscript out loud, while the scribe listened to the dictation and copied it onto new palm leaf. Some manuscripts show signs that the scribe read the source manuscript and copied the text by sight. But, for many manuscripts, it is not known whether the copy ever was in any contact (i.e., in the same room or on the same desk or floor) with the source text or whether the teacher was reciting the text from memory. This scribal practice allowed for the manipulation, expansion, rearranging, and pedagogical use of Pali and vernacular source texts in nonstandardized ways.

By opening up these manuscripts and reading the colophons, one also confirms their idiosyncratic and highly independent order and the mixed training and background of their scribes. For example, if one looks specifically at colophons of pedagogical manuscripts (*nissaya*, *vohāra*, and *nāmasadda*), one sees a world of traveling, humble students with mixed training. A great fear that manuscripts would be lost and misordered also existed. One colophon on a *kammavācā nissaya* from Wat Bichai in Lampang reveals little about the identity of the scribe or patron, but it offers a clue as to how it was used and stored. The scribe states that he copied/composed it in order to make the text easier to "understand clearly and memorize" for "ordinary people" (*puthujjana dang lai*) who possess a weak wisdom (*mandapañña*). Then he states that, with the manuscript finished, he was placing it in a chest on the evening of the eleventh day of the second month of the Year of the Cock (1909) in order to prevent its destruction. The novice scribe, Phinda, who inscribed (*likkhitta*) by himself (*duai ton eng*) under the charge of Chao Dhammasena, claims to have skill and training in writing (*khian*) but that he needs more skill and training, which writing this manuscript would give him. He repeats again that he hoped the manuscript would remain safe inside the room and not be mixed with other folios (*glāt glā*) forever and ever (*niccam niccam dhuvam dhuvam*). Since Phinda requested that the manuscript not be removed, he was afraid not only that his work would be mixed up but that it would be lost entirely. However, this manuscript must have been removed often. Physical wear and tear and the fact that it was a manuscript used to guide a sermon show that it was used frequently. Here one might sense the fear that would have been generated when Kesarapañño's teacher mixed up the manuscripts at Wat Lai Hin.

One often finds manuscripts that have been composed or copied at one monastery and then moved to another hundreds of kilometers away. Furthermore, at Wat Sung Men many of the colophons show that the text was produced by a student who was in residence in one monastery, like Wat Nam Wan or Wat Sri Chum, but was training at Wat Sung Men. For example, a colophon of a Dhammapada *vohāra* manuscript indicates that Kañcana would farm out work and teach students at monasteries near his own. So Wat Sung Men can be seen not as an isolated school but as a central campus connected loosely to regional campuses near it. This network of schools is common in urban monasteries throughout Thailand and Laos, and from this colophon (and many others) one can see that it was common in rural temples as well. This manuscript is a good example of how from a few lines of text one can draw a large amount of information about the institutional history of a monastic school and the relationship between monasteries. There are fifteen fascicles in this manuscript. The colophons collectively at the end of each of the fascicles indicate that there were at least three scribes involved in the production of this one manuscript and that they hailed from at least three different monasteries.

An excerpt from a colophon of one of the fascicles reads: "[This fascicle] was finished very late in the period of the morning drum (7:30–9:00 a. m.) on the twenty-fourth day, [according to the] Dai (Tai) [system of dating], in order to [gain merit] for myself [and] for [my] four older and younger brothers and sisters. The young brother is named Phinarassa Bhikkhu and the older is Uttararassa Bhikkhu."[44] There are spelling anomalies and several ambiguous statements in this colophon.[45] It is clear that space was dear, because the colophon ends on the last line and the scribe has to write very small and in the margin to finish the colophon without going on to another leaf. There may have been a concern for saving leaves (although the opposite is also common, as scribes were compensated for producing manuscripts by the line, and some clearly tried to use as much space and as many lines as possible so as to make more money). Another quizzical feature is the time. Finishing a manuscript at this time, especially if this was a monk, is unlikely, as this part of the day in a monk's life is busy with issues of eating, prayer, and cleaning. One fares better with the colophon at the end of fascicle 15. Valuable information regarding the date, provenance, author, and patron is often spread over several colophons in a long manuscript. The end of the fifteenth fascicle reads as follows: "Hence, this *dhamma desanā* (*dhamma* sermon) is beneficial for the masses, [that means] many people. [That is the sermon] that was given on that day. The Udenavatthu, the first [story] in the Appamādavagga, is finished, completed. The form and the meaning are completely straightforward (lit.: bald). . . . The novice Abbhiya wrote [this]." This colophon reveals three things. First, the author's name is Abbhiya, if this is indeed the same scribe who copied the first fascicle. Since the handwriting/inscribing is slightly different and the manuscript is very long, they may in fact be two different people. Abbhiya does not say whether he or the donor is the scribe or who is his abbot or preceptor. He simply says that he "wrote" it, not copied it (although to "write" usually means to "copy" in Northern Thai and Lao manuscripts). From the information provided, he is the author, although this is open to question. Since he was a novice, he could have been listening to a sermon or lecture and taking notes. Second, the name of the monastery is not mentioned, but the date, the vocabulary, the orthography, and the fact that it was found at Wat Sung Men lead me to believe that its origin is the area of Luang Phrabang. Most of Kañcana's manuscripts came from Laos. Third, the author calls the story the *Udenavatthu* and does not specify which section of the *Udenavatthu*, namely, the *Sāmavatīvatthu*. The chapter name is therefore incorrect.[46] The *Sāmavatīvatthu*, the story of a consort named Sāmavatī, lauds her faith and dedication. Instead of using the title of the story, Abbhiya uses the more general title, *Udenavatthu*, which suggests that this author was in possession of a different *Dhammapada-atthakathā* source text that did not list the titles of the individual stories in the Udena cycle. All of these points indicate the lack of standardization in regional monastic education and manuscript production.[47]

In general, the mixed Pali and vernacular colophon and others at the end of the other fascicles on this manuscript show that the text was produced at one monastery and then given to Wat Sung Men for protection and storage and for the service of a school with more students. Manuscripts moved as frequently as did students and teachers, and therefore rural schools must be seen as similar to schools in Chiang Mai, Vientiane, and Luang Phrabang. They existed in a loose network of open campuses that shared teachers, texts, and students across the larger Tai-speaking world of eastern Burma, Laos, parts of southwest China, and Northern Thailand. These networks, while certainly affected by the economy and by warfare, were generally independent of the machinations of leaders and borders.

Not only do these colophons reflect fear of loss, the collective production of manuscripts, and the connections between monasteries, but they also indicate that manuscripts were for the education of the audience (in this case, instruction on performing a regular monastic ritual, *kammavācā*, and an explanation of why it was performed) as well as for helping students practice writing and for compensation. Their purpose sounds like that of a science fair project or a book report popular in modern American schools where a student is given an assignment to teach others about a basic scientific law or inform them about a good book, and while doing this project the student personally learns about the law or book and possibly wins a prize. This same sentiment is seen in a colophon from a *kammavācā nāmasadda* (also called a "sab") manuscript from Luang Phrabang, which I translate as follows: "I am *kasila abhatto* (amassed with toil and difficulty) and am not able to be a [good] servant (*dāsa*), a guard that protects the glorious king of the people. *Āma saccam* (Oh, this is the truth) good sirs, the *Kammavācā Sab* is finished . . . [it was] written (*liccana*) by [internal or external] adolescent supporters [of the monastery]. [It took] all night [to complete]." This colophon is a typical example. Scribes, whether they were novices, monks, or specially trained and well-educated laypeople, usually composed texts from dictation. This author dictated this text to "adolescent supporters of the monastery," meaning to students. The teacher would sit in a room, often his personal *kuṭi* or the *vihāra*, or in a *sala*. The young scribes/students would gain merit (*puñña*) by copying the manuscript from dictation or copying by reading for themselves, for high-ranking nobles or the monarch, for their own families, or even for all beings. The teacher/author/dictator would gain merit from composing the text and facilitating its inscription. Since this particular manuscript "took all night," perhaps this teacher was running a draconian manuscript production center in order for the monastery to make money. This colophon, however, is a rare instance in which the student scribe mentions his own troubles. He fears the king, who may have been the person who ordered the texts since this manuscript was found at the royal museum in Luang Phrabang, and he laments his own financial situation. Occasionally in Lao and Northern Thai colophons there is an apology from the scribe/student or author for the mistakes he made and the lack of skill he possesses. However, this obvious request for financial assistance coupled with the condemnation of those who seek out praise suggests that this person was both in need of and ashamed of his need of money.

Another manuscript from Chiang Mai, the *Nissaya mātikātthakathā*, composed in 1569, reflects the collective effort common in monastic schools. Here there was clearly a change of scribes partway through the text, as easily seen in the change of handwriting, but it seems to have had little effect on the methods of translation and commentary in this text. Even though it is unclear whether this text was copied aurally or visually, it is clear that either the person chanting the text to be copied or the physical text of the source text was uniform and composed by one person but inscribed by a group of students. A monk can sponsor a text by donating labor (his students) and time. All of this is quite common in Laos and Northern Thailand. Many scribes often worked on one text, and when copying the text they would add their own notes and correct previous mistakes. The fact that many scribes, students, and teachers often work on one manuscript shows that scholarship and learning in monasteries was not a solitary endeavor.

As in the medieval scriptoria of Ireland and France, many monks would sit together copying, composing, and editing one text, following the dictates of their sleep schedules, their access to material, their teacher's perception of their particular skills, requests by patrons, the need for many students to practice reading and writing using a limited number of texts and prepared palm leaf, and the instructions of their teachers. Monastic teachers today often read out Pali texts, which students are then asked to translate word by word in notebooks and out loud. I observed this at Vat Ong Teu, Wat Phra Singh, Wat Sung Men, Vat Xainyaphum, Vat Naxai, and many other monastic schools. Where Pali language classes are taught in larger monasteries, like Wat Mahathat, Wat Chedi Luang, Wat Suan Dok, and Wat Rakhang, in Central and Northern Thailand, the teacher reads Pali passages from a printed textbook of which the students also have copies. The vocabulary list (Pali and direct vernacular gloss) is given at the end of the passage. The students and the teacher read the passage out loud together, and the students translate each word of the Pali with a vernacular gloss. The teacher either moves on or reads the proper translation with syntax, depending on his knowledge of Pali grammar. Some teachers I have observed do not know Pali grammar very well, but they teach effectively by simply following the vernacular glosses provided in the text. I am getting ahead of myself here, however. That is enough said for now.

3 Kings and Universities

The Siamese began to colonize the region to their immediate north in the late nineteenth century. With this colonization came the reform of monastic education. Before looking at these reforms, I summarize the basic political history of this colonization. Historically this region was more culturally and economically connected to Laos to the east and the Shan and Khoen regions to the north and west than it was to the Siamese in the south.[1] It had been a collection of independent and tributary city-states self-designated as the kingdom of "Lan Na" and populated by various groups of Thai-speaking peoples. In the early twentieth century, Siam, which had been slowly gaining administrative and economic control over the North under the "monthon" (a type of "sphere of influence") system, formally established seven provinces (*changwat*) in the region (*phak*) of Northern Thailand. This removed institutional and economic power (and, more slowly, symbolic and ritual power) from local royal families. Since the early twentieth century local Northern Thai (Chao Lan Na / Khon Muang) leaders have pledged their allegiance to the Thai government centered in Bangkok. However, regional teachers and students have resisted or ignored what Victor Mair calls the "culture of the capital" and have been able to maintain their diverse local pedagogical interpretative traditions.[2]

How the North Became Thai

Prince Damrong of Siam composed the first Thai "official" history of the conflict between Laos and Thailand in 1926 (*Chotmaihet rang rop khabot Vien-*

tiane). Beginning with Damrong's history came other histories that separated the Lao people living in (present-day) Northern Thailand and Northeastern Thailand and those in present-day Laos. Charles Keyes writes that "despite the fact that well over half the population of Siam, the boundaries of which were fixed during the colonial period, had previously been called 'Lao' by the Siamese, Prince Damrong literally wrote the Lao out of Thai history."[3] Prince Damrong himself wrote that "people in Bangkok have long called [the peoples of Northern Siam] Lao. Today, however, we know they are Thai, not Lao."[4] The Lao on the left side of the Mekong became Thai, and according to Thai history texts they always had been "naturally" Thai. Keyes asserts that these official histories create "national narratives that are a 'product of modern nationalisms.'"[5] The present political borders are mapped onto the past and ethnicities and languages are subsumed under these nations, erasing their shared histories. Lao and Thai become natural, eternal, and, therefore, real divisions, even though there is little evidence that they existed in precisely this way historically.

Before this coercive and/or defensive ethnicization, reference to the people who occupy modern-day Northern Thailand and Laos simply as "Lao" had a long history. The Siamese colonization of Lan Na was a slow process, and for most of the nineteenth century the North was considered culturally Lao and of little importance to the Siamese. Ayutthayan chronicles refer to the area of Northern Thailand as the "country of the Lao." The oft-quoted Daniel McGilvary, when referring to Siamese relations with Chiang Mai, wrote in the late nineteenth century that "the Siamese [Central Thai] had never interfered with or assumed control of the internal affairs of the North Lao states."[6] His book *A Half Century among the Siamese and the Lao* groups the Northern Thai with the Lao in Northern Thailand. In referring to the people (in what is today Northern Thailand), he writes that "the substantial character of the Lao as a race will I have no doubt enable more to be accomplished thro' native assistance than in many other lands."[7] Lillian Johnson Curtis, a missionary in Chiang Mai, Lampang, Phrae, and Nan between 1895 and 1899, wrote *The Lao of North Siam.* She continually observes in her book the customs of the people of the cities and villages of Northern Thailand as distinctly Lao and not Siamese. For these missionaries, Northern Siam or Northern Thailand was Lao. Even as late as 1919, the Christian missionary Jessie MacKinnon Hartzell referred to the language of Nan and Phrae as "Lao," even though she referred to the region and the people as "Northern Siamese."[8] Furthermore, she referred to two of her local contacts as Ai Sen and Pi Teing, evidence of the mixing of Thai and Lao languages, which persists until this day. *Ai* is "older brother" in Lao, and *Phi* is "older brother" in Thai. The American Presbyterian missionary groups in Northern Thailand in the mid-to-late nineteenth century were called members of the "Laos Mission." The missionary newspaper was printed and published at Payap University in Chiang Mai at the first printing press in all of Northern Thailand and was called *Laos News*, as distinct from the reports of the "Siam Mission" in Central Thailand. Mary Backus (1884), Carl Block (1884), Etienne Aymonier (1884–85), George Younghusband (1887), and Reginald Le May (1913), missionaries, scholars, and travelers, all used the term *Lao* in their published accounts when referring to people living in present-day Northern Thailand.[9]

These missionary groups were actively supported and promoted by King Chulalongkorn of Bangkok with land grants in order to help spread the teaching of the Central Thai or Siamese language through missionary printing presses. The king saw the missionaries as a civilizing and nationalist influence. Still, the Northerners were not seen as Siamese or Thai. Hartzell speaks to the way Bangkokians would poke fun at her when she spoke Lao in Bangkok and referred to the Northern Thais (or Lao) as "ewoot cak paa [*sic*]" (monkeys of the jungle).[10] Efforts were made to write dictionaries for the North that incorporated and suppressed the Lao elements of the Northern language.[11]

Because of the cultural and linguistic association of people in Northern Thailand and Laos and the long relationship that has developed among the Burmese, Shan, Khoen, Yuan, and Lao people through economic, religious, and intellectual exchange, authorities in Siam / Central Thailand have instituted programs to make the North more Siamese. These programs were resisted, however. For example, Krishna Charoenwong notes that Central Thai education administrators and policy makers met much resistance when they tried to establish the Central Siamese educational system in the North, the biggest problem being the Siamese royal government's policy of Central Thai–language schools. Krishna writes that "they [Northern Thais] did not understand central Thai. This created serious obstacles in communication with the government and within private sectors . . . it resulted in two rebellions: Prayapraasingkhraam's in 1889 and the Shan Rebellion in Phrae in 1902. . . . Lan Na people did not enjoy dependence on the central Thai government . . . one of the most important factors in the tension . . . was that they spoke different languages as well as had different cultures."[12] In 1893 Central Thai was made the official language of the Siamese-controlled Lan Na region. In 1903, after much resistance, the policy was changed slightly. The Lan Na language and Yuan script could be taught in schools as a subject, but the royal policy states that central Thai remains the medium of instruction.[13]

Individual city-states in the North remained independent from Siamese rule long after their "liberation" from the Burmese in 1774. For decades, however, they "enjoyed full autonomy, conducting foreign affairs, carrying out administrative responsibilities, and mobilizing local resources for whatever tasks they sought to accomplish. The Northern Thai nobles could enter into treaties with their neighbours such as the Red Karen and Muang Pong, and, initially, could negotiate with the British. They controlled the land, the forests on it, and all internal matters—justice, defense, corvée, ceremonial life, and revenue administration."[14] While Chiang Mai royal leaders were expected to attend royal funerals in Siam and perform a water ritual showing their allegiance to Siam, they were for all intents and purposes independent. For example, in 1836, the greatest single year of manuscript production in the North, a British mission in Chiang Mai negotiated a border between Tenasserim in modern-day Burma/Myanmar and Lan Na. Thongchai Winichakul writes that the British authorities in India were concerned about the drawing of this border because they thought it would threaten Siam.[15] "Strikingly, not only was Chiangmai ready to make a treaty without Bangkok's approval, but for the sake of friendship [with the British] the king of Chiangmai also happily gave away a portion of territory as a present which the British did not request."[16] It was not until after the Bowring Treaty of 1855, in which the British gained timber contracts in Siamese territories, that the Bangkok royal house attempted to interfere in the internal affairs of Chiang Mai and other Northern towns. However, these treaties were tentative and provisional, because of the very real chance that the Northern royal leaders would choose to side with Burma and the British. For example, Ratanaporn Sethakul reports that in 1865 King Kawilorot had a royal messenger from Bangkok killed. In 1869 the Siamese court refused to interfere, at the request of the American counsel, when two Christian converts were executed by Kawilorot. The Siamese stated that "they (the royalty of Northern Thailand) have their own laws and customs, which they enforce as they see fit. They do not use the same laws as Bangkok."[17] Even in 1883, King Chulalongkorn states that "Chiang Mai is still not an integral part of the kingdom."[18] It was not until 1900 that the tribute system ended and the "Regulations on the Administration of Northwestern Monthon" were issued, making Chiang Mai and many surrounding cities part of the Kingdom of Siam.[19]

Northern Thailand and Laos certainly considered themselves sovereign from Siam and Burma for long periods of time. These were separate states with their own linguistic, religious, intellectual, pedagogical, artistic, and historiographic traditions, even though these regions overlapped ethnically and people living in certain towns simultaneously paid tribute to two competing overlords.[20] Chiang Saen was at one time under the "overlordship" of Chiang Mai, Kengtung, Luang Phrabang, and Siam. Many towns in modern-day Laos were once paying tribute to the Vietnamese, Siamese, and Cambodians and to Chinese bandits (Ho) in the nineteenth century.[21] The royal authorities in Bangkok realized there were these historical divisions between the North, Laos, and themselves and also recognized the possibilities of absorption or loss of control that came with traditional shifting and overlapping allegiances. Siam instituted numerous reforms, including those regarding language and education, in a gradual process, as Thongchai writes, of "displacing the traditional local autonomy, especially in the tributaries, by the modern mechanism of centralization. The tempo, strategies, problems, and solutions varied from place to place. But the final outcomes were the same: the control of revenue, taxes, budgets, education, the judicial system, and other administrative functions by Bangkok through the residency."[22]

While Thongchai's assessment of Siam's invention of Thai-ness as part of its absorption of the north, northeast, and southern parts of modern-day Thailand is fresh and astute, he does not concern himself with the deep continuities between the premodern and modern periods and the underlying intellectual links between Laos, the North, and Siam that belie the linguistic, historical, political, and social differences. This book seeks to expose these epistemological links that are often hidden in studies based on spatial and temporal frameworks. By focusing on the pedagogical methods, rhetorical style, educational material, and homiletics of the region, I draw connections between these disparate and often contentious peoples and places that are otherwise masked by historical vicissitudes. Although the history presented above shows great divisions between Siam and Northern Thailand and Laos, I hope to show that there are reading cultures and interpretative communities that operate without borders and outside the view of kings and university administrators.[23]

How Soon Is Now? The Modern Siamese Reform of Monastic Education

In order to understand the history of modern monastic education in the North, the parameters of the modern period need to be addressed. There is a trend in Southeast Asian studies to focus on the rupture between the present and past, the early modern and modern, the precolonial and postcolonial, and the pre–printing press and printing press periods.[24] For the Buddhist history of Northern Thailand, the question of when modernity began is complicated. Northern Thailand was only tangentially colonized, although there was influence from American Christian missionaries in the nineteenth century and from British, Dutch, and French traders and travelers as early as the sixteenth century. Industrialization, global advertising, and tourism did not seriously impact the region until the late twentieth century. Marking the advent of modernity with the arrival of Westerners in the region reveals an orientalist Eurocentric perspective, however. Can one talk about modernity without talking about the West?

For my purposes, the use of Pali and its relation to the modernization of monastic education are more useful ways of discussing the emergence of modernity. Steven Collins notes problems with the designation "modern" when periodizing Buddhist history. He states that in some cases it was the reaction to Western colonialism and science, but more importantly that the modern period began when Pali "ceased to be an obvious and viable linguistic and textual medium to express contemporary Buddhism." This is the period when Pali "became both a learned and dead language: somewhere, depending on local circumstances, between the beginning of the nineteenth and early twentieth centuries."[25]

This observation offers scholars a new way to think about the link between Westernization and modernity and to examine alternative modernities, rhizomatic participatory ways of being modern. For me, the question for this region is not when Pali became a "dead" language but what does "living" Pali look like? What does it mean to "learn" or to "know" Pali? Pali texts in both the premodern and modern periods were used for different purposes (prestige, power, display, ritual performance, ethical inquiry, cadastral technology, protective magic, philosophical reflection, psychological coping, etc.) and in different ritual, private, and educational contexts. In many of these contexts and for many of these purposes, "knowing" how to read or write Pali was not necessary. Like most young monks and novices, I could chant hours of Pali before I ever learned the grammar. Like most monastic students, I used Pali incantations to bless motorcycles, houses, newly married couples, corpses, and so on before I could identify grammatical inconsistencies. I could explain individual Pali words in sermons, without being able to write a Pali poem or read a Pali story. The line between literacy and illiteracy is vague. Historically, entirely new texts were rarely composed in Pali after the mid-sixteenth century; however, the need to gloss, comment on, invoke, and instruct Pali terms and abridge texts in specific ways persisted and persists.[26] This is where the "languaging" of Pali happens. The line between the death and life of Pali is blurry and remains so to this day in monastic education and religious scholarship. This approach allows one to move beyond field-wide discourses that associate modernity with loss and that see Thai Buddhists as victims of Westernization.

Perhaps a move can be made from trying to define when modernity began to tracing continuities and disruptions in epistemic flows. Instead of identifying when the modern began and what enabled its emergence, one needs to observe local epistemes that were impacted/influenced by the use of printing presses, industrialization, tourism, communication technology, religious ecumenicalism, human rights, and other Western and non-Western accoutrements of modernity. One also needs to trace which intellectual agents did not engage in coterminous modern self-transformations of literary, epistemological, enlightenment-rational, textual, and pedagogical approaches to teaching and learning. Instead of asking when modernity began, perhaps one should ask why it did not. Perhaps, instead of asking what modernity has destroyed, one should ask what has survived and flourished. The trajectories of multiple modernities need to be traced.

Generally, I wonder why historians and anthropologists of Southeast Asia tend to see a break between the premodern and modern without offering detailed examples of bridges between the two. The reasons for changes in education, political policy, health care, literacy, notions of nationhood, and Buddhist practice from the premodern to the modern period have been discussed extensively by leaders in the fields of Southeast Asian history and religion (or scholars choose to work on either the modern or premodern period). Rarely are efforts made to trace the connections between them beyond the use of the vague term *traditional*. For example, Maurizio Peleggi, Nidhi Aeusrivongse, Milton Osbourne, Sulak Sivaraksa, Anthony Reid, B. J. Terwiel, John Butt, Thomas Kirsch, and Benedict Anderson, among others, emphasize the changing face of Southeast Asian culture and religion based on the disruption of colonialism, capitalism, globalism, technology, or Christianity.[27] While massive changes are undeniable, these are rarely explicitly coupled with detailed attempts to see what meaning-making systems, literary tropes and themes, exegetical practices, indigenous systems of data compression, and conceptions of history and nation persist. What is lost and what is gained by looking for ruptures between the premodern and the modern? While changes in institutions, printing, communications and media technology, national border formation, and bureaucratic administration are undeniable, these types of changes are mapped onto assumed epistemological changes in teaching, expressing, and learning.

The Sangha Act of 1902

Looking at the study of Thai Buddhist education, perhaps the most common markers for change from the premodern to the modern are the reforms of King Chulalongkorn and Prince Wachirayan, culminating in the Sangha Act of 1902. Yoneo Ishii, Tamara Loos, Stephen Zack, Patrick Jory, John Butt, and David Wyatt, and Venerable Khammai Dhammasami all invoke this royal administrative act as one of the signals that Thai Buddhism was entering into modernity, or perhaps that modernity was impacting Thai Buddhism.[28] The main crux of this act was the formalization and centralization of Thai Buddhist education and administration.

In the nineteenth century the Siamese kings Rama IV (Mongkut) and Rama V (Chulalongkorn) made great efforts to formalize the Buddhist ecclesiastical system and educational practices in Siam and in their vassal states in the north, northeast, and south. This was part of the nation-building and social control process to suppress regionalism, strengthen the country against foreign missionary influence, formalize the curriculum, and "modernize" the entire education system. Siamese ecclesiastical ranks, textbooks printed in Siamese script, monastic examinations, the Pali Buddhist canon, and teachers approved from Bangkok and Central Siam were disseminated to the rural and urban areas in Siam and its holdings. Monks from the recently pacified north, northeast, and south were brought to Bangkok to study in two new monastic universities (Mahachulalongkorn and Mahamakut). Localized forms of expression, language, curricula, and script were considered irrelevant to this formalization and centralization. The Sangha Act and the Royal Education Acts sponsored by King Chulalongkorn of Siam forced Northern monks to be under the authority of the higher ecclesiastics (Mahatherasamakom) and the leader of the Siamese Sasana (Sangharāja), and mandated that curricula be dictated and written (in Siamese script and language) in Bangkok. One of the most significant features of Buddhism in modern Thailand is its apparently well-organized and centralized institutional structure. Since Siam (later Thailand) is the only country in Southeast Asia that was "never colonized," the nation-building project in which religious reform played a major part could be considered a success. Although the Buddhist ecclesia has grown in wealth and institutional stability since 1902, still there are deep fissures in Thai Buddhism that existed before 1902 and persist today.

Royal reform of Buddhist monastic education is not particularly modern. Consistently, from the earliest thirteenth-century records to 1902, Siamese kings and high-ranking monks had seen it as their duty to collect and edit Buddhist texts, rewrite Buddhist history, purge the Sangha of corrupt persons, and rein in renegade, independent-minded practitioners. By 1902 these techniques had become more efficient and widespread. In 1902 King Chulalongkorn and Prince Wachirayan, an ordained monk who had become the supreme patriarch of the entire Thai Buddhist Sangha, removed the role to educate the Thai people from the Sangha and regulated the organization of monastic education. Those two, working with another half brother, Prince Damrong (the minister of the interior), released the act on the administration of the Sangha (Acts of the Administration of the Buddhist Order of Sangha of Thailand: 2445 [1902], with later adaptations in 2484 [1941], 2505 [1962], and 2545 [2002]). Before this Sangha Act, monastic education and administration in Thailand was neither formal nor centralized. It depended largely on the aims of the monks of each monastery. The Sangha Act was designed to make those residing in a monastery "in service to the nation" and to deflect criticism from European missionaries and Japanese envoys who denounced the poor and idiosyncratic state of Thai Buddhist education and organization.

The details of the Sangha Act represent largely administrative rules dividing the Buddhist ecclesia into formal ranks and assigning national, provincial, and district heads of the Sangha. They are still in effect today. Each of the regions (north, south, central, and northeast) has a formal hierarchy of monks, and they all report to the Mahatherasamakom. Individual monasteries are still run by abbots (*chao awat*) and deputy abbots (*rong chao awat*), but after 1902 they had to report regularly to their district and regional heads. All monks had to be registered with a particular monastery and were issued identification numbers and cards. Prince Wachirayan, commenting on the act, states that "although monks are already subject to the ancient law contained in the Vinaya [Buddhist Book of Precepts], they must also subject themselves to the authority which derives from the specific and general law of the State."[29]

In 1902 around eighty thousand monks became subject to the law of the royal government of Siam, which controlled their admission to monkhood, their right to ordain, the size and status of monastic ground, and the ranking of monks. There was sporadic resistance in the form of renegade monks in the north like Krupa Sri Wichai and rebellions of holy men in the northeast until 1924. There was also Western influence on Thai Buddhism.[30] King

Chulalongkorn was quite impressed by Western scholars of Buddhism and sought to reform the canon and teaching of Buddhism in Thailand based on a strict historical and canonical understanding of Buddhism. King Chulalongkorn's massive survey of monasteries in 1886 led him to conclude that the Buddhist teaching in the region was "full of nonsense" because it was found that "the Jatakas and other *nithan* [folktales] formed the basis of religious instruction for most of the kingdom."[31]

In order to suppress rebellions by local "holy men" (*phu mi bun*) against Central Thai authority in these regions the Siamese king ordered that local manuscripts of *jātaka* and stories of these holy men be burned and that the Central Thai Sangha authority under the king be enforced.[32] Prince Wachirayan also believed that reform was necessary to ensure that Siamese Buddhism could purify itself. He believed, as did the king, that Buddhism was simpler and more pure in the distant past. "True Buddhism" was that designed by the Buddha himself in India twenty-four hundred years earlier. The state-centered and state-sponsored reform movements of King Mongkut, Prince Wachirayan, King Chulalongkorn, and Prince Damrong, among others, portrayed Thai Buddhism as overly corrupted by those claiming magical and fortune-telling powers and, thus, in need of renewal. Prince Wachirayan in particular believed that there was an ideal past when Buddhist practice did not involve protective magic, when all monks studied Pali for many years, and when the Buddhist ecclesia and benevolent Buddhist kings worked together for the common people.

Besides administrative organization, the most significant feature of the 1902 reforms was the examination system for monks and novices.[33] Prince Wachirayan publicly stated that the Pali canon was the most important source of Buddhist ethics, law, and history. However, when formulating his exams and writing his textbooks for monks, the canon actually played little role. In fact, there was very little real difference between the examinations and texts used before Wachirayan and after.

The canon and the 1902 reforms seemed not to have ushered in the modern era (at least not in monastic education) that Ishii, Wyatt, and others suggest they did. There is little evidence that the Pali canon was available and accessible to the majority of Thais previous to 1902. The canon was rarely found as a set in one monastery, and the authoritative parts of the canon were not commonly agreed on at any time in Thai history. Ideally, Wachirayan wanted to make the canon more prominent; to facilitate this goal, he promoted the study of Pali grammar. He composed six volumes of Pali grammar, as well as several guidebooks for students, including the still standard *Navakowat*, outlining what he saw as basic Buddhist ethics; the *Buddhasāsanāsubhāsit*, a selection of short, pithy Buddhist proverbs from the canon; a Buddha biography; and a guide to the Vinaya. These textbooks, all written in simple and straightforward Thai, began to form, ideally, the standard curriculum for monks in Siam.[34] Monks in both monastic universities were encouraged to take examinations in Pali and Thai that were designed by the prince and based on these and other anthologized Buddhist texts. Therefore, in the early twentieth century these textbooks were the basis for the new *nak dham* Buddhist examinations. The prince instituted three grades of *nak dham*, or "student of the Dhamma," which remain relatively unchanged today. These examinations are in Thai and were prerequisites for the Pali examinations. Interestingly enough, most of the examinations were on commentarial texts like the *Dhammapada-atthakathā*, *Maṅgala-atthadīpanī*, and Visuddhimagga and on Thai handbooks and anthologies, not on canonical texts themselves.[35] While these *nak dham* examinations and essays do not involve exact, word-for-word translation or memorization and are not based on Pali-language texts (but mostly on Thai translations), the *parian* examinations involve the literal reproduction of an original Pali text (again, not canonical texts) from the Thai and vice versa. The eighth-level *prayok* examination involves over 160,000 words of memorization.

In comparing texts to those used by King Rama II in the early nineteenth century one sees little change. First, commentaries, and even commentaries and histories composed in Northern Thailand, not canonical texts, constituted the textual material for most of the examinations. Second, narratives from the *Dhammapada-atthakathā*, very similar in style and subject matter to narratives from the *Jātaka-atthakathā*, which King Chulalongkorn had claimed were "full of nonsense," were an important source for the exams. In fact, King Chulalongkorn himself wrote an introduction in Thai (largely copied from British scholar Caroline Rhys-Davids's English introduction) to the *Jātaka-atthakathā* in 1903, and therefore his judgment of the texts in 1886 seems to have been either rash or based on his assessment that these stories inspired rebels. Despite royal rhetoric about the purity of the canon and a lauding of the Westerner's help in discovering and preserving the canon, extra-canonical narratives and translocal and local commentaries still played a dominant role in the state's new monastic curriculum and examinations. Third, very few monks, nuns, or novices ever actually sit for these examinations (as I discuss below), and less than a handful every year ever take the highest levels of the examinations. Most of the students who do actually take the examinations take the lower levels and hence study the *Dhammapada-atthakathā* and anthologies more than they do Pali canonical texts.

The prince opened an academy at his own royal monastery in Bangkok, Wat Boworniwet (Bovornivesa), called the Mahāmakuṭa Rājavidyalāya (Mahamakut Monastic University). This institution later expanded into one of the two major monastic universities in Thailand. From this base and from his institution of a Thai curriculum, he began to change the Pali examination system. First, he instituted written examinations. This change enabled a larger number of students to sit and take the examination at the same time. For example, the first cycle tested fifty-three students in one day, a number unheard of in the old system. Second, he revised the subject matter of the Pali examinations. While keeping the Dhammapada commentary and the *Maṅgala-atthadīpanī*, he chose canonical texts for the upper grades from the Vinaya, Sutta, and Abhidhamma piṭaka.

The vast majority of monks in the capital still took the old Pali exams and were trained at the major monastic university, Mahāchulalongkorn Rājavidyalāya (Mahachulalongkorn Monastic University) next to the grand palace on the river. It was not until 1913 that Prince Wachirayan's system was standard for all monks in the kingdom. By his death in 1921, the examinations were held at eleven Bangkok monasteries. This worked well for nation building since any monk who wanted a national ranking had to travel to and was usually trained in Bangkok. These ranks were important because they could lead to employment after a monk disrobed. In order to work for the civil service, teach in government schools or universities, or enter secular bachelors, masters, and doctoral programs, one had to pass these examinations if one had been a Buddhist novice in one's youth. In 1911 if a monk had not passed any examinations he could be forcibly disrobed and sent to the military.

Modern Monastic Educational Institutions in Thailand

Despite these institutional and elite changes, there is no record indicating that many monks were forcibly removed on a large scale because of examination failure rates. Indeed, if they had been, very few monks would be left in Thailand. These rules have never been enforced systematically. A bending, breaking, and altering of the rules is found in every monastery on a daily basis. Monastic life is subtle and intensely personal. Much movement is observed within the walls. Friends are helped; students are quietly dismissed or promoted. Monastic examinations have slowly become less relevant. Many monks can spend their entire careers, even in the royal monasteries in Bangkok, without passing any of the upper-level examinations. In rural monasteries, especially in the North and South, royally sponsored examinations and the canon play little role.

Scholars typically overestimate the influence of the Central Thai ecclesia and the government's Ministry of Religion and Culture on the practice of Thai Buddhism. The Central Thai government's sponsorship of ecclesiastical examinations and suppression of local religious practice (especially Lao) and training of Thammayut missionaries have had only limited influence over the past century. The Sangha Act, like other public displays of the progressiveness of the Siamese royal presence (e.g., lavish train stations, public clocks, public parks, secular universities, royally sponsored dictionaries, and photographs of royalty in European suits) had little effect outside the capital and did not fundamentally change the lives of the urban and rural poor.[36] The new Buddhist education created by the elite has had little commerce among the vast majority of monks and novices in Thailand today. According to national statistics, of the 267,000 monks and 97,840 novices in Thailand in the year 2000, only 9,775 were enrolled in monastic universities (less than 3 percent). Of the 9,775 enrolled, only 351 are studying beyond the bachelor degree level and only a handful are studying for their doctorates. The Northeast, the poorest and least populated of the four major regions of Thailand, has the largest number of monks and novices in the country (over 40 percent of the total). The North has only 20 percent of the total. The northern sixteen provinces (of which only seven were ever part of the kingdom of Lan Na) and the twenty-six northeastern provinces produce the lowest number of university students. They sit for monastic examinations much less frequently than do Bangkok monks and novices even though Bangkok and the surrounding provinces supply only 16 percent of the total number of monks and novices in the country. The South has the least, and only 6 percent of all the monks and novices reside there.

Before monks and novices can enter monastic universities they study at primary and secondary monastic schools. There are 31,071 monasteries in Thailand, but only a small percentage of these monasteries actually run schools. Of these, 3,554 (11 percent) have *rongrian pathom* (elementary schools); 78 percent of this 11 percent are in the North and Northeast. In Central Thailand only 1.66 percent have monastic elementary schools. The North and Northeast have 21,629 and 160,991 monastic elementary students, respectively (many are lay students), while Bangkok and the surrounding provinces have fewer than 8,000 students enrolled at monastic elementary schools. The largest number of monastic students in modern Thailand study in Pariyatidhamma secondary schools. Within these schools are three major divisions: Paliseuksa study (Pali language, liturgy, and texts); Dhammaseuksa (ethics and general Buddhist history and teachings); and Samanaseuksa ("common," secular subjects).[37] Most schools teach only Buddhist subjects, but some also teach *garuhat* (household or lay subjects). It should be noted that texts from the Pali canon and the Pali grammar in general are almost completely absent in elementary and secondary monastic schools. Pali is limited to lifting (*yok sab*) Pali words from an idiosyncratic selection of texts and basing lessons on them.[38]

These statistics are striking because they reflect the sparse influence that the Sangha educational reforms—especially the textbooks, curriculum, and examinations of the late nineteenth and early twentieth centuries—have had on the state of Buddhist education in the country. Less than 30 percent of all the monasteries in the country have schools; only 16 percent have anything more than elementary schools. The North has a much lower percentage than does the Northeast and even a lower percentage of monks and novices in residence. Many novices and monks reside at one monastery and travel to attend classes at another nearby. Many have never attended school formally and study with their abbots, older novices, and senior monks. If they do attend a neighboring monastic school or government school, it may be for only two to three years. The vast majority of formally or informally trained monastic students never sit for state-sponsored monastic *nak dham* or *parian* examinations. Of those who sit, even fewer pass the exams. As a monk in the Northeast myself, I never prepared for examinations, and none of the other monks or novices, including my abbot, had ever studied in a formal monastic school or taken examinations. Even though we were members of a Thammayut monastery, we did not have any of the official textbooks written or compiled by Prince Wachirayan or his successors for Thammayut students. We did not have a full (unopened) copy of the canon. I taught English at a local Mahanikaya (the "sect" to which 95 percent of Thai monks belong) elementary school for several months in rural Thailand. None of Prince Wachirayan's sponsored textbooks were available at that school either. This lack of resources does not mean that education (reading, writing, etc.) was not important or promoted in our monastery or in the local Mahanikaya monastery. It certainly was, but the elite and royal reform movement had little influence on what we studied or how we studied or taught. This is quite common throughout Thailand and even more so in Laos and Northern Thailand, where monastic education is largely informal and idiosyncratic. The rise of Buddhist Sunday schools, as well as meditation centers, mosques, Christian mission schools, and government schools, further reflects the sparse influence that the Sangha educational reform has outside the elite monasteries of Bangkok and a few other major urban centers. The reforms of the kings and princes of the nineteenth and early twentieth centuries have little effect on Buddhist education throughout Thailand today. However, as I discuss, this does not mean that novices and monks do not receive an education.

Studies by Jory, Wyatt, and Ishii, among others, that posit a rupture between pre-1902 and post-1902 Buddhist education are certainly accurate if one sees Buddhist education as royal, institutional, canonical, elite, and Bangkok centered.[39] However, this approach has certain limitations. First, it focuses only on the changes ushered in by the elite in Bangkok. Second, it does not examine the actual impact institutional changes have on the reception of Buddhist learning among students (except for misleading records of examination scores and the granting of certain monastic ranks). Third, it does not offer any real understanding of the nature of Buddhist education before these institutional changes. Wyatt and Ishii in particular state only that Thai Buddhist education before King Chulalongkorn's reforms was amorphous, informal, idiosyncratic, and decentralized. While there certainly is little information available about Buddhist education before the nineteenth century, there has been no effort to look directly at the texts used in premodern education to discover possible rhetorical styles, pedagogical techniques, or curricular parameters. Fourth, although this cannot be said of David Wyatt and Craig Reynolds, it treats the royal reformers and elite monks of Bangkok as simplistic, "oriental" thinkers, who could do nothing but ape the West. Just as French reformers and researchers were diverse in their approaches to Lao Buddhism, Prince Wachirayan, King Chulalongkorn, and others had many different approaches to Thai and Pali religious scholarship. They supported the editing, printing, and copying of vernacular as well as classical texts; they appealed to scholars in Burma and Cambodia and developed a sophisticated way of testing and teaching. They were active agents of change, not just victims of it.[40]

How Thai Is the North? Modern Monastic Education in Northern Thailand

There has been much written on the influences on Prince Wachirayan, King Chulalongkorn, and Prince Damrong in formalizing the Buddhist education system in Thailand. I do not overly rehearse it here. I want to emphasize two points that are often overlooked. First, the powerful effect of indigenous pedagogical methods and the use of vernacular commentaries and guidebooks are largely discounted by historians. No study has been done of the differences between Northern (or any other region) monastic education and Central monastic education in either pre- or post-1902 Thailand. Second, it is assumed, because there was a reform instituted by the elite in Bangkok in 1902, that this reform actually changed the way monastic education worked on the ground. The statistics above and my observations and interviews show that this was simply not the case. These reforms were not actually implemented in any significant way. Ideologically and institutionally change has occurred, but practically, it has not.

Although the nineteenth-century reform of Buddhist education was centered in the royal monasteries and courts of Bangkok, it was eventually tested in the North. Long before the efforts in the 1950s and 1960s to stamp out the communist insurgency through the monkhood, King Chulalongkorn saw Buddhist education as a way to peacefully pull the rural areas under the umbrella of the emerging Thai nation. On September 18, 1898, Damrong, under the king's orders, held a meeting to discuss the educational situation in the countryside. The meeting was centered on textbook dissemination and administrative reform based on the model put forward by the Ministry of Education. Because of the lack of resources in the provinces, all education, religious and secular (although this division was still not absolute), would be expanded through the rural monasteries. The monasteries could provide education that ensures "knowledge, capabilities [skills], and good behavior . . . all thereof these benefits should be more widespread. They are fed and nourished by the study of reading and writing, science, and the *Dhamma*." However, changes in rural monastic education needed to be transformed because "the traditional monastery education . . . had failed to achieve these ends. The old system was too diffuse, too fragmented, and too independent-minded to meet the needs of the times." To this end, Prince Wachirayan recommended that the rural monastery must not be considered a place for religious education only. The royal government needed to "consider all monasteries as schools, register them as such, and consider all their pupils as school students. 'During their general education in the monasteries,' boys should learn to 'use the writing system of the country [i.e., Central Thai / Siamese], arithmetic, to earn a living, and to know good from bad.' Each of these schools should itself hold annual or semiannual examinations."[41] These monasteries were to be monitored and given textbooks. Their students' progress on examinations would determine whether individual monasteries received more or less funding. To ensure better instruction and preparation for examinations, the monks were to be better trained and organized. However, the royal planners saw the dangers in pushing reform too far and too fast in the provinces. Wachirayan, having been a monk for almost three decades, warned that the Sangha should feel independent and their traditional hierarchy respected. Moreover, the more the Sangha was guided instead of controlled, the "drain on government funds will be lessened."[42] Funding was a constant concern, and the rural monastery was seen as a resource that could be utilized with little capital expenditure. The greatest expenditure was for textbooks. At first, Damrong suggested that twenty thousand copies of each level of text be printed and distributed free of charge to the monasteries and then after two years the government would charge a small amount for the texts at a small profit.[43] Government texts would prepare students for government examinations.

Besides the textbooks and examinations, the government interfered little in Buddhist educational practice in the outer provinces. These textbooks were poorly distributed and rarely replaced by new editions, and students seldom sat for any type of official examination. In terms of higher monastic education, especially Pali education, the provinces were largely unaffected until the 1970s and 1980s, when some rural monks were moving to Bangkok to receive higher monastic training and compete for ecclesiastical ranks. A few royal monasteries in the provinces felt the reform in the early part of the twentieth century. For example, the king appointed monks to ecclesiastical administrative offices only if they resided at royal monasteries (loosely meaning monasteries directly supported by royal coffers and more formally meaning monasteries ritually dedicated by the king and given a royal seal). Most of these royal monasteries were located in Bangkok, but some were in provinces as far away as Chainat and Phetchaburi (both over two hundred kilometers from Bangkok). "Far more numerous, and extending over the whole kingdom, the commoner monasteries remained completely unorganized, surviving independently through the support of the provincial notables and people."[44] Even though, after 1902, all monks and monasteries were under the control of the government in Bangkok, the actual effects of that control were minor. However, slowly over the twentieth century the best and brightest of the monastic students, lay or ordained, were drawn to the secular and monastic universities of Bangkok in order to gain prestige for their family, obtain lucrative government jobs or business contacts, or, in terms of monks, an easier urban life coupled with the chance for prestigious ranks and for classes with reputedly the best teachers standing in front of the best-stocked, officially sanctioned, bookshelves. Most of these reforms were relevant only to monks at major monasteries in Bangkok.[45]

Since 1902 and the rise of the printing press and centralized publishers of Buddhist educational material, the dissemination of official Buddhist educational material in the form of textbooks, examination standards, ecclesiastical ranks, and so forth has been one-way, from the capital to the countryside. Monasteries in Chiang Mai, especially Wat Suan Dok, Wat Chedi Luang, and Wat Phra Singh, are now surrogate agents of this dissemination. Wat Suan Dok is the location of the Northern regional campus of Mahachulalongkorn University. Its curriculum and texts are identical to those of the central campus in Bangkok. Its large library holds books printed in Bangkok, including two sets of the Tipiṭaka in Thai script. Many of its teachers were also trained in Bangkok. Wat Phra Singh also follows this curriculum, and students from both monasteries share teachers and library resources. Students from other monasteries, such as Wat Chiang Man, also can attend these schools. The instruction is in Central Thai, and the texts are in Thai and Pali. The local Yuan / Northern Thai language is no longer the medium, and the texts and textual genres that formed the basis of premodern monastic education in the urban and rural North are often only the purview of the local antiquarian and codicologist.[46] Today, students from rural areas in the North travel, as did Krupa Kañcana 170 years ago, to Chiang Mai (and often Bangkok) to study. As the cities of Chiang Mai and Bangkok grew over the past century so did their power over Buddhist education.

Because of its royal status, central location, and ritual power, Wat Chedi Luang had been an educational center as early as the fourteenth century, and that status led to its being chosen as the central school in Northern Thailand for the Thammayut sect/lineage and the Northern branch campus for Mahamakut Monastic University in the twentieth century. The Thammayut branch university at Wat Chedi Luang, like its older sister school in Bangkok, Mahamakut Monastic University, which was started by Prince Wachirayan in the nineteenth century, attracts some of the best and brightest students in the Theravada world to sit and listen to teachers sitting on the golden preaching chair. Mahamakut's curriculum is nearly identical to Mahachulalongkorn's in Bangkok. Prince Wachirayan wrote in 1887 that Mahamakut University should "use the new curriculum and written examination system [and that] Wat Mahathat [Mahachulalongkorn Monastic University] should follow it exactly."[47] He encouraged donors to give the same books to both monasteries. He instituted the *nak dham* and *parian* examinations there, as well as the Pariyatidhamma secondary-level curriculum and administrative structure.[48] While there have been some minor changes made to the system because of sectarian debate and attitudinal, ritual, and aesthetic preference, the education system for both Mahachulalongkorn and Mahamakut monastic universities and the secondary school systems that feed them are largely interchangeable. Mahamakut, like Mahachulalongkorn, opened up provincial campuses beginning in 1898. These regional campuses did not have many students until the 1980s. Wat Chedi Luang became one of these provincial campuses in the twentieth century as the Siamese royal family gained more influence in Northern Thailand.[49]

In Chiang Mai, about 45 percent of all university-level monastic students study at the Mahachulalongkorn Monastic University branch campus at Wat Chedi Luang (55 percent at the Mahanikaya sect's branch campus at Wat Suan Dok). Not all the students reside at this monastery; many reside at other monasteries in the city but travel to Wat Chedi Luang for classes. Similarly, teachers are drawn from many different monasteries.[50] Initially, teachers for these schools were trained exclusively at the Bangkok campus, but eventually regionally trained monks became instructors. Since the Mahamakut and Mahachulalongkorn system used Thai-language textbooks printed in Bangkok and designed a Siamese-centric curriculum, the regional provincial campuses had to adopt this system, and these texts further eroded the traditional monastic education system of the North.

The changes that have happened over the past century should not be overly emphasized or dramatized. Most monastic students in the rural North or other rural areas in Thailand never study in the cities, never sit for Pali examinations, and never achieve high ecclesiastical ranks. In fact, many leave the monkhood after their secondary education is completed, sometime between the ages of eighteen and twenty. The latest government statistics support this finding.[51] According to the latest statistics compiled in 2002, in 1999 there were 7,421 Mahanikaya and 124 Thammayut monasteries in the sixteen Northern provinces serving a total of about 12 million Buddhists. Most of these monasteries are in Chiang Mai (1,107 and 23, respectively), followed by Chiang Rai (855 and 9), and Lampang (652 and 9). Provinces with smaller populations, like Phrae and Nan, have many fewer monasteries (Nan, 389 and 1; Phrae, 286 and 3). Of these, even fewer run schools of any official sort.

In looking specifically at Dhammaseuksa schools and students (i.e., students who take Buddhist courses), statistics show that there are 1,595 monastic schools in the North that offer at least three years of Buddhist courses.[52] There are 5,157 teachers and 88,724 students. Of these 1,595 schools, only 101 offer secondary-level Dhammaseuksa courses, with 1,701 teachers (736 teachers are monks and the rest are laypeople) serving 21,218 students. Therefore, only 25 percent of students at monastic schools study Buddhist subjects past the age of twelve to fourteen. Of these 21,218 students, only 1,111 graduate from a monastic, Pariyatidhamma high school. That is a graduation rate of 5 percent. Most of these graduating students are in Chiang Mai (356), with fewer in places like Nan (153) and Phrae (88). When one looks at students who focus on Paliseuksa, or Pali grammar, reading, and writing, the numbers drop significantly. Of the 21,218 students in secondary-level monastic schools, only 30 percent take the Pali courses. For 8,033 Pali students, there are 592 teachers (with only 36 Pali teachers in Phrae).[53]

In looking at Monastic Universities in the North, one finds that the effects of Bangkok-centered royal reform are even less significant.[54] At the Northern campuses of Mahachulalongkorn Monastic University (Mahanikaya) there are 31 teachers for 656 students. Of these 656, only 100 are in their fourth year. For Mahamakut (Thammayut), there are 28 teachers for 353 students and only 59 in their fourth year. Furthermore, these universities have been in operation for only thirty years. The reforms of 1902 took decades to reach the North, and even today they are relatively insignificant.

In looking at Sangha examinations for all of the North, statistics show that of those who took any Pali courses in secondary- or tertiary-level monastic colleges and universities only 280 passed the third-level (*nak dham*) examinations and only 89 passed any *parian* examination over the sixth level. That means that less than 1 percent of Pali students in all of the North actually pass the highest-level examinations and only 3 percent pass the basic-level examinations. Of the 21,218 students at monastic schools in the North studying all Buddhist subjects, less than one-third of 1 percent pass the highest Pali exams. Most students simply do not sit for these examinations. The royal reform of monastic education has influenced, according to the government's own published statistics, very few of the 12 million Buddhists in the North.

These statistics are deceiving in many ways, however. They do not take into account the highly mobile population of monastic students in the North. They do not reveal the subtleties of the motivations, career choices, and objectives of individual students. Statistics, by their very nature, remove agency. Furthermore, it is unclear whether all the monks from the Dhammakāya Nikāya are included. These monks have been quite successful recently in passing these examinations.

To this end, I make a few cautionary statements. First, students' decisions on whether or not to take monastic examinations might relate to their career choices. Students planning to disrobe and pursue a lay career, for example, in business, science, or law, may seek monastic degrees (secondary, bachelors, masters, or doctorates), and these can be better achieved by taking fewer Pali courses and more secular courses. These degrees can also be achieved without taking most monastic examinations. Students often choose monastic education based on economics. A family may not be able to support all their children, and monastic education can be one of the few avenues out of a life of poverty. Once a level of education is achieved, a student may leave the monkhood and enter secular schools. Second, statistics do not take into account the relationships between students and teachers or the differences in ways certain courses are taught. For example, one major change in Northern Thai (and Central Thai) monastic education in the past twenty years is the influx of lay teachers into monastic schools on the one hand and the participation of monks and novices in secular schools on the other. For example, monks in the North occasionally attend courses at the secular Chiang Mai University or the Christian Payap University.[55] Other monks move to study at secular universities like Naresuan University in Phitsanulok or Khon Khaen University in the Northeast. Teachers and students trained in secular schools often have different pedagogical methods, different approaches to texts, and different ideals as to what counts as valuable and practical information. Third, extracurricular activities at modern monastic schools offer alternative views on Buddhism and religion in general. Now there are "field trips," training in Web-site development and Internet use, and chances to meet foreigners indirectly through "pen pals" or directly, at "monk chat" (a program that allows foreign travelers to talk informally with monastic students in English). The impact of these new educational opportunities will surely be seen over the next decade. Fourth, ordination, throughout what is now called Thailand, has always been a temporary career for most. Some monastic students may ordain for three months, three days, or, in some cases, three hours. There are even formal printed curricula for students who ordain for fifteen days or three months at Mahamakut Monastic University.[56] Therefore, these students may attend monastic school for a short time and then enter or return to secular school. Fifth, and finally, the wide variety of secular courses at monastic high schools and universities, like biology, psychology, and world history, has obscured the parameters of monastic and secular education.

Recently, Shawn McHale made an important observation in his study of print culture and state repression in Vietnam. According to McHale:

> When one initially examines Vietnam from 1920 to 1945, it seems to make little sense to contest the notion that French repression was brutal. But the French colonial state was not all-powerful. Its laws gave a limited amount of freedom to book and newspaper publishers. Its police did not always operate effectively. In short, the French colonial state failed at hegemony. When one examines the kinds of material that the French administration censored, it becomes clear that it cared little about the vast majority of morality tracts, Buddhist tracts, novels, or popular songs. . . . Given this mixed success and the state's lack of interest in other realms of print culture, Vietnamese were able to stake out zones of autonomy from the colonial state.[57]

As I suggested in chapter 1, a similar assessment to McHale's could be made for the effectiveness of the French in Laos. Historians should not equate the rhetoric of elite reform with actual changes on the ground. Kings, colonists, and ideologues talk about reform and even support institutions that supposedly carry out the policies of reform. However, the reception and implementation of that reform are not guaranteed. In short, the harsh repression or even the paternalistic amelioration of Buddhist teaching, writing, and learning was not of great concern to the French.

Just as French colonial reform did not radically change the way Lao and Vietnamese Buddhist teachings were disseminated or the nature of their content, the Siamese royal reforms on Buddhist education did not usher in a completely new modern era. Chapters 2 and 3 emphasize that the reform of religious education by Siamese kings and later by the Thai monastic and secular elite was part of the larger nation-building process. However, this process has been one in which many, if not most, monastic educators have not taken part. In examining specifically the Northern region during the pre- and post-1902 periods, one must develop a new approach that looks beyond, or perhaps beneath, that of national and institutional history. Many approaches are possible; I am suggesting one—the curricular approach to the history of Buddhist monastic education. To this approach I now turn.

PART II

Proximate Mechanisms

Toward a Curricular History of Monastic Education

4 Genres, Modes, and Idiosyncratic Articulations

The study of kings and buildings, the stuff of institutional histories, is not enough if one wants to understand how Lao and Northern Thai monks learned and taught Buddhism. Kings and colonists may have built buildings, but teachers and students filled them with sound. To understand the ways monks made meaning and transmitted Buddhism one must look at the records of their day-to-day educational activity—*nissaya*, *vohāra*, and *nāmasadda* manuscripts.

When I first began to read manuscripts alongside monks and lay experts in Laos and Central and Northern Thailand I was struck by several strange features of these documents. These texts were both easy and difficult to read. They were easy because the words and phrases were common, but since the texts were bilingual (Pali and Lao, Northern Thai, Khoen, Leu, or Shan) I had to keep adjusting between two languages. In the history of Buddhism in Southeast Asia, not many teachers and students conversed or composed texts in Pali; certainly Pali texts were composed, analyzed, and employed, but often not as complete texts. However, the invocation of Pali words and phrases has been continually important for social prestige and ritual technology. The texts were easy to read also because they were repetitive and rhythmic. They were difficult because the grammar and spelling were poor and the palm-leaf pages were often broken, unclear, and physically damaged through overuse.

My teachers and I had similar problems in reading *nissaya* and other manuscripts, but slowly, over time, our eyes grew professional.[1] We found these manuscripts difficult to be read, physically damaged, and poorly edited because they were lecture notes and often were written by one teacher with a group of other teachers and students in mind. We were reading the notebooks that teachers shared, used, and reused. They were composed to guide professional sermon givers, and hence are idiosyncratic and difficult to read by those outside the system. The students who benefited from these sermons often did not or could not read them in manuscript form. These texts, therefore, were used by a few teachers, but listened to by many. The repetitive structures, orthographic variants, and excessive glossing seen in these texts are a record of how monks taught and were taught. They are what teachers felt their students needed to know in order to pass down the tradition and provide vision and safety to the community.

Nissaya, *vohāra*, and *nāmasadda* pedagogical genres reflect modes of thought, pedagogical techniques, and commentarial practices specific to a place and given time. These manuscripts have also influenced the way knowledge is assessed, organized, and written about in the modern period. An educational history based on methods and modal entities will emerge through a study of pedagogical manuscripts.[2] These texts cannot be placed into neat categories. They must be seen as particular moments in a history of articulations of Buddhism. They do not describe Buddhist thought systematically. They do not clearly represent a Buddhist episteme or a commentarial tradition. Instead, they evince the ways local agents were reaching back and reaching toward Buddhism.

Over the past six years, I have examined hundreds of *nissaya*, *vohāra*, and *nāmasadda* manuscripts in detail. Each manuscript I read (only a handful of which I am able to discuss here) is important not only for its content but also as a socio-archaeological object that offers clues to its socio-pedagogical context, namely, to how it was composed, taught, copied, stored, initiated, and concluded. After reading a number of individual manuscripts, I saw among them certain shared pedagogical methods, commentarial services, and physical features. I came to see these individual texts not only as important idiosyncratic articulations but also as modal entities that help to define the content of local curriculum and pedagogical techniques. Over time, these modal entities can be seen as defining the contours of the epistemic mode—the way this genre of texts influenced major trends in producing and teaching information. Seeing the individual text, the modal entity, and the epistemic mode together, one can trace the social history of the manuscript. This is small work. These are puzzle pieces. What do these manuscripts teach researchers? Simply put, they show that Lao and Northern Thai teachers were not primarily concerned with transmitting whole canonical Pali Buddhist texts; rather, they drew Pali terms and phrases from a wide selection of canonical and extra-canonical texts in order to teach their own idea of Buddhism. Instead of transmitting an integral and received tradition, they took bits and pieces of the received tradition in service of their own local rituals, ethics, and social concerns.

Such selective appropriation and reapplication of Pali are characteristic of Buddhist communities across Southeast Asia. In order to understand the role of the individual intellectual agent in the region, it is necessary to understand the processes that guide, but not govern, the use of texts and language. Each teacher and student at a monastic school in seventeenth-century Phrae or twenty-first-century Luang Phrabang has brought his or her voice to the translocal text in hand. This detailed examination reveals what Mikhail Bakhtin referred to as *heteroglossia.* Heteroglossia "implies dialogic interaction in which the prestige languages [Pali, Sanskrit, Chinese, Arabic, Javanese, Classical Malay, Mon, Royal Thai, French, Russian, Dutch, etc.] try to extend their control and subordinated languages to try to avoid, negotiate, or subvert that control. 'Language is not a neutral medium that passes freely and easily into the private property of the speaker's intentions. . . . Expropriating it, forcing it to submit to one's own intentions and accents, is a difficult and complicated process.'" Bakhtin emphasizes that all discourse "lives on the boundary between its own context and another, alien context. Each and every time it is uttered, a word is recontextualized, pulled in a slightly different direction, imbued with a different inflection. . . . The [classical, translocal] word enters a dialogically agitated and tension-filled environment of alien words, value judgements and accents, weaves in and out of complex inter-relationships, merges with some, recoils from others."[3]

The study of pedagogy and curricular history below reveals this process of heteroglossia. It returns history to individual teachers and students who shaped Buddhist thought and practice in constant negotiation with the confines of the languages and pedagogical methods they inherited. Or as Ernst

Gombrich put it, "The language reacts back on the speaker." Language and the modes in which it is expressed always have a "creative share" with the individual motivations of the author.[4] Studying a curriculum means studying the way inherited language, pedagogical method, and epistemological attitude play together with shifting socioeconomic and political contexts and individual intentions.

Important Terms

Nissaya, *vohāra*, and *nāmasadda* are idiosyncratic lecture and sermon notes structured around the selected translation of words and passages from individually chosen canonical and extra-canonical Pali texts. However, these pedagogical manuscripts, while reflecting idiosyncratic translations and commentaries of individually selected Pali source texts, are preserved in monastic libraries and may have been used by multiple teachers over time. The intention of the text is not the sole property of the original composer. It is spread across all the teachers who use the texts and notes over time. And since these are lecture notes based on older, mostly Pali, texts, the intention is spread across hundreds of teachers over many centuries. To use someone else's individually crafted lecture or sermon notes may seem strange, but in a culture where the physical entity of a manuscript and the skill of a Pali translator, and the relationship between student and teacher, are highly valued every effort was made to preserve manuscripts. Even today in Laos and Thailand the same value of preservation and protection is seen for printed books. Children are taught from a young age in both countries that they should never place a book on a floor or physically mistreat printed material. Furthermore, in premodern Northern Thailand and Laos the literacy rate, especially in classical languages, was low. Therefore, manuscripts of idiosyncratic lecture notes, composed by literate monks, in a mixture of vernacular and Pali languages were valuable because they were palm-leaf manuscripts, difficult and expensive to produce, and "owned" by monks, and to many people they contained de facto the words of the Buddha.[5] The way manuscripts were stored, bound, titled, and anthologized shows that many monastic and lay archivists were unable to read either the script or the language of the manuscripts or were sometimes concerned more with their value as objects than with their content.[6] This intent, of course, does not mean that content was unimportant, but just that it was not the only important aspect of a manuscript. The fact that there were genres of pedagogical manuscripts in both vernacular and Pali shows a deep creative engagement with content and an understanding that individual teachers were not simply faithful stewards but also creative interpreters of the Buddha's words.

To describe these texts as idiosyncratic should not convey the idea that these pedagogical texts were completely individual reflections. These texts can be grouped into a genre based on certain common traits. First, because they are notes and glosses based on source texts, their authors were controlled in some ways by the source texts and languages from which they drew. For example, while two manuscripts of a *Dhammapada nissaya* composed by different authors can be very different, because of their shared source text, they will have certain similarities.[7] Second, the methods of glossing and the commentarial services of *nissaya*, *vohāra*, and *nāmasadda* authors are similar. Third, since the texts' function was to serve as notes to be used by a teacher or preacher, they must employ common terms, tropes, and metaphors that are familiar to their respective audiences. Even though these manuscripts are an individual teacher's reflections on source texts, they were useful also for other teachers and readers and not just the original author (just as graduate students often use the lecture notes of their advisors when teaching a course and adapt them according to their own background and preferences). Also, lectures and sermons work well because there are certain shared assumptions held by the audience and the speaker.[8] Working with these general assumptions, a later teacher could read these lecture notes and use them as a guide for composing his own lecture. Pedagogical manuscripts are idiosyncratic, but they are general and useful to others besides the author or teacher.[9]

In this study *lecture* refers to the lesson a monastic teacher delivers to monastic students in a classroom setting. *Sermons* are like lectures, but designed to be delivered to a broader audience including the laity. The differences between the terms *homily* and *sermon* are more complicated. These differences can be profitably applied to didactic traditions in Laos and Northern Thailand. In the European tradition, homilies differ from sermons in two ways. First, homilies are given in liturgical and ritual contexts, whereas sermons can be ad hoc, secular, and initiated without having a ritual, calendrical, festal, solemn, catechetical, or liturgical occasion.[10] Second, homilies are exegetical, whereas sermons can be given without reference to a passage of Holy Scripture. Modern English usage of these terms erased these two distinctions beginning in the seventeenth century. The distinction between the ritual locus and exegetical function of homilies and the extempore, non-ritual, and often secular character of sermons remains today among Catholics and Protestants. While a Baptist or a Lutheran sermon is the primary reason for a community gathering on Sunday, the Catholic homily is always embedded in ritual and is certainly secondary (it is the only major section of the Catholic mass that is optional and is often removed in daily morning masses) to the transformative function of the formulaic ritual ceremony. Protestants go to the sermon hall or church to hear a sermon. Catholics go to mass where they may hear a homily as one part of the formal liturgy.

In following this lexical distinction, Lao and Northern Thai pedagogical texts, both in the premodern and modern periods, should properly be referred to as "sermonesque." Creative, didactic, often ethical, and occasionally political, sermons are common in the region. Sermons are given in a variety of contexts and styles. In the most common a monk will offer a sermon, although this is never required as a duty, on *wan phra* (often referred to as the "Buddhist Sabbath," occurring four times a month according to the phases of the moon). Here, the preacher begins by prostrating three times to the image of the Buddha and to any senior monk in attendance, then gives a short benediction in Pali of his choosing, perhaps followed by one or a selection of short Pali and occasionally vernacular recitation, and then immediately offers a sermon that does not directly relate to any specific passage of scripture.

After the sermon, often a popular Buddhist narrative about an ethical question, or social issue, the preacher offers a short final benediction. The congregation is free to enter and leave as they please, and the preacher is not controlled by any external time restraints or ritual necessities. These sermons are not connected with the heavily ritualistic duties of the monk, such as conducting a funeral, reciting the *paṭimokkha* during the *uposatha* ceremony, and morning and evening recitations (Lao: *tham vat xao*, *tham vat yen*). Sermons are an optional part of the monastic calendar. There are certainly formal aesthetic requirements, such as the prostration and the wearing of the *saṅghāti* (formal folded shoulder robe), but generally, the sermon is not part of standard Lao and Northern Thai Buddhist monastic rituals.

Furthermore, sermons do not need to be exegetical. The Pali benediction and the selection of Pali recitations chosen by the preacher are rarely mentioned or referred to in the sermon. Sermons define and explain Pali words drawn from canonical and noncanonical texts. They also often summarize Pali narratives and philosophical or ethical tracts found in the Pali canon and commentaries. However, these texts do not have to be formally recited before the sermon or directly referred to in a literal and sequential manner. There is usually a disconnect between the sermon subject and the Pali liturgy, and sermons are not a part of daily Buddhist liturgies. Indeed, from my observations at some rural monasteries there are almost never any formal sermons today, and one can assume safely that this was the case in the premodern period.

That said, research among the vast manuscript archives in Laos and Northern Thailand reveals examples of what can be called homilies. The *nissaya*, *nāmasadda*, and *vohāra* manuscripts that were based on Pali ritual texts, like the *kammavācā*, and *paritta*, and even many Abhidhamma texts, demonstrate that these were used as written guides to oral homilies—meaning sermons given on ritual occasions and involving the exegesis and glossing of Pali texts that related directly to the ritual in question. They work by drawing selected passages and terms from canonical and noncanonical Pali source texts and explaining the semantic meaning, grammatical features, ethical import, and social context of the source according to their authors' own political and social needs.

In this study, the terms *translation* and *gloss* are also troublesome. *Nissaya*, *vohāra*, and *nāmasadda* lie somewhere between vernacular and classical texts. The authors of these pedagogical texts took Pali source texts (although occasionally the source is locally produced), either physically present or in mind, and drew words and passages from the source for glossing. Sometimes these glosses are expansive, and the author comments on the grammar and secondary and tertiary meanings of terms or compares them to other known Pali terms. *Nissaya*, *vohāra*, and *nāmasadda* are rarely, if ever, close/literal translations of the classical source. They also are not translations of the entire source. Most often, only certain words and short passages are selected and others are ignored. In this way, *invocation* is a better term in these instances than is *translate*. The vernacular and the Pali play together on the leaves of a *nissaya* manuscript. Often, vernacular words are glossed with Pali terms not found in the invoked classical source. Like Dante's notion of Italian as the *vulgari eloquentia* that was more *illustris* (in the sense of illuminating) as a language for communicating with the masses, pedagogical manuscripts break down the notion of translation from classical into vernacular and undermine the inviolability and supremacy of Pali.[11] The vernacular and the classical may better be seen as two octaves in the same musical score than as a source text in a classical language and a secondary (i.e., once removed and less accurate and valid than the source) vernacular translation.

It would be prudent to elaborate on the way these authors understood language in general. *Nissaya*, *vohāra*, and *nāmasadda* authors could be classed as modist linguists, or modistae. The modistae was a school of twelfth-to-fourteenth-century European linguists who held the notion that "a word, once it has been imposed to signify, carries with it all of its syntactical modes, or possible combinations with other words . . . words themselves are the product of a primary act of imposition by which a particular utterance is connected with some thing or property of a thing . . . the word carries its *modi significanti* through a second act of imposition encoding all of the general syntactical roles it can play in connection with other words and expressions."[12] There seems to be no question in the minds of Lao and Northern Thai authors that it was possible to gloss Pali words and that there was a universal grammar that existed between the two languages. The source was open to manipulation, alteration, insertion, and expansion. Everything that could be said in Pali could be rendered in Lao or Northern Thai. This should not suggest that Pali was or is seen as identical in status to the vernacular. In fact, the mere knowledge of Pali terms and the ability to memorize, translate, and explain Pali words are the mark of great prestige in the region. Pali is understood locally as the language of the Buddha himself and holds certain powers in magical rites and religious rituals. Moreover, despite the fact that authors of pedagogical manuscripts believed that they could directly translate Pali words without loss of meaning, some Pali terms were given much more than a direct gloss. The expanded glosses and comments edified the audience, displayed the skill of the author, and provided a platform from which to offer a lecture on more general subjects. However, at the most basic level, these authors saw languages as translatable and understandable across grammatical and geographical barriers.

Nissaya, *vohāra*, and *nāmasadda* reveal a tendency to invoke the whole of Buddhist source texts, but they teach only individual parts. Often, the source text is reduced to a title, like *Sattaparitta*, *Mūlakaccāyana*, or *Mahāvagga*, and a few passages or terms. The source text is not present in *nissaya*, *nāmasadda*, or *vohāra*; it is neither accurately conveyed nor systematically addressed. The idea of the whole source text is invoked, but only a few of its parts are translated and taught. For Lao and Northern Thai monks, Pali texts were often things of reverence, prestige, wisdom, and beauty. The composers cite the first line of a source (often inaccurately, according to scholarly critical editions, which themselves are often inaccurate) and then move on to focus on individual terms or phrases from one part of the source. These were triggers to help the audience and the teacher either to remember parts of the text or to usher in a certain explanation based on the definition and commentary on that particular word or phrase. The idea of the whole text was invoked by these triggers and sustained by a selection of terms according to the needs of the teacher. However, the whole was rarely translated. *Nissaya*, *vohāra*, and *nāmasadda* served as detailed outlines to lectures or sermons expanded on in performance. Understanding the way these pedagogical genres work forces one to see vernaculars, not as linear descendents of the classical, but as hybrids that, in Bahktin's words, "interanimate" one another.[13] This approach, one can hope, will breathe new life into the lumbering debate between those who see the cultures of Buddhist Southeast Asia as inextricably "Indianized" and those who see it as deceptively autonomous.

Source Texts: The Content of Premodern Curricula

The primary content of the monastic curriculum for Laos and Northern Thailand consisted of ritual (both protective and daily monastic liturgies), grammatica, and ethical and romantic narratives. The composers of *nissaya*, *vohāra*, and *nāmasadda* commented on a wide range of source texts, but the collections are dominated by vernacular and Pali narratives from canonical and noncanonical *jātaka* and *Dhammapada-atthakathā* anthologies, vernacular stories like the *Madhurāsajambū*, ritual texts such as the *Sattaparitta* (*Sutmon*) and the *Kammavācā-uppasampadā*, and grammatical texts.[14] In some collections historical and cosmological texts were numerous. Strangely, the *Maṅgalatthadīpanī*, a commentarial text, composed in Chiang Mai in the early sixteenth century and so important to modern Thai elite monastic education, was not as popular in the earlier manuscript tradition.

The choice of texts to use in *nissaya*, *vohāra*, and *nāmasadda* form can reveal a great deal about the needs and values of the communities that composed them. The choice reflects those aspects of Buddhism that were deemed more important and most necessary to teach, especially in the vernacular.[15] *Desanā* (Thai/Lao: *thet*) employ similar methods today. *Nissaya*, *vohāra*, and *nāmasadda*, like *desanā*, are structured around lists of vernacular synonyms for Pali terms or glosses and illustrative explanations of the source text in question. *Nissaya*, *vohāra*, *nāmasadda*, and *desanā* also leave many Pali terms untranslated and simply explain their semantic import in a particular text or lesson.

The choice of source texts provides insight into which texts were considered particularly efficacious for pedagogical purposes. Indeed, by the time these pedagogical texts were composed, the Northern Thai and the Lao had centuries of familiarity with and belief in Buddhism. These texts may be seen as articulations of a highly local understanding in an attempt to make sense of a world in which Buddhism constituted the overarching, dominant system of ideology and practice. These texts are negotiations between the classical and the vernacular, the translocal and the local. They incorporate local elements into a nonnative literary structure. Further research along these lines might lead one far in determining the different modes of interaction between these shifting epistemes. By looking closely at *nissaya*, *vohāra*, and *nāmasadda* manuscripts, one can see the evolution of Pali and vernacular local Buddhist literature as processual and dynamic, reflecting strong ties to the past and engagement with the present.

The narrative source texts are entertaining stories. They may not systematically explain Buddhist ethics or doctrine or provide an accurate history of the Buddha's life, but they draw from funny, frightening, and memorable stories of magic, family crisis, wealth, and love. The use of narratives as teaching tools has been well documented.[16] Canonical and extra-canonical *jātaka* are still the most popular religious texts in the region, and performances of the *Vessantara jātaka* (*Thet Mahachat*) at festivals (*Bun Phra Vet*) or upon request, and television and cartoon adaptations of these tales, are very popular.[17] Bosaengkham Vongtala notes that stories, many of which were collected in various versions of the *Paññāsa jātaka*, are often requested by laypeople at religious ceremonies and family events (weddings, funerals, house blessings, tonsure ceremonies, etc.).[18] Therefore, monks have to be taught these stories, as I was when I was a monk, so they can explain them in Lao or Thai. It is well known that monks in the region are judged on their ability to relate a good story; in the region, however, the monks have not felt obliged to accurately relate a story handed down from the Pali canon and commentaries. Instead, their story changes with each retelling. Narratives, especially in the vernacular, were a major part of the regional religious curriculum.

Ritual texts are often used at ceremonies such as house blessings, ordinations, and the beginning and end of the rains retreats. Their content, therefore, provides the perfect subject for sermons (*desanā*) by a teacher for the benefit of his followers on these occasions. Two examples of this class are the *Sutmon nissaya* and the *Kammavācā nissaya nāmasadda*. The latter explains the meaning of the Pali chanted at one of the most common of Buddhist rituals—the ordination. The ordination ceremony is a time of great celebration and interaction between monks and laypeople. The *Kammavācā nissaya nāmasadda* is still employed by monks as a guide to giving a sermon on the importance of ordination. The *Sutmon nissaya* is based on one of the best-known collections of ritual prayers in South and Southeast Asia. It became the platform on which many sermons were based. The *Sutmon nissaya* is a collection of mantras chanted for protective purposes at a number of Buddhist ceremonies. Therefore, it provides a logical subject for a sermon following the ceremony.

Besides narratives and ritual texts, many pedagogical manuscripts that I have read are drawn from the Abhidhamma, seemingly for the purpose of teaching Pali grammar (which is one of the main activities of any large monastic school). The *Atthakathāmātikā nissaya* is a partial gloss of the *mātikā* (index) of the *Dhammasaṅgaṇī* (traditionally the first volume of the Abhidhamma). Even though the *mātikā* is not a grammatical text, the author of the *nissaya* used these texts as a matrix on which to build grammatical lessons. A *Nāma nissaya* from Chiang Mai is a grammatical text loosely based on Kaccāyana's grammar composed in India. The text's purpose is not to provide a clear Pali grammar lesson in Northern Thai. Its importance lies not in how closely it follows and faithfully reproduces Kaccāyana, but in how it does not.

Based on manuscript inventories and my examination of manuscript collections, it is clear that the choice of sources to gloss and comment on in the vernacular was not standardized across the region or even from one monastery to the next. While narratives, ritual texts, and grammatical texts tend to be the most prevalent, there are occasionally *nissaya*, *vohāra*, and *nāmasadda* on Pali verse extracts from the Abhidhamma, the Visuddhimagga, and the Vinaya. Moreover, two manuscripts with the same title copied around the same time period are often completely different in content. Moreover, two *vohāra* or *nissaya* written at the same monastery on the same source text in the same year can have major differences depending on the skill of the scribe or the aspect of the source text the author wants to emphasize. These authors rarely translated complete Pali texts. The sections of Pali source texts that are translated are manipulated for pedagogical purposes. When the source text can be identified, it is usually not a complete text but a summary of that source text that lifts out Pali words or phrases and then translates them, while leaving many words untranslated. Furthermore, narratives are occasionally left incomplete, passages seemingly vital to the plot are missing, and certain characters are emphasized while others go unmentioned. Manuscripts of the *Atthakathāmātikā nissaya*, *Atthasālinī nissaya*, *Kammavācā nissaya nāmasadda*, *Dhammapada vohāra*, and *Dibbamon nissaya* are all incomplete translations of Pali source texts and parts of their commentaries and subcommentaries, if available. The *Sutmon nissaya* is a commentary on selected passages of the Thai *Sattaparitta* (*Chet tamnan*), which is itself a collection of *paritta* texts. There are apparently no extant Pali source texts for the *Madhurāsajambū nissaya*, *Lokabhāsā nissaya*, *Maṇḍapakaraṇa nissaya*, and *Sakuṇa nissaya*, to cite just a few examples.[19] The tradition is diverse. Not only did the composers expand and manipulate their source texts, but individual *nissaya* were rarely copied from other *nissaya* on the same source text. These manuscripts were largely individual creations. Still, despite the diversity, certain features that define the genre are discernible if a number of manuscripts are compared.

Nissaya Manuscripts

Nissaya, *nāmasadda*, and *vohāra* genres overlap in style, pedagogical method, and social use. Since there has never been a study of all three genres, I highlight here the minor differences for readers interested in the details of textual history and for the sake of clarity. Whereas *nāmasadda* manuscripts are characterized by close, word-by-word glosses, *vohāra* cite longer passages of twelve to twenty-five words from Pali source texts and then offer expansive and creative vernacular translations and commentaries. *Nissaya* fall in between the two genres and often cite four to ten words before offering glosses and creative asides. These differences are ones of degree, not kind. All three genres are linked by the use of trigger words, in a method known locally as *yok sab* (lifting words), albeit linked in slightly different ways.[20] These ambiguous differences were acknowledged by the original authors and scribes who often conflated these two titles in the colophons of the manuscripts—*nisaisab* (Pali: *nissayanāmasadda*); *nisraiwohān* (Pali: *nissayavohāra*); and *sabnissai* (Pali: *nāmasaddanissaya*). Individual authors and later scribes were not corralled by these governing features associated with particular genre rubrics, nor did they consider their supposed parameters sacrosanct. A good way to understand the function of these genre designations is to compare their use to that of terms such as "study of," "analysis of," and "notes toward" that are found in the titles of journal articles written in English. Although some scholars take the subtle differences between these titles seriously, others seem to apply whatever title "sounds good" for their essay. Teachers in Laos and Northern Thailand wrote *nissaya* (as they did *vohāra* and *nāmasadda*) as preparation for sermons and guides to understanding source texts (premodern CliffNotes). These are not merely translations or commentaries. They are pedagogical texts that teach parts of Pali source texts and invoke wholes. *Nissaya* manuscripts generally range from one fascicle (*phuk*) with approximately 9 folios to twelve fascicles with over 250 folios. They work by lifting individual Pali terms from a source text and glossing them in a repetitive way.

Nissaya means "support." It is an old term, found in the Vinaya, meaning on the one hand the relationship between a young monk or novice and his teacher (*ācariya* or *upādhāya*) or on the other hand the period of training, support, or dependence of a newly ordained monk, usually lasting between five and ten years.[21] *Nissaya* also has the wider meaning of "resource" or a means of support on which monastic life depends (related to the term *paccaya*). There are also common compounds with the word *nissaya*. For example, *nissaya-sampanno* means having sufficient assets or "a good credit rating." *Nissaya-ācariya* is one of the five types of teachers (*pabbajja-ācariya, upasampadā-ācariya, nissaya-ācariya, uddesa-ācariya* [or *dhamma-ācariya*], and *ovāda-ācariya*). Here the *nissaya-ācariya* is specifically a guide or a tutor on whom "one takes dependence." This type is seemingly different from the *uddesa-ācariya*, who gives textual instruction, although, at present these two types are often conflated.

Nissaya manuscripts were supports, resources, or guides written by a teacher for a student or a small group of students to guide their translation and study of Pali texts and thus enable them to explain Pali concepts in sermons to fellow monks and to lay audiences.[22] *Nissaya* are not conducive to being read as connected narratives or teachings, because they are interspersed with Pali words and their definitions, asides, synonyms, and a short explanation of their grammatical forms. They are disjoined texts, and to read them straight through would be like reading the "Anna Livia Plurabelle" episode of James Joyce's *Finnegans Wake* if every third word were followed by its dictionary definition in Italian. They read not as sermons, stories, or instructions but as notes for telling stories, giving sermons, or explaining instructions. They are supports for those who have to read and explain Pali texts to an audience and therefore give us a rare window into the practices and intellectual approaches of a premodern Buddhist teacher in the region. They are to Southeast Asian studies and Buddhist studies scholars what Isaac Newton's lecture notes would be to historians of European science.

The choice of source text depended on its popularity for use in sermons and ceremonial chanting or on the message a teacher wanted to communicate, while the purpose for writing it was to instruct its audience on the meanings of Pali words and phrases. From my experience listening to, reading, and giving sermons; talking with monastic teachers; and attending monastic university pedagogical training courses, I doubt any *nissaya* was read out loud verbatim as a sermon or as a narrative. Instead they were guides to consult when explaining the meaning of words and phrases. There are local verbatim translations of texts like the Dhammapada, *kammavācā*, and *Sattaparitta*, as well as Pali and vernacular commentaries. There is no reason to have a separate genre of manuscripts called *nissaya* unless they served a separate purpose.[23]

If *nissaya* were ever read silently, which was most likely rare, they would only be useful as a companion text to a Pali source. They would be a handy running commentary, but since *nissaya* often diverge from known source texts and are generally not found bound with, next to, or even in the same monastery with their supposed source manuscripts, these *nissaya* were texts in their own right—they were inspired and influenced by the structure, ideas, and lexicon of a particular source text, but they were not read alongside them very often. Even today, monastic teachers rarely read the way international scholars of Buddhism do—they often read when preparing a lecture, debate, recitation, or sermon. The texts, commentaries, literal translations, dictionaries, concordances, and secondary analyses found in scholars' offices are rarely found in monastic cells or libraries. This function might explain the lack of multiple copies of any individual *nissaya* manuscript.[24]

I offer one example of a *nissaya* manuscript that is based on a local collection of protective prayers (*paritta*) and displays the features discussed above. This text, titled *Nisai sūtra manta*, from Chiang Mai in Northern Thailand states that it was copied in cūḷa sakkarāja (CS) 1192 (1830).[25] It starts off with a long passage praising the qualities of *arahants* who have crossed the "great ocean" and reached enlightenment, as well as the honoring the god Indra (Sakka). Next comes the story of how the gods, Brahmans, and ogres (*yakkhā*) asked the Buddha about the nature of auspiciousness. Then the author states that these words protect the chanter from fire, poison, thieves, demons, drowning, ghosts, and the "diseases of the countryside." There are also long lists of animals, insects, and diseases that this *paritta* is effective against, similar to an advertisement printed on the side of a bottle of vitamins or headache medicine.[26] The chanter should also concentrate on the qualities of the Buddha, Dhamma, and Sangha and the groups of ten and thirty perfections. Not until the eighth page of the manuscript is the *Maṅgala sutta* mentioned as a *paritta*. From here the author translates selected words from the source, often out of order, with vernacular synonyms or cognates in a repetitive process.

The author then moves onto a selective and repetitive glossing of other *paritta* like the *Ratana sutta*, *Āṭāṇāṭaya sutta*, and others found in different order in different collections throughout South and Southeast Asia.[27] For example, at the conclusion to the *Ratana sutta* and the beginning of the *Karaṇīyametta sutta*, the author gives vernacular glosses for words like *yāni*, *idha*, and *bhūtāni*, but not for other words in the *Ratana sutta* verse like *samāgatāni* and *yāniva*. There is no attempt to avoid repetition in a highly repetitive *paritta* like the *Ratana*, because repetition was often a useful tool. If this composer wanted to avoid repetition, he could have stopped glossing these words long before the end of the text.[28] Furthermore, this manuscript uses many vernacular synonyms as well as additional Pali words to introduce and conclude *paritta*. For example, at the end of the *Ratana sutta* section he writes "Ratanasuttam niṭṭhitam ko laeo paripuṇṇam ko puan muan kon" (the *Ratana sutta* is finished; that is, [it is done] already, completed; that means it is already complete). This repetitive translation comes from the fact that the composer employs two Pali synonyms and two vernacular words to gloss one action. Authors of *nissayas* based on the *Chet tamnan paritta* collection(s) would often give one title to the manuscript (e.g., *Kampī suat mon nissaya*), but the contents of individual manuscripts would be widely different, with some *paritta* texts emphasized and others ignored. For example, this *nissaya* glosses texts from the standard Central Thai *Chet tamnan paritta* collection, but the *Khandha sutta*, often found in others, is not included. The *Dhajagga sutta*, *Āṭānāṭaya sutta*, *Angulimāla paritta*, *Bojjhanga paritta*, and *Pakiraṇaka gāthā* are included.

Near the end of the manuscript another story is introduced that I have yet to identify and that is, as far as I can tell, not included in the known Central Thai, Northern Thai, Khmer, Shan, Burmese, or Lao collections. This is not strange, since numerous manuscripts I have come across are anthologies of seemingly randomly collected texts and manuscripts that start off copying or translating one Pali text and expand into copying or glossing others.

Nāmasadda Manuscripts

The only significant difference between *nāmasadda* and *nissaya* manuscripts (Sanskrit: *nāmaśabda*, Lao/Thai: *nāmasab*) is that *nāmasadda* texts offer a more literal word-by-word translation of Pali source texts; however, this tendency is not consistent enough to state definitively that these two types of texts had significant differences.

For example, an *Atthasālinī nāmasadda* from Luang Phrabang, like most *nāmasadda*, draws short passages from the Pali source (a Pali commentary on the Abhidhamma) and translates them word-by-word, usually with vernacular synonyms, cognates, or simply repeating the Pali word. This eleven-fascicle (over 280 folios) manuscript begins with the first line of the *Ganthārambhakathā* (a section of the *Atthasālinī*) and remains faithful to the *Atthasālinī* until the third folio, where it begins to pick and choose words, often departing from the order of the source text. The details of the *nidāna*, the "introduction," to the *Atthasālinī*, which has been such an important text for modern scholars of Buddhism, are passed over, with only an occasional passage cited. Moreover, the passages cited are similar to repeated phrases from the *mātikā* of the doublets and triplets that follows the *nidāna*. It does not show signs of following the *Atthasālinī-atthayojanā*, the *Mohavicchedanī*, or any of the *ṭīkā* (subcommentaries).[29]

This manuscript seems to have been used not as a simple running vernacular translation but more as a set of mnemonic triggers or cues for a person orally teaching the text. The format would also be useful for a student interested in learning how to break up compounds, since the text presents a Pali clause lifted from the *Atthasālinī* and then divides the compounds and translates each member accordingly. This text would help a student study Pali grammar since it also demonstrates a great effort to show the grammatical relationships between members of the compounds using words like *beua* for a dative relationship, *tae* for an ablative, and so on.[30]

Another palm-leaf *nāmasadda* manuscript from the Fang district in northern Chiang Mai Province called the *Nissaya nāmasadda ākhyāta* was composed sometime in the early nineteenth century. This manuscript, like many others, has both *nāmasadda* and *nissaya* in its title. It is interesting because it is clearly based on a section of *Kaccāyanavyākaraṇa* Pali grammatical text but was not bound with any other sections of the source or its attendant *nāmasadda*. It was found at Wat Phra Thatchomgiri as a text consisting of two fascicles. Although it was found bound as two complete texts, there is no introduction and no colophon, and it was probably originally part of a larger manuscript. Since manuscripts were borrowed and split up for easy carrying, this section was probably removed from a larger grammatical text by a teacher and never returned.[31] This manuscript is repetitive, and even though its title is the *Ākhyāta* (a lesson on the use of verbs), it actually is a lesson on the rules of Pali noun gender (from the *Nāmakaṇḍa* section of the larger *Kaccāyanavyākaraṇa*), through example rather than by technical explanation, and draws randomly from a source text. One verse, based on the seventy-first verse of the thirteenth-century Pali commentary from Sri Lanka called the *Padarūpasiddhi* and the sixth verse of the *Kaccāyanavyākaraṇa*,[32] reads

> ālapane si seño si an long nai alapana mai jeu wā // pubba oyya long wai ā // āgho () itthī linga mai jeu wā gha // [*sic*]

"Si" in the passage beginning with ālapana it is called (vocative) // before oyya place "ā" (plus) gho () has the feminine gender and it is called "gha."[33]

This passage is followed by a litany of repetitive examples illustrating this grammatical rule, like *bho rāja*, *bho purisa*, and *bho satta* (in this context meaning "venerable king," "venerable man," and "venerable being"), many of which are not present in the *Kaccāyanavyākaraṇa* source, but some of which are found in the *Padarūpasiddhi*. Therefore, this *nāmasadda* is a creative gloss on two Pali sources, with its own examples added. This is not a mere translation.

Without going into a discussion of the way Pali grammar rules work, the abbreviations commonly used in the texts, or the orthographic inconsistencies in this verse, it is important to note that the author was probably dictating this manuscript, since there are mistakes common to a local pronunciation. The haphazard, commonly misspelled and indirect reference to this verse and others from the *Kaccāyanavyākaraṇa* also suggests that this author was drawing from memory rather than examining an actual copy of the source texts. The source was more likely an ideal, but non-present, source text referred to by the author. In this way, *nāmasadda* are like *nissaya* and *vohāra*: they are like maps based not on actual territory but on a landscape constructed from memory, hearsay, local landmarks, and imagination.[34]

Vohāra Manuscripts

Vohāra, in Northern Thai (Yuan), Central Thai (Siamese), and Lao, has the general meaning of "idiomatic" or "common" speech—or, more formally, "oratory," "rhetoric," or "eloquence." It is also the formal term for royal literary style, like the *vohāra* or "style of speech" of King Chulalongkorn. This meaning is connected to the way kings would orally dictate their literary works to scribes. The Thai and Lao meaning comes from the Sanskrit *vyavahāra* for "common" or "quotidian" and the Pali *vohāra* for "popular logic," "common use of language," or "general way of speech." It is most often found in the title for a judge or a magistrate (*vohārika*). When Thais use the term *wohān di* (good *vohāra*), it means that an author has great skill in employing the appropriate words at the appropriate times. It does not necessary imply using Khmer, Sanskrit, or Pali words, but means simply the ability to wield words effectively—to be a wordsmith. This definition of the term *vohāra* is often used when describing orally performed poems and plays. Arthid Sheravanichkul informed me that the term *vohāra* is sometimes used to connote the specific ways "old words" (Sanskrit, Pali, or Khmer) are used effectively in rhyme, as metaphor, or for alliteration, and so forth. He states that "in some contexts *vohāra* can mean the use of 'mechanical techniques,' including using foreign words, decorative words, figures of speech, verse forms, etc." In reference to its use in sermons, he writes that "in a sermon a monk likes to begin with a Pali *gatha* [verse], and he will quote some words during the sermon . . . this is to show that he is well educated and the sermon sounds more 'luxurious.' In some contexts, such as in the sermon, quoting Pali words is required and its gives prestige to the preacher."[35]

These descriptions are applicable to the *vohāra* genre of manuscripts in Thailand and Laos. This genre of manuscripts defines the manner in which any words are drawn from a source text and transformed into common speech for reading or, in the premodern period, for oral delivery regardless of their content. However, the way in which *vohāra*-type speech is used is specific. *Vohāra* authors, like judges and lawyers, need to draw on seemingly ancient sources of knowledge and wisdom (constitutions, royal law codes and edicts, canonical scripture, ancient revelations, etc., in classical languages) in order to justify and add weight to their present judgments. *Vohāra* authors lifted words and phrases from what were considered "ancient" texts and used these words and phrases to anchor a sermon in the vernacular. Often in Theravada Buddhist studies Pali is seen as the only classical language in Southeast Asia; however, in Laos and Thailand, Khmer, Sanskrit, and Pali all function as classical languages that have ritual, legal, historical, and pedagogical power. They all need to be mediated through the common vernacular. Even though Khmer may have been spoken at the court and almost all writing in Thai before the nineteenth century was in Khmer (Khom) script, over time Khmer words were understood less and less and needed to be glossed in Thai. Seeing Sanskrit, Pali, Khmer, and even Mon as equally powerful and legitimate classical sources reflects in some ways why most Thai and Lao have no problem combining Brahmanical (from either India or Cambodia) and Buddhist rituals, magical techniques, and symbolism. In fact, when the Thai and Lao use the word *Pali*, it is commonly in the compound "Pali-Sanskrit." *Pali* as a word often does not stand alone in common speech.

Secular authors and court poets used a method similar to that of monastic *vohāra* writers, but instead of primarily Pali texts, they lifted Khmer and Sanskrit words (as well as Pali) and invoked the names of powerful deities, kings and queens of the past, bodhisattvas, and magical material objects like golden conch shells, rings, elephants, horses, and swords. They also invoked the famous acts of bravery of kings of the past to establish lineages, justify marriages, and glorify royal qualities. These ancient stories and the ritual power of Khmer and Sanskrit words are equivalent to Pali canonical and extra-canonical texts for *vohāra* monastic authors. For example, secular texts like *Lilit Phra Lo*, *Samut ghot kham chan*, *Aniruddha kham chan*, *Lilit ong kan Chaeng nam*, and *Yuan pai* all have *vohāra* qualities such as lifting Pali, Sanskrit, and Khmer words and glossing them in common Thai or Lao. Classical Thai "secular" drama became very efficient in this method by creating compound words merely by placing together two synonyms, often one Khmer,

Sanskrit, or royal Thai and one common. This case is one where a compound comprises a classical (Khmer, Pali, or Sanskrit) word and a vernacular gloss. This method is seen in the compounds *sanuk sanan* (very fun), *salak samkhan* (very important), *thon sai chon dat*, *lakhat lakheun*, *gan wao*, and the like. One word is from a classical language and the other from the vernacular. The repetition of these glosses gives cadence, rhythm, and rhetorical force to the oral delivery. Thai literature scholar Chonlada Reuangraklikhit emphasizes that the secular royal poems of the Ayutthayan period often use repetition to place stress on important terms and invoke the names of powerful gods, the names of certain characters, or particularly powerful turns of phrase.[36] Amara Prasithrathsint echoes Chonlada, showing how repetition and reduplication are common features of Thai interlinguistically.[37] Reduplicated forms of verbs evolve into forming adjectives and adverbs. It seems that Thai has grown lexically through repetition, and therefore the *nissaya* method can be seen as perfectly suited to Thai rhetorically and even at the very level of syntax and morphology.

Rhetorical questions are also often used repetitively to add weight to the reflections of heroes and heroines. This repetition is seen not only in Pali, Khmer, and Sanskrit words but also in vernacular words, as when two lovers are speaking or a battle is being described. For example, in the poem *Lilit Phra Lo*, even though it is famous in Thai literature for beautifully using "common speech," one finds several examples of repetitious royal honorifics like *rāja* and *srī*, as well as names and even common verbs, question words, and nouns like *chang phuak*, *krai seu*, and *chuai du*. These words are repeated in a romance tale like *Lilit Phra Lo*, as they are in oral poetic versions of the *Vessantara jātaka* like the *Wessanton kham luang*.[38] These romance and adventure poetic narratives are described by Thai literary scholars as having "*vohāra* qualities," and these qualities are similar to the *vohāra* qualities of Buddhist texts. Words are lifted, glossed, and repeated over and over again.[39]

For the sake of space, I concentrate on Buddhist *vohāra* only from Northern Thailand, with an understanding that there are methodological similarities with *vohāra* versions of secular texts as well as *vohāra* from Central Thailand and Laos. The first example is a *Dhammapada vohāra* inscribed in 1831 at Wat Sung Men in Phrae Province by a monk named Pinarassa and a scribe named Paññati Bhidheyya (although the colophon is unclear).[40] The first twenty to twenty-four folios of this manuscript present a slightly different type of rhetorical style and translation/commentarial method than that seen in *nissaya*. It is based on the *Maṭṭhakuṇḍalīvatthu* (narrative commentary on the second verse of the Dhammapada and the second story in the *Dhammapada-atthakathā*). It also draws from a similar version of the story in the *Vimānavatthu-atthakathā* and the *Petavatthu-atthakathā*. It seems that the author was simply recalling sections of the story from memory or working from a local version of the text unknown outside of the region. First are long sections (12–25 words) from the Pali source cited verbatim, followed by long vernacular texts (70–260 words). These long vernacular passages translate the preceding Pali, but unlike *nissaya*, and in many ways *nāmasadda*, there is less of a use of Pali synonyms or vernacular cognates in this translation. Moreover, this *vohāra* translates, not the source text, but only these selected passages. Often the space between these passages is small, skipping only five to ten words, and occasionally long passages from the source are neglected. *Nissaya* certainly do not translate verbatim every part of their respective source texts, but they do, largely, provide a vernacular summary of the source text and primarily employ Pali synonyms and vernacular cognates in a running gloss. *Nissaya* do not provide a literal and detailed translation and are clearly not meant to be read without a previous knowledge of the source or as a straight narrative, because the narrative is broken up by the repetitive loops, commentarial explanations, word glosses, and so forth. However, they do provide the "gist" (*chai khwam*) of the source text. They do not simply pick selected passages and only translate and comment on them. This, instead, is what a *vohāra* often does. One could possibly feign a sense of the plot by reading only these cited Pali passages and stringing them together. However, much of the detail of the narrative, a number of characters, and even the central ethical import of the text are lost because often long sections of the source are neither cited nor glossed.

An example from one passage reads as follows:

(f.*ghao*.v) akkocchima avadhimanti imaṃ dhammadesanaṃ satthā jetavane viharanto tissattheraṃ ārabbha kathesi so kirāyasmā bhagavato pitucchāputto mahallakāle pubbajite buddhasāsano uppannalābhasakkā-

> raṃ paribhuñjanto thulasuriro akkoṭitapacchakoṭitehi civarehi suyyena vihāramajjhe uppaṭṭhānasālāyaṃ nisidi // satthā mak wā satthavāho nāyako sabbañu phra buddha cao ton pen nāyanāṃ mū satta hi mām kon cāk dān plā an mī con geu vaṭṭhansān hi ni thoeng nibban an satri nai jevaṇṇa ārāṃ brarob soeng tissathen pen hen ārammaṇa haeng dhammasesanā an ni an Sangitikāthāyya hāk khwaet gatha mai Tuai kalyaṇa gatha ādipai wā akkocchima avadhimaṃ

"Akkocchima avadhimam." The teacher told this dhamma sermon about the Elder Tissa while residing in Jetavana. He, it is said, the son of the aunt of the Lord, despite being quite old, he left home and entered the ascetic life. In the order of the Buddha, enjoying the honor of being reborn, he sat in the assembly hall in the middle of the *vihāra*. According to most, he was a corpulent man with wrinkled robe. The *Satthā* (the teacher) means a *satthavāho* (a caravan leader), a *nāyako* (a leader), a *sabbañu* (an all-knowing one), the Lord Buddha, that is, [one of] the group of *nāyanāṃ* (leaders), indeed *Satthā* (teacher) of me. The people who are from the forest are poor. That is *vaṭṭhansān* (those possessing head ornaments?), indeed. Nibban, the woman in the forest retreat of Jevaṇṇārāma, who is known to Tissa the Elder. She is the one who sees the dhamma sermon in the forest retreat. This is from the *Sangitikāthāyya* (the collected verses), that is, the *Kwaetgatha* that means the verses of the *Kalyaṇa* (the verses of the good one). It explains the "akkocchima avadhimam."

Following this passage there is an approximately 240–word section, consisting almost entirely of vernacular words, before another Pali passage is cited. This vernacular section is a long and expanded translation/commentary of the passage I just cited. Unlike *nissaya*, this *vohāra* does not follow the source, but only glosses and comments on selected passages. After the first few words, it ceases to cite and provide glosses for words from the source text. The percentage of cited Pali words and sections is approximately 12 percent (much less than the average *nissaya* and *nāmasadda*). This percentage is reduced when proper names and exact cognates such as *bhikkhu* and *thera* are not counted. However, this percentage is difficult to compare to that regarding *nissaya* texts, because over 90 percent of the 12 percent are in one connected passage. *Nissaya* work by interspersing Pali words among vernacular glosses and cognates. In this example, there is also much less use of the Northern Thai words *reu*, *an wā*, or *yan* ("this means") to indicate when a Pali word is being glossed. This is likely due to the fact that the reader or audience had just read or heard the Pali passage and did not need to be told that the glosses and the expanded vernacular translation that followed referred back to it. Moreover, the few individual Pali words that are cited generally do not come from any known recension of the source.

Despite the differences, the author of this *vohāra*, like the authors of *nissaya*, made many additions to the source text. For example, in this section, one learns that the author either believed this story or actually obtained it from a text known as the *Sangitikathā*. Whether it was an actual text or simply a reference to collected verses in general is impossible to tell. It may be an unknown local anthology. The author also provides another name for the source, namely, the *Kalyaṇagatha*. In addition, the author also adds information through glossing; for example, the gloss of the word *sattha* is not simply "teacher" but also "caravan leader." The author also glosses the word *nibban*, clearly a cognate of *nibbana*, as "woman" (*satri*). One also learns that the people who live in the forest are poor and that they wear a headdress of some sort (the manuscript is unclear here). These are details not provided in the cited section of the source or in any other known source. Besides unknown local sources (which could be simply the personal additions of the local author), there are also certain sections of this larger manuscript that are drawn from other sources outside of the *Dhammapada-atthakathā*. That I had to draw on many source texts to understand certain passages means that the author may have remembered selected passages from memory. When he delivered the Pali text from memory, he conflated several sources. The author was not paying allegiance to one source. He understood the meaning of the passage for him and wanted to convey his own interpretation to his students, who did not have a strong understanding of Pali vocabulary. Unlike *nāmasadda* and *nissaya*, the Pali text is presented in long blocks, and no grammatical explanations are given. It was designed for students, perhaps lay students, who were not studying Pali grammar and were not being trained to give sermons or lectures themselves. *Nissaya* and *nāmasadda* usually supplied more comprehensive vernacular translations. *Vohāra* require very creative teachers very familiar with the sources.

Orthography: Manuscripts Written to Be Spoken

A detailed examination of the orthography of these manuscripts reveals some interesting findings. First, the spelling of common words is in no way standardized across different manuscripts or within any single fascicle. For example, the word *haeng* (of) is spelled three different ways in the *Dhammapada nissaya* from Luang Phrabang. Often the spelling changes two to three times on one folio. Pali words are also often spelled several different ways. For example, the word *puggala* (person) can be spelled *pugalā*, *puggala*, or *pugla* on the same leaf. Furthermore, the Tham script, in which the Lao manuscripts are composed, is nonstandardized, has many influences from Khoen and Leu speakers, and commonly uses different letters to represent letters like *g* or *t* across manuscripts or within one.

The instruction (or forced labor) at monastic schools rarely produces uniformly trained students. Colophons reveal a lack of standardization and students using a variety of dialects and having different skills. For example, in a *Dhammapada nissaya* manuscript the colophon gives alternate spellings for the name of the text itself. It states that the author aimed to teach the *gāthāsāt* at one point and then at another point he writes the *gāthācatt*, and then at another point he writes *amaregātha*. These titles are equated with one another in the colophon. The first title means "one hundred verses," but it is confusing because there is no known text with that title and because it is equated with the title "four verses" or "six verses," depending on whether one assumes the scribe/author was meaning to write *catu* (four) or *chatta* (six). The second possibility might help one to understand *sāt* (one hundred). If this was a Lao speaker, which most people from Nan (where this manuscript was produced) at that time were (and largely still are), then *sāt* is the pronunciation of *chatta* (six) in Lao. The author might have gone on to correct himself by writing *catt* following *sāt*. He equated the two titles with each other using the Northern Thai word *reu* (or / "it is called"). Since, *c* and *ch* are pronounced the same way in Pali, switching *catta* to *chatta* is easy, as most manuscripts are orally produced. Finally the author writes the numeral six after the title *Amaregāthā*. *Amaregāthā* is not the sixth chapter of the *Dhammapada-atthakathā* or of other related narrative collections. It could have been a local name. He also calls it the twenty-third section at one point.

The confusion does not end here though. There are also colophons at the end of other fascicles in this manuscript, and they are written in a different hand (most manuscripts seem to have been produced as a group endeavor). The colophons on the first two fascicles are by a scribe, the monk Ananchai Bhiikhu, who is more familiar with the Yuan script, even though he has trouble writing certain letters and uncommon consonant clusters. He also gives different spellings for the title of the text and even gives two spellings for his own name. Clearly, the sponsor and monk, Phra Godung Chao, was not bothered (if he read the colophons) by this lack of standardization or the number of people involved. In fact, the more people involved in making the manuscript, the more merit generated. Furthermore, this could have been a training exercise for his students. Since palm leaf is relatively difficult to prepare for inscribing, it would have been more efficient to train many students on one manuscript, like many automobile repair students train on one engine or many medical students observe a surgery on a single human body. Phra Godung Chao played the role of the sponsor who directed the completion of the manuscript and the teacher who read the source text or terms to his students/scribes.

Orthographic inconsistencies also abound in manuscripts composed in the Yuan (Northern Thai) script. This shows that (1) there was no overarching authority in place that determined what was the proper spelling of different words; (2) that scribes were poorly trained in both vernacular and classical composition; (3) that spelling was phonologically determined, and that scribes wrote texts that were dictated to them and changed the spelling of words based on what they heard rather than having a standardized way of spelling any individual word; and (4) that the highly mobile nature of monks and of the population in general led to speakers of Shan, Khoen, Leu, Lao, Yuan, Thai, Khamtu, Mon, Hmong, Burmese, and other languages living and working together.[41] There is overwhelming evidence collected from many different pedagogical manuscripts. These examples are so numerous that they would be best demonstrated in a chart that would have the added benefit of providing a guide to the mutable orthography of manuscripts of the region.[42] However, a script chart, no matter how many alternatives it offers, creates a false sense of consistency or base standard from which scribes were deviating.

These orthographic inconsistencies are not just found in *nissaya*, *vohāra*, and *nāmasadda*. They are found in magical, medical, astrological, and ritual commentaries and in canonical texts in Pali and the vernacular. They are numerous and often present a word spelled three or four different ways on one line of a folio. While inconsistency in script can be attributed to the four reasons listed above, an unsystematic way of teaching various spellings suggests that these frequent, unsystematic, and widespread orthographic inconsistencies are reflections of the oral composition/orthophonic spelling of these texts and the lack of an overarching editing, publishing, or educational system or standards. Heightened attention to orthography demonstrates the benefits of using manuscripts rather than printed texts or transliterations when studying Southeast Asian religion and literature. These apparent "mistakes" actually provide valuable evidence on how these texts were composed. They demonstrate that there was a lack of large-scale educational institutions to enforce the use of certain spellings and scripts over others. Historical evidence of a highly mobile monastic population is reinforced, since letters (as well as vocabulary) from Shan, Yuan, and Burmese scripts are found interspersed throughout Lao manuscripts and vice versa, and strongly suggests that these manuscripts were composed orally/aurally. What the modern scholar sees as orthographic anomalies, the original composer and scribe did not. These texts were for oral performance and teaching, not for reading silently alone. The spelling is phonetic.

William Johnson's study of Latin and Greek orthography and manuscript text layout is helpful here. First, he emphasizes that all scripts are "inadequate in conveying prosodic and paralinguistic features like tone of voice, facial expression, eye contact, body language, and other elements that make spoken utterances quite different from written scripts. Writing not only records incompletely the locutionary act (what is said) but is poor as a conveyance of the illocutionary force (how the speaker intends what is said to be taken)."[43] This is especially true with early Roman and Greek manuscripts, which have no breaks between the words (*scriptio continua*) or punctuation, paragraph markers, highlighting or underscoring marks (all qualities shared with Northern Thai and Lao manuscripts). This type of writing makes it extremely difficult (and some argue impossible) to read silently, because of the lack of a "Bouma shape," or separate word unit or sign that acts as a point of "ocular fixation" so that the natural saccadic movement within the bounds of parafoveal vision—fifteen to twenty letters in Yuan or Tham script—is not overtaxed. According to the bounds of this basic human cognitive/ocular ability, Northern Thai and Lao manuscripts would be extremely difficult to read silently (as they were for me and my teachers) at any semi-rapid pace. Moreover, these manuscripts often break words at the end of lines with no apparent attention to syllable breaks or word separation. This lack of morphemic boundaries cannot proceed line by line efficiently without the text being read out loud. Finally, Johnson helps one to understand that many manuscripts were written (or dictated and copied by a scribe) with the intended, usually "professional," reader/audience in mind (the way a physician writes prescriptions for a pharmacist) and hence do not have to have every word spelled out or be overly concerned with proper orthography.

Physical Features: The Importance of an Ugly Manuscript

The physical features of the manuscripts show that *nissaya*, *vohāra*, and *nāmasadda* were used by monks giving sermons and were actively used for teaching. Some scholars who work with Chinese, Old English, Spanish, and Pali manuscripts acknowledge the importance of apparent "mistakes" in the manuscripts they study. Instead of immediately correcting errors in grammar and syntax or repairing damage done to a manuscript leaf, some scholars are beginning to act like forensic scientists, paying attention to anomalies in their subject rather than immediately correcting them. For example, Susan Cherniack in her study of manuscript production in Sung China notes that "the role assigned to the Western textual critic is to . . . purge the text of its accumulated filth and disease."[44] Cherniack believes that textual scholars often correct manuscript errors and overlook the fact that traditional Chinese scholars and scribes saw their role as trying to improve and update the texts on which they worked. Therefore, what modern philologists see as corruptions, they saw as improvements.[45]

One should also pay attention to the literal context of the text. Fred Robinson has argued that one needs to pay attention to how manuscripts are bound and preserved. He was able to gain some insight into the way manuscripts were classified and used in instruction by looking at what other texts they were bound together with in archives.[46] Similarly, the binding of *nissaya* manuscripts in monastic libraries offers some clue to their use in instruction and their function. For example, fascicle 1 of the *Dhammapada nissaya* from Luang Phrabang is a complete translation of *Dhammapada-atthakathā* 1.1, but at its end is attached the explanation of another, yet unidentified, narrative. This narrative was translated by a different scribe (evident from handwriting samples and the number of lines per leaf), but it has similar orthographic alternatives and syntactical patterns. This reveals that the scribes were receiving dictation or some form of instruction from the same teacher (or at least very similarly trained teachers). Moreover, since the additional narrative is not complete, nor is the following narrative in the Pali *Dhammapada-atthakathā* source, the text may have been meant more as a lesson on certain terms drawn from the source text (or from the teacher's memory of the source). The instructor was not following the normative *Dhammapada-atthakathā* and may have been either working from a no longer extant anthology of Pali narratives based on the *Dhammapada-atthakathā* or relating stories in random order from memory.

In addition to the manuscripts' archival neighbors, one also needs to pay greater attention to the physical conditions of texts. Katherine O'Brien O'Keeffe argues that "the disembodiment of text [from its material form] . . . limits the optimum recovery of medieval texts and their contexts . . . each manuscript is time specific and embodies the poem as a particular reading. The poem cannot exist without the medium which transmits it."[47] Her hyper-attention to the physical features of the manuscripts has allowed her to see the different contexts in which the poem *Solomon and Saturn I* was read. John Dagenais, studying the manuscripts of the *Libro de buen amor* (a fourteenth-century Spanish composition), notes that there is no known author or date of the text, but the physical features of the manuscripts go far in determining the history and the origins of the text. The many glosses, marginal notes, illuminations, and so forth in the *Libro* led Dagenais to rethink the way he approached medieval texts in general. He calls for a greater awareness of what the actual manuscript can reveal about the scribe, the possible readers, the institution that produced the manuscript, the expense of the material, and so on.[48]

In keeping the work of Dagenais, O'Brien O'Keeffe, Robinson, and others in mind, one can see that these *nissaya*, *vohāra*, and *nāmasadda* manuscripts were commonly used and not meant for display. They were not particularly beautiful, well-preserved gifts; collectors' items; or symbols of the glory of Buddhist teachings. There are no illustrations of note or aesthetic intrigue. The folios are broken and often do not have covers (when they do they are neither decorated nor gilded, painted nor carved); one rarely finds extensive or beautifully composed (stylistically or aesthetically) colophons. Silk manuscript covers and decorative binding cords are largely absent, and the texts are often missing folios or whole sections. Non-pedagogical manuscripts seen in the regional monastery museums at Wat Phra That Lampang Luang and the Wongburi Mansion Museum in Phrae, and Northern Thai manuscripts on display at the National Library of Thailand are occasionally beautifully produced. However, pedagogical manuscripts are not ceremonial/ritual manuscripts like the Central Thai *Phra malai* or the Burmese *kammavācā*.

Nissaya, *vohāra*, and *nāmasadda* manuscripts do not afford these accoutrements of wealth and prestige. They are idiosyncratic, noncanonical, vernacular, and aesthetically and stylistically plain. Their leaves are cracked, showed signs of being frequently handled, and display poor handwriting (inscribing). They can be compared to a modern high school algebra or economics textbook, not to a leather-bound, gilt-edged collector's edition of the *Decameron* or a velvet-wrapped, acid-free, silver-chained, double-scroll copy of the Torah or the velum Book of Kells. This inelegant textbook or instruction manual quality of *nissaya*, *vohāra*, and *nāmasadda* manuscripts indicates their everyday function as pedagogical texts, read and used by monks to prepare for or give a sermon. This use is easily seen today, as monks throughout Thailand hold printed, wood-pulp paper manuscripts while giving sermons, occasionally referring to them with a downward glance. These printed manuscripts are very inexpensive (one fascicle costs about twenty baht, the equivalent of about forty U.S. cents), lack adornment and illustration, are poorly edited and printed, and are usually vernacular and Pali bilingual texts.[49] There is no evidence of their widespread worship. *Nissaya*, *vohāra*, and *nāmasadda* in particular are important for the fact that they are not beautiful or painstakingly constructed. They have marginalia, corrections, additions, and so on. They were used and not well preserved. Unlike many Pali manuscripts, there are very few colophons where the scribe asks that the manuscript not be altered.[50]

In the premodern period, as in the modern period, when manuscripts were finished they were placed, often, in large wooden boxes (Northern Thai: *hip*; Lao: *hīt*) or closets (*tu*) that were illustrated with scenes from popular *jātaka* (which may have been the subject of oral lessons for the illiterate as well). These boxes, as well as single manuscripts, were then placed in libraries (*ho trai* / *ho tai*), which were, and are today, wooden or stone structures often constructed on wooden stilts. These small buildings were mostly windowless, with low ceilings and one door and built high off the ground to protect the manuscripts from insects and thieves. Today one also finds old Buddha images stored in these libraries, and many of them have small altars as well that monastic and lay visitors pay obeisance to before they remove a manuscript. These libraries are not conducive for sitting and reading because of the lack of floor space, headroom, and light. In addition, without windows, the heat inside the libraries can be stifling. The outsides were, and are today, often decorated with popular scenes from *jātaka* (often extra-canonical) or scenes from the Indic *Rāmayāna*. Looking at the photographs, the reader will notice that these libraries were often inaccessible without ladders. Ladders, owned by the abbots and kept safely away from the libraries, could only be acquired by asking the respective abbot to use them. Some libraries, especially in Central and Northeastern Thailand, were built on stilts in ponds, to protect them from fire and insects. Once I saw a monk fall into a pond in Ubon Ratchathani (Northeastern Thailand) when the ladder he used to access a library on stilts slipped. He joked that these ponds protect libraries from big insects that wear orange robes. The insides of the libraries are dark, and to see, a monk would need either to hope that enough light would come from the small door or to use a candle. In the modern period, the danger of fire from candles is avoided by using flashlights, but severe danger from fires persists since it is common for monks to soak the wooden stilts in gasoline to protect them from climbing insects. Since many monks and scholars I know are heavy smokers, this might not be the wisest method.[51]

Pedagogical Methods

These three genres (*nissaya*, *vohāra*, and *nāmasadda*) encompass many of the services most commonly associated with commentaries, and their unsystematic shifting between commentarial methods shows how teachers used them pedagogically. The first method of all three genres is the glossing of individual words. This glossing is repetitive and runs throughout the text. For example, the *Madhurāsajambu nissaya* from Wat Sung Men provides glosses of the most basic Pali words, like *ahaṃ* (I) and *dhamma*, as well as less commonly known words like *parasuddha* (*parisuddha*; pure). The glosses range from simple synonyms in the vernacular to long explanations incorporating other Pali words (which may or may not be glossed). The *Dibbamon* (Pali: *Dibbamanta*) *nissaya* at Vat Mai in Luang Phrabang operates more like a bilingual dictionary than it does a textual translation. This is the function usually associated with *vohāra* or *nāmasadda* texts, but some *nissaya* provide it as well. One passage reads, "Siddhi man gong ko dī kammaṃ an ko geu wā kām ko dī dhammaṃ an ko geu wā dhamma ko dī saccaṃ an ko geu wā sacca ko dī nibbanaṃ ab geu wā nirabbān . . . (*siddhi* (means) powerful, *kammaṃ* is action, *dhammaṃ* is dhamma (law, truth, etc.), *saccaṃ* is sacca (truth), *nibbanaṃ* is nibbana") (f.1.v.1–2). Here is an example of the many ways Pali words can be rendered in Lao. First, *siddhi* is given the Lao gloss of *man gong* (strong/powerful). Second, *kammaṃ* is glossed with its Lao equivalent *kām*. Third, the glosses for *dhammaṃ* and *saccaṃ* suggest that there is no Lao lexical equivalent (although there are several, and *dhammaṃ* is usually written as *dham*). The gloss merely removes the ending (accusative singular masculine) of the Pali word. However, the last word (*nibbanaṃ*) is translated with a hybrid Sanskrit (*nirvaṇa*) and Pali (*nibbana*) lexeme—*nirabbān*.[52]

New material is often added by individual teachers in litanies.[53] This type of litany expansion is seen in the *nissaya* of the *Dhammapada-atthakathā* 252. Here there is a list that mentions beautiful garments, jewels, and so on removed magically from a ram's mouth; in the *nissaya* translation these items are expanded to include local terms for specific fabrics and the mention of silver as well as gold. The list of foods taken from the ram's mouth is shortened and ghee and sesame are not mentioned. This may be explained by the general lack of sesame and ghee in a Lao diet (although there are Lao words for these foods) and therefore a lack of understanding of their value by the author or audience. The same explanation can be given for the addition of specific fabrics, since silk and cotton production and the artistic skill associated with it have been extremely important to the Lao economy and symbols of its local identity.

In this text, words are idiosyncratically selected, entire sections are skipped or added, and glossing is repetitive and sometimes contradictory. It is more akin to an expository discussion of random terms from a source text presented by a teacher during an orally performed lesson (i.e., a lecture) on a source text of his choosing. Anyone who has taken a literature class on the *Tempest*, Saint Paul's Epistles, or the *Ṛg Veda* will recognize this style. These texts contain many cryptic terms or terms that must be understood to interpret the larger import of the text. A teacher serves his or her audience not only by explaining themes, historical context, and symbols but also by defining certain important terms. Sermons are often long and expansive Pali vocabulary lessons.

The second pedagogical method is grammatical explanation.[54] A *Kammavācā nissaya* manuscript from Wat Pichai, Lampang Province, Northern Thailand, reads, "Sammāpetvā ko hai pati ao duai dī lae hai mī chai-ya an loem sīa ying dī " ("*sammāpetvā* means that he caused the *pati* (lord) to hand (it) over (immediately) and he caused (him) to have a complete and successful victory") (f.*kāi*.v.2). The word *heu* (Central Thai: *hai*) indicates the causative in Northern Thai. Most grammatical explanations are of the locative, ablative, or nominative plural using the words *nai* (in), *chāk* (from), or *xāk* (Lao), and *dang lāi* (all/many), respectively. Furthermore, the imperative is consistently indicated with the word *jeung* or *jong* (old Lao). However, there are dozens of examples of Pali words, not in the nominative singular present, that are never grammatically indicated in the vernacular. This could indicate a poor knowledge of Pali grammar, but in most cases the grammatical form of the Pali word seems to be understood by the translator and simply not indicated because it can be understood in context. This follows Lao and Northern Thai grammar in that it only indicates tenses and modals if they are not apparent from the context. Words like *cha* (will / shall) and *laeo* (already / in the past) are often considered superfluous.

Oftentimes the *nissaya*, *vohāra*, and *nāmasadda* author seems to be presenting a lesson on a particular grammatical form and seems to be more concerned with that grammar lesson than in providing an accurate gloss of words from the source text. If one looks at the manuscripts pedagogically one can suggest seriously that they were often designed to be a student-centered grammar lesson, drawing material from a source text. In this way, the source text becomes the servant of the translation and reverses the general notion of the superiority and inviolability of the "original." Source texts that were not originally designed to be grammatica, like the *Abhidhamma mātikā* or the *Saccasaṅkhepa*, are employed to teach the reader/audience how to read compounds, and the translator gives only the semantic meaning of the Pali terms when it serves this pedagogical grammatical end. Vivien Law and Suzanne Reynolds have shown that Latin passages from the Bible were used as guides to teach Latin grammar in late medieval Europe.[55] Vernacular glosses, very similar to *nissaya* texts, form the vast majority of texts in medieval European archives. This reflected an attempt to "merge moral and educational competence."[56] For French or English students in the thirteenth century, learning to read meant learning to read Latin, but the way to learn to read Latin was through vernacular glosses of classical and religious texts. This is why the Psalter and the Pater Noster were used to teach grammar more than was Donatus's Latin grammar.

The third commentarial service is the clarification of word order. For example, the *Dhammapada nissaya* from Luang Phrabang reorders the words of the initial sentence of a verse from the *Dhammapada-atthakathā*. Throughout *nissaya*, *vohāra*, and *nāmasadda* this manipulation of Pali word order is commonplace. In order to identify where an author is changing the word order of the source text, that source text needs to be identified, which is often difficult if not impossible. Moreover, when the source text can be identified, the translation is often simply a translation either of some selected passages or words or of a summary of the source text that is not extant in Pali and perhaps may have been written by the translator himself. The *Aṭṭhasālinī nissaya* is a good example of the former, and the *Nāma nissaya* and the *Lokabhāsā nissaya* are good examples of the latter.

The fourth commentarial service is as a thesaurus of Lao or Northern Thai vocabulary.[57] Often throughout *nissaya* a Pali word is given several definitions or at least a list of synonyms. An *Atthasālinī nissaya* from Chiang

Mai gives numerous different definitions for the word *dhamma*. In a *Dhammapada nissaya* (fascicle 7), there is a translation of the word *bhariyā* (wife) (f.1.v.1), which illustrates this service well. In a *nissaya nāma* from Wat Phra Thatchomgiri in Chiang Mai, one finds other lists of vocabulary that blur the line between thesaurus and dictionary. The gloss of *bhariyā* reads, "Itthi reu phū ying // vadhu reu lūk saphai // bhikkhuni reu bhīkkhuni tang itthivadhu bhikkhunī long sicho (?) haeng pubba ao tth ao dh long wai ao i wai" ("*itthi* (means) woman, *vadhu* (and) the *bhikkhuni* (means) nun, all of these, the *itthi*, the *vadhu* (and) the *bhikkhuni* come (?) previously (one) took 'tth' (and) took 'dh' (and) placed them (?) (and) took 'i' (and) placed it") (f.1.3). This example (from a manuscript that is damaged and unclear) demonstrates not only that some *nissaya* provide lists of semantically related lexical items but also that they offer instructions on how to write or, more likely, to pronounce the words. Although I am unsure, the passage that follows the list of "woman, daughter, nun" seems to be the translator's note of how the words can be spelled differently (i.e., replace "tth" of *itthi* with "dh"). The fact that "tth" is in *itthi*, "dh" is in *vadhu*, and "i" is in *bhikkhuni* might suggest that they were abbreviations for these words. Abbreviations in Northern Thai are not universally taken from the first syllable of the word. In an *Aṭṭhakathāmātikā nissaya*, the word *vipāka* was given the synonym *vipaccaṃ*. Later in this manuscript (f.*jī*.1), in another long and repetitive passage explaining how to read different types of compounds, one finds the term *sahāvihāra* translated with the synonym *savitakka*. Dozens of other examples may be found of these synonyms, demonstrating how *nissaya* (and *vohāra* and *nāmasadda* in many cases) could have worked as a thesaurus or a dictionary for students learning how to listen to or read and write in Pali and the vernacular.

There is a fifth commentarial service that I have found only in the manuscript of the *Madhurāsajambū nissaya*.[58] One Pali sentence reads, "Khemimaggayam kampiya rukkha rucei dāmana manipabhābhidhammāgga samaṃ manamānicca" (f.*ka*.v.1).[59] This verse makes little or no sense as it is, and although individual words like *rukkha*, *magga*, and *abhidhamma* can be isolated, without grammatical endings, it is a litany devoid of syntax. Still, the author of the *nissaya* divided the words and provided endings. The semantic resonance of the Pali or the Northern Thai gloss is not important here; instead, what is important is the way the author of the *nissaya* provides declension markers for Pali words without markers, most often placing them in the accusative singular masculine. Furthermore, he "corrects" or provides alternate spellings for certain Pali words like writing *khemaṃ* for *khemiṃ*, *pavara* for *pabhābhidhamma*, and *ruci* for *rucei*. The clarification of *sandhi* is also interesting, because *pabhābhidhamma* is divided into two unrelated words, *pavara* and *visuddhiṃ*. *Manamānicca* is simply rendered as *niccaṃ*. Thus this Pali passage and its translation would make any good Sri Lankan, German, Japanese, or British Pali scholar shudder because both the Pali sentence and its translation butcher canonical Pali grammar and spelling. One could simply relegate this manuscript to the dustbin as an example of the poor Pali training in medieval Northern Thailand or designate it as the product of an exhausted and amateurish scribe. This I believe would overlook some of the most significant facts about the languages of Northern Thai and Pali in Northern Thailand and the creative and pedagogical aspects of translations in the region in the premodern period. Moreover, since dozens of examples of "good," normative Pali are available in this and other *nissaya* and in other manuscripts written around the same period and from the same temple, one cannot simply say that the training of this particular author was poor or that the author was completely unaware of his unorthodox translation. In the process of dividing words the author does not simply add endings and split up the Pali words and provide vernacular translations. He adds Pali words that are not found in the Pali sentence he is glossing. Moreover, he not only adds Pali words and ignores others but also provides vernacular glosses for those Pali additions. Therefore, as he translates, he is composing a new Pali text. This text is more than a translation. It becomes what I like to call an "implicit grammar," or an "emergent text," meaning an attempt to make a language instead of being the product of a preexisting one. Here one sees the early stages of the vernacular-Pali creole that is modern Lao and, especially, Thai. It is a commentary on the author's own translation and not one of any "original" Pali source text.

Rhetorical Style: Repetition and Reinforcement

While reading numerous *nissaya*, *vohāra*, and *nāmasadda* manuscripts slowly, I soon became aware of certain repetitive syntactical structures, which actually taught me how to read the text. There was gradual lexical replacement at strategic intervals in these structures that allowed me to memorize Pali vocabulary and their vernacular glosses without a concerted effort, very much like popular songs that slowly add new words within familiar syntactical structures. Two examples may suffice to illustrate my point. In a *Kammavācā nissaya* from Luang Phrabang is a gloss of the Pali word *gandā*.[60] First, the novice asks, "What does *gandā* mean?" and receives the answer in bold—"It is a boil, it is something swollen, it is a *nap* (?); namely, these things are in the body (*sālile*) in the body, (which is) the flesh of you (*te*) of you that spreads over (you)." In this gloss of the *gandā* are two additional Pali glosses of the words *sālile* (sārire) and *te*. Furthermore, between the question and the answer is another phrase that reads "*ābādha* (disease/mistake) means diseases in general; namely, that have characteristics like this." This phrase is repeated again on the next line and then the definition for *gandā* is repeated again in an abbreviated form. Therefore, the reader reads the gloss of *gandā* twice as well as reads the gloss of *ābādha* twice. *Ābādha* had already been glossed in the manuscript several times before. Moreover, when the glosses of both *gandā* and *ābādha* are repeated, alternate spellings of *sālile*, *sahāva*, *pān*, and *tūma* are used—*sārire*, *sabhāva*, *bān* (the phonetic equivalent of *pān*), and *tūm*. Finally, inserted within these glosses are glosses of common Pali words like *te*, *evarūpa*, and *sārire*, which had already been glossed several times before and are simply reinforced here. If this seems confusing, it is because texts like this one were not meant to be read silently; these texts were accompanied by an oral commentary. The repetition assisted the teacher in emphasizing the importance of certain terms.

On three leaves of a *Dhammapada nissaya* from Vientiane that dates from 1720 (f.*khāi*.30–f.*khām*.v.1), the Pali words *Meṇḍaka* and/or *seṭṭhi* are mentioned forty-seven times. Meṇḍaka is the name of one of the characters in this narrative, and *seṭṭhi* is a treasurer or a wealthy person. Almost every time Meṇḍaka is mentioned, he is called a *seṭṭhi*. While this in itself is not surprising, it is interesting how many times Meṇḍaka is mentioned and that his name is glossed in Lao nearly every time he is mentioned.[61] For example, although Meṇḍaka had been introduced and reintroduced dozens of times in the story (f.*khao*.4–5), one finds: "*Tasmim cā samaye nai kāla* (and at that time) at that time when Meṇḍaka the householder who is known as

Meṇḍaka the Wealthy one, the one who has excellent and important merit in greater amounts than all five others who also have ample amounts of merit *sampatti* is a *seṭṭhi* (he obtained the [position] of a wealthy person); namely, a person who is important within that city among *pañca* (the five) people who have great amounts of merit. Meṇḍaka *nāma* (he is known as Meṇḍaka), that is Meṇḍaka the Wealthy One." By reading or listening to line after line of glosses embedded in the narrative, the reader or audience would surely not forget the name Meṇḍaka or the fact that he was a wealthy person or a treasurer *seṭṭhi*. I imagine that any Lao teacher giving a lecture or sermon based on this *nissaya* would do so in order to emphasize the generous nature of Meṇḍaka. Meṇḍaka was rewarded because he gave to the *sangha* and to his people. This seems to be clear evidence of a premodern Lao method of "passing around the collection plate."

This selection from the *Dhammapada nissaya* has sixty-three words, seventeen of which are Pali. However, if the name Meṇḍaka and the title *seṭṭhi* are not counted, then this number drops to nine out of sixty-three words, or approximately 13 percent. Therefore, one cannot say that the number of Pali words written out and glossed is consistent throughout this manuscript, and it appears that the decision of when to write a Pali word and supply a vernacular gloss is idiosyncratic and depends on the author. For example, why would the author decide to write out and gloss the Pali numeral *pañca* (five) and not, for example, the Pali word *nagara* (city)? Why write the Lao word *pun* (merit) and on the next line write the Pali word *puṇṇa* (merit / name for the slave of Meṇḍaka), from which *pun* is derived? This cannot be called a vernacular gloss since the vernacular appears first and is not directly correlated with its Pali equivalent. There is no apparent underlying cause for this choice. The standard hierarchy between the Pali source text, as well as Pali words and vernacular glosses, and translations is either neutralized or reversed. The vernacular and the classical languages play together like well-matched tennis players, but the second-seed vernacular upsets the top-seeded classical in this match. This pedagogical method is a defining feature of Lao and Northern Thai *nissaya*, *vohāra*, and *nāmasadda* texts in general. It would be going too far, without evidence as to the conscious or subconscious intentions of the author, to say that he purposely attempted to devalue the Pali text. In fact, the opposite is more likely. He strung Pali words and phrases through the vernacular to maintain a link with the prestigious and ancient Pali source text but used the vernacular to communicate with and edify his audience. The Pali text is invoked, but it is reduced to a bank of words and phrases, not an intact or inviolable text. Here a lesson on the importance of giving is offered through the example of Meṇḍaka. The repetition of phrases and words at frequent intervals allows the audience and scribe to learn certain important words like *aham*, *nāma*, *satthā*, *buddha*, *seṭṭhi*, and *dhamma*, as well as to remember the main characters of the text. Any other reader (listener) or scribe would be able to remember numerous Pali words and relate the main themes and characters of the story without reference to the text.[62]

Repetition is a well-known feature of Pali texts in general, especially texts like the *Maṅgala sutta* and *Dhammapada-atthakathā*; however, *nissaya*, *vohāra*, and *nāmasadda* employ repetition in different ways.[63] First, repetitive phrases in *nissayas* do not mimic the Pali passages of the source texts being translated (if the source is even known or exists). Second, repetition is not for the purpose of ritual praise, does not involve meter, and rarely is associated with litanies or qualities or directives. Third, because they are vernacular translations that often, but certainly not always, lift Pali words and phrases from the source texts, they do not simply provide vernacular glosses for the Pali words but actually write the Pali words followed by their vernacular glosses and then repeat this gloss within the context of the text.

This repetition of both Pali and vernacular words is seen clearly by focusing on what I call "reinforcement." Certain Pali words are consistently glossed in *nissaya*, *vohāra*, and *nāmasadda* even though their gloss must have been commonly known. For example, in the *Paññāsa jātaka nissaya*, the first-person nominative pronoun *aham* is glossed dozens if not hundreds of times with the Northern Thai word *khā* (I). One would assume that once the word has been glossed it would be remembered by the reader/audience or would only occasionally have to be retranslated; however, even in the last fascicle (tenth) of a *Sutmon nissaya* one reads the phrase "ahaṃ reu khā" (I means I) numerous times. In the *Madhurāsajambū nissaya* the Pali second-person nominative (and often accusative) plural pronoun *tumhe* (you all) is one of the many relatively simple words glossed dozens of times with identical vernacular translations over fifteen fascicles. In the *Saccasaṅkhepa nissaya* the word *navaka* (ninefold) is repeated seven times in less than two lines of one folio (f.*gu.*1–2). Other common words like *puggala* (person), *āha* (he/she said), *evaṃ* (thus), and *sutvā* (having heard) are given the same vernacular gloss over and over again. These terms are memory triggers for a teacher giving a sermon and also serve to reinforce for the audience the sound and meaning of certain selected terms. The teacher associates these repeated terms with the selected source text, and after the sermon the source text and terms are forever associated in the memory of an alert audience.[64]

The South and Southeast Asian Science of Words

The philological detail in this chapter helps to establish the oral and pedagogical function of these three pedagogical genres and to demonstrate how they are a highly valuable historical source for defining the premodern curricula of the region. It would be fruitless to attempt to isolate the direct sources for these methods or the urtexts of Lao and Northern Thai pedagogical manuscripts. These texts are defined by their methodology, not their content. It seemed of no concern to the authors whether they had the most original text, because they had no problem changing the sources with which they were working. This is not a history of institutions, but a history of proximate mechanisms, of textual modes, pedagogical methods, and rhetorical styles.

The interpretative communities and practices of South and Southeast Asia, since the post-Vedic period, have been fascinated with the science of words. Since the earliest *nirukta* texts, which explained and glossed Vedic texts, through the great commentaries of Buddhaghosa and Dhammapala, up until the time of the Sri Lankan *sannaya* and Burmese, Siamese, and Tai-Lao *nissaya*, *nāmasadda*, and *vohāra*, Brahman and Buddhist scholars have made it a priority to explain, gloss, etymologize, compare, and expand the meanings of individual words and phrases drawn from texts in Sanskrit, Prakrit, and Pali.[65] This tradition does not differ much from the Jewish and Islamic traditions or the work of classicists today. Knowing the basic terms and being familiar with the "classics" of their field is the first duty of scholars. How this is done is quite different from community to community. For Lao and Northern Thai monastic teachers, the foundational terms for Buddhism were not sacrosanct; they were mutable tools applied in different situations.

While commentaries on syntax, prosody, plot, or argument structure exist and have been important in the South and Southeast Asian textual traditions, their prevalence is secondary to individual lexeme and verse commentaries. *Nissaya*, *nāmasadda*, and *vohāra* are merely a part of later developments of this larger science of words. It shows that perhaps Pali was losing its importance as a language of composition and instruction in Southeast Asia. Generally, there was either a loss of interest in studying, teaching, and writing in Pali or a decline in the Pali language skills of scholars in Northern (and Central) Thailand and Laos after the sixteenth century. That Pali word commentaries and grammars have continued to be produced in great numbers and that virtually every major monastic and protective Buddhist ritual is still performed in Pali casts doubt on whether the cultural importance of Pali has ever seriously waned. However, the significant decline in writing original works in Pali does indicate a shift in priorities. *Nissaya* and *vohāra* (and to a lesser extent *nāmasadda*) are creative and original texts even though they are partly translation and partly commentary and not completely new works. This decline in Pali writing and the rise of the vernacular in education and ritual does not necessarily indicate the presence of some sinister outside force like invading Burmese or deleterious colonial or Western influence. The decline of commentaries and other texts written in Pali need not be considered a sign of "loss." In fact, the decline of Pali composition and the growth of vernacular glosses and commentaries may reflect a desire to spread the Buddha's teaching (and the economic and political influence of the Sangha and the political powers that supported it) to a greater audience. Invoking the power and prestige of the classical but teaching in the vernacular may have been designed to increase the number of young people being ordained. Vernacular glosses would have also helped train these new monks and novices quickly. Teaching new novices and monks how to invoke Pali words in sermons would allow them to impress their lay audience with their Pali skills, without necessarily training each student to read, write, and speak Pali fluently. It is often assumed that Theravada monks know Pali well; however, the vast majority throughout South and Southeast Asia do not, but they can invoke and explain Pali terms in the vernacular. This situation is similar to Catholic priests and Latin, to Indonesian and Malaysian imams and Arabic, and to Hindu Brahman swamis and Sanskrit. Most often these religious intellectuals cannot read, speak, or write well in their religion's respective classical language, but they are familiar with basic terms, stories, and scriptures that they have learned through vernacular commentaries.

Often too much importance is placed on the particular language of a text and too little on the role of the text and how it reflects and helped create a particular interpretative community. Even though *nissaya*, *nāmasadda*, and *vohāra* are vernacular texts, they should not be considered as outside of the millennia-old tradition of commentary in South and Southeast Asia. In fact, the commentaries on which Buddhaghosa, the most famous composer of Pali commentaries, based his work were in the vernacular language Sinhala. These include the *Sīhalaṭṭhakathā*, *Mahāpaccariya-atthakathā*, *Kurundī-atthakathā*, and *Uttaravihāra-atthakathā*, among others. According to legend, around the fifth century the great commentator had "burned" these vernacular texts when he was finished with his work. Buddhaghosa states, "[I] perform my task well . . . from these [Sinhalese] commentaries after casting off the language, condensing detailed accounts, including authoritative decisions and without overstepping any Pali idiom. . . . [I am] . . . now rejecting the Sinhala language, adopting the graceful language that accords so well with the order of the text. . . . I proceed to expound the meaning of my text, omitting all unnecessary repetitions."[66] Despite his derisive attitude toward the Sinhala vernacular, the vernacular has clearly played an important role in the Pali commentarial tradition of which *nissaya*, *nāmasadda*, and *vohāra* are a later example. This interplay between vernacular and classical languages is seen throughout the textual traditions of South Asia, where Sanskrit texts were commented on, translated, criticized, and expanded in multiple vernaculars.

The pedagogical methods found in these manuscripts are most likely the result of influences of traditional commentarial styles in Sanskrit and Pali from South Asia combined with local literary experiments with alliteration, repetitive patterns, and so forth and served as a model for composing instructional manuals for giving sermons and for creating language "textbooks" or "readers." Understanding the specific origins of *nissaya*, *nāmasadda*, and *vohāra* is not as important as seeing them as part of a long history of commentary and interplay between the vernacular and the classical.

5 The Culture of Translation

In 2002, one hundred years after the Sangha Act was announced, I found myself listening to a sermon on the Dhammapada at Wat Rakhang (Khositaram). I was fortunate to have found an apartment down a narrow alley from this royal monastery, which sits on the riverbank directly across from the Grand Palace. Wat Rakhang is home to one of the largest monastic schools in Thailand and shares teachers and students with Mahachulalongkorn Monastic University nearby. It is the former home temple of the Sangharāja, the supreme patriarch of Thailand.

This sermon was about a story in the *Dhammapada-atthakathā*; however, I quickly noticed that the preacher was not reading from a textbook of the Pali story or from an old manuscript of the story. Instead, he was holding a faux palm-leaf manuscript made out of cardboard. Rather than being inscribed with a stylus in Yuan, Tham, or Khom script, the text was produced with a laser printer in modern Thai script. It mimicked the exact dimensions of a traditional palm-leaf manuscript—it was long (about twenty-two inches) and narrow (about three inches) and had twelve bi-folios (the exact size of most premodern single-fascicle manuscripts).

As the preacher was giving the sermon he would occasionally glance down at the cardboard manuscript and "lift" (*yok*) a Pali word and explain that word in modern vernacular Thai. The text of the sermon did not relate the story verbatim, but summarized the main narrative and then discussed important terms from the story. As I listened I could not help seeing the parallels with *nissaya* and *vohāra* manuscripts. It seemed as if I was witnessing how premodern *nissaya* must have been used centuries before. After the sermon

I asked the preacher if I could see the cardboard manuscript. As I read the manuscript my suspicions regarding the connection between this modern manuscript and premodern *nissaya* and *vohāra* were confirmed. On the first leaf were instructions telling the preacher to give the sermon using the "*vohāra* method." I return to a full description of this modern manuscript of the *Dhammapada-atthakathā* in chapter 7. The subject of the present chapter is to trace connections between premodern *nissaya* and *vohāra* and their modern manifestations more generally—to trace the process of Pali languaging over time. These connections entail not merely the contents of the texts but also their pedagogical methods, aesthetics, commentarial services, rhetorical strategies, and generic features.

Why Did *Nissaya*, *Vohāra*, and *Nāmasadda* Disappear?

There is no evidence of new *nissaya*, *vohāra*, or *nāmasadda* composition after 1920 in Laos or Northern Thailand. These genre rubrics seemed to have disappeared. This is partially due to the fact that many manuscripts were lost in the burning and looting of Siamese monasteries and royal libraries by the Burmese in the eighteenth century. Although there is little evidence that speaks to the degree of the loss, it is known that pedagogical manuscripts were part of the Siamese tradition. However, the manuscript equivalent of notebooks and lecture guides (*nissaya*, etc.) were the first to be replaced by the European stylebook, wood-pulp paper, and eventually wire-bound notebooks. Since these texts were used as guides and notes in oral/aural performance in monastic schools, they may have become obsolete with the rise of the printing press (first used in Siam in 1835 and decades later in Laos and Northern Thailand) and published editions of liturgies, histories, grammatica, dictionaries, glossaries, concordances, anthologies, and textbooks and the first printings of the Pali canon in both the classical and the vernacular. With published texts came the critical edition.[1] With the reign of King Mongkut came stronger notions of the proper, literal translation and the ability for students and teachers to own their own copies of texts (i.e., one no longer needed a senior and literate monk to translate or explain a Pali text orally). With printed copies of Buddhist texts and guides to those texts, students could read silently and hold their own copies of a particular text. The industrious student could read and translate Pali on his or her own. In a common monastic classroom today, especially in a large urban monastery in Northern or Central Thailand, a teacher refers to passages and page numbers in student textbooks, rather than orally describing the contents of his own manuscript. Certainly, in monastic classrooms, like any classroom setting, some students follow quite diligently, while others doze off, secretly try to read comic books or magazines, or pass notes to their friends.

The change that came with the rise of printed Pali and vernacular Buddhist texts did not happen to nearly the same extent in Laos. There are no state-sponsored or widely distributed Buddhist textbooks (if any are used they are usually brought in from Thailand) and few monastic printing presses. There is not even a full Lao script edition of the canon in Pali or Lao translation (although one of the first books printed in Lao was a Lao translation of the Christian New Testament). Furthermore, the literacy rate in Laos is still quite low when compared to that of its neighbors.[2] This may be why *nissaya*, *nāmasadda*, and *vohāra* manuscripts are still occasionally used in Laos for teaching. Overall though, with the rise of printing and the state's distribution of monastic textbooks and editions of the canon, it seems that the time of pedagogical manuscripts has ended.[3]

Other reasons for the disappearance of *nissaya*, *nāmasadda*, and *vohāra* as separate genres may be rooted in the takeover of Northern Thailand (or Lan Na) by Siam and the replacement of these traditional pedagogical texts by *desanā* (sermons), *nangseu plae* (translations), *phochananukhrom* (dictionaries), *khu meu triam sop* (examination preparation handbooks), and *tamra* (textbooks).[4] Although *nissaya* and *vohāra* as separate but closely related genres have disappeared, they have manifested themselves in modern textbooks and sermons. The genre of the *nāmasadda*, which can be translated as "word book" or "glossary," may have been made inefficient by dictionaries, used by teachers in preparing lessons on the meaning of terms in individual Pali source texts. *Nāmasadda* have been replaced by dictionaries, thesauruses, literal translations, facing-page translations, encyclopedias, and other aids to reading, studying, and preparing lessons in monastic schools.[5] Today, glossing Pali terms in the vernacular is still a common feature of Thai and Lao lectures and sermons, and traditional glossing passed down orally, not modern dictionaries or glossaries, is the most widely used source and method.[6]

All was not lost, however. The long-standing interpretative and homiletic practices of these pedagogical genres can be seen in the modern practice of lecture and sermon making and the larger craft of didactic prose in Laos and Thailand. The particular repetitive rhetorical style and the choice of source texts and commentarial services that characterize premodern pedagogical genres continue to pervade the modern textual and pedagogical practices of the region. While certain very prevalent texts known as *nissaya* and *nāmasadda* died out, the interpretative communities, reading cultures, and methods that produced them certainly did not. The *nissaya*, *nāmasadda*, and *vohāra* genres have been conflated into one general approach to Buddhist teaching—the *vohāra* mode.

From Genres to Modes

Literary genres are created long after the particular aspects (*eidos*/genus) that define them emerge. Aristotle did not group literary works into a series of genres until these particular types were well-established members of antiquity's cultural milieu. The work of making genres is descriptive, not prescriptive, and analytic, not creative. However, once a genre is established and its rules well known, it can become at best standardizing and at worst stultifying. Aristotle and Plato concerned themselves with defining the rules of the genres of tragedy, epic, comedy, and iambics and employed meter measurement, content, character type, "unity or plurality of action," and "duration of events."[7]

Following this practice, I have attempted to define the major features of *nissaya* and *vohāra*. However, these genres have many features that overlap, and it is difficult to define *nissaya* or *vohāra* as genres based on their content because their content follows that of their disparate source texts. Moreover, there is no evidence for any explicit attempts by the literati and exegetes themselves to define the parameters of premodern Northern Thai and Lao genres. I have never come across a *nissaya*, *vohāra*, or any other manuscript in which the author has consciously reflected on his attempts to follow certain *generic* rules, explicitly mix genres, or create new ways of writing.[8] In *nissaya* and *vohāra* even the most basic and original distinctions between genres—poetry and prose—are often broken down when a prose gloss or explanation is made from passages composed in verse.

One must ask then, are genre rubrics useful? Does defining *nissaya* and/or *vohāra* as belonging to a particular genre of literature take one any further in understanding their function in premodern religious, social, or intellectual history? Does one learn anything more about the interpretative communities that employed them? It does if one is trying to identify the continuities between the premodern and the modern. It helps to see modern Asia not simply as a colonially corrupted region eternally victimized by the "West" with its cultural forms, literature, and pedagogical methods as "traditional" leftovers maintained only by tourism and the stubbornness of old monks. *Nissaya* and *vohāra* are reflective of a pervasive episteme and intellectual and aesthetic attitude toward the translocal, externally validated sources of knowledge (Pali texts, both canonical and extra-canonical). The *vohāra* mode is not merely a persistent leftover but a "mode of approach" to a selection of texts chosen and transmitted locally. The *vohāra* mode is constitutive of the way new information is brought in, filtered, and taught.

Tzvetan Todorov and Alastair Fowler see genres as useful in tracing change and continuity. Todorov points out that the postmodern tendency to see genre rubrics as anachronistic is related to a general assumption that texts subvert or deconstruct well-established genre rules. Genres, Todorov emphasizes, "are useful for seeing disruptions and changes, as well as continuities."[9] Genres are discursive and hence are useful for seeing how a writer at a particular time and place situated his or her work. Later writers could be creative within the rules defined previously. Fowler sees genres as dynamic and moving from specific ways of describing and writing texts to more general modes of discourse. This is what he calls "generic modulation." Genres, like elegies, pervade culture, and the elegiac mode is a way writers of one culture can render a text. Genres, and their subcategories and repertoires, tend to combine with other genres and repertoires over time. For example, the river poem contributed to the emergence of the country house poem and then to the Georgic verse essay.[10] Genres can also incorporate other genres; new genres can emerge when an author changes the function of his or her work or includes several features from different genres under one title. This change from genre to "modal entity," or the evolution of one genre into many repertoires, is a process of creative engagement. In this way, pedagogical genres are reflective of a premodern sensibility in regard to classical sources and contemporary audiences. These genres survive as a pedagogical mode in the modern period. Genres evolve into modes. The practice of composing *nissaya* may have disappeared, but the *vohāra* mode remains an active pedagogical practice and epistemological approach.[11]

WHERE HAVE *NISSAYA* GONE? MODERN *VOHĀRA*

At a small private book dealer's house in the suburbs of Bangkok I came across a remarkable little book. This book fills in a gap in the literary record. I soon came to discover that it represents many types of books that were being produced at a time when the transition from pedagogical manuscripts to modern handbooks for the average student was taking place. This book, published in 1931 at Tha Phra Chan Press, one of first modern publishing houses independent from the royal court in Thailand, is titled *Maṅgalatthadīpanī yok sab plae.*[12] Just in the title one sees a definite link between the *yok sab* (lifting words) method explicitly used in *nissaya*, *vohāra*, and *nāmasadda* manuscripts and the modern use of the term *plae* (translation). This text is nearly identical in style, format, and method to premodern pedagogical manuscripts. However, now instead of a manuscript with notes in the margins and a wooden cover, one finds a red-cloth cover and the use of footnotes and parentheses. This little book and many others like it that I have found in the used-book sections of markets across Thailand, in the personal libraries of monks, or in the archives of monasteries like Wat Phra Singh, Wat Boworniwet, or Wat Phra That Haripunchai reveal that the *vohāra* genre persists. It simply has evolved into a more general mode of discourse that undergirds religious and secular oral presentation. One can see *vohāra* using the *yok sab* method in modern handbooks for teachers, sermon guides, handwritten notebooks, audio/video-recorded sermons, and so on. Since *vohāra* were essentially "oral texts," one needs to compare oral text to oral text—educational context to educational context. *Vohāra* were created for and in response to oral presentations, summaries, expansions, and adaptations of source texts whether they are canonical, commentarial, vernacular, or classical. They exist in a group setting. They are cues to unwritten oral expansions and asides and are responsive to contemporary events, personal biases, political agendas, idiosyncratic wonderings, and audience reactions. These encounters may float above the texts, but they are part of the history of Buddhist education.

Modern *vohāra*, Pricha Changkhwanyeun states, are vernacular commentaries on Pali texts that work by drawing examples, glossing words, summarizing contents, or relating events in the past to contemporary concerns.[13] Their main concern is to define and explain terms used in the Pali source texts. Good *vohāra* composers, like the contemporary monks Phra Debwissuddhimedhi or Phra Kalayāṇo, have a knowledge of words. They not only composed a number of *vohāra* but also wrote a dictionary for Buddhist laity that helped explain certain Pali words. This knowledge of Pali words, Pricha asserts, is the ultimate sign of intelligence and diligence in Thailand. It allows the author to relate words found in one story to the same words found in others and also to generate synonyms as well as guess obscure terms in other texts by relating similar words. It demonstrates the interconnectedness of the words of the Buddha and the ability of the author to synthesize a large amount of material for his audience. Premodern *nissaya*, *vohāra*, and *nāmasadda* cited Pali terms, glossed them, provided synonyms, and gave different prefixes and suffixes in a repetitive fashion. These are the services Pricha associates with modern *vohāra*. In fact, his descriptions of modern *vohāra* are closer to premodern *nissaya* than to *vohāra*. Modern *vohāra* follow the conventions of sermons and are explicitly tied to orality. He writes that "in order to explain what a *vohāra* is, we must see it as a type of Buddhist teaching that has existed since ancient times[;] its purpose was and is to divide and highlight the details, as well as supply examples and make comparisons [between Pali words] . . . the defining of words is a method of clarifying a passage and the way each preacher emphasizes the most important parts [of the text according to his opinion].[14] He continues: "The reason for dividing, highlighting the details and providing examples [of Pali terms drawn from source text(s)] that were particularly interesting was to instruct those with little knowledge like villagers and young students."[15] The author/preacher adapts each *vohāra* to the level of the audience and abbreviates or expands the number of the types of words drawn from the source text(s) to their level. This system allows the author/preacher to constantly make the source text(s) relevant to the concerns of the audience.[16] This reflects a creative engagement with the source as opposed to a slavish reproduction of it.

The preacher is a teacher, not simply an objective medium through which the classical flows.

This creativity is best expressed in the way one preacher can explain the same words and passages differently. For example, Phra Debwissuddhimedhi first explains words through their "roots" and then moves on to anonyms, synonyms, and examples. His 1995 *vohāra* sermon reads:

> *Paṭiccasamuppāda* rendered in the widest sense means that all things are interconnected (lit.: they live together [the law of causality]). That is they arise together and the reasons for their arising are connected generally. Still, when we speak directly about how the term relates to human life, *paṭiccasamuppāda* means the process of the arising of suffering.[17]

This passage continues defining *paṭiccasamuppāda* in several different ways. The word is repeated many times. Then Pricha cites three other ways in which Phra Debwissuddhimedhi defines the word *nibbana* in of his *vohāra* sermons:

> One type [of translation/commentary used in this *vohāra*] is that of *paṭisedha* (anonym). That is to show the meaning [of the word in question] by giving its opposite, showing what it is not, the bad side [of it], the various useless [i.e., nonsensical] meanings [of it] . . . such as [in the case of the word *nibbana*] *nibbana* means the end of *rāga* (passion), the end of *dosa* (ill will), the end of *moha* (delusion). *Nibbana* is the extinguishing of existence. *Nibbana* is the end of craving. (3)

Following this passage, Phra Debwissuddhimedhi defines *nibbana* with several synonyms like *ajara* (agelessness) and *amata* (immortality) and

> nibbana pheua sadaeng theung kun laksaṇa khong nibbana nan nai bāng ngae bāng dān chen santa (sangob) paṇīda (praṇīt) suddhi (khwām parisut) khema (khwām kesom) pen ton

[This type of translation/commentary] of *nibbana* is for showing the qualities and characteristics of *nibbana* from various sides and various angles, for example, it is *santa* (peaceful), *paṇīda* (scrupulous), *suddhi* (pure) [and] *khema* (tranquil). (3)

Here the author of the *vohāra* uses Pali adjectives to define *nibbana*. Finally, metaphor is used:

> *Nibbana* is like the *arahant* which in turn is like the cow who leads the herd across a passable place in the current until they reach the other side. It is like a person who crosses the great ocean or a large mass of water that is very dangerous until he stands safely on the opposite shore . . . *nibbana* is like a flat, smooth and delightful plain which provides cool shade, like a far-off land that is free from peril . . . *nibbana* is a city known as Udompuri (The Abundant City) and Nibbananagara (The City of Nibbana). (3)

Many of these types of translation/commentary are found in *nissaya* and *nāmasadda* texts. Pricha's work confirms that *vohāra* are explicitly connected to sermons. The examples also show that modern *vohāra* also use repetition as a pedagogical tool. These passages certainly are representative, and, if the full text were shown, this repetitiveness would be even more apparent. In these examples, however, the texts are not titled *vohāra*; instead, the premodern text has become a modern mode.

Phraya Upakit Silapasan's *Lak phasa Thai* is a compendium of the history, proper usage, and genres of Thai. He enumerates five types of *vohāra* used in modern Thai homiletics. The first is *panyai wohān* (Pali: *paryāya vohāra*)—an exact translation of idioms according to a teacher as part of a speech or a lecture. This type of explanation is often embedded in historical works or narratives as an aside for the audience. The second is *bananā wohān* (Pali: *vaṇṇanā vohāra*)—a type of lamentation of emotional reflection on a particular event. It is "subjective and not meant to be taken as fact" (*mai champen tong chai khwam ru kon kwa het phon ton doem thao thai nak*).[18] It is designed to invoke an image of that particular thing in the mind of the audience. The third and most important for these purposes is the *desanā vohāra*. Like the first two types, it invokes the definition of terms in creative and lengthy ways. It is directly connected to sermons (*desanā*) used by monks as a method of explaining Pali and vernacular religious terms and as a way of emphasizing certain terms and explaining them in detail (*bisadan yak hai khao kao chai lae hen khwam ching*). This helps the audience to use Pali words (often in verse) in everyday vernacular. A good preacher should use rhythmic and repetitive sayings like "wela nam ma fong pla kin mot wela nam lot fong mot kin pla" (when the water rises the fish eat the ants, when the water dries up the ants eat the fish) as an aid to the audience's memory. The fourth is the *sathok wohān* (*sādhaka vohāra*)—an explanation of terms employing comparisons "for easy listening, believing, and understanding" (*hai khao fang ngai hai khao chai lae cheua theu*). This last type, *upāma vohāra*, explains terms through metaphor.[19] Phraya Upakit associates all of these types of *vohāra* with oral performance and teaching, with the choice of which words and passages to "lift" from the source depending on the needs and objectives of the teacher/preacher.[20]

Where Have *Nissaya* Gone? Modern Lectures and Sermons

There are no extant manuscripts called "sermons" (*desanā*) in the Northern Thai manuscript archives (although there are a few in Laos). In premodern manuscript colophons, like some discussed in chapter 2, scribes explicitly call the *nissaya*, *vohāra*, and *nāmasadda* texts a *dhamma desanā* (dhamma sermon). But from my reading of a large number of *desanā* printed in the past few decades in Thailand, they are very similar to *nissaya* and *vohāra*, in the manner of repetitive lifting of individual Pali words from a particular text and of employing several methods to explain the word in the vernacular. Anyone who has listened to numerous sermons in Thailand or Laos and has listened to sermons on audiocassettes and compact discs knows the repetitive glossing that characterizes sermons in the region. The connection between these premodern pedagogical texts and *desanā* is direct in one case in Luang Phrabang, where one manuscript titled *nisai-desanā* is found.[21] This manuscript works by glossing Pali words from an unknown source and explaining them repetitively through metaphor, grammar, original usage, and synonym.[22]

The "Phra Dhammadesanā Biyakarakathā" by Phra Kawiwarayan and Phra Briyatthirakhun's "Phra Dhammadesanā Dhammacārīkathā" are transcripts of two modern sermons that are based on the repetitive and meticulous (but often fanciful) glosses of individual Pali words and phrases. It also may be noted that audiocassettes of sermons or nightly radio and television broadcasts of sermons in Thailand generally have the style of repetitive lessons based on the creative and multiple glosses of Pali words. Taped sermons by Phra Phayom, Phra Kittiwuṭṭho of Chonburi, Luang Ta Mahabua

Ñāṇasampanno of Udon Thani, and Achan Cha from Ubon Ratchathani Province are very common and particularly good examples of this style. Phra Phayom is famous for adding ad hoc humor, and Phra Kittiwuṭṭho is well known as a conservative political firebrand. The infamous monk Phra Yantra Amaro of Nakhon Sri Thammarat (and later Kanchanaburi), now living in exile in California, would often base whole sermons on the translation of one Pali term like *taṇhā*.[23] The nun Maechi Sansanee Sathirasut often emphasizes the importance of understanding the basic Pali terms of Buddhism before beginning a life of meditative contemplation.

Luang Ta Mahabua Ñāṇasampanno, perhaps the most famous and influential monk in all of Thailand, delivered a sermon on July 4, 2002, at Chulalongkorn University in front of a crowd of hundreds. It was based on the gloss and explanation of the Pali word *kilesa* (defilement). He began by defining *kilesa*, which he pronounced interchangeably in Pali and Thai (*kilet*), as a "bad dream" that persists during the waking hours and attacks your mental health. Through alliteration and word association he progressed into explanations of the word *loka* (world) as an active entity that acts on a person and generates *kilesa*. Keeping the geographical theme, he glossed the vernacular word *khopkhet* (horizon or border). He saw *khopkhet* as necessary attachments like wives, husbands, and children and as good things because they were checks to *kilesa*. A husband who was loyal to his wife would not intoxicate himself and lose money gambling. His attachment to his wife is a border or limit that works against *kilesa* (a rare promotion of attachments in a Buddhist sermon). *Hiri-ottappa*, the Pali compound commonly translated as "shame and guilt," was also given a long explanation as a positive quality because the two components reminded one of the dangers of *kilesa*. The person who possessed *hiri-ottappa* was a person who instinctively knew the meaning of *kilesa*. *Hiri-ottappa* was possessed by anyone with faith (*khwam cheua* or *saddha*). Then *kilesa* was translated with lists of its "ingredients" like *krodha* (anger), *icchā* (jealousy), and *akusala* (unskillful or bad things). Luang Ta Mahabua's sermon defined both vernacular and Pali terms that were in turn given as synonyms or used as part of an explanation of another Pali or vernacular word. This style consists of definitions within definitions and glosses within glosses. Furthermore, his sermon was repetitive. He always returned to the term *kilesa*, and his definitions of words used to define *kilesa* were also repetitive. *Hiri-ottappa*, *khopkhet*, and other terms were repeated and glossed several ways as part of the larger explanation and definition of *kilesa*. Moreover, like the rhetorical style of *nissaya*, his sermon did not have an introduction or conclusion. It progressed through ever-widening repetitive lexical loops. He also ended the sermon abruptly, seemingly because he was tired. It seems that the sermon could have continued in this style, perpetually driven by word association, reinforcement, and expanding definitions and by repetition of words and phrases in slightly altered form. After ninety minutes of speaking without notes and with his eyes often closed, I realized that the reason he did not need notes or any mnemonic aids was because he could simply use word association, circular and interconnected glossing of terms within terms, and repetition to continue speaking without need for pausing, memory recall, notes, or visual aids. The glosses were triggers to define other words.[24] Less experienced monks often need handheld notes (in the shape of a palm-leaf manuscript) to remind them of which Pali words to lift.[25]

This method is highly efficient and effective. Experienced monks do not need any other guide to a sermon besides a series of closely related trigger words. Individual words are lifted, and the process begins in slow, lexical, associative chains and cycles. There is no introduction, body, or conclusion; it is an organic speech that serves to discuss and teach important terms. These are not fully mapped trips with beginnings, rest stops, and destinations. They work by following signs from spot to spot. This method allows a monk to prepare a sermon quickly and to speak melodically and effortlessly if he has been trained over years by the same method. It has the added advantage of giving prestige to the monk by displaying him as a well-educated, classical wordsmith. It is a well-known fact that monks are judged on their sermon skills, not so much by what they teach, but by how long and how effortlessly they can speak and by how they manipulate Pali words and use puns, alliteration, rhyme, and difficult or rare words. My own abbot, Luang Phu Sompun, in the villages surrounding our monastery on the Lao-Thai border was renowned for the length of his sermons and his ability to speak for over three hours without notes and with pauses only to spit out his betel nut juice (*nam kiao mak*). He prepares his sermons by reading modern Pali-Thai dictionaries and word commentaries, other printed sermons, and anthologies of Pali narratives. More formal monastic classroom lectures are often similar to sermons, except that the audience in the modern period often holds textbooks or handbooks and the teacher is interrupted by questions.[26] It allows one to see Lao and Thai teachers as individual intellectual agents instead of as a faceless mass of monks "influenced" by an amorphous translocal religion. Buddhism was transcreated and transmuted in this region one word at a time.

Although the *nissaya* mode is the most common pedagogical method in modern and premodern regional Buddhist discourse, there are many different Thai and Lao styles for giving sermons. Other modes include informal and humorous styles like that of Achan Cha, Phra Phayom, or Luang Pho Khun. Achan Cha's sermons, like *nissaya*, are structured on the lifting of Pali words, but he often lifted colloquial Thai and Lao words and explained them in terms of classical Pali terms.[27] Popular author and teacher Phra Mahawudhijaya Wajiramedhi, from Chiang Rai (Northern Thailand), combines rural humor and a sophisticated command of modern religious studies theory in his sermons and in his more than twenty books, like *Dhamma lap sabai* (Anger Management) and *Dhamma bandan* (Inspiration). These books offer creative English and vernacular Thai glosses for traditional Pali Buddhist terms. Phra Phayom in particular has become widely known in Thailand for his humor and for linking Buddhist ideals to contemporary political, social, and economic concerns and even to pop culture. John Hartmann and Louis Gabaude have collected many of Phra Phayom's writings, including *Siang tham siang thip*, *Phasa khon phasa tham*, and *Tae khwam ching*. One example from Hartmann's translation of a Phra Phayom sermon reads: "And as to the second commandment, who is more evil? As for stealing, who is more degenerate—monks or villagers? With villagers, you have to chain down toilet scoops!"[28]

Where Have *Nissaya* Gone? Modern Monastic Textbooks and Handbooks

The methods found in the Pali grammar textbooks are similar to those of *nissaya*. They generally provide Pali words and their vernacular translation using dozens of examples, but they avoid lengthy grammatical explanations or technical grammatical terms. The case of a particular word is occasionally identified, but instruction generally takes the form of giving long lists of examples. A survey of the Pali textbooks popular in Thai monastic schools shows that no matter the level of the text, beginning with *Mathyom seuksa pi thi neung* (equivalent in the American system to a seventh-grade text for students ages twelve to thirteen) up until *Mathyom seuksa pi thi hok* (twelfth grade), Pali grammar is taught in a similar way. A series of Pali words displaying a certain grammatical suffix is followed by their translation in modern Thai. There is rarely any explanation, and textbooks offer repetitive drills in which students must translate single words or short clauses from Pali into Thai. As the student advances the passages tend to become longer, and what little introduction and explanation there may have been completely disappears. Moreover, the lessons are drawn randomly from both canonical and noncanonical texts. The most popular selections are from *paritta* prayers that, from chanting during liturgies, would be familiar to novices, monks, nuns, and laypeople. In fact, the most common translations of Pali texts available (besides Buddhist comic books with stories drawn from *Jātaka*) are bilingual, word-for-word translations of Pali liturgies and *paritta*. There are many editions. They can be bought easily in any major bookstore in Thailand.[29] In Thailand, as in Laos, teachers' own notebooks are often the only text in class. For example, at Wat Rakhang's girls high school in Bangkok and Narīrat Girls High School in Phrae (as well as in boys high schools throughout the country), the freshman Thai language and literature class involves teaching the Pali origin of common Thai words. There is no explanation of Pali grammar. Indeed, the teachers I spoke with had never studied Pali grammar or philology. In these courses, Thai words are given in lists drawn from stories and articles the students read in class. These Thai words are given their Pali antecedent (taken from the teacher's edition of the textbook at Wat Rakhang and from the teacher's handwritten notebook at Narīrat High School).[30] A teacher at another high school told me that she often teaches Northern as well as Central Thai words in her gloss of Pali terms.

Besides Pali grammar textbooks, examination preparation handbooks used by young nuns (*maechi*), monks, and novices reflect *nissaya* textual practices. The *Buddhasasana subhasit chabap matrathan* is an examination preparation book that states it is "for teachers and students of the dhamma" (*samrap khru nak dhamma dhamma seuksa*) and is "easy to read, easy to understand for beginners" (*an ngai khao chai ngai chan to*). Throughout the text Pali verses are cited from a variety of source texts (a chrestomathy) and then followed by a literal translation. The *nissaya* is found below this literal translation. For example, for the Pali passage "uṭṭhā navato satimato sucikamassa nisammakārino saññatassa ca dhammajīvino appamattassa yasobhicaḍḍhati" there follows, "the word *yasa* translates as importance or excellence, that is the importance of a person, the excellence of a person, this can further be divided into three types: *isariyayasa yasa* which means the status, for example, *yasa thahan* (the [high] rank of a member of the army), *yasa tamruad* (the [high] rank of a police officer), etc. . . . these *yasa* are given to a person who has worked hard, that is to someone who has worked hard in their studies."[31] This example and others reflect a high level of repetitive reinforcement, expansion of meaning, use of examples, combination of the lifted term with other Pali terms, the use of both Pali and vernacular synonyms, and selectivity on the gloss. It is interesting that only one minor term from the Pali passage is cited for gloss and commentary. Furthermore, the Thai gloss spells the word *yasa* with a *so sala* (*ś*), as does the Sanskrit word *yaśa*, which is how the Pali word *yasa* is spelled in Thai. This word is pronounced in Thai as *yot*. These are qualities common in all *nissaya*, *nāmasadda*, and *vohāra* manuscripts.

The *Khu meu triam sop* (Handbook for Examination Preparation) follows a similar method, but it foregoes the citation of the Pali source verse and literal translation and merely offers a selection of important Pali terms drawn from a selection of source texts and gives expanded vernacular glosses. For example, under the section on the *majjhimāpaṭipadā* (practice of the middle way) are a series of Pali words listed, the lifting of the terms for the eightfold noble path and vernacular translation, and the four noble truths cited and translated repetitively.[32] In other sections, lists of Pali terms are followed by expanded vernacular glosses. In examinations for young monastic students, source texts are barely invoked; important Pali terms are chosen from a selection of source texts that are rarely ever read or even held by the students. Just as the composers of *nissaya*, *vohāra*, and *nāmasadda* selected terms from source texts in an idiosyncratic manner and often did not abide by the actual source's vocabulary, grammar, syntax, or sequence, these test-prep handbooks reduce the Pali source to a bank of selected terms and gloss them repetitively. The vernacular translation, the teacher's explanation, and lifted words are present. The source text is not.

In Laos, guides for monastic and lay students of religion also may be descendents of the *vohāra* mode of translation and commentary. However, while they are based on the selection and expanded translation of certain Pali terms, in general they neither repeat the Pali word to the same degree modern Thai textbooks do, nor do they employ Pali words as synonyms for the original word lifted. In general there is a lack of Pali words cited and translated in religious handbooks for the lay and the ordained in Laos. This is certainly reflective, in part, of the very poor state of Pali textual publishing in Laos (it is basically nonexistent, although many Lao monks study Pali seriously and Buddhist rituals still use Pali texts) and the dismal state of the publication industry in Laos in general.[33] Individual monasteries do occasionally publish their own books, but these are small and have been poorly edited, typeset, and bound. Most Lao monastic instruction is through handwritten notebooks. The largest collection of textbooks is found at Vat Ong Teu, but most of these textbooks are Thai and remain unopened on library shelves.

Some Lao student handbooks, however, are used in monasteries, and they echo *nissaya* and *vohāra* methodology. One of these books, published by Vat Sisaket in Vientiane, is the *Khu meu Phra Song Samanen Vat Sisaket* (Handbook for Students at Vat Sisaket). It is a series of Pali prayers that students are instructed to memorize for certain rituals, and it does contain sections that cite certain Pali terms from unknown source texts (based on commonly known Pali words chosen by the author) and provide expanded translations. For example, in a section titled *Kan payat kiao kap ngan viak* (The Economy of Work), *citta* and *viriya* are lifted and given expansive and creative glosses. However, there is a noted lack of repetition and Pali synonyms.

This same lack is seen in the few modern Lao sermons that have been published, although many Lao sermons I have attended are structured around the repetitive glossing and explanation of Pali terms. For example, the *Baeb hian taeng thesana san mathayom seuksa Song* (Textbook for Writing Sermons, Monastic Secondary School Level) provides a series of examples of sermons on a wide range of subjects. They begin by citing a very short Pali verse and then explain its meaning in a vague and expansive manner with many asides and tangential statements. When the explanation is exhausted another verse is selected. Occasionally, there are other Pali terms and verses cited from unknown source texts (the memory of the teacher) and employed to explain the import of the first verse, but this is rather infrequent. There is also repetition of the Pali words from the verse and repetition of certain Lao words used to explain the verse. The original verse is always mentioned again at the end of the sermon.[34] The *Dhamma panyai* (Dhamma Lectures) by Phra Thavon Bumpasoet is closer to the *vohāra* mode, meaning it lifts Pali words loosely from the Pali sources in an idiosyncratic order and provides expansive translations marked by repetition and the use of Pali synonyms, but neither the repetition nor the number of commentarial services employed is to the level of most *nissaya* or modern Northern and Central Thai examples.[35]

Why modern Lao religious handbooks and printed sermons do not reflect a major influence from *nissaya* translation practices, while modern Thai source do, is unclear. That there are so few Lao examples to cite, and that my Lao informants and own experience listening to Lao sermons did confirm likely *vohāra*-mode antecedents, makes me hesitant to place much weight on the few modern Lao texts that I have come across. Moreover, Lao modern handbooks are based on the "lifting" of Pali words and phrases, and since these handbooks are meant for reading and not necessarily for guides when giving sermons, printing the repetitions would be uneconomical. In practice, repetition of lifted words in sermons and lectures is common, and many monks prepare sermons with their own notebooks or even by using palm-leaf manuscripts.

I want to state emphatically that the lack of Pali repetitiveness and the general lack of commentaries and translations of Pali texts in Laos does not reflect a weak state of Pali study in Laos or the lack of interest in Pali by Lao monks. As I discuss in chapter 1, political changes have hurt the free practice of Lao monastic publishing, and there is a major lack of printing presses and word processors (although there is a new computer room at the Monastic College in Vientiane and monks/novices are frequently seen in Luang Phrabang and Vientiane's Internet cafés). In my experience chanting, ordaining, and talking with, listening to, and learning from Lao monastic and lay scholars, the state of interest in and study of Pali is alive and well in modern Laos despite a lack of books and governmental support. Laos has often been judged (and still is) by foreign scholars (including Thai) of Pali as a country lacking in Pali scholarship. This judgment is not based on interviews with actual Lao teachers or made by scholars who can actually read or speak Lao. Instead it is based on titles in manuscript catalogs, which, as I have shown, are inaccurate. Moreover, the judgment is based on an assumption that the only good Pali text is one that is close to a Sri Lankan/Indic "original" and that Pali Buddhist texts are superior to vernacular or bilingual texts. This prejudice for the original "true meaning" or "original intention" over the living, evolving traditions still plagues much of early and Theravada Buddhist scholarship and does not acknowledge the creative work of individual Lao monastic teachers and scholars. The preference for the Pali also has caused Lao vernacular Buddhist and Buddhist-inspired literature and rituals to be overlooked.

It is well known that vernacular secular literature, particularly romantic and adventure narratives, is more prevalent in Lao monastic libraries than are Pali texts or Pali-Lao manuscripts like *nissaya* or *nāmasadda*. The *nissaya* in Laos, while certainly not identical to their Northern Thai counterparts, may be more influenced by Northern Thai, Shan, Khoen, Burmese, and Leu monks who moved to and settled in Laos between the fifteenth and eighteenth centuries than by an indigenous literary form. The *vohāra* mode may never have been incorporated or seriously adopted by Lao scholars to the same degree it was in Thailand. So while Lao and Thai monastic curricula are still very similar, since the late nineteenth century the close intellectual interchange has seriously declined through a combination of internal and external forces.[36]

Where Have *Nissaya* Gone? Modern *Hoi Kaeo* / *Roi Kaeo*

It was common for local writers in Laos to string together an alternating and repetitive series of vernacular and Pali words like "jewels on a necklace" (i.e., *hoi kaeo*) for reasons of education and aesthetic appeal.[37] The *hoi kaeo* method of composing bilingual texts in the region is most likely the result of the mixing of traditional Lao and Northern Thai poetry (which works on the practice of repetitive patterns of alliteration, tone alternation, and rhyming) with Pali word commentaries. The result is a unique linguistic feature that allows the reader/audience to remember certain Pali and vernacular lexical items easily through repetition, alliteration, and rhyming. Moreover, the *hoi kaeo* system combined with the type of excessive glossing shown above reflects one of the pedagogical functions of *nissaya*, *vohāra*, and *nāmasadda*—to tell entertaining, melodious stories or give ritual instructions or ethical sermons while teaching Pali and vernacular vocabulary and certain important Buddhist concepts.

In Thailand today, *roi kaeo* simply means "prose." *Roi kaeo* is also a type of chanting style that incorporates Thai and Pali words. However, when monks are describing their homiletic methods they often use the terms *vohāra* and *roi kaeo* together and see the methods as closely related (see chapters 6 and 7). *Roi kaeo* is written, and *vohāra* is oral. Therefore, one of the most common methods for orally presenting secular and Buddhist stories is by repetitively stringing Pali and vernacular words together like jewels on a necklace. This is also seen in secular stories where the term *kham sroi* is used to denote the use of repetition to add rhythm and to stress importance.[38] *Kham sroi* is related to *roi kaeo*, as they both mean jewels strung on a necklace—it is the repetitious quality as well as the quality of the verbal jewels strung together that make the literary or didactic piece noticeable and memorable. Early *vohāra* and *nissaya* manuscripts and *hoi kaeo* poetry in Laos were textual expositions of monastic and lay lexical skill. Wordsmiths were respected in both arenas (in fact, the actual physical arenas were also similar, as poets often perform(ed) on the grounds of monasteries). They are connected through function and style. In modern Thailand, since *roi kaeo* now refers to "prose" in general, it is my suspicion that the *roi kaeo* style characterized the earliest prose writings in Thailand. Some of the oldest prose texts in Thai were generally these bilingual *nissaya*, *vohāra*, and *nāmasadda* texts. Most early Thai literature was in verse. Since the earliest non-verse writing was characterized by citing Pali words and then following them with vernacular glosses and expanded translations, *roi kaeo* may have evolved from describing a particular way of stringing together Pali and vernacular words to prose. In general, monastic oral performances take on two forms—sermon and chanting. A sermon is most often in *nissaya* or *vohāra* style. Chanting is most often taken from texts composed in verse (either protective mantras or poetic versions of Buddhist narratives like the *Vessantara jātaka*). *Roi kaeo*, I suspect, originally was the general term used for non-verse oral performances by monks—sermons and lectures guided by *nissaya*, *vohāra*, and *nāmasadda*. The Pali words were the jewels and the vernacular words were the links of the chain that held the jewels together, but separated from each other, on the necklace. While the practice of composing traditional *hoi kaeo / roi kaeo* has apparently died out in Laos and Thailand, its remnants persist in sermons, religious textbooks, and speeches and it informs the larger practice of prose writing in the two countries. In Northern Thailand and Laos, *nissaya* are the earliest and clearest examples of this general textual and oral practice and may be the oldest form of didactic literature in the region.[39]

Contemporary Students and Teachers: *Nissaya* Not in Hand, but Still in Mind

That authorship is extremely difficult to determine in premodern Southeast Asia is well known. The fact that writers not only avoided (often) mentioning their name but often took the names of their teachers or famous teachers in the distant past (so in South and Southeast Asian studies students often come across two authors named Bhāṣā, two to three named Dhammapala, etc.) further compounds this difficulty. Scribes often mentioned their name but not the name of the author of the text they copied. Furthermore, textual and temporal authenticity for a work was easier to claim if the original author was the Buddha himself or one of his famous disciples. Ownership of ideas was simply not as strong of a concept before print culture (and if one reads the published religious works in Thailand or Laos today, it quickly becomes evident that citations are few and far between, that often authors completely copy or plagiarize previous writers' work, and that many other texts are written by a group or dedicated to an abbot who may have had little to do with the actual writing). Borrowing or copying was not considered an academic or economic crime in Southeast Asia before the rise of print culture and the economy of books and publishing.

To situate oneself in a teaching lineage was a much stronger motivation than it was to claim creative skill as an individual author. The monk as teacher is particularly honored and is considered to be a representative of the Buddha. A teacher (*ācariya/kalyaṇamitta*) is the interpreter of the words and texts of the Buddha through sermons, lectures, rituals, protective and curative magic, the settling of arguments, and the offering of advice. He does not need to prove that his lessons come from a legitimate edition of the Pali canon (although this was used as a political tool by several kings in the region) or from a specific authoritative teacher. Texts in monastic education are rarely read alone; they are mediated through one's teacher. This teacher does not even need to read or write Pali fluently (the vast majority cannot, although they can chant numerous Pali prayers). For example, as a monk I performed several rituals, gave blessings, drew protective *yantra*, gave sermons "lifting" Pali words, and chanted Pali every morning and evening; however, I did not study Pali grammar formally until after I had disrobed.

If one understands the *nissaya* and *vohāra* genres as a mode, one can see that Pali and the vernacular did not necessarily occupy completely different realms of authority (as many scholars assume) or usage in the past and do not in the present. Neither language seems to be dominant for the purposes of rituals or narratives. Certain rituals must be performed in Pali, but there are vernacular sections as well as asides during, before, and after the ritual. In listening to any sermon, ritual chanting, or classroom lecture in monasteries in the region, one hears a monk easily move between Pali and the vernacular, often maintaining the same rhythm, cadence, and physical posture. Monastic lectures to novice students are constantly moving back and forth between Pali and the vernacular like *nissaya* and *vohāra* manuscripts. Surveys of any medieval or modern monastic library or bookstore demonstrate that Pali and vernacular texts happily share space and volley back and forth on the pages of most manuscripts and religious books.

Most of the nuns, novices, and monks I talked with were not familiar with *nissaya*; when shown the examples (often in transliteration since most monks cannot read the Yuan or Tham scripts), they said that they "looked like" sermons. In Laos today, the term *vohāra* is commonly used in reference to the method of orally describing a text. Some Lao monks also use the term *nissaya* (*nissai*) when describing their homiletic methodology. However, the most general term for giving a sermon is *desanā* (*thet*), or for a lecture in a monastic school they simply use the word to teach—*son*. In July 2000 I visited the abbot of Vat Naxai in Vientiane looking to examine a few of the hundreds of manuscripts in the multitiered *ho tai* (library). I requested to see the *nissaya* manuscripts. Instead of taking me to the library, he led me to his *kuṭi* (monastic cell) and handed me the only manuscript that he had in his room—a *Kammavācā nissaya*. I asked why he had removed that particular manuscript from among the hundreds of others. He told me that he was reading that particular manuscript from the library in order to prepare a sermon on the importance of ordination, since the beginning of the rainy season was only days away (the traditional time most monks ordain). He wanted to become familiar with the important terms in the ritual.

Professor Bualy Paphaphanh of the National University of Laos, a monk for many years before 1975, sketched out in several meetings a picture of monastic education in the 1960s that was very illuminating. He stated that education was generally focused on preparing monks for ritual and performance. Certainly, texts were used, and reading and writing were important, but the curriculum and teaching methods were focused on the public life of the monastery. Monks were expected to be prepared for chanting at funerals, performing *jātaka*, and chanting before and after sermons. It was in monastic schools also that he was first introduced to the Tham script and local Lao "secular" tales of romance and adventure. Achan Seng Ngonevongsa, presently a Lao monk in Southern California, and originally from the rural Vientiane province, generally confirmed Bualy's impression. He added that the treatment of Buddha images and the details on how to perform protective rituals (of which he performs now in California) were the heart of his education in Laos. He, unlike Bounteum Sibounheuang and Thong Xeuy, whom I mentioned in the introduction, did not learn Tham script or receive detailed textual education. In fact, he had never heard of a *nissaya* manuscript.

At Wat Sri Chum in Phrae a monk named Phra Suwat, with skills in Pali grammar and Yuan script, told me that *nissaya* and *vohāra* were basically the same type of text and that these two genres were used to teach Pali texts. He said that *vohāra* were for the laity since they explained texts and that *nissaya* explained the meanings of particular Pali words and were for the instruction of serious students. According to him, *nissaya* were more detailed, but he admitted that he did not read them often because it was easier to learn the meaning of Pali words orally from one's teachers and to learn the craft of homiletics by observing one's mentors. He said *vohāra* were for the laity and therefore were more common for monks to use since impressing the laity was essential to the survival of Buddhism (and the economy of the monastery). When I asked him why there were no new *nissaya* texts written in the modern period, he said that monks just called *nissaya* and *vohāra* "thet" (*desanā*)—

sermons. These previously separate genres had been conflated in the modern period. Phra Sane, the director of the Pali department at Wat Suan Dok (the Northern Branch of Mahachulalongkorn Monastic University) generally concurred with Phra Suwat. He said both *nissaya* and *vohāra* were for lessons for monks and novices. They could also be used to guide sermons for the laity, but only if the lesson was on a specific Pali text. *Nissaya* were not used anymore, since there were modern printed manuscripts and modern translations of the Pali texts in Thai. The difficulty of reading *nissaya* manuscripts led monks to rely on modern printed *desanā* and commentaries since they explained the meanings of individual Pali terms more clearly. *Vohāra* were still written by some monks to prepare lessons on texts in a general sense, but were now a method and quality of delivery more than a separate textual genre. The parts of the text cited and explained were determined by the teacher himself according to his preference, level of education, and opinion.

Phra Dhammo from Uttaradit Province in Northern Thailand told me that his teacher used manuscripts that explained the meaning of Pali terms through the *yok sab* method, but his teacher simply called the manuscripts *kamphi* (religious texts) and did not use the specific terms *nissaya*, *vohāra*, or *nāmasadda*. In comparison, Phra Narādhīpa Kittiñño from Wat Phra That Cho Hae in Phrae had heard of *nissaya*, *vohāra*, and *nāmasadda* manuscripts and associated them with oral instruction. He made a distinction between *nāmasadda* that were specifically for teaching Pali grammar and those for teaching ethics, history, and so forth. Phra Khru Palatnopalandha Thitadhammo and Maechi Wirawan from Wat Rampoeng in Chiang Mai were familiar with *nissaya* and *vohāra* manuscripts. The former, they said, were used in the past for Pali instruction, while the latter were for sermons on general topics. Today, they said, they were generally called *desanā*. The abbot of Wat Sung Men, Phra Adhikārasuvit Paññāvidho, did not seem to think that there was much difference among the three genres. They were all just aids to the reading and teaching of Pali texts. They were "help" (*chuai leua*) to the teacher. However, like teachers I spoke with at many other monasteries, he stated that monks did not like to use these old manuscripts because they were hard to read (he knew Yuan script and actually teaches a Yuan reading class on Sundays at Wat Sung Men). Today, he stated, it was much easier to use modern cardboard manuscripts that were similar to *nissaya*, but were clear, printed, and durable. Most monks, novices, and laypeople did not understand the old script, and so new printed manuscripts were more "convenient" (*saduak*). These new printed manuscripts are structured like *nissaya* and *vohāra*, in the way they cite Pali words from specific texts and explain them in the vernacular. The abbot at Wat Sung Men used modern manuscripts printed in Yuan script, while the abbot of Wat Lai Hin was reading the printed manuscript (in modern Thai script) of the *Temiya jātaka* the last time I met him, in June 2002. They both stated that *nāmasadda* texts were specifically for teaching Pali to monks and novices and textbooks were used today.

Seven novices, ranging in age from thirteen to seventeen years, from Wat Sung Men filled out a survey I had designed (in Thai) on Pali education. Their answers to the questions (1) "What are *nissaya* texts?" (2) "For what reason are *nissaya* texts used?" (3) "What are *vohāra* texts?" and (4) "What are *nāmasadda* texts?" were nearly identical, and they had clearly copied from one another. Like any high school students, they were concerned more about having the "right" answer than about expressing their opinion or avoiding cheating. It soon became apparent that these answers were all copied from Phra Thong Di Achicitto, their forty-two-year-old teacher. Their answers included a couple of divergences (in brackets):

(1) Kamphi [reuang rao] kiao kap kan patipat kan prabriti khong bhiksu [samanen] ([A *nissaya* is] a religious text [or narrative] that concerns the [proper] practice and conduct of a monk [or novice]).

(2) Phra bhiksu samanen hai patipat kan pen rabiap riap roi somkhuan kae samanen rop khong ton ([*Nissaya* texts are for teaching] a monk and a novice to practice and conduct themselves in a proper way appropriate to their status as a novice in order to [guide] themselves).

(3) Kham sang son reu kam tang tang thi phra buddha cao trasaru wai hai kae buddha sawok ([*Vohāra* texts are] the various teachings of sayings that the Buddha passes on to his disciples).

(4) Phasa pali phasa magadha thi mi nai abhidham pitok thi yak lae sut tang tang thi plae pen phasa thai (Pali or Magadha language [texts] that

> are from the Abhidhamma Piṭaka that are difficult and various *sutta* that are translated into the Thai language).

Although these answers are vague, they do point to an association of these genres with the everyday teaching of monks and novices and, at least in terms of *nāmasadda*, to texts that translate selected Pali source texts in Thai. Generally, however, I discovered in conversations with novices and through my survey answers that novices called all Buddhist texts *kamphi/gambhīra*, tipiṭok (tipiṭaka/canon), or *nangseu sāsana* (religious book). Neither the genre titles nor the specific differences between them were important. It was also assumed that the knowledge of Pali (chanting well and using Pali in sermons) was the supreme intellectual achievement of a scholar monk.

Two of the most helpful interviews I was granted were not with monks but with lay experts: a Pali teacher with thirty-two years of experience at the Abhidhamma Jotika College for the advanced study of the Abhidhamma at Mahachulalongkorn Monastic University, Anuson Bhuribhiwatanakhun, and his colleague Maechi Chirapa. They explained that *nissaya* and *vohāra* were merely different degrees of the same translation and commentarial process that monks used to explain terms and passages from Pali texts. A *vohāra* manuscript was merely a selective gloss of a Pali source, while a *nissaya* was evidence of an abbreviated translation and explanation of an entire text. A *nissaya* did not fully translate all the words of the source text, because during a lesson on a particular text a teacher may want only to highlight certain terms or sections but generally would try to follow the sequence and main themes of the whole source. This explanation is very close to what premodern manuscripts reveal. Anuson and Chirapa did not limit their explanation to texts called *nissaya* or *vohāra* only. They said that any translation could be called a *vohāra*.[40]

Anuson and Maechi Chirapa stated that the *vohāra* was just a basic translation into the vernacular of a selected word or passage from a Pali source (*kham pali ma su phasa thi tong kan*). The *nissaya*-type translation selects the term and uses it as a trigger to begin teaching a lesson related to that term. This expands the translation. Despite the fact that a *nissaya*-type translation expands the meaning of the source term, it is actually called a *kham yo* (abbreviation), because it only translates a few selected words according to the teacher's needs, knowledge base, and preference.[41] The *vohāra* tends to be longer because lengthy selections or the entire source is translated, even though, they admitted, *vohāra* translators are often selective in their translations. In terms of the function of these two types of gloss, they said that even though they could guide the private reading of a Pali source text, they are more often used in lessons or sermons for monks, nuns, and novices and interested laypeople who may not know or may be learning Pali. When taught in lessons the texts were referred to as *desanā*, a particular style of *desanā* based on a particular Pali source. When asked why the texts are no longer called *nissaya* and are rarely referred to as *vohāra*, they told me that the terms *kham plae* (translation) and *kham adhibai* (explanation) had replaced these old genre rubrics.

Anuson actually considered *nissaya* and *vohāra* as comprising a "fifth piṭaka" (collection of texts). He supported his point by drawing from Buddhaghosa's description of the four types of Buddhist literature from the sixth-century *Samantapāsādikā*, which reads: "katamaṃ catubbidhaṃ suttaṃ suttanulomaṃ ācariyavādaṃ attanomatinti" (Which four? (1) *sutta*, (2) [those texts] that agree with *sutta*, (3) the words of the teachers [disciples of the Buddha], (4) [those texts] that are compositions of one's own). Anuson stated that these are the four piṭaka in contrast to the more commonly known "three piṭaka." The fifth piṭaka consists of vernacular translations of these four types. For Thai people, he emphasized, the fifth piṭaka was the most important.

Phra Sompong, the head of the Pali Grammar Research Institute at Mahachulalongkorn Monastic University, was generous with his expertise and time throughout my research. He confirmed my thesis that *nissaya* had played a twofold role in the monastery before the rise of the printing press and standardized examination systems and curricula. His teacher, an octogenarian monk of Burmese birth, Phra Dhammananda, at Wat Tham-Ma-O in Lampang, had used *nissaya* manuscripts in the 1960s and 1970s as *khu meu* (handbooks) for *phra puat mai* (newly ordained monks). This was a common practice, he said, in Northern Thai monasteries. First, the abbot or an older monk would train the younger, less experienced monks and novices with *nissaya* through oral instruction. Second, *nissaya* could also be used as *bantheuk triam son* (guides to prepare a lecture). In this case, a monastic lecturer could read them before or use them as notes during a sermon on a certain source text. This is why Phra Sompong believed these texts were called *nissaya*—they were "supports" to teachers and students studying Buddhist texts. As for the choice of source texts, he said that this was more orderly than it appeared from the manuscript collections. Teachers, in the past, would usually start off with the *paṭimokkha* (monastic rules) and move through the *kammavācā* texts (major monastic rituals). From there, grammar or narrative became the subject according to the teacher's skills and preferences.[42]

Languaging Pali in the Translation Culture of Laos and Thailand

Thailand and Laos have a translation culture. The practice of translation, or better—languaging (the "shaping of old texts in new contexts")—was the "poetics" of religious literature in the region.[43] Vernacular narrative collections, *nissaya*, *vohāra*, and *nāmasadda*, as well as *ānisaṃsa* (blessings), *paritta* (protective mantras), and *xalǭng* (guides to ceremonies), all draw from the Pali canon. Even if the source text was originally composed in the vernacular, an ideal Pali source was "invoked." Change has been subtle and slow, as change always takes part in lineage, tradition, and community. Maverick pedagogues and explicitly radical reinterpretations have been only marginally accepted. Even the most radical teachers, like Buddhadasa and Siri-maṅgala, employ the rhetoric of eternal return to the original intent of the Buddha; however, they are constantly languaging Pali, putting the utterances of the language into new and disparate contexts.

In the twentieth century, new vocabulary to meet the needs of foreign concepts and technological innovations was generated through the invention or adaptation of Pali/Sanskrit words based on classical rules concerning prefixes, and roots.[44] In fact, it can be argued that scholars like Jit Bhumisak and Kings Rama VI and IX, among other Thai scholars, actively created a new "hyper-Sanskrit" or "hyper-Pali" to incorporate new words from languages such as English and Japanese. Hundreds of examples of this new Sanskritized Thai for concepts and subjects such as "democracy," "oncology," "parliament," and "globalism" may be found in modern Thai dictionaries.[45] Sanskrit, Pali, French, and English were also employed by different authors at different times to consciously identify the author of a particular text with a particular political stance, economic motive, or educational background. The conscious incorporation, employment, and teaching of Sanskrit and Pali vocabulary, whether as "established loans" or "deliberate borrowings," have been pervasive rhetorical practices. By studying the phenomena over time, one can see these individual choices and practices turn into modes of writing and reading.

This process of languaging is very specific, but not systematic. The word *yok* is used for the activity of "lifting" Pali words and passages from a text and incorporating or commenting on them in another text. These lifted words, removed from their original source context, take on the adapted meanings assigned to them by the original "lifters" and subsequent "citers." These lifted words, if repeated enough and incorporated into vernacular syntax slowly, become part of the vernacular vocabulary and cease to be seen as loan words (e.g., "kindergarten" or "coup d'etat" in English).[46] Originality and individual creativity are obviously prevalent; here it is creativity in Goethe's or Walter Benjamin's sense of the term—a creative reformulation or recombination of words spoken by the Buddha and his disciples. No one says anything new; they just say it in a new way. When they do say something new, they rarely admit it.

An American teacher like me does not come from a culture of translation. English is taken for granted as the language of news, advertising, academia, literature, science, air-traffic control, and commerce. Americans rarely experience the impact of translation cultures when they travel. English is their advantage, their passport to other places. Other people learn their language; Americans, in general, do not learn theirs. In Thailand and Laos, translation plays a dominant role in every aspect of public culture. If one takes a walk down any street in Bangkok, Chiang Mai, Khon Kaen, Phitsanulok, Vientiane, Ubon Ratchathani, or Luang Phrabang, one will immediately notice that many signs are written in both Thai/Lao and roman script. Usually the signs are not merely transliterations or phonetic equivalents (although this is common as well) but also (often incorrect) translations. In Chinatown Bangkok (Sampeng), Chinese characters usually are on the signs as well. Bilingual signs for Pepsi, Tylenol, Nescafé, Lipton, Colgate, Dutch Mills, Cadbury's, Kentucky Fried Chicken, 7–Eleven, and Gillette flank the sides of alleys and roads, and people walk past with t-shirts reading (in roman script) "Catholic

Youth League"; "Cleveland, Ohio, 1983 Summer Camp"; "Diesel Brand Clothes"; "Red-Bull Energy Drink"; and "Manchester United." Even Thai uniforms are often in English as well as Thai (e.g., "Rajapat Institute of Technology," "Mae Burapa Fish Sauce Factory," and "Department of Education"). On public transit, at least that built after 1990, signs appear in both Thai and English; advertisements on bus stops are in both Thai and English for Thai-made products like Sun Silk Shampoo and Comfort Brand Socks. The native-English-speaking population of Thailand is less than one percent. Tourists are usually interested more in products made in Thailand in the "traditional way" (read: at Chinese factories and sold in newly built quaint bamboo huts with signs saying "Asian Style Today" or "Traditional Tribal Buddhist Art") than in styles mimicking Western brands. Bilingual signs speak more to Thais and Laos than to foreigners or expatriates. Any Thai or Lao person (like a person from Quebec, India, or Singapore) is constantly confronted with bilingual signs. Whether or not he or she translates every sign or even notices them cannot be determined, but the point is that the work of languaging is everywhere.

The academic, monastic, commercial, and governmental publishing industries also practice and promote translation in Thailand and Laos. The leading Thai journal of art history and archaeology, *Muang boran*, contains articles written by Thais for those who can read Thai, but its table of contents and the abstracts for each article are translated into English.[47] Mahachulalongkorn Monastic University, a school where all classes are taught in Thai and every student must be a fluent speaker of Thai, has published a curriculum in English. I asked the staff whether any of them has ever read it; they all said no. Books for Thai novices are often translated into English (e.g., *Sāmeṇera sikkhā: The Novice's Training*). A series of English-language translations of Pali *sutta* and grammar books for young novices is available. Titles of government reports and the titles of news programs and local conference advertisements (in Thai with Thai audiences) often are translated into English. There are sections of newspapers that teach a new English phrase a day. I recently attended a meeting at a rural secondary school where I taught English in 1993. The meeting was on new methods in teaching biology. Besides me (I showed up unannounced at the last minute to visit an old friend), the meeting was attended only by Thai speakers from the teaching staff at the high school. The sign for the meeting hung above the podium and was made of Styrofoam. It gave the title of the meeting in Thai and then, in much bigger script, in English. Nobody spoke much English (except for a few English technical loan terms like "physics" and "assessment"). When I asked the person who made the sign why there was an English translation, he said, because it "looks nice. Is it spelled correctly? If I knew you were coming I would have tried to spell it better." English words are pervasive for medical science, for military, electronic, and industrial equipment, and in everyday conversation in Thailand and Laos, just as they are in a vast majority of Asian, South American, European, and African countries. The legacy of the British Empire and American military and economic dominance have made English the new Pali/Sanskrit of Thailand and Laos and the only global language.

The pervasiveness of English is not a secret, nor is it unique to Thailand or Laos. To compare the English "cosmopolis" to the Sanskrit "cosmopolis" would require a much larger study. However, the manner in which the particular culture of translation has been influenced by methods and rhetorical practices (of which *nissaya* are the earliest regional examples) is important for understanding the persisting legacy of these textual practices. The specter and prestige of Pali have remained in the region for more than one thousand years. However, Pali texts have never remained stable in the hands of local teachers.

6 Canons and Curricula

So far, this book has been, as Brian Axel argues, an "ethnography of archives." However, unlike Axel, I do not see monastic manuscript archives as solely "privileged sites of knowledge production" or as the sole repositories of truth.[1] I do not privilege manuscripts as evidence because they are commensurate with my post-Enlightenment reverence for the immutable text. Instead, I see pedagogical manuscripts as questioning the inviolability of sacred and timeless scripture. These manuscripts question the nature of the Buddhist canon. In daily interactions between teachers and students, the classical was not simply reproduced and archived but reimagined and realigned in conversation through local stories, rituals, and memories. If one looks for the pedagogical texts that actively transformed, questioned, *languaged*, and pulled apart the artifacts of the classical textual tradition, then one can radically change the way the study of Southeast Asian Buddhism is approached.

Whither the Canon?

In 1983 Charles Keyes wrote, "The evidence from monastery libraries in Laos and Thailand reveals that what constitutes the Theravādin dhamma for people in these areas includes only a small portion of the total Tipiṭaka. . . . Moreover, the collection of texts available to the people in the associated community are not exactly the same as those found in another temple."[2] Steven Collins used this statement and the research that supported it to develop his notion of a "ritual canon." The "ritual canon[s]" are the collections of texts used at any particular monastery in the "actual ritual life in the area concerned."[3] The term *practical canon*, inspired by the work of Collins, was coined by Anne Blackburn in her 1996 dissertation on the *Sāratthadīpanī* from Sri Lanka and shows how the choice of texts to copy, translate, teach, and preserve, both canonical and noncanonical, Pali and vernacular, in any given community actually must be seen as defining the particular canon of that region and time period.[4]

What Keyes observed in 1983 can be confirmed today with even the most cursory inventory of the major monastic, royal, and governmental manuscript libraries of Laos and Northern Thailand. Generally, the most popular texts were the *ānisaṃsa* (Lao/Thai: *anisong*), which are blessings used in ritual and magical ceremonies; *paritta* (incantations for protection); *xalǫ̜ng* (ceremonial instructions for both lay and religious ceremonies); apocryphal *jātaka* (noncanonical birth stories of the Buddha); stories drawn from the *Dhammapada-atthakathā*; *kammavācā* (ritual instructions and rules); local epics (including the *Xieng Mieng* cycle of stories, *Thao Hung Thao Chuang*, *Xin Sai*, and *Om lom daeng kiao*); excerpts from the Visuddhimagga and *Maṅgaladīpanī*; grammatica (excerpts from the *Padarūpasiddhi*, *Kaccāyanavyākaraṇa*, and local grammatical handbooks); and *tamnan* (relic, image, and temple histories).[5] The first three categories of texts have clear reasons for being the dominant texts preserved in the region because of their everyday use in house, buffalo, temple, and bodily blessings, and for their usefulness in cases of revenge, fear, and lust (love potions and incantations are included here). The *tamnan* are mostly, but certainly not exclusively, vernacular histories that have political, economic, social, aesthetic, and educational reasons for being popular. *Nissaya*, *vohāra*, and *nāmasadda* versions of the *Maṅgaladīpanī* are strangely rare, and they do not appear to have been used in everyday teaching, although their memorization by advanced students may have been common, as it is in the modern period. Ritual, narrative, and grammatical texts were the most common choices for composing *nissaya*, *nāmasadda*, and *vohāra*. That Pali canonical texts are most often in the minority in these collections is important to observe.[6] This is where *nissaya*, *vohāra*, and *nāmasadda* find their place. They are evidence of the way the canon, in the loosest sense of the term, was taught in a lecture or a sermon. The adaptation took place in writing the *nissaya*, *vohāra*, and *nāmasadda* to prepare the sermon and in the extemporaneous and expansive commentary that accompanied the oral presentation.[7] The Tipiṭaka "left the library and entered society through the sermon," as Skilling and Prapod succinctly put it. The sermons, as well as graphic images in mural paintings, were the vehicles by which people came to know the ideas and narratives of the Tipiṭaka.[8] A full study of a curriculum involves examining these points of encounter where the canon was negotiated by the teacher in oral performance.

These points of encounter, manipulation, and creative engagement reflect an episteme where classical and canonical texts are neither sacrosanct nor static. The canon, in practice, is fluid and open. Just as monastic library collections and the choice of source texts for pedagogical use are wide-ranging and most often noncanonical, in modern Thailand and Laos Tipiṭaka (Tripiṭaka/Tripidok) refers, not just to the traditional "three baskets" (i.e., the canon) assembled by the Mahāvihāra school in Sri Lanka over fifteen hundred years ago, but to all types of religious books.[9] The monk who holds a printed copy of a vernacular commentary on a noncanonical text while he gives a sermon is considered to be reading *Phra Tripidok* (canon). Lao monks refer to *nissaya*, *vohāra*, and *nāmasadda* as *gampi tipidok* (canonical scripture).[10] In 2006 a *Nangseu Phra Traipitok samrap phu roem seuksa* (Tipiṭaka for Beginners), in a handsome case and teakwood stand, was published by Chulalongkorn University in honor of the king's birthday. The entire Rama VII edition was chanted in February 2007. A monastic student's textbook from Rong Phim Kansasana, a popular press for religious textbooks in Bangkok, publishes a book titled *Bramuan dhamma nai Phra Tripidok* (Dhammic Lessons in the Tipiṭaka) by Suddhiphong Tontyaphisalasut, who draws from a mixture of canonical and extra-canonical sources sporadically without addressing which texts are canonical and which are not.

There is no religious bookstore in Laos that "sells" a Tipiṭaka (in Lao, Thai, or Pali). Vat Ong Teu, the central monastic college of Laos, has a copy of the Burmese script edition that is dusty and unused. Vat Mai in Luang Phrabang has copies of a Thai script edition and a Yuan script edition from Bangkok and Chiang Mai, respectively. They both have remained locked in cabinets until this day. At Vat Ong Teu, the Thai edition is still sealed in plastic wrap. Pali grammars and readers in Thailand generally contain unmarked passages from both canonical and extra-canonical texts.

Some modern Thai books like the *Phra Tripidok sangkhep* (The Abridged

Tipiṭaka) contain simple descriptions of canonical texts, and monastic Pali exams are separated into canonical and noncanonical sections (although the most difficult exams and those that, if passed, give the highest respect are noncanonical). Moreover, the *Tamnan Ho Phra Samut* provides a detailed history of the copying and/or printing of various Thai editions of the Tipiṭaka from the mid-nineteenth to the early twentieth century that generally follow the parameters of the Sri Lankan canon (although many editions also include the major commentaries, expanding the canon from approximately forty-five to ninety-one volumes). This source shows that the parameters of the canon were formed partly in response to Western scholars' notion of an *editio princeps* and partly informed by locally diverse notions of the canon. Still, what is important is that the idea of the canon for most Southeast Asian Buddhists is simply wider than is commonly understood in the West or by largely Western-educated Buddhist studies scholars at Asian universities.[11]

Over the course of Lao and Thai history, several efforts have been made to assemble texts under the rubric *tipiṭaka.* In chapters 1–3, I discuss some of these efforts by Lao and Northern Thai kings and monks between the fifteenth and the twentieth centuries. Each collection in this region has included different texts. Even in nineteenth-century Siam, the region most "influenced" by the West (by Jean Baptiste Pallegoix, T. W. Rhys-Davids, Adolf Bastien, Joost Schooten, and many other missionaries, emissaries, and Buddhist studies scholars), there were debates over what should and should not be in the canon. The examination system and source texts used for monastic education in Siam were not particularly canonical. In recent years, the names and numbers of texts included in the Tipiṭaka have become relatively fixed in Thailand (there still is no Lao Tipiṭaka). There are three new electronic versions of the latest version of the Theravada canon in Thai script. The model for these versions is the 1997 (frequently updated) electronic canon in roman, Devanagari, Burmese, Thai, Sinhalese, Mongol, and Khmer scripts produced by Vipassana Research Institute and based on the so-called Chattha Sangaya (Sixth Council) edition from Burma. This edition includes commentaries and subcommentaries in the electronic equivalent of 135 volumes. Two digital Thai script editions of the Pali canon have been produced. The first was made by the intensely mission-focused and international

Dhammakāya Foundation in Pathum Thani, Thailand. The second was developed by staff at the Mahidol University computing center, in Thailand, under the direction of Supachai Tangwongsan.

Evidence from monastic holdings, translation practices, and *nissaya*, *vohāra*, and *nāmasadda* texts leads one to believe that this fluid and more comprehensive sense of the term *tipiṭaka* was even more prevalent before the introduction of the printing press (1830s) and foreign notions of what constituted the Theravada canon.[12] But even in the modern period there is a difference between the Pali canon as referred to by international scholars and global Buddhist missionary movements and the idea of the canon on the ground. In Thailand, and even more so in Laos, the Tipiṭaka (*Phra Tipidok* or *Kamphi Tipidok*) is seen as identical to *lak sut* or *lak seuksa sāsana* (basic Buddhist curriculum). In fact, nearly every nun, monk, and novice I spoke with considered these terms synonymous. In 2001 Phra Ajahn Mahabua Kham Sariput, the "dean" of the Sangha Monastic College in Vientiane, told me that when he designed the new curriculum (*lak sut*) for the college (which is now available as a photocopied handbook in the main college office), that the *lak sut* was the Tipiṭaka for students.[13] The textual sources for the teachers' notebooks used in class are mostly vernacular versions of local Buddhist histories, extra-canonical *jātaka*-type narratives, glossaries of Pali words (*nāmasadda*), *paritta* protective texts, and folktales. These notebooks, like the pedagogical manuscripts that came before them, employ the *nissaya* and *vohāra* mode and methods. These idiosyncratically assembled and shared notebooks, glossaries, summaries, and anthologies presented orally as the Tipiṭaka have created a notion of the canon that is very different from the international one. Even though most of the texts used for the curriculum at the only monastic college in Laos are extra-canonical, for directors, teachers, and students curriculum is canon.

My interviews and surveys with monastic students and teachers throughout Laos and Northern Thailand (as well as many in Central and Northeastern Thailand) confirmed this fluid conception of the canon. For example, to groups of students at different monasteries in Nan, Phrae, Lampang, Chiang Rai, and Chiang Mai I handed out a survey that listed twelve canonical and extra-canonical texts in random order. I asked the students and teachers to check the box next to the texts that were in the Tipiṭaka (*Phra*

Tripidok/Tipidok). This list, using the standard Thai spelling and script, included *Maha Vessantara jātaka* (*Maha Wessanton chadok*), *Kaccāyana-vyākaraṇa* (*Mun Kacchai*), *Vohāra Abhidhamma mātikā* (*Wohan Aphitham mātikā*), *Dhammapada-atthakathā* (*Thammabot Atthagatha* or *Nithan Thammabot*), *Paññāsa-jātaka* (*Ha sip chat*), *Kammavācā nāmasadda* (*Kammawacha sab*), *Nissaya nāma* (*Nisai nam*), *Maṅgala sutta* (*Mongkon sut*), *Vinayasangaha* (*Winai Sangaha*), *Sāsanāvaṃsā* (*Sāsanāwong*), *Traibhūmīkathā* (*Traiphūm*), and *Ṭīkā Atthasālinī* (same). The results were shocking. Not one student or teacher to whom I gave the survey got all the answers "correct." In fact, most assumed all the texts were in the canon except for the *Kaccāyanavyākaraṇa* (although over 40 percent did think that text was in the canon as well). About 37 percent did not check the box next to the *Ṭīkā Atthasālinī*, but when I interviewed the students and teachers afterward, many admitted never having heard of that text. Most international Pali scholars would see that actually only two of the twelve texts listed above are in the canon and that the rest are Pali commentaries, grammatica, extra-canonical *jātaka*, a Thai cosmological text, and a chronicle composed in nineteenth-century Burma. Lao students and teachers were uncomfortable with surveys (I produced a Lao-language survey for them), so I relied mostly on formal and informal interviews using the same questions. The results were very similar. The internationally accepted Pali Text Society edition, the Vipassana Research Institute edition, or other versions of the canon are not only different from local manuscript collections, curricula, and so forth, but the difference between canonical and extra-canonical or even Pali and vernacular Buddhist texts is unknown and largely of no concern to local students and teachers (especially in rural Northern Thailand and Laos). The canon to them encompasses all Buddhist texts. If the text has a Buddhist title, is in Pali, or lifts Pali words, it is *buddhavacana* (words of the Buddha), *lak sut* (the basic Buddhist curriculum or foundational texts), and *Phra Tripidok* (the Tipiṭaka)—that is, the canon.

Texts are considered part of the canon not just because of their title or subject matter but because of the way they are aesthetically presented. The introduction in the previous chapter described a monk preaching with a faux, cardboard manuscript in his hand. The monk sat on an *āsana*, or preaching "throne," about one foot above the laypeople kneeling below. He held a text that looked like a palm-leaf manuscript (even the light-brown color and stiffness of the cardboard made it look more like a palm-leaf manuscript than it did white paper).[14] His saffron robe had neat accordion folds flowing evenly away from his shoulder (any monk knows it is difficult for a robe to fold perfectly). He voice was low and steady. The large, multitiered altar next to his seat was littered with Buddha images in various poses, wooden elephants, candles, incense, flowers, and plastic stupas. Every inch of the room's walls and high ceiling was painted with murals of various flying spirits (*kinnaree*), monasteries, abstract lotus flower patterns, and traditional rural Thai scenes, and the wooden shutters had golden filigree designs. The floor had the traditional ubiquitous red carpet.

This room, the monk, and the faux manuscript looked "Thai" and "Buddhist." It was a predictable space. Modern faux manuscripts used for preaching (and often for use in monastic classroom lectures), like Thai Buddhist architecture and aesthetic accoutrements, have changed little (except to the discerning eyes of art historians) in the way they look. The aesthetics of the room and the monk "made" the text, in a way, canonical. Since that sermon, I make it a regular practice to ask audience members at sermons and at lectures the name of the title of the text they were listening to and whether or not it is in the Tipiṭaka. Usually they cannot remember the title (they remember the contents, but the title is often not emphasized by the preacher), but almost universally they state that it is indeed in the Tipiṭaka, even though, of course, it often is not. The common Thai and Lao notions of the canon show the difficulty of defining what constitutes a canon and the more insidious problem of allowing a "defined" canon to lead a scholar into assuming that the canon is universally read, understood, held, preserved and unaltered by the religious community that ideally adheres to it.[15]

From Commentary to Canon to Curricula

Pedagogical manuscripts incorporate many of the features of what Buddhist studies scholars include under the rubric of "commentary."[16] Commentary is done for the purpose of "altering the course of the reader's cognitive, affective, and active lives by the ingestion, digestion, rumination, and restatement of what has been read."[17] Reading "specialists" in many traditions, especially Buddhist India, guide readers through their own particular interpretation of a "canonical text" through commentary. Commentary is thus a "belief-forming practice."[18] Paul Griffiths provides his own definition for what constitutes a commentary, that being (1) apparent and direct relation to some other work or, what Michael Fishbane calls "multiple and sustained lexical linkages," and (2) that these linkages should "quantitatively" dominate the text so that if they were removed the work would become incomprehensible.[19] It should be clear that *nissaya*, *vohāra*, and *nāmasadda* are forms of commentary according to Griffiths's definition.[20] However, Griffiths is generally writing about commentaries written in the same language as the object text. A commentary in one language on a source text of a different language does not necessary change the style or purpose of the commentary. Furthermore, some of the *nissaya*, *vohāra*, and *nāmasadda* available seem to be written on Pali texts that never actually existed before that time. They often have multiple and sustained linkages to a source text, but that source text is either unidentifiable or almost completely divergent from any extant version of the source. Sometimes the *nissaya*, *vohāra*, and *nāmasadda* follow a known source at points and then make long detours away from it. Sometimes they make a conglomerate vernacular commentary on an ad hoc anthology of excerpts from various sources. *Nissaya* expand the purposes of a commentary by explaining a text, justifying its importance in the tradition, and absorbing and replacing the original.

Repetitive glossing, or the introduction of new vocabulary as additions to stock phrases of texts, shows that the composers of *nissaya* wanted to use the commentary as a way to teach language and help scribes or the audience to remember stories. This defined what was important to know as a Buddhist in that community. More important, by seeing the *nissaya*, *vohāra*, and *nāmasadda* as primarily educational, one can see how the very choice of what texts to translate and comment on was a way of serving the intellectual and social needs of medieval Laos and Northern Thailand. The choice of what texts and what words from a particular text to comment on and translate in *nissaya* and *vohāra* form can tell a great deal about the needs of the communities that composed them and what aspects of Buddhism were deemed more important and most necessary to teach. If commentaries define what a particular community considers "canon," then Lao and Northern Thai pedagogical manuscripts define a set of texts that were considered "canonical" for the sake of Buddhist education.

Nissaya, *vohāra*, and *nāmasadda* are evidence of what can be called a type of curricular canon operating in premodern Northern Thailand and Laos. This canon did not exist in the minds of the writers and audience, but these texts were the ones taught and copied in the vernacular. They can be called vernacular commentaries on an ad hoc canon composed of Pali canonical material, Pali commentaries, vernacular folktales, apocryphal *jātaka*, locally assembled anthologies, or collections of prayers. This certainly stretches and qualifies the understanding of commentaries. Since certain types of texts were used for different purposes (*paritta* for life-cycle rituals and warding off malevolent spirits; *jātaka* for calendrical rituals such as New Year's festivals, weekly sermons, calling for rain, and *visakha pūja*; and *kammavācā* for ordination ceremonies, the establishing of a new monastery, etc.), one can say that there were multiple, overlapping canons of texts. Since these genres clearly incorporate pedagogical methods and may have been employed to teach both vernacular and classical vocabulary, syntax, phonetics, and so forth, taken in the living context of reading, translating, copying, commenting, and teaching, they simply constitute a particular Buddhist curriculum. If one favors the study of the canon over curricula, then one effectively favors a study of texts and ideas over opening an evolving conversation with communities and learning from traditions, interpretations, and textual practices.

I see texts in a curriculum, as Rich Freeman does of texts in general. Speaking of the literary culture of Kerala, India, Freeman writes, "Texts do not just reflect or represent the extratextual activities of their surrounding culture; rather, texts are immanent activities and practices of that culture, and work to constitute it as well. Textual practices, and the genres that order them, may thus alternately maintain, refigure, or actively change their social contexts."[21] *Nissaya*, *vohāra*, and *nāmasadda* authors never explicitly stated that they valued the vernacular over Pali, but through their textual and pedagogical practices they slowly communicated to their monastic and lay audiences that the vernacular was a legitimate vehicle of the classical. These pedagogical texts invoked the power of Pali consistently and tied local to translocal, but at the same time they gave power and legitimacy to the vernacular and local interpretation. The act of collecting local Pali and vernacular folktales and *jātaka* and binding them together with foreign canonical and extra-canonical texts, or the act of stringing Pali and vernacular synonyms together on one line of a manuscript or in one line of sermon, slowly justified local literature, expertise, language, and performance. If the vernacular was a legitimate conduit for Pali, then local teachers were legitimate surrogates for the Buddha. The earliest translators and commentators of Laos and Northern Thailand developed an attitude toward classical and canonical Buddhist texts in which their ritual power, social prestige, and cultural and ethical import was respected and consistently invoked, but their integrity and completeness was disregarded. This understanding of texts as mutable tools for community building and "movable bridges" of personal, extemporaneous expression can be seen in conterminous treatment of translocal Buddha images, chronicles, relics, and rituals—they were consistently transformed in bits and pieces locally, but represented as whole and original.

Nissaya diverge from standard definitions of commentary. First, commentaries in the Pali tradition are usually understood as being in the same language as the source text. Still, it would be overly reductive to call them vernacular commentaries. Second, *nissaya*, *vohāra*, and *nāmasadda* often diverge widely from their particular source text often to the point that they seem to be rewriting the source text, inventing entire sections, or writing a commentary on a source text that may have never existed as a separate text in Pali or vernacular. Third, they often contain internal subcommentaries on their own commentaries of a source text, and it is occasionally difficult to determine whether the author was attempting to teach the meaning of a passage from a source text or comment on his or her own explanation of the source text. Fourth, the source text is employed as a platform to teach grammar, vocabulary, and concepts, which is almost completely divorced from the semantic meaning or original purpose for which the source text seemed to be composed. In this way, the source text plays the role of a canvas that serves only to provide a space for the author of the *nissaya* to paint his own picture. At many points, source texts no longer guide the sequence, structure, or subject of the commentary. This practice could be compared to a tourist who strolls through a Bangkok monastery, inspired by its architecture, images, history, royal pedigree, and residents, to compose a long journal entry on all and sundry subjects in no particular order.

These pedagogical manuscripts and textual practices often change the discursive mode of the source. They make narrative thought systematic and systematic thought narrative. Collins has argued that Buddhist knowledge can be divided into expressing either systematic or narrative thought. He writes that "in Buddhist systematic thought, the beginning and end points of an exposition can differ, as can the ordering of the intervening items, without any basic change in the meaning. . . . [I]n narrative, by contrast, differences in any of these three things must have an effect on meaning; and significant differences may lead one to say that the story has a different meaning."[22] In another, as yet unpublished, piece Collins continues, "Systematic thought is constituted by ideas, related by logical-mathematical or other non-sequential principles." These can be rational arguments, irrational "sets of binary oppositions," or in the discursive form of "logical-rhetorical argumentation, or questions and answers." Narrative thought, in comparison, "is constituted by plot, character, etc., as well as by ideas, and it requires one or another specific sequential ordering, not as expository necessity but as part of the particular way it produces meaning."[23] *Nissaya*, *vohāra*, and *nāmasadda* often transform Buddhist narratives into systematic glosses of the names of characters, short explanatory commentaries on events in the story, or launching pads for grammatical lessons. In other cases, systematic texts like the *nissaya* on the *mātikā* of the *Dhammasaṅgaṇī* or the *Nissaya suat mon* change systematic texts into narrative ones by relating or invoking stories about the first time the Buddha uttered these teachings or about how they can be used to protect against the dangers of snakes and tree spirits. Simply put, if commentaries define a canon, then the *nissayas*, *vohāra*, and *nāmasadda* define a canon wholly different from that of the Pali Tipiṭaka.

Pedagogical manuscripts also differ greatly from systematic commentaries in the way they elide the importance of authorship. Anyone seriously interested in Southeast Asian Buddhism knows the names of the great Pali commentators like Buddhaghosa, Dhammapala, Sirimaṅgala, and Ñāṇakitti, among others. Each of these commentators had his own style and method of interpretation, so much so that one can even use the appellation "the Buddhaghosa school" or the "Sirimaṅgala approach." However, authorship is often unknown for most pedagogical manuscripts in Laos and Thailand. Furthermore, "originality" is unimportant for those composing or using pedagogical manuscripts. Of course, each monk who composes and each teacher who reuses a pedagogical manuscript when giving a lecture or a sermon brings his own unique interpretation and approach to the text. However, this is not a value that the author or teacher emphasizes or that most members of the audience laud. *Nissaya*, *vohāra*, and *nāmasadda* are important, not for what they say, but for the tradition, authority, "ancient" knowledge, and power to which they give access. Pedagogical manuscripts give access to the powerful words known broadly as the Pali Tipiṭaka (*Kamphi Traipitok*). This is not a specific group of texts, but a foundational ideal about what is right and true. These pedagogical texts can be seen as pickaxes that expose veins of gold. The teachers who use them are not authors but miners.

The word *curriculum*, from the Proto-Indo-European root "kers I" and more directly from the Latin *currere* (to run), is related to other English words like *current*, *recourse*, *incur*, *occur*, *corridor*, and *discourse*. Its Proto-Indo-European root connection to a school's curriculum was not regular until the late nineteenth century. It is first recorded in English dictionaries in 1909. It was first associated with instructions for carriage driving. It is evocative of action. This is how I am using the term. A curriculum is used and adapted. I have tried to offer a curricular history of monastic education in Laos and Thailand. A curriculum must be seen as incorporating more than the primary texts that are found in monastic school libraries, that are found in the canon defined by local elite ecclesia, or that are "externally validated" by scholars and the leaders of other religions. Scholars interested in the history and development of monastic communities and the religious epistemes or cultural ecumene that they constitute and are constituted by would do well to see how texts are used in lectures and sermons on a day-to-day basis. Seeing the way words are lifted by teachers from canonical and extra-canonical texts and anthologized, cited, combined with other words, and used in oral exposition in both classical and vernacular languages is essential to writing a textual anthropological study, or, better, an anthro-philological study, of monastic education. The translocal sources provide the vocabulary, and the local traditions put that new vocabulary into sentences that respond to contemporary situations and with syntax informed by indigenous attitudes toward reading and teaching. When one sees the method and choices of this lifting in the context of political, colonial, and economic forces, as well as influenced by the evolving formats and attitudes toward texts and learning in general, then one can write a history of monastic education that assigns change not simply to elite reforms but to broad regional linguistic and ethnic taxonomies, translocal religious movements, colonial chauvinism, print technology, examination records, and official canons. Stepping into the premodern monastic classroom through the words, methods, physical features, and rhetorical styles of pedagogical palm-leaf manuscripts can be as telling as observing teacher handbooks, student guidebooks, the writing on blackboards, and the CD-ROMs used in examination preparation and listening to lectures and sermons in modern classrooms and sermon halls. This enables one to see teachers and students as active agents in their own education, not as mindless consumers—servile and indoctrinated consumers of a translocal belief system.

It is important to note that the terms *commentary*, *canon*, and *subcommentary* are somewhat misleading. Not all subcommentaries, for example, are in a direct chronological line, basing their comments and analyses on commentaries or canonical texts that came before them. Many comment only on certain parts of a source text or multiple source texts using different methodologies. Moreover, canonical source texts and their commentaries are rarely handed down together, copied together, found bound together, or found even in the same monastic library. For example, the *Atthasālinī-atthayojanā* clearly draws from the *Atthasālinī* but not from the *Mohavicchedanī*, which chronologically precedes it. There are words like *naccagītassa* and *caturritthiyo* that are in the *Atthasālinī* and not in the *Mohavicchedanī*.[24]

It is important to emphasize that manuscripts were spread across hundreds of different monasteries and that some texts were considered important at one site but not at another. The *Atthasālinī-atthayojanā* and the *Mohavicchedanī* clearly had different lineages, and the *nissaya* under discussion seem to have been influenced by the former, which makes sense considering they were both composed in Northern Thailand. Furthermore, one *Atthasālinī nissaya* that I examined from Vat Mai in Vientiane (Laos) does not follow a Pali version of the *Atthasālinī* manuscript found in the same monastery. They were copied/composed at different times, by different scribes, and where the *Atthasālinī nissaya* does not draw long clauses from the Pali *Atthasālinī*, it contains mistakes not seen in the Pali *Atthasālinī* manuscript found in the same monastery. Finally, commentaries did not simply pass from Sri Lanka to Burma to Thailand. Throughout the nineteenth century, Thai monastic emissaries brought subcommentaries and handbooks from Thailand (Siam) to Sri Lanka, such as Ñāṇakitti's sixteenth-century Northern Thai *Atthasālinī-atthayojanā*, which was brought to Sri Lanka in 1890.

This stroll through the linguistic and codicological world of *nissaya* has shown that there are many ways to define a canon. I have hoped to emphasize the importance of seeing how texts were used in an educational context to think about what could have been the nonstandardized and peculiar curriculum of a certain region and certain time. Between the sixteenth century and the present, a concerted effort has been made to translate and comment on Pali texts, both canonical and extra-canonical. This constant referral to and manipulation of Indic textual methods, rhetorical styles, tropes, themes, and ideals of the past in order to explain and manage the present were part of the general commentarial and translation (oral, textual, architectural, and artistic) culture of Southeast Asia. *Nissaya*, *vohāra*, and *nāmasadda* obfuscated and elucidated source texts with inventive methods of teaching vocabulary, grammar, and occasionally meanings of a seemingly random collection of Pali texts. These were texts that not only gave the definitions of Pali words and phrases but also taught their readers/audience how to incorporate Pali terms into Lao or Yuan / Northern Thai syntax. They invoked the ideals of Pali and "India." The pedagogical methods and physical features of the manuscripts show what sources the authors of these texts listened to, read, collected, and handled. Therefore, they have to be seen as intertextual—constantly referring to other texts, oral commentaries, and ritual / liturgical contexts. One must understand the gestures and the aesthetics that surround any pedagogical text. I surmise that from this evidence, one can begin not only to outline the premodern curricula of the region but also to trace their modal affects in the modern period.

PART III

Vernacular Landscapes

Teaching Buddhism in Laos and Thailand

7 From Manuscript to Television

If one were to walk into most any Thai bookstore, look at most any Thai Buddhist-themed Web site, scan most any Thai Buddhist curriculum, or examine most any Thai manuscript archive, one would see the Dhammapada. Laos, although lacking in its number of Web sites, universities, bookstores, and curricula, is also a place where the Dhammapada is ubiquitous. *Some form* of the Dhammapada has been widespread for at least five hundred years. If one looks at Thai, Mon, and Khmer epigraphic evidence, some form of the text goes back another thousand years. Still, all Dhammapada are not created equally. Despite its importance for students and teachers in Laos and Thailand, the nature of the "text" of the Dhammapada and how it has been read, summarized, anthologized, and transformed through various pedagogical methods and mediums have not been explored.[1]

At first glance it would seem that the Dhammapada in modern Laos and Thailand is radically different from its premodern antecedent. Several key changes have been made in the text and the manner in which it has been conveyed over the past five centuries. First, a pre-twentieth-century emphasis on narrative commentarial sections as a pedagogical subject has been replaced by a valorization of canonical Dhammapada verses. Prior to the twentieth century, the verses as a separate or complete collection had little commerce among teachers and students. In the premodern period the Dhammapada verses were rarely collected as one text. Second, manuscripts of some form of the Dhammapada are most often in the vernacular, not in Pali. The most common way to render and teach the Dhammapada prior to the modern period was the *nissaya* method, which is a vernacular gloss and explanation of Pali words and phrases from the source. Third, the manuscripts of the Pali Dhammapada and vernacular Dhammapada commentaries and glosses nearly always include extra-canonical material and are anthologies of local and canonical material. The Dhammapada changed over time in Thailand, until the advent of the printing press slowed, but did not put an end to, its expansion. Fourth, the mediums for teaching the Dhammapada have changed in response to technological advances, colonial and royal reform, the influence of Western ideas of the Buddhist "original canon," the rise of the primacy of Pali over vernacular commentarial texts, and changing social concerns; however, these changes need to be qualified based on the audience and the manner of the instruction. These primitivist, textual, cultural, and moralist biases have been well documented in the study of Buddhism in Sri Lanka.[2] In more recent years, the Dhammapada's role in education has expanded into television programs, popular anthologies, bilingual editions, handbooks, Web sites, and avant-garde dramas. In Laos, even though the printing of the text has not been common, the Dhammapada is one of the primary sources for sermons and monastic school lectures. Stories from the *Dhammapada-atthakathā* are also the subject of temple murals. In Thailand there are abundant copies of the complete Pali Dhammapada (verses and commentarial narratives) thanks to the efforts of the Thai royal family and to Sri Lankan and British Buddhist scholars who brought copies to Thailand in the late nineteenth century.

Although the mediums and content have changed significantly, the methods used to instruct the Dhammapada have remained largely the same since the sixteenth century. Instruction still operates on a system of drawing selected Pali words from the text and offering expanded creative glosses and analogies to contemporary issues. Reading, it seems, still involves looking for the terms, themes, and narratives that best convey a point orally. Moreover, commentarial narratives on the Dhammapada are still the primary content for lecturers and sermon givers. Seeing how the Dhammapada is taught in an oral context is essential in avoiding convenient and facile reification of unrealistic barriers between the past and the present and the East and the West. Many scholars have identified how the "Western scholarly interpretation of Buddhism" was subsequently adopted by Sinhalese and Thai Buddhists and became the official view of Buddhism locally.[3] However, as Blackburn emphasizes, this monolithic aping of the West can be overemphasized and may remove the multivocal, inconsistent, and dynamic agency of colonized Buddhists.[4] It is wise not to overemphasize this change lest one become blind to some fundamental continuities in the various ways Buddhism has been taught to Buddhists by Buddhists.

The first Buddhist text translated into a Western language, Latin, was a Dhammapada, "Dhammapadam ex tribus codicibus Hauniensibus Palice edidit Latine vertit," by Viggo Fausbøll in 1855.[5] The history of the Dhammapada in the West and a full bibliography are sorely needed, but that must be left for another day.[6] However, just because the text is popular among students and scholars in London and Bangkok, Los Angeles, Sydney, and Savannakhet does not mean that the text is taught and printed the same in all contexts. As American historian David Harlan argues, studying texts in their sociohistorical context is not purely instrumental where "complex texts are reduced to mere tokens and documents."[7] One context is not sufficiently explanatory for how the text should be taught. Instead, texts are always parts of multiple contexts, multiple readings, and educational settings, which, I argue, one would do well to compare. The context in which a text was first composed is not the text's only context, and certainly not even its most important. One also needs to pay attention to the intention not only of the original text's author but to that of others as well. Questions regarding texts need to shift with shifting contexts. Understanding the ways Lao and Thai Buddhist readers and teachers have creatively translated and taught the Dhammapada will provide insight into how sociohistorical forces have influenced the local reading and teaching of Buddhism and offer a more sophisticated way of seeing the changes and continuities of Buddhist exegesis. This study does not simply teach scholars more about local exegetes, translators, and instructors. In the end, my hope is that it will force scholars to think about how they read, learn, teach, and translate the Dhammapada in their classrooms, libraries, and offices, as well as what they choose to count as historical evidence. There is much to learn from local teachers about what counts as the Dhammapada. In this regard, learning from the ways Laos and Thais learn the Dhammapada is not only a historical investigation; it is also an intertextual and self-reflective project.[8]

Instability and Freedom: The Premodern Vicissitudes of the Dhammapada

The Dhammapada is one of the oldest and best recognized texts of South and Southeast Asian Buddhism. In pre-twentieth-century Laos and Thailand it was a central subject of commentaries, sermons, and inscriptions.[9] However, before the twentieth century there is little evidence of many "complete manuscripts" of the Pali Dhammapada in Laos or Thailand.[10] While there are a few manuscripts that contain most of the 423 verses, the text is found most commonly in *nissaya* form. *Nissaya* almost never provide a complete translation of the original text, and parts of the text are often found in numerous different monastic libraries. For example, a manuscript found in one of the regional microfilm catalogs has "Dhammapada mad #4" as its title. One would assume that this is the fourth section or chapter of the Dhammapada. However, the actual manuscript is a Thai translation of several (disconnected) stories drawn from the Pali *Dhammapada-atthakathā*. Extra-canonical material is also included in this manuscript. Each section of the Dhammapada is called a *mad*. Each *mad* is of different length, ranging from twelve to forty-two fascicles or one to two fascicles. From the available manuscript catalogs there seem to be a total of sixteen *mad*. These *mad* do not correspond to the Pali Dhammapada's twenty-six *vagga* (chapters) or 423 verses. Moreover, not one monastic library contains all sixteen *mad*. Each *mad* seems to have been composed independently of the others by different local scholars at different times in different places. Many of these *mad* have been mislabeled and often have numerous missing or severely damaged leaves. In addition, one manuscript can have several *pecia*. I believe that any attempt to collect "all" of the *mad*, place them in sequential order, and translate them as one text would be misleading as to how they were composed and collected. It would create a false sense of "completeness." I am confident that these *mad* were not composed in order, by one author, and at one place or ever bound together as one large manuscript. These vernacular narratives and word commentaries seemed to have circulated independently and were considered complete texts in and of themselves and never read as a complete (i.e., all sixteen *mad*) text. That I have found only sixteen *mad* in different places in no way means that sixteen was the total number of *mad* of the

Dhammapada in any of these regions. In addition to the several *mad* for the Dhammapada, there are also numerous *mad* for the *Dhammapada nissaya*. These scattered *nissaya* manuscripts were used for instruction and creative retelling of particular stories from the commentarial sections of the Dhammapada. *Nissaya* are evidence of the first Dhammapada guidebooks in Laos and Thailand. Finally, it is very difficult to determine the actual content from the title of the manuscript on the wooden cover, in the colophon, or in the margin on the first leaf. For example, there are manuscripts with the title "Dhammapada," but they do not contain the Pali verses. Usually they are vernacular glosses (*nissaya*, *vohāra*, or *nāmasadda*) of some stories from the *atthakathā* and other local narratives.

I discuss one example, a mixed Pali and Thai manuscript titled *Dhammapada nissaya* (Northern Thai: *Nisai Dhammapot*), to help understand this reception and transformation between the sixteenth and the late nineteenth centuries. The manuscript, composed in 1836, comes from Phrae Province in modern-day Thailand. It is a long manuscript, with over ten fascicles and 175 folios.[11] The title suggests that this manuscript is a gloss and explanation of the Pali verses of the Dhammapada; however, it is actually a *nissaya* loosely based on the *Khadiravaniyarevatattheravatthu* from the *Arahantavaggo* of the *Dhammapada-atthakathā*. Details and events from another story seem to have become inserted in the process of translation. The main narrative is based on the ascetic powers and great devotion of Revata and his ordination as a *bhikkhu* (monk). The Pali story also relates the Buddha's trip to the Khadiravana retreat. Revata was the youngest brother of the eminent disciple Sāriputta and was held back from ordaining by his mother, because she did not want all her children to abandon her for the mendicant life. However, Revata, not wanting to marry and raise a family and take care of his mother (because he realized the impermanence of all things), secretly ordained. After ordaining, Revata displayed his ascetic power by creating luxurious dwellings for the Buddha and his followers while staying in the Khadira forest. The Buddha told the skeptic Visākhā about the wonderful powers of Revata.

There are numerous other narratives taken from the *Dhammapada-atthakathā* in these ten fascicles. The order of *mad* does not follow any previously known order of the Pali *Dhammapada-atthakathā*, and the choices of narratives to comment on and translate from do not follow the order of stories or chapters in the Pali source text. For example, the last narrative glossed in this manuscript (fascicles 9 and 10) is the *Culla-ekasāṭakavatthu*, which is not situated near the *Khadiravaniyarevatattheravatthu* in the canonical Dhammapada or its commentary. However, it is also a story that involves Vipassī Buddha. Since a number of the narratives in this Dhammapada manuscript mention Vipassī Buddha, this may have been the underlying reason for grouping together these seemingly disparate canonical and noncanonical narratives. This is further supported by the fact that Vipassī is emphasized more in these stories than in the Pali versions. From this example, it is important not to assume that two manuscripts with the same titles have the same contents or to assume that the Pali title is anything more than a loose guide to the actual contents of the largely vernacular text. In fact, this is rarely the case, and it is never the case with *nissaya* versions of the Dhammapada. The narratives chosen by the authors of any of the manuscripts of this Dhammapada do not follow the order of the *Dhammapada-atthakathā*, and narratives from different chapters of the *atthakathā* are bound together. The choice seems to be based on a preference for certain stories or based on plot or other similarities rather than on any traditional translocal order.

In looking directly at the Revata narrative, one sees that as the story progresses the author gradually cites fewer and fewer Pali words from the source text. By the end of the fascicle there is little to connect the manuscript to any known Pali source, and even the final verse in Pali is not cited. This author begins his translation through direct and sustained citations from a source (whether present or in mind), but gradually he ceases to maintain that connection, although the basic and abbreviated contents of the story are still present in the vernacular. In this section, certain details, like the mention of the city of Bandhumatī and an unusual emphasis of the life of Vipassī Buddha (the nineteenth of twenty-four), suggest strongly that the author was drawing on material from the Vipassī section of the *Buddhavaṃsa* (21) and the story of Dipankara and Vipassī from the *Dūrenidānakathā* of the *nidāna*. The *nidāna* is the introduction to the Pali *jātaka*. On the one hand, combining details and narrative events from stories in both the *nidāna* of the *jātaka* and the *Dhammapada-atthakathā* reveals that the author may have had a very different collection of stories, called the Dhammapada, as his source text. On the other hand, he composed the *Dhammapada nissaya* by using Pali trigger words and phrases, which in the process of oral translation would invoke a mixture of different stories with similar characters, locales, and events. Hence, he might not have had a physical manuscript of the Pali source text. If he did have a Pali source text, then this is evidence that another recension of this story, different from the Sri Lankan recensions, was available in the region. It seems most likely that the author did not have a Pali source text present and was not translating but recalling a Pali story or parts of stories from memory and hearsay and dictating them in the vernacular, since he does not directly quote any lengthy passages and does not follow one story consistently. It would be understandable if the author were using the Pali trigger words written and glossed to combine details and events from these two stories. Both the story of Dipankara from the *nidāna* of the *jātaka* collection and the story of Revata from the *Dhammapada-atthakathā* involve the Buddha Vipassī and Revata. Moreover, the fact that the city of Bandhumatī is mentioned in this text although it is never mentioned in the Dhammapada is because it was the birthplace of Vipassī. The Buddhas of the past were often known by their tree, height, life span, birthplace, and other basic biographical details. The author of this text seems to have been telling the story of Revata using certain Pali words to anchor and order the narrative, and when Vipassī was mentioned as part of the Revata story from the *Dhammapada-atthakathā* the author recalled or confused the two stories and added information about the life of Vipassī that was not mentioned in the *Dhammapada-atthakathā*. If trigger or key words were used to translate this manuscript, they also might have been used to guide the collection of narratives in this particular collection. If one sees trigger words or particular details, like the names of cities, particular Buddhas of the past, or certain acts of charity or ascetic power, present in previously unrelated stories as organizing principles then this might explain why two stories like the *Culla-ekasāṭakavatthu* and the *Khadiravaniyarevatattheravatthu* are bound together in this manuscript. They both involve Vipassī Buddha. Moreover, the plot details and characters of the former are found in versions in the *Milinda-panha*, the *Aṅguttara-atthakathā*, as well as the *Dhammapada-atthakathā*. The version from the *Aṅguttara* commentary takes place in the city of King Bandhumatī, which may be another linkage between this story and the Revata story. It is easy to see how the events of two stories both involving Revata and Vipassī may have been conflated. This tendency to conflate different legends from the lives of one famous holy man is very common in Thailand, where legends and retellings of legends in highly divergent forms are found in books on the lives of famous monks and in sermons. Any speaker of Thai who has spent time in the amulet markets and monastic cells in this region can attest to the popular pastime of relating the miraculous events of famous monks living and dead, legendary and historical. Accuracy and sources never seem to be a major concern to the storytellers. Their power as moral and ritual exemplars has ethical and discursive force. Where these stories came from is of little importance to this study, because most stories in these collections are found in numerous narrative collections in Sanskrit, Pali, Chinese, and so forth. However, the organizing principles in the mind of the author who combined these stories into one collection are telling. For scholars to define the parameters of Buddhist, local, and India literature in Northern Thailand and Laos, they must understand this creative anthologizing of stories as defining the idea of the canon or the curriculum of Buddhist education in the region. Since narratives are the most common way Buddhism is taught in Southeast Asia, and narrative texts are some of the most prevalent in manuscript collections, examining what stories were collected and how they were manipulated, expanded, contracted, and conflated provides a good picture of the subjects and themes of Buddhist education in the region. The intellectuals of the region did not simply reproduce, translate, collect, and preserve the Pali canon and commentary, but they creatively engaged with that wide corpus and contributed to it through creative and expansive translation and anthologizing.[12]

A brief selection from the manuscript demonstrates how this works. I do not translate the Pali into English, so the reader can see how the Pali breaks up the vernacular:

> This *dessanā* meaning this *dhammadessanā* is distinguished by being a "paddha gathā" that is "'ātīkalyāṇa." This means [the verse] "gāme vā yadī vārañeni" and "āyasmā hi sāriputto." This refers to "sāriputtathera,' the honorable one, [who] has reached *āyu* (proper age) and has already placed down *vatthū* (clothes), material goods, silver, and gold of all types

> amounting to 87 *koṭis*, after he caused to ordain . . . [he brought together his three sisters to ordain]. Only Revata still lives in the house and this child, his older [brother wants] to ordain. (Approximately: f.*ka*.r–f.*kha*.v)

The decision of when to write out a Pali word and supply a vernacular gloss is idiosyncratic and depends on the author and the words that he wants to mention and gloss. From the manuscript this sermon giver wanted to emphasize the importance of gifts to the Sangha; however, a number of other themes could be expanded on orally. Most *nissaya*, including this one, have approximately 5–20 percent Pali words. The vast majority of Pali words from the ideal source are not lifted or glossed.

The standard hierarchy between the Pali source text and the Pali words and vernacular glosses and translations is either neutralized or reversed. What is not seen from this short selection is the degree of repetition. Clearly, they were used for emphasis in an oral exposition. They almost form the chorus of the sermon, which is returned to over and over again. Despite this repetition, the actual narrative would be unclear and useless for reading alone. It needs oral commentary and explanation. These repetitive words are triggers and clues to what the sermon giver emphasized for oral commentary.

Whether the author of the *nissaya* was drawing material from the *nidāna* or from any other known source directly is difficult to say. It is more accurate to say that the author was drawing from a common bank of terms, names, and narrative sequences from various sources including the *nidāna*, *Cariyapiṭaka*, *Buddhavaṃsa*, local folktales, his own memory, and stories from his teachers. There are enough terms or passages to associate details and events from this manuscript with some version of the Revata story, but this story should be seen as inspirational and not prescriptive. A great number of new *jātaka*-type narratives were being composed in this region, many including random bits of information, tropes, characters, plot elements, morals, and so forth. The authors of *nissaya* were freely borrowing details, characters, and events from one another and from the collective bank of well-known narratives (both canonical and noncanonical, vernacular and Pali-Sanskrit). This free borrowing of whole narratives or elements is certainly not unique to Thailand. The *Dhammapada-atthakathā* and the *jātaka* possess many stories from Sanskrit narrative collections such as the *Pañcatantra*, *Mahābharata*, and the *Hitopadeṣa* or from Buddhist Sanskrit and Hybrid Sanskrit collections. Many of these same stories, of course, worked their way into the collective memory of Persian and European storytellers. Great stories are always stolen, always adapted, and always shared.

Lao *Dhammapada nissaya* manuscripts, like the one composed in 1720 in Vientiane examined in chapter 4 and several other *Dhammapada nāmasadda* and *vohāra* manuscripts from Laos, Nan, and Phrae, reveal that the authors were often not closely following any known source text, but were instead glossing a very few selected words from the known Pali sources alongside hundreds of other Pali words not found in the known sources. They are mostly anthologies of stories drawing a few words and phrases from nonsequential parts of the source, but representing themselves as the entire source. The authors used certain known terms, names, and narrative sequences as triggers to compose their own texts. The introduction, the titles of the chapters, and so forth served as anchors to the texts. The *Dhammapada nissaya* from 1720 Vientiane, for example, draws on the names of the characters from the Meṇḍaka narrative, but it adds new content and takes the story in new directions using these characters as launchpads for their own creative expansion. These are partly new texts based on new ideas, new vocabulary, new creative anthologizing, new audiences, a new stage of Pali, new intentions, and a new sociohistorical context. Since these texts are in *nissaya* form, they were used as a guide to an oral sermon/lecture. This is the way that most monastics and laity were introduced to the Dhammapada. It is certainly the way most Thais are introduced to the Dhammapada today. Sermons often draw the first line from the story of the *Dhammapada-atthakathā* and occasionally a verse from the text and then explain each word in the vernacular, accompanied by stories, anecdotes, historical lessons, jokes, and links to contemporary events. The source text serves the needs of the teacher, the translator, the anthologizer, the politician, or the poet.

After seeing evidence from one manuscript, one may ask if there is any relation to the actual Dhammapada at all. Given that the *nissaya* only draws on selected passages, is repetitive, does not mention the "original" Pali verse, has extensive vernacular asides, draws from multiple versions of a story, and is useless as a connected narrative, can this even be called a text in the Dhammapada lineage? I argue that since local communities saw this as part of the Dhammapada tradition, the fact that most people in the region (literate and illiterate) over time were taught that this text was part of the Dhammapada (or even "the" Dhammapada), and that the *nissaya* author was clearly drawing from some version(s) of the *Dhammapada-atthakathā*, one cannot discount it unless one believes that texts should be read only in the form of a critical edition or that context and reception are of no use to historians, textual scholars, philologists, anthropologists, and the like. Is the Dhammapada valuable only as a complete text? What counts as a complete text? Is a partially oral text part of a textual tradition? Can there be a partially oral edition?

The Rise of the Verse: The Dhammapada in Modern Laos and Thailand

Manuscript evidence shows that the Dhammapada grew and changed in Laos and Thailand before the twentieth century and the rise of the printing press and royally sponsored monastic reforms. It also demonstrates that the commentarial narratives, not the verses, were the primary vehicles for teaching the Dhammapada. These narratives were creative anthologies drawn from a bank of common stories, themes, terms, and names, rather than a standard collection based on the normative Pali *Dhammapada-atthakathā*. Before the modern period it seems that these versions of the *Dhammapada-atthakathā* were presented to their audience as normative. In fact, in modern sermons, these anthologies are still often called the "Dhammapada" and for the nonspecialist one would assume, and my interviews confirm this, that they are considered normative. From the mid-nineteenth century to the present a shift occurred in which the verses began to receive more prominence in terms of printed editions, royally sponsored canons, Web sites, and anthologies. The narrative commentaries have become more standard and have witnessed changes in format under influence from the West. However, the use of the Dhammapada in Buddhist education and homiletics has changed little.

In the late nineteenth and early twentieth centuries it became more common for the verses of the Dhammapada to be published separately from the narratives of the *Dhammapada-atthakathā*. This was certainly a new phenomenon in the way the Dhammapada was rendered in writing. The several editions of the Tipiṭaka and Pali commentaries sponsored by the royal family between the 1780s and the present separate the verses and narratives (although the content of the canons has shifted from edition to edition). This separation of the verses and the narratives, as well as the creation of a "standard" edition of the *Dhammapada-atthakathā* in 1916 by the Liang Chiang publishing house in Bangkok, changed the manner in which a teacher or student could possess the text. This standard *mattatan* edition of the Dhammapada's verses and narratives has been reissued twice recently, once in 1972 and again in 1987 by the Mahamakut press. There are six volumes in each paperback set.[13] The first is based on Prince Wachirayan's nineteenth-century edition, which was translated into Thai by the novice Udit Sirivanna Parian, who is now an American-educated businessperson. Udit and another novice named Adisak Thong Khwan Prian also published a small handbook for the study of the verses of the Dhammapada, which helps students learn how to translate the verses into Thai.[14] Specific instructions are provided on the nature of verb endings, noun declensions, word order, and syntax that are not seen in any pre-1902 manuscript versions. The main guide is for translating the verses, while only the last two chapters mention methods of translating the narratives. In both six-volume sets and the handbook, Udit states that he abides by the more authentic *plae doi payanchana*, or "literal translation method," versus translating for the spirit of the text. This method was rarely employed in pre-1902 Thailand exegetical practice. However, the standard is now "literal." To emphasize the superiority and grammatical integrity of the original Pali, the handbooks emphasize the eight submethods used to translate the text: according to the nouns, according to the verbs, according to compounds, and so on. The Dhammapada, instead of an evolving and ever-changing part-Pali, part-vernacular collection of narratives, has been limited to a translocal Pali text with literal Thai translation. The Pali original and the Thai translation are grammatically fixed. The text is standardized and not available in local scripts, and the verses and the narratives are separate. Moreover, both the 1972 and the 1987 editions, through their formatting, have changed the experience of reading the text. The verses are now printed in many modern editions in bold and formatted separately from the narratives (or bound as an edition without narratives). There is a table of contents separating the stories. English punctuation has been added, so there are quotation marks, paragraph breaks, parentheses, periods, and so on, copying Western editions of the text in roman font. Included in the standard printed editions are photographs of Bodhgaya and the stupa at the Mahāvihāra temple in Sri Lanka, and the cover of one edition is from a nineteenth-century Sri Lankan painting. The only way to know that this text is Thai is the script. The Dhammapada has been internationalized in Thailand. In manuscripts there was no way to know without reading through every story (or more likely listening to every story) where one story ended and the next began. There are no tables of contents, paragraph markers, punctuation, or font changes. Colophons provide little more than the ritual dedication, date, and title of the entire text, all according to local customs.

This internationalization is also reflected in new mediums used to teach the Dhammapada, especially the verses. First, there is a nightly television program called *Dhamma Samrap Brachachon*, which highlights Dhammapada verses and then gives literal Thai translations. There is no mention of the narratives. Also, ITV, one of Thailand's major television networks, ends its broadcast day with a picture of a Buddha image and soothing New Age music over which a Pali verse from the standard Dhammapada is given. This type of daily affirmation or chicken soup for the Buddhist non-soul style of presenting the Dhammapada valorizes and promotes the verses in Pali and removes them from the local tradition of teaching, binding, translating, and expanding on the text. Avant-garde dramas, like Patravadi Mejudhon's *The Buddhist Bible* (she uses an English title, although her play is in Thai), invoke verses from the canonical Dhammapada without touching on the commentarial verses. She told me she wanted Thais to see the true core of Buddha's word made accessible to the younger urban generation. She also reads the Dhammapada in English. There are also several Thai Web sites, most sponsored by university Buddhist study groups, which emphasize the centrality of the Dhammapada and promote its verses instead of the narrative commentaries. For example, Mahidol University study group uses verses from the Dhammapada, disconnected from their narratives, which it claims teaches students "the core truths" of Buddhism.[15] A Thai real estate company run by Luanchay Vongvanit has started the Dhammathai Web site in order to provide the "essence of Buddhism" in an accessible manner. The Web site provides the verses of the Dhammapada in English and Thai. There is no mention of the narratives. This is a massive change considering palm-leaf manuscripts rarely emphasized the verses.

Perhaps the best example of the changes that came with new printing technology, Western formats, and the growing internationalization of Buddhist literature is the Lao Young Buddhist Association's edition of the Dhammapada printed in 1973, two years before the communist takeover and in the middle of a civil war in Laos.[16] This book, which commemorates the eightieth birthday of the Lao Sangharāja, Somdet Phraphoutthajinorot (Thammayana Mahathera), is replete with photographs of the Lao royalty and the Sangharāja, and letters, in French and Lao, from Prince Souvanna Phouma, the Sangharāja, Bounthip Janthamontri (the secretary of the Young Buddhist Association), the French translators R. et M. Demaratray, and the Lao translator K. Viphakone. It also has roman-Lao script charts, an introduction, and a table of contents in English and Lao. The verses are presented in four languages, Pali, Lao, French, and English, and are printed on the same page for easy comparison. The source of the Dhammapada verses and the English translation is the Mahabodhi Society of India, under the supervision of the Sri Lankan monk Narada Mahathera and funded by the foundation of Paul Geuthner in Paris. As far as I have been able to tell, this was the only four-language Buddhist text published in Laos and the only multilingual edition of any Buddhist text in Laos. This text never became a part of the study of Buddhism by monastic students in Laos, and the text was not distributed en masse to schools. Indeed, I have never seen a copy in any monastic school library in Laos. I retrieved my copy from an expatriate Lao man in California. Its existence was a surprise to the staff at the National Library of Laos and the Sangha Monastic College of Vat Ong Teu. This unsuccessful quadri-lingual verse edition was not simply a victim of the communist revolution and the resulting decline of monastic education between 1975 and 1995, although that certainly was a negative factor, but it was also incongruous with Lao traditional approaches to the Dhammapada. As in modern Thailand, the interest in the "original" and "international" version of the Dhammapada verses has remained limited to the internationally oriented urban elite and has not entered into the daily curricula of monastic education. The original verses, the "Buddhist Bible," have had little commerce in monastic education past and present.

A Modern Dhammapada: Orality and Homiletics as History

The rise of the Dhammapada verses and the creation of standard editions of the verses and narratives would seem to indicate a massive shift in the modern period. This shift can seemingly be placed squarely on the shoulders of the West and its intellectually colonized royal and monastic admirers. However, neither the Lao nor the Thai simply copied the West, and nor do the apparent changes to the written text of the Dhammapada and *Dhammapada-atthakathā* reflect the continuities in pedagogical methods, examinations, and sermon giving.

Most Buddhist educational reforms have remained ideological, institutional, and relatively innocuous in the daily teaching of Buddhism in Thailand. The same can be said of changes in the instruction of the Dhammapada. Certainly, the text has been standardized and formatted differently. It was set in several editions of the canon. Still, the way the text is taught and its role in education have remained relatively intact.[17] One saw how the *atthakathā*, not the verses, are essential to the monastic examination taker. Therefore, there is little change here except for the institution of written examinations in 1913 (and in the 1930s under the French and 1990s under the Marxists in Laos) and the focus on standard and grammatically fixed editions of the narratives. Still, most laity, nuns, and monks do not take these examinations. In the introduction I related a story of my experiences in a monastic high school classroom in Savannakhet, Laos. Here stories from the *Dhammapada-atthakathā* serve as a font of terms and themes from which teachers draw for daily instruction. This is the way most monastic and lay students/audiences come into contact with the *Dhammapada-atthakathā*, through sermons and lectures at monastic schools or in sermon halls. These sermons are where the *nissaya* pedagogical method and the creative expansion and adaptation of the Dhammapada persist.[18]

The difficulty with studying the evolution of Buddhist texts in Thailand is that it is hard to define the nature of a text. I began my research comparing manuscript versions of the Dhammapada (which include *nissaya*, *vohāra*, *nāmasadda*, and verse-only and Pali-only narratives, the last two being rare and not widely circulated) to modern editions of the Dhammapada (Pali verses, Thai translations of the verses, editions of the *Dhammapada-atthakathā* used for examination preparation, and handbooks to the grammar of the *Dhammapada-atthakathā*). There was a great disconnect in content, medium, formatting, grammar, orthography, and rhetorical style. However, listening to sermons and attending monastic classes based on the Dhammapada or listening to teachers who invoked the Dhammapada (verses and narratives) to strengthen their point revealed a deep continuity between the premodern manuscripts and the modern sermons. The problem was comparing only one type of "text." If scholars compare only the palm-leaf manuscript versions of the Dhammapada (or any other text) to the modern printed editions of the Dhammapada (or any other text), then this reifies the common assumption that modern editions are simply newer manuscripts using a different medium. This is an easy assumption to make since most of the time scholars read palm-leaf manuscripts in transliterated printed form, or if they actually read the palm-leaf manuscript, it is from a copy made from a microfilm roll and read in French, British, Danish, Australian, Japanese, or American archives or in monastic libraries and national archives in Thailand, Laos, Sri Lanka, India, and so on. This reading is done seated alone under electric light attended by dictionaries, concordances, or CD-ROMs. The practice and experience of reading a printed text alone are mapped onto the experience of reading a palm-leaf manuscript. The size and paper and the clarity of the script seem to be the only difference. This is a very important part of textual and philological research, of which I am a practitioner, but it is not the only way to study texts. This experience and practice miss the fundamental orality and social experience in studying, listening to, worshipping, and teaching a palm-leaf manuscript. For many, the Dhammapada is not read in a text, but vibrates in the air between the sermon giver or lecturer and the audience. It was and is an aural/oral experience. The context in which the premodern Dhammapada manuscripts (especially the *nissaya* versions) were composed, copied, taught, and studied was oral and homiletic in nature. It was part of the ritual, meditational, and devotional life of a Lao and Thai Buddhist, as it remains so. Therefore, it is of limited value to compare premodern manuscripts used in educational settings to modern printed editions. Differences can be noted. Corrections to the past or to the present text can be made. Chronological textual stemma can be created. Judgments of textual integrity can be made. But to what end? What do any of these answers reveal about how Thais have read and taught these texts and how that has changed over time? What does one learn of appropriation? Of course, these endeavors are not useless. Indeed, I strongly aver that they are fundamental in the process of research. However, they are not adequate for tracing educational history and defining the contours of a Buddhist reading and teaching culture.

In order to trace the history of Buddhist education and the texts used in that education one must compare premodern manuscripts used as guides to sermons, lectures, and training (ritual, monastic, astrological, magical, and medicinal) to modern teacher handbooks, sermon guides, handwritten notebooks, audio/video-recorded sermons, and so forth. It would also help to compare these to student notebooks and textbooks. One needs to compare oral text to oral text—educational context to educational context. These texts are created for and in response to oral presentations, summaries, expansions, and adaptations of source texts, whether they are canonical, commentarial, vernacular, or classical. They exist is a group setting. They are cues to unwritten oral expansions and asides. They are responsive to contemporary events, personal biases, political agendas, idiosyncratic wonderings, and audience reactions. These encounters may float above the texts, but they are part of the history of Buddhist education.

By listening to sermons both in the city and at rural temples, reading transcripts of sermons delivered by monks all over the country, or attending classes at monastic high schools and grammar schools that teach the Dhammapada, one can see the creative reading, exegesis, expansion, and anthologizing of the Dhammapada witnesses in premodern manuscripts and through the *nissaya* method. In these sermons and lessons in the nonelite monastic schools and sermon halls, teachers most often do not work from a standard edition of the Dhammapada but instead tell stories from the *Dhammapada-atthakathā* and then lift words (*yok sab*) from the story and offer creative glosses and expanded oral narrative subcommentaries.

These sermons are becoming relatively standard as well. They can be purchased throughout the country in faux manuscript form. One popular sermon guide, the *Nithan Thammabot*, is published by Liang Chiang, but it is different from its other *mattatan* editions and those standard editions published by Mahamakut. It is an anthology of stories from the *Dhammapada-atthakathā*. Like premodern *nissaya*, the collected stories in this *Nithan Thammabot* edition are not identical to the canon. The creative *nissaya* method of presenting the Dhammapada stories orally lives on in this popular guide for sermon givers. Its shape mimics that of a palm-leaf manuscript and shows the importance of the traditional manuscript that is to be held when a monk gives a sermon (the text is the same width and length as a traditional palm-leaf manuscript and folded into a libretto book). The "feel" of a manuscript is maintained not only through size but also by weight, as the pages are made of stiff cardboard and make holding it similar to holding stiff palm leaf. There is also a space on the back of the text where the text's donor can write in his or her own name. Therefore, new colophons are being created every time this printed text is donated. It also comes in codex form as a two-volume set, but this version is not as popular for sermon givers. The title is misleading, as it is not all the "stories of the Dhammapada" (*nithan* [from the word for "story," not the Pali text *nidāna*] *thammabot* [Dhammapada]) but actually short introductions to some of the stories. In the beginning there are instructions on how to give a sermon based on these summaries and a selection of important terms. The text has twelve *phuk* or *kan* (Pali: *gaṇḍha*, English: fascicles). A list of techniques for giving sermons states that it is in the *vohāra* style, which is nearly identical to the *nissaya* style. Both the *nissaya* and *vohāra* methods use the *yok sab* technique of lifting Pali words and phrases from a canonical or extra-canonical source text / anthology (or a bank of Pali words and phrases in mind) and expanding on them orally with a high degree of repetition for emphasis and stylistic flow. It gives insight into the ways canonical texts are anthologized and taught in the modern period. Taught here are not the Dhammapada verses but only twelve selected and abbreviated stories from the *Dhammapada-atthakathā*. For example, the *Maṭṭhakuṇḍalīmāṇapa* story is introduced as being good for teaching on various occasions and is followed by the story of *Nāng Kālīyakṣinī*, which has the identical instructions on how to give a sermon. Here one sees that across the twelve *phuk* the stories that are chosen are mainly about the benefits of giving to the Sangha or about how listening to the dhamma cures disease and brings wealth. These were consistent themes in the *nissaya* Dhammapada(s). For the monk using the text, instructions on how to give a sermon are offered at the beginning of each *phuk*. Since the instructions are identical, it shows that the *phuk* can be used and shared separately from the set. This gives an indication as to why so many scattered and shared palm-leaf *phuk* are found in pre-modern Laos and Thailand. The instructions state that there are four techniques for giving a sermon: "[(1)] *sandassanā* is the sermon that helps the listener clearly understand that which is (true); (2) *samādapanā* is the adapting (drawing out / *nom nao*) of meaning in order to help the listener use the teachings in practice; (3) *samuttejanā* is giving the listener confidence and motivation in his or her practice; (4) *sampahansanā* is the instilling in the listener a sense of happiness, joy, hope, and enthusiasm."[19]

Following these techniques are the five objectives a preacher should have: "(1) offer the listener something he or she has never heard before; (2) help him or her understand more clearly things he or she has heard before; (3) help his or her doubt abate; (4) help him or her develop the right view (*khwām hen tūk tong*) according to the dhamma; (5) help them liberate their mind from confusion (in order to begin to lessen the power of *kilesa* [moral stains] and *taṇhā* [craving])."

Then the text provides explicit warnings and inspiration to the sermon giver:

> Before you [the sermon giver] begin this sermon on the stories of the Dhammapada in prose using the *vohāra* sermon style, [you should know that] this text uses modern vernacular colloquial language, but should be given properly as a sermon ought to be, because this is part of the world heritage of the wisdom of Buddhists. This is designed to draw out the dhamma and explain it clearly so that the audience will understand it easily and clearly. You should only speak for about twenty-five minutes. This sermon is important because it summarizes the main theme of each story. Its objective is to be convenient for the sermon giver and to be used easily in his teaching of essential information in accordance with the theme of the story. It supports the sermon giver by allowing him to use his own language [expressions, turns of phrases, accent] however he sees fit and in any way that facilitates learning and appreciation from the audience. This ensures that the dhamma penetrates and seeps into (*saek seum*) the listener and becomes part of his or her way of life. This is designed to

> sow the seeds of virtue in the heart and mind of the people so that the roots of virtue grow from the heart and mind. This will make each person and the whole society happy.[20]

Here one sees an example of what Jeffrey Samuels calls "attracting the heart" and how the stories from the Dhammapada are designed, in this text, to be adapted by and inspiring to the sermon giver.[21] The sermon giver must use the *vohāra* style as well as be attentive to the needs of his audience.[22] The text that is negotiated by the sermon giver and his or her reading exists somewhere in the space among the text, the reading, the teaching, and the reception—never stable, never alone on paper. Seeing this modern Dhammapada text and these premodern *nissaya* manuscripts as a sermon and lecture guides is essential to understanding how the vast majority of Lao and Thai teachers and students come in contact with the Dhammapada through reading and listening to *nissaya*-, *vohāra*-, and *nāmasadda*-style sermons and lectures.[23] The structural mechanisms of institutional adaptations and contested ideological reimaginings did not cause, in any significant way, the proximate mechanisms of pedagogical methods, rhetorical styles, or subject matter of Buddhist lessons to radically shift. Looking at the homiletic and pedagogical practices, one can see a deep continuity.

One sees that the teacher and the student transform, manipulate, and expand the core, and that is the core of their idiosyncratic reading/listening. This core is transformed to the degree that it is no longer a core or no longer from the canon. The idiosyncratically appropriated text, the sermon guide, the handbook, and the lifted series of terms are enough. The teacher's reading and the audience's reception are tantamount. The integrity of the original text (whatever that may be) is secondary. The core, whether a canonical or commentarial source, is an ever-shifting body of ideas and narratives. The forces of the core text and the forces of changing contexts, intentions, mediums, opinions, agendas, and abilities are always in play while reading and teaching. The source text and the text of the sermon guide cease to be simply texts, but become practices. Therefore, studying the Dhammapada is a study of shifting practices of circulation. The study of appropriation is part of a study of circulation. Studying a text's circulation and appropriation means studying shifting contexts and not just external sociohistorical contexts, not just ideological and institutional changes and contexts, but the personal and internal contexts (training, worldview, language skills, moods, epistemological approaches, etc.) of the sermon givers, students, and teachers.

8 Philosophical Embryology

Different Dhammapada have been used in a variety of ways in sermons and lectures. The content, verses, or commentarial narratives are used by different teachers in different mediums to communicate different messages. However, these are not the only ways texts are changed in the pedagogical process. Not only do content and format change, but the purported raison d'être of a text can be changed by teachers as well. For example, texts containing ethical lessons can be used for protective house blessings and chronicles can be used for grammar lessons. These changes are common. Often there is a disjuncture between the contents and the purposes of texts in monastic education. However, it is only a disjuncture if one values texts only for their semantic meaning and not for their usefulness in ritual transformation. In this chapter I offer one example of this disjuncture—the Abhidhamma. Different texts in the Abhidhamma genre have been used for funerary rites and for the magical generation of new ephemeral fetuses despite their semantic content. The *Nissaya atthakathā mātikā*, the *Abhidhamma chet kamphi*, and the *Abhidhammatthasaṅgaha* (three commentaries on the canonical Abhidhamma—the "philosophical" section of the Theravada Buddhist canon) offer instructions of how to ensure favorable rebirth through refined and ritually protected new fetuses.[1] In this way, in ritual and in the classroom, Buddhist philosophy moves from the realm of cerebral reflection, physical description, epistemological taxonomies, and ethical/psychological speculation to ritual technology and physical transformation. It demonstrates a unique way in which Abhidhamma texts are read, transformed, taught, and applied in matters of life and death by Southeast Asian Buddhists.

The Abhidhamma Genre

Scholars have long argued over the dating, canonical status, mode of compilation, method of recording, and provenance of the Abhidhamma. There is no doubt among practitioners that they represent the pinnacle of the Buddha's own insight into the complexity of the human mind. According to most scholarly and traditional descriptions of the Abhidhamma, there are seven sections (alternatively called "groupings," "treatises," or "volumes"), which are listed in different sequences depending on the school of Buddhism. These seven sections (*Dhammasaṅgaṇī*, *Vibhaṅga*, *Dhātukathā*, *Puggalapaññatii-pakaraṇa*, *Kathāvatthu*, *Yamaka*, and [*Mahā*]*paṭṭhāna*) comprise the third "basket" of the Tipiṭaka. These sections or groupings were most likely compiled over several centuries by a diverse group of commentators. Traditional accounts (found in manuscripts and still found in most major introductory textbooks) state that the Buddha proclaimed the seven sections while residing in the Tāvatiṃsa heaven over a period of three months. The Buddha's audience for this exposition was his mother and the worlds of the deities.

The seven sections are characterized by long taxonomic lists that cover a wide range of subjects generally relating to the relationships between the sense receptors, emotions, mental states, analytical modes, physical elements, the nature of perception, and conditional relationships between thought, sense, and action and the genesis and result of these conditional relationships. They also include early Buddhist debates, the refutation of various opinions, and specific commentaries on passages from other sections of the Tipiṭaka. Quite simply, these massive tomes attempt to describe in detail the psychological nature of the individual and to link that nature to virtuous/non-virtuous actions and soteriological potentials. Their mastery, if possible, is a mark of intellectual, ethical, and social prestige for teachers and students.

The content of these sections has been the subject of commentary and debate in Southeast Asia. Commentaries composed or transmitted in Burma, Laos, and Thailand include the *Atthasālinī*, *Mohavicchedanī*, *Sammohavinodanī*, *Gūḷhatthadīpanī*, *Pañcappakaraṇaṭṭhakathā*, *Līnatthavaṇṇanā*, *Abhidhhammāvatāra*, *Abhidhammatthasaṅgaha*, *Maṇisāramañjūsā*, *Nāmarūpa-pariccheda*, and *Saccasaṅkhepa*, among others. Not surprisingly, considering the content of the seven source texts, none of these commentaries includes instructions on how to generate ephemeral fetuses. None promotes the recitation of Abhidhamma texts at cremation ceremonies or states that individual syllables from the Abhidhamma can be used for ritual protection. However, despite the content of the Abhidhamma and its major commentaries, Lao and Thai monastic teachers have used the Abhidhamma in just these ways. An education on the Abhidhamma in Laos and Thailand is an education not only on the ethical and mental nature of the individual but also on ritual birth and death.[2]

Mātikā/Matrix/Mother

I first came across the ritual and embryological way of reading Buddhist philosophy while translating a palm-leaf manuscript of the *Nissaya atthakathā mātikā* (*Nissaya* on the Commentary of the *mātikā* of the Abhidhamma) composed in 1569 in Northern Thailand.[3] Assuming that I was going to translate a commentary on the first section of the canonical Abhidhamma, I was immediately struck by the strange use of language and the abbreviated structure. This text could not possibly have been a useful commentary for instructing monks and laity on philosophy or psychology. The *mātikā* is the first part of the Abhidhamma. It establishes the subjects for the Abhidhamma's description of the mind's intentions, influences, and moral and immoral tendencies. It is a "table of contents" of sorts that seeks to establish the important subjects for those beginning a study of higher Buddhist philosophy of mind. I figured the commentary would quickly move from the discussion of this table of contents to the actual content of the Abhidhamma. However, the commentary remained at the level of the table and seemed to be more of a technical vocabulary lesson than a work of philosophical analysis. I later discovered that this vocabulary was essential, not only for explaining (often orally) the nature of the senses, intentions, and so on, but also for creating a ritual fetus.

The choice of the *mātikā* itself is strange for a commentator.[4] Its contents are simply short phrases and terms. There is no explanation of the terms. There are no pronouns, speakers, narrative, and so forth. Despite the contents, however, the *mātikā* of the *Dhammasaṅgaṇī* (the first book of the Abhidhamma) is one of the most important parts of any text in the Theravada

Buddhist canon. As K. R. Norman states "The *mātikā* is an outline of a universal system of classification comprising the whole analytical teaching of the Buddha . . . the greater part of the *Dhammasaṅgaṇī* is an expansion of the *mātikā*."[5] Shwe Zan Aung stated in 1908 that in Burma the *mātikā* was "considered by scholars as indispensable to the study of the remaining six books. The importance of the digest [*mātikā*] may be inferred from the fact that there are no less than six Burmese *Akauks* ([vernacular] analytic works) on it."[6] The *Atthasālinī* on the *Dhammasaṅgaṇī* was the earliest major commentary composed by Buddhaghosa.[7] The *mātikā*, the *Dhammasaṅgaṇī*, and Buddhaghosa's *Atthasālinī* (followed by the commentary on the *paritta*) have been the subject of numerous commentaries and subcommentaries, of which the 1569 Northern Thai *nissaya* is one of the latest premodern examples.[8] The *Mohavicchedanī* was written only on the *mātikā*. Oskar von Hinüber shows how the *mātikā* permeates and structures every section of the *Dhammasaṅgaṇī*.[9] This would make the *mātikā* summary and study guide for the Abhidhamma more than an introduction or "table of contents," as Caroline Rhys-Davids translated the term.[10]

The *mātikā* is a list of terms useful for memorizing the text and commentaries, and translations of it are guides to explaining certain basic terms that are essential for understanding the complex psychological analyses of the *Dhammasaṅgaṇī* and the Abhidhamma as a whole.[11] This outline was designed, as Aung states, to be "elaborated by a later genius on the line laid down by Him [Buddha]."[12] *Nissaya* often work in the same way, isolating and repeating terms seemingly to serve as triggers and guides for those giving a sermon or teaching a class—rendering the *mātikā* a platform on which a teacher could create his own speech. When I first read through the *Nissaya atthakathā mātikā*, I was struck by the way the author would repeat over and over certain terms but not translate them. By seeing the *mātikā* as a lexical foundation on which expansions are based, the repetition of important and powerful terms makes perfect sense. The author of the *Nissaya* would have wanted to emphasize the terms in the *mātikā* through repetition, rather than translation, because his students would have needed to be familiar with these technical terms if they were to comprehend any teaching based on material from the Abhidhamma. Pe Maung Tin, in the preface to the English translation of the *Atthasālinī*, referred to these as "word definitions . . . very tedious (and sometimes pointless) to a Western scholar [but they] are all-important to the Buddhist student, who must know the meanings of conceptual terms before he can grasp ultimate truths."[13] However, it is not just the semantic meanings that unlock ultimate truths. They are triggers for expanding on the terms for the purpose of giving a sermon or examples in grammar lessons or for chanting the text from memory. They are also transformative ritual terms used in constructing an ephemeral fetus. The *nidāna* of the *Atthasālinī* states that the Buddha declared the *mātikā* foreseeing that 218 years after his death Tissathera (a commentator) would expand on the text according to the order laid down by the *mātikā*. Therefore, as the text states in several places, the *mātikā* would be "endless and immeasurable."

The most recent study of the *mātikā* tradition, by Rupert Gethin, offers an intriguing and convincing suggestion that the *mātikā* should be seen as a "matrix" or "mother" (which follows the actual etymology of the term, from the Sanskrit—*mātṛkā*). *Mātikā* can be translated as "having the qualities of a mother." Gethin notes that the "translators of Buddhist texts have often taken the word to mean something like 'summary' or 'condensed content' . . . it is the underlying meaning of 'mother' that seems to inform the use of the term here. A *mātikā* is seen not so much as a condensed summary, as the seed from which something grows. A *mātikā* is something creative—something out of which something further evolves. It is, as it were, pregnant with Dhamma."[14] Gethin cites a passage from Kassapa of Cola, the composer of the *Mohavicchedanī*, who writes, "In what sense it is a *mātikā*? In the sense of being like a mother. For a *mātikā* is like a mother as a face is like a lotus. For mother gives birth to various different sons, and then looks after them and brings them up, so a *mātikā* gives birth to many different dhamma and meanings, and then looks after them and brings them up so that they do not perish."[15] This *Nissaya atthakathā mātikā* manuscript from Northern Thailand, and *nissaya* in general, works very much like this matrix. Teachers based lectures on the gloss of terms from a Pali source text. These terms and their glosses would be expanded on in oral performance. Therefore, every teacher could add to the matrix of terms as he saw fit, thus making the chosen set of terms a deep, if not bottomless, font of subject headings in which to creatively expand. The composer of the *nissaya* saw their work as giving birth to many different dhamma and meanings. Now one can see why it would not be strange to employ the Abhidhamma as ritual text to create new ephemeral fetuses. Today in Laos, and most Lao monks tell me it has been the same as far as they or their teachers could remember, the *mātikā* is chanted at funerals alongside other texts. In many ritual handbooks printed in modern Laos the *mātikā* is included as a quick reference to monks preparing for funeral recitation.[16] Here the *mātikā* is a mother who magically creates new bodies.

Lifting Syllables: The *Abhidhamma chet kamphi* and Funerary Rites

The most obvious time to construct a new fetus is at a funeral. Death demands new birth. A knowledge of the foundational "motherlike" words from which the entire Theravada Buddhist philosophical complex arises enables a teacher not only to transmit information about the nature of thought, desire, sensory perception, emotion, and intention but also to create new life. This is explicitly seen in another genre of Abhidhamma commentaries—the *Abhidhamma chet kamphi*. The *Abhidhamma chet kamphi* (Seven Books of the Abhidhamma) is a genre of texts well known by both the elite and the common people in Laos and Thailand. There are several versions, of which no comparative study has been done. The text was most likely composed long before the eighteenth century, and few copies have survived.

The title *Seven Books of the Abhidhamma* is misleading, as this text does not contain the entire seven volumes of the Abhidhamma. I consulted several palm-leaf and modern pulp-printed paper editions of this text, of which I discuss three in particular here. The first is a palm-leaf manuscript from 1771, composed at Wat Sung Men in Phrae (present-day Northern Thailand). This manuscript is the longest and most detailed version: four fascicles composed in Thai Yuan script. It states that the text can be transmitted in four different ways: (1) "adhi," or perhaps "originally" or verbatim; (2) "attha," or for its "core meaning"; (3) "desanā," or as a sermon; or (4) "paṭivedha," or exegetically interpreted for its underlying meaning. The wise, it is said, understand the words of the Buddha in all four ways. The Buddha himself gave a sermon in the heavenly realms in this manner. He meant it to be understood on multiple levels, and the deities could understand the deepest (Pali: *gambhīra*) meanings. The text starts by relating the story of the Buddha residing near Benares with five disciples. It then moves on to discuss the first time the Buddha orally delivered the seven books of the Abhidhamma to his mother and to the gods and goddesses in the Heavenly realm (*devaloka*). From this story it moves on to offer the first few verses from each book of the Abhidhamma in Pali, followed by a short (often only a few words) gloss in Northern Thai (Yuan). Many verses are skipped, and some are only partially cited.

It is difficult to determine how this text was used. The verses could have been used as triggers to signal the recitation of the entire Abhidhamma, or recitation of these sections could ritually be used to represent the entire corpus. The selected verses are sequentially connected and could be timely reminders to teachers of the entire seven books. This text rarely glosses words into the vernacular, but instead simply uses the vernacular to separate the Pali words and remind the reader of his or her place in the recitation. Occasionally the vernacular explains what that section of the text is about. For example, a short section in the third fascicle explains that the *nāyamātikā* of the *Dhātukathā* regards the division of the *khandha* that make up the human person. Still, most of the manuscript is in Pali. This text was most likely designed to be a guide to a reciter as opposed to a sermon giver. The emphasis on the Pali verses, the lack of glossing, and the minimal exegetical comments suggest a manuscript designed to teach students how to chant the Abhidhamma. Many of the verses are close to or identical to those cited in the standard Thai *Royal Chanting Book*.

The Royal Chanting Book (*Suat mon chabab luang*) has been the main text used for decades by monks chanting at rituals. It has been in print since 1878 and has appeared in sixteen editions. Although first distributed only in Bangkok, it is now available throughout the country and can be found in most monasteries (although some rural monasteries I have been to do not possess a copy). There is a translation of the Pali in Thai, and several different publishers have produced the book in hard- and softcover. However, this handbook for monks has only recently included a section titled "Abhidhamma." In the early twentieth century, the chanting book contained little more than the standard seven or twelve *paritta* texts common throughout the Theravada world. However, the recent editions include a whole range of Pali verses drawn from both canonical and noncanonical texts that are used in everyday Buddhist ceremonies. These new sections have been added because they are common throughout the country, and the book has expanded to include a fuller range of texts used by monks at rituals. The "Abhidhamma" section is simply seven paragraphs, each containing the first few lines of each of the seven books. There are some minor changes that make the texts more suitable for chanting. For example, the *Dhammasaṅgaṇī* section begins with the first triad of the *mātikā*, before moving to the beginning of the first chapter of the main text, the *Kāmāvacarakusala* of the *Cittuppādakaṇḍa*. Similar minor changes are seen in the other sections. These sections are repetitive and lend themselves well to melodious and easily memorized passages for recitation. For example, a section from the last book of the Abhidhamma, the *Mahāpaṭṭhāna*, reads,

> hetupaccayo ārammaṇapaccayo adhipatipaccayo anantarapaccayo samantarapaccayo aññamaññapaccayo nissayapaccayo upanissayapaccayo purejātapaccayo pacchājātapaccayo āsevanapaccayo kammapaccayo vipākapaccayo āhārapaccayo indriyapaccayo jhānapaccayo maggapaccayo sampayuttapaccayo vippayuttapaccayo atthipaccayo natthipaccayo vigatapaccayo avigatapaccayoti.

This passage is simply a list of the main "relations" or "causal conditions" (*paccaya*) to which a human being is subject. Twenty-four are enumerated and expanded on in the *Mahāpaṭṭhāna*. According to Abhidhamma teachings, life can be reduced to conditions (actions, sense objects, association, disassociation, dependence, practice, previous birth, etc.). That a life is no more than these conditions would be a sobering, but timely, subject at a funeral. The seven short passages of the "Abhidhamma" section are useless on their own. To an untrained ear, they would simply be a list of similar sounding words. They either have to be expanded on in oral vernacular commentary or listened to, not for their semantic meaning, but for their meritorious power at the time of death. They are most often chanted at a funeral in Pali only, and then the words are lifted and used as the basis for a vernacular sermon after the funeral. The sermon, however, is not necessary; only the Pali recitation is. Sermons at funerals are not necessarily connected to, or even mention, the texts chanted. These sections from the seven books mirror those cited in the *Abhidhamma chet kamphi* manuscript from 1771 Phrae. This usage is not limited to Phrae, however. These sections were commonly chanted (especially at funerals) in this form in Laos and Northern and Central Thailand for over 230 years.[17]

This text could have been used as a teacher's guide to help students chant the *Abhidhamma mātikā* and to explain to them in brief the sections that they were chanting. It could have also been used by a teacher to explain the nature of the Abhidhamma to beginners who may have asked what they were chanting. It also could have been the basis of a vocabulary lesson on the nature of birth, development, and death. I imagine the text was used in all these ways, as it is today throughout the country. Sections of the Abhidhamma, especially from the *Dhammasaṅgaṇī*, are the common texts chanted at funerals. In modern times the Pali sections of the *Abhidhamma chet kamphi* are only chanted, and the actual Abhidhamma source text is not chanted. These verses are chanted while monks stand in front of the funeral pyre (*sut na fai*). Sections from the longer *Abhidhammatthasaṅgaha*, discussed below, are often chanted at the beginning of the funeral. This chanting is done in Pali, which the vast majority of laypeople and monks cannot understand. However, the semantic meaning of the chanting matters little compared to its powerful ritual value. Funerals are perhaps the most common and frequent times for public Pali chanting in Thailand and are occasions when large groups of laypeople come in contact with monks. The Abhidhamma is one of the most commonly heard and least understood texts.

Another manuscript, quite different from the *Abhidhamma chet kamphi* from Phrae, brings one closer to an understanding of the connection between philosophy and fetuses.[18] Instead of citing verses sequentially, this manuscript only cites the titles of the books of the Abhidhamma and then links those titles to parts of the mind and body. Rather than serve as a guide to the reciter or teacher trying to briefly explain the main contents of the Abhidhamma, it is designed to be a ritual guide to the text. However, despite this difference, it is also used at funerals. This manuscript is titled the *Abhidhamma chet kamphi ruam*. Like the Phrae manuscript it has Pali and Northern Thai sections. It draws Pali terms from the Abhidhamma and breaks them down into syllables to be used in protective incantations and to connect the sounds of the words to particular parts of the body. One particularly interesting example for the purposes here is that given by the breakdown of the word *Dhamma-*

saṅgaṇī. It begins, "*San* [from *Dhamma-SAN-gani*] . . . It refers to the thirty-three factors of the mind in the *Dhammasaṅgaṇī*. *San* was in the right side of the first man for seven days. Then, departing from the left side, it entered the womb of the first woman through the top of her head. . . . *i* [final vowel of *Dhammasaṅgaṇī*] became the waist [of the first child]." In nineteenth-century versions of this text these syllables are associated with the body of the Buddha and with gaining the Buddha's power and protection. Today these syllables are still important for chanting a protective incantation. For example, *Vi* from *Vibhaṅga* is traditionally associated with a drop of sesame oil that was on the tail of a deer at the beginning of time. This drop of oil, through processes represented by the five other syllables, eventually led to the formation of the ideal human body. Without this body neither the Buddha nor any other human being would have come into existence. Therefore, the seven books of the Abhidhamma are directly connected to the first human being. When chanting these books (made easy by chanting only the first syllables), the body is protected and released from suffering. Each of these syllables relates to a specific form of bodily protection. For example, *san* of the *Dhammasaṅgaṇī* is related to the "eye." Therefore, if a person who is born or dies on a Sunday chants or hears the *Dhammasaṅgaṇī*, he or she will be protected from "demerit accrued through the eye [faculty of sight]."[19] He or she will then have a good rebirth in a heavenly realm. If a person is born or dies on a Monday, the *Vibhaṅga* should be chanted, and so on. One version of this text states that if a monk does not know the seven books of the Abhidhamma (presumably through the syllables), he will go to hell after he dies and will be considered a "fool" by the Buddha. This helps one to understand why lifting and explaining (or chanting) words from the *mātikā* was so important in the 1569 and 1771 manuscripts examined above. This vocabulary was invoked ritually to protect the body at the time of death and to ensure a favorable rebirth facilitated by a newly created fetus. Here vocabulary from the Abhidhamma is broken down into syllables. This emphasis on the syllables of the Abhidhamma book titles is also expanded into other syllables related to the thirty-two parts of the ideal human body, the five *khandha*, and the five elements (water, earth, fire, wind, and atmosphere). They are connected to persistent ideas in Southeast Asian Theravada Buddhism of the relationship between the human body and the words spoken by the Buddha. They are also related to the origin of humankind and the protection of the body in this world and the next.

At a funeral, chanting the syllables helps guide the body, whether born on Sunday, Monday, or so on, to a good rebirth. This is also related to a little known funerary custom where monks write the four syllables on a small piece of paper. These stand for the four major subjects of the Abhidhamma (as outlined in the *Abhidhammatthasaṅgaha*): "ci" for *citta* (mind), "ce" for *cetasika* (mental factors or concepts), "ru" for *rūpa* (material form), and "ni" for *nibbana*. This piece of paper with the four syllables is placed inside the corpse's mouth to guide the dead person to a favorable rebirth.[20] These four subjects, because they were important for chanting or at least abbreviating at funerals, became standard to study in the major monasteries of Bangkok. Also common is for sections of the Abhidhamma to be chanted as monks walk alongside the corpse as it is being taken for cremation. Of course, this is all nominally related to the belief that the Buddha himself chanted the entire Abhidhamma in the Tāvatiṃsa heaven to his mother after her earthly death. The Abhidhamma is certainly not just useful for teaching Buddhist "philosophy" or psychology.

The last *Abhidhamma chet kamphi* version I look at here is published by Liang Jiang in Bangkok. There have been several printings, the most recent in 2001. The first seven sections have the titles of the seven volumes of the canonical Abhidhamma. These are not short summaries of the contents of these canonical texts, as I first suspected, but actually a short narrative of when the Buddha preached the contents originally, followed by the first three lines of the canonical text and then followed by an explanation of some of the important terms in the text. At the beginning of each section are also sermon instructions to the monk using this text. Then the syllables representing the seven books are given. The text is sold in modern Thailand to those who want to donate it to monasteries at the time of a funeral. This manuscript is a blend of the first two. It is a guide to a preacher and briefly explains the main contents of the seven books of the Abhidhamma in vernacular. These explanations are initiated by the first Pali verses of each of the seven books.

The chanting of syllables from the Abhidhamma is also common at Lao Buddhist funerals. The consistency of these practices has been well documented and is now established in print in numerous Lao monastic guidebooks known as *Ku meu Pasong-Samanen*, which are found at monasteries throughout Laos. These guidebooks have sections called the *Abhidhamma chet kamphi* that list the seven short recitations to be chanted at funerals.[21] In Laos and parts of Northern Thailand, these syllables are directly related to parts of the body. In Laos, in particular, the seven texts are also associated with animals, which in turn protect the parts of the body. For example, the *Dhammasaṅgaṇī* is connected to the eye, which is protected by the rhinoceros; the *Dhātukathā* is connected to the nose, which is protected by the tiger; and the *Mahāpaṭṭhāna* is connected to the internal organs, which are protected by the lion, and so on. This system of connecting syllables to the sense organs, parts of the body and mind, and even protective animals has been a central feature of Abhidhamma teaching and learning in the region for over four hundred years and seems to have been particularly prevalent in teaching the Abhidhamma in Laos.

A connection also is made between protective *yantra* ("mystical or esoteric" drawings that incorporate syllables) and incantations drawn from the Abhidhamma and funeral rites. Bizot and Lagirarde note that the syllables from the title of the Abhidhamma are essential for drawing *yantra* (usually by placing the syllables in circles) as well as for recitation at a funeral. They write, "The recitation of the Abhidhamma at the moment of death is indispensable for giving birth to the new body." The seven syllables marking the seven books of the Abhidhamma, "sam [for Dhamma-SAM-gani], vi, dhaa, pu, ka, ya, pa," he states, "mark the beginning of the development of the fetus through the production of the mental faculties . . . the seven books are pronounced at the time of death[;] these books are the *mātikā*, or the mother, that enable rebirth."[22] Here, they show the connections among syllables (often placed inside drawn circles on *yantra*) of the Abhidhamma, the body, the senses, and death. This connection is seen in the rituals described in the *Saddavimala*, a text that was very popular in the nineteenth century in Laos. Here, the titles of the seven texts of the Abhidhamma are chanted to create an ephemeral fetus. These texts offer instructions for a creation ritual in which the seven syllables of the seven books of the Abhidhamma are chanted.[23] Another Cambodian ritual observed by Bizot in the 1970s takes place in a cave, which is a simulacrum of a womb. In the ritual, the syllables of the Abhidhamma are chanted. The books of the Abhidhamma are said to be connected to the navel of a woman. The way to access the womb and unlock its generative powers is through meditation, especially the control of the breath. After associating different parts of the body with different Pali syllables, each participant takes part in ensuring a successful rebirth.[24]

Perhaps the most radical example of the disconnect between the content of the Abhidhamma and the use of the text is seen in the illuminated manuscript tradition of Central Thailand (Siam). Here, there are thousands of beautifully illuminated extant manuscripts that contain the text of the *Abhidhamma chet kamphi* or short excerpts from the opening sections of each of the seven sections in Khom script. The text is not surprising, but the illumination is. The paintings are most often depictions of the ten birth tales (*Dasajātaka*), the *Phra Malai* story, or the *Vessantara jātaka*, but the text written between the paintings on each leaf of the manuscript is from the Abhidhamma (most often the *mātikā* of the *Dhammasaṅgaṇī and* the *Vibhaṅga*, or the short seven sections of the *Abhidhamma chet kamphi*). One would assume that the text (often in Khom script) and the paintings are on the same subject. To have a manuscript whose text and illumination have nothing to do with each other seems counterintuitive. It would be like the text of Saint Thomas Aquinas's *Summa theologica* with illuminations of the nativity of Christ. However, it makes sense if one understands that the most common event at which to offer gifts of manuscripts is the funeral. The ten *jātaka*, the most popular of the birth stories of the Buddha, offer guidance on how to live a meritorious life and ensure rebirth as a bodhisattva or even a future Buddha. The *Phra Malai* story, which is sometimes depicted alone or as an addendum to the *jātaka*, is about a monk who visits various hells and heavens and speaks of life after death. The Abhidhamma is the text most often chanted at a funeral. So while the text's invocation (although not necessarily its message) is essential for the ritual creation of a new life, the illumination is important to guide a sermon on the proper life and the possibility of enlightenment in future lives. Therefore, even if a monk could not read Khom script and/or Pali and simply memorized the ritual chanting of the *Abhidhamma chet kamphi* or *mātikā*, he could offer a vernacular sermon on the *jātaka* aided by the paintings of the stories. The most common title for these manuscripts is *Mahābuddhaguṇa* (The Great Qualities of the Buddha), which is seemingly vague enough to represent texts taken from the Abhidhamma and illuminations from the *jātaka* and the *Phra Malai* story. Here, the manuscript, both image and text, can be used as a trigger for sermons that are appropriate ritually and ethically at the time of death.[25]

In short, the epistemological understanding of the Abhidhamma as esoteric and spiritual mother arises from the same approach to knowing what the Abhidhamma actually means. It is not only informative and descriptive; it is also transformative and protective. It is necessary, not just for being a well-educated student of Buddhism, but also for the amelioration and ultimate liberation of one's mind and body. The connection seen between the *Abhidhamma chet kamphi* from 1771, the nineteenth-century illuminated manuscripts of the *jātaka*, and the modern Liang Jiang version from Bangkok is rooted in an understanding throughout the region of the Abhidhamma as a life-giving mother. It was important, then and now, for monks to understand the grammar, the words, and the syllables in order to help the laity at the time of death, to put their training to practical and existential use. As one can see, there are fundamental continuities in the epistemological approach to the Abhidhamma and the way it has been taught in Thailand despite the changes brought by modernity to the study and teaching of Buddhism.

Memory Circles: The Abhidhamma Jotika's Guidebook

The way the Abhidhamma is taught and used in rituals in Thailand is diverse, but one can certainly see continuity from the past to the present despite massive institutional changes, state control of the Sangha, printing technology, canonization, and so-called Western influence. One can also see continuity in pedagogical methods unaffected by centralization and reform. This continuity is clearly observed in this last example that I give of an Abhidhamma text. It is a modern handbook used at the Abhidhamma Jotika College of Mahachulalongkorn Monastic University. One of the most basic and popular textbooks is the *Handbook for the Study of the Abhidhamma* (*Khu meu kanseuksa Phra Abhidhamma chan chulabhidhammikatri*) by Phra Platawisut Kuttachayo.[26] It is a study of the *Abhidhammasaṅgaha*, the most ubiquitous summary on the entire Abhidhamma in Buddhist Southeast Asia. The *mātikā* and *Abhidhamma chet kamphi* are not the only types of Abhidhamma text chanted or used in funerary rites. The *Abhidhammasaṅgaha*, a twelfth-century Pali commentary on the Abhidhamma, has long been associated with funerals in Thailand. The *Abhidhammasaṅgaha*, or at least the *si na* (four subjects), is chanted at the beginning of the funerary rites, when the corpse has yet to be removed from the home.[27] The *Abhidhamma chet kamphi* is chanted at the time of the actual cremation. These subjects were important to study not only at elite royal monasteries, as is seen in monastic university textbooks as early as 1926 (this is the earliest copy I could find; however, the textbook was probably first printed in 1912), but also in rural Northern Thailand, as evidenced by their connection to a ceremony in 1569 that neither the rich nor poor can avoid.

The first seven chapters of the handbook contain a study guide to the *cetasika* (a group of mental factors) outlined in the first part of the *mātikā*. The final section of the handbook is drawn from a standard modern biology textbook that describes the process of procreation and birth. This section comes complete with detailed drawings of fetal development, the umbilical cord, the uterus, and so forth. Here, ovulation, chromosomes, and spermatozoa are mentioned as the origin of the process that leads to sense faculties, mental formations, perception, and other cognitive events based loosely on the five *khandha* and the *paṭiccasamuppāda*. The process of death is connected to the process of life both cognitively and physically. This handbook describes the cognitive and physical evolution from life to death. Obviously, the original *Abhidhammasaṅgaha* has been long abandoned by the end of the handbook. However, this final chapter relates to the *Abhidhamma chet kamphi*'s use at funerals to ensure a good rebirth. In fact, the guide to chanting the Abhidhamma at a funeral is taken not directly from the canonical Abhidhamma but from the *Abhidhammasaṅgaha*. The syllables representing the four central terms of the *Abhidhammasaṅgaha* are those placed in the mouth of the corpse. Moreover, the introduction to the Thai-script edition of the nine chapters of the *Abhidhammasaṅgaha* explicitly connects this commentary to funerals and to the death of the Buddha's mother. The introduction states that the Abhidhamma "contains teachings that ordinary men cannot easily understand"; therefore, the *Abhidhammasaṅgaha* is chanted instead. Short sections are often heard at funerals instead of canonical passages. The

Abhidhamma Jotika's guide to the *Abhidhammasaṅgaha* is designed not only to teach the Abhidhamma in brief but also to help monks understand the basis of their chanting at funerals. This handbook is also associated with the different versions of the *Abhidhamma chet kamphi* through its use of syllables. These are the primary pedagogical methods of the text, and they form the basis of examinations on this handbook.

The handbook emphasizes the syllables of the core text. First, one of the first verses from the *Abhidhammasaṅgaha* (*Gantharambhakathā* in the *Cittaparicchedа* of the *Bhūmibhedacittam* section) is cited: "Tattha cittaṃ tāva catubbidhaṃ hoti kāmāvacaraṃ rūpāvacaraṃ arūpāvacaraṃ lokuttarañceti mīmāṃsā" (First, therefore, mind is fourfold: the mental abode that is characterized by desire, the mental abode that is characterized by material form, the mental abode that is characterized by formlessness, the supramundane mental abode"). This passage is translated into Thai literally (although the Thai translation does not note that kāmāvacaraṃ, rūpāvacaraṃ, and arūpāvacaraṃ also refer to cosmological realms). From there, this one verse is expanded and each of the four abodes of the mind is broken down. When I say "broken down," I do not mean "explained." The term *citta* is followed by a list of six *citta* in Palized Thai (*akusalacit, ahetukacit, kāmāvacarasobhaṇacit, rūpāvacaracit, arūpāvacaracit,* and *lokuttaracit*: "unwholesome mind" (or "consciousness"), "causeless mind," "wholesome mind characterized by senses," "mind characterized by material form," "mind characterized by formlessness," and "supramundane mind").

Each term from this list is further broken down into a list of three or four terms, each according to their ethical import. For example, the term *akusalacit* (unwholesome mind) is broken down into eight types of mind characterized by greed, two types of mind characterized by delusion, and two types of mind characterized by hatred. The last member of the first list (*lokuttaracit* / supramundane mind) is further broken down into two lists, each with four members. The first list is of the well-known four paths of a nearly enlightened being (stream-enterer, once-returner, non-returner, and *arahat*). The second list is of the well-known four fruits (ends of the four paths) of enlightenment. There is little surprise here for a student of the *Abhidhammasaṅgaha*. After these lists are established, each member of the list is further broken down into its member's first syllables.[28]

Their first syllables in Pali are *so, sam, a; so, sam, sa; so, vip, a; so, vip, sa; u, sam, a; u, sam, sa; u, vip, a; u, vip, sa.* These syllables are then placed in drawn circles divided into three sections. These circles are placed in a row and then placed in alternative assemblages. They are shuffled around like billiard balls. These syllables in circles are reminiscent of *yantra* mystical drawings, common in the region for use in protective rites. They are useful as mnemonic triggers but also for training in the epistemological and technical foundation of protective incantations and for the practical act of transforming a dead body into a new ephemeral body reborn into a new life. These syllables are important not just as signs of longer words but also as symbols of conceptual ways of approaching the contents and power of the Abhidhamma as life giving. For this reason, the handbook not only abbreviates the words of the Abhidhamma (as summarized in the *Abhidhammsaṅgaha*) associated with the mystical syllables placed inside the mouth of a corpse, chanted at funerals, or drawn on *yantra*, but it also has a chapter describing the biological processes of birth. The Abhidhamma is the mother that bears new children.

This handbook is a modern repository of pedagogical techniques and rhetorical approaches that were used as early as the sixteenth century in Thailand. Just as the *Abhidhamma chet kamphi* is used to chant at funerals, the Abhidhamma Jotika handbook is used to help students learn the major Pali terms for sermon giving and funeral chanting. The students are given a basic list of terms and clauses from which to expand on orally. They use the syllable method to memorize these verses or groups of verses. These verses serve as the basis for chanting these sections of the text and also can be used as triggers for vernacular exegesis in a sermon. The students are tested on their ability to memorize these syllables; however, in practice, they need to be able both to chant the initial verses of all seven books of the Abhidhamma and to offer sermons explaining their import to nuns, monks, and the laity at funerals. The process of memorizing the syllables in the circles, although not explicitly taught in connection to drawing *yantra*, most likely grew out of a long tradition of memorizing, chanting, and drawing syllables for the sake of protective rituals. The ritual to create a new fetus specifically involves the Abhidhamma's syllables. This tradition is seen most clearly in the inclusion of biological sketches describing the development of an actual fetus in the Abhidhamma handbook. In order to create an ephemeral fetus, one needs to understand how a biological fetus develops.[29] This text is a perfect example of how "Western" science has been incorporated relatively seamlessly in Buddhist notions of birth and death. Both are seen as true and not as mutually exclusive.

At first glance the versions of the *Abhidhamma chet kamphi* and the Abhidhamma Jotika handbook for the *Abhidhammasaṅgaha* are so different in form that they would seem to confirm the general scholarly consensus that there was a massive rupture between the premodern and modern worlds of Buddhist education in the region. Physically, the texts are on palm leaf in Yuan or Tham script, on cardboard libretto, and in modern paper-pulp codex. The Abhidhamma Jotika draws on modern biology textbooks to explain some Abhidhamma concepts and is replete with scientific sketches of the ovaries and spermatozoa. Institutionally, the 1569 manuscript of the *Nissaya atthakathā mātikā* from Phrae was taught unsystematically in various independent Northern monasteries and did not form part of an official, royally sponsored curriculum that was aimed at passing state examinations. The Abhidhamma Jotika handbook is an official textbook used at the central monastic university and at many participating Abhidhamma education centers. The *Abhidhamma chet kamphi* is a sermon and ritual guide for funeral rites, which are neither nationally consistent nor monitored. These texts were composed at different times in different scripts in different regions by monks in very different institutional settings. However, rhetorical features and pedagogical methods tie these texts together and reflect a regional epistemological approach to studying, teaching, and ritually using the Abhidhamma. These texts do not see the contents of the seven volumes of the Abhidhamma as the sole reason for studying these texts. Ritual is also important. Rituals are often seen as governed by texts. Ritual in this case creates new texts. Furthermore, commentaries are given equal value to canonical texts. Individual terms and syllables can be used as bases for rituals, grammatical lessons, and sermons. The canonicity, completeness, and interpretation of the Abhidhamma are secondary. Finally, these texts are also linked because they are all designed as written guides to oral exposition and cannot be understood outside their performative use. Abhidhammic rituals bridge the study of Buddhist philosophy and embryology. Philosophy, in this case, does not simply describe or speculate; it creates.

Conclusion

The combination of institutional and curricular evidence (or structural and proximate mechanisms) provides a picture of monastic education in Laos and Northern Thailand. In this picture one sees laywomen and laymen, novices (*samanen*), nuns (*maechi*), and monks (*phra*) attending (depending on their haphazard schedules and family, ritual, and social demands) a wide range of lectures and sermons. These lectures and sermons have been fully integrated into the liturgical, ritual, performative, social, and aesthetic responsibilities of monastic life. The focus of these lectures and sermons generally has been on the importance of giving and etiquette, the protective power of Pali words and syllables, and the adventures of famous bodhisattvas, millionaires, and queens. They work to create an ideal Buddhist agent who is both tied to an invoked and invented Indic tradition and pulled by the changing needs of the community. The student and teacher negotiate this tension using pedagogical methods and rhetorical tactics.

Modernities and Trajectories

Lao and Northern Thai lectures and sermons follow a regional pedagogical method—*yok sab*—lifting words from narrative, ritual, and grammatical texts through the medium of *nissaya*, *vohāra*, and *nāmasadda* manuscripts. Teachers sit in open-air pavilions, on the verandahs of their monastic cells, or in the main hall holding these pedagogical manuscripts.[1] They occasionally glance down to lift a Pali word and offer an expansive and repetitive vernacular lesson. Generally, these lectures and sermons have not been part of a graduated educational system replete with examinations and course schedules. Until the monastic examination systems instituted by Burmese and

Siamese kings, there is little evidence that there was one way of marking a monk as "educated." The teachers have often been independent masters. Students have depended heavily on the guidance of their teacher without recourse to a regionally known standardized body of facts and texts. Despite institutional changes (in classrooms, examinations, textbooks, and universities) brought by Siamese royalty, French colonial scholars, and Lao Communist reformers, these pedagogical methods have remained strikingly consistent over the past five hundred years.

A curricular study of monastic education reveals the way the Pali language and Pali texts are treated locally. One can see how Pali is "languaged." Pali words and texts provide a useful and adaptable technology. Buddhist stories and lessons are useful as commonsensical and often entertaining guidelines rather than as dogmatic prescriptions. Stories are slowly changed in transmission, as different parts are emphasized and different conclusions met. Most Pali canonical texts that were not seen as useful for these ritual and ethical needs often remained untranslated in monastic or royal archives. Many canonical Indic Buddhist texts remained part of the intellectual heritage of Buddhism but not part of the living interaction with students of religion. When they are part of monastic education, they are in vernacular anthologies, like the *Buddhasāsanāsubhāsit* and the *Navakowat*, composed by Prince Wachirayan in the late nineteenth century. This is not simply a "high" and "low" division of religion. Many advanced and "elite" Buddhist texts, like sections of the Abhidhamma or the Visuddhimagga, were invoked, discussed, and translated by both rural nonelite teachers and monastic university professors. Many "low," seemingly unsophisticated texts like protective *paritta* and entertaining narratives have maintained their place in the elite monastic curriculum. Since the *nissaya* method and the choice of texts are flexible, monastic education has been dynamic—guided by these broad needs and approaches.

In this way one can question the uses of the terms *tradition* and *modernity*. Pedagogical practices in Southeast Asia reveal that tradition, as Talal Asad argues, is not simply a "stage of development" but contested and adaptable trajectories in the interpretative process.[2] Similarly, modernity is not a single tradition but "an integrated set of practical knowledges" that is not simply connected to Westernization.[3] Western scholars have a hegemonic tendency to see modernity as singular and Western. Asad, like Bakhtin, sees the discourses of tradition and modernity as hybrids themselves and not so easily separated into successive stages of development or self-reflection. Malcolm Miles and Wolfgang Welsch argue that "'modernity per se . . . does not exist . . . [only] varying concepts of modernity' the relation of which is continuous and reactive, smooth and fracturing at once. Once we see modernities as conceptual formations rather than delineations of a period, we can see the play of continuities in the place of boundaries."[4]

The *nissaya* method allows subtle changes to happen text by text, teacher by teacher. In *nissaya* and other pedagogical texts, tradition (canon, classical languages, translocal orthodoxy) and local understandings, intentions, and interpretations merge in a heteroglossic discourse. The convenient scholarly paradigm of "translocal canon versus local knowledge" needs to be questioned if not abandoned. Instead, scholars need to listen to each "utterance" in the monastic lecture. These utterances include historical contexts, gestures, audiences, notions of prestige, accents, and social positions. *Nissaya* in the past and their homiletic descendents in the present are records of these various utterances.[5] Local Buddhist utterances are not solely determined by the classical Pali Buddhist traditions. Buddhist teachings had to live up to the needs of the Lao and Northern Thai teachers. The teachers did not have to live up to an ideal Buddhism.

Since at least the sixteenth century, local teachers generally have not tried to teach an immutable preestablished body of knowledge, transmitted in a canon. Intellectual trends, ritual needs, and performance styles have developed in the arts of reading and teaching, but generally, outside of the halls of modern Siamese monastic universities, there has been no explicit preconceived notion of what a good Buddhist should know. These universities have had little impact on the education of most students in the region. Instead, ritual needs to stave off sickness and to protect children, homes, and livestock have often been paramount. More broadly, the social-psychological anxieties of death, rebirth, love, and poverty have driven the choice of texts to teach. This does not mean that the lofty soteriological goal of *nirvaṇa/nibbana* or the profound ethical conundrum over compassion and indifference is elided. However, it shows that the importance of the quotidian concerns of protection, prestige, and power cannot be discounted. For many students and teachers, curing their mother's illness, achieving financial security for their family, or ensuring that young men join the monastery is a more pressing concern, and a no less important task, than is the ascetic and detached pursuit of enlightenment. Still, these goals are not mutually exclusive. They are merely different idioms. Donald Swearer has argued that these ethical dialectics exist at the very "core of Buddhism." The dichotomy between "the ideal of an ultimate personal transformation and the need to address the entire range of life experiences bracketed by birth and death" shows that the "lived tradition of Buddhism, like all classical religions, is not so tidy. It teems with paradox, myth, legend, and symbol not so easily rationalized into a logical system."[6]

From the widest perspective, the picture drawn here of monastic education reveals that Buddhism should be studied, not as an object with particular features, but as a series of overlapping processes. The study of curricula is a study of the ways in which these processes (pedagogical techniques and technologies) drive and are driven by teachers and students in everyday educational (and often ritual) moments. Buddhism is not a set of facts, a knowledge artifact, that is reproduced in classrooms; it is mutable epistemic lineages consisting of activities and interests that have been shaped over a long period of time by every teacher and every student who speaks a text anew. Tracing these lines of evolving interpretation, tracing the methods and forms teachers use in the process of interpretation, is the study of Buddhist curricula.

The way I have displayed the picture of monastic education in Laos and Northern Thailand reveals my approach to Southeast Asian studies in general. Approaching regional studies through transnational information flows and interpretative lineages allows scholars to begin to break out of what Arjun Appadurai calls the study of "trait geographies," or "inherent properties of peoples, soils, cultures."[7] Nations and peoples are seen as "clusters of traits." If scholars approach the study of culture, religious and otherwise, through processes, then they can start comparing epistemological modes that seemingly lack similar traits. For example, the manner in which the concept of universal kingship is localized in the Javanese *Arjuna wiwaha*, the Northern Thai *Jinakālamālīpakaraṇam*, and the Khmer "Sdok Kak Thom Inscription" belies the fact that they were composed centuries apart in different languages, in different locales, by authors with different class and religious traits. The way battles and revolutionary heroes are memorialized in Hue, Savannakhet, and Yangon reveals complementary processes of selling nostalgia despite the fact that the Vietnamese speak Vietnamese, are culturally influenced by the Chinese, and fought the French and the Americans and that the Burmese are Indianized, fought the Bengalis and the British, and speak Burmese. The manner in which beauty contests are advertised and judged in rural Mindanao, urban Bangkok, and hyper-urban Singapore reveals more about processes of gender formation than does looking at women's "rights" status in the official government dictums. The study of "process geographies" will hopefully help scholars to reconceptualize Southeast Asia as "a place" despite its fundamental trait differences in religion, language, agricultural products, government forms, and ethnic populations.[8] The study of curricula is one way to trace these processes.

New Directions and Possibilities

There are many things not seen in this picture of monastic education, however. First, very little is known about women's space in this educational arena. Certainly, women were not absent from monastic education. Manuscript colophons indicate that laywomen were involved in sponsoring the production of pedagogical and other manuscripts. Moreover, female characters, often protagonists, were central in narrative texts taught at monasteries and were often the subject of murals in Central Thailand (at Wat Pathum Wanaram, Wat Thepdhitaram, Wat Nang Chi, and Wat Pho, to name a few). In fact, one of the oldest known Pali chronicles in Southeast Asia was about Queen Cāmadevi of Northern Thailand. Her story and many other vernacular and Pali stories depicted women as ascetically powerful and politically active. Generally, when women have been the subject in Southeast Asian Buddhist studies, they are depicted as victims, not intellectual shapers of discourse. However, any person who spends time in a Thai monastery knows that in the modern period women play a prominent role in monastic education. However, this is a subject that has been overlooked. My next project (together with Steven Collins) examines this role and is beyond the scope of this book.

Another aspect of monastic education that may seem conspicuously absent from this book is the place of meditation. It is the subject of an ongoing study of mine, but I can note here that texts that guide meditation, narratives that promote the value of meditation, and descriptions of meditation training centers, meditation teachers, and different meditational techniques are largely absent in premodern pedagogical manuscripts. In fact, meditational guidebooks are largely absent in modern monastic examination systems and academic curricula. This absence certainly does not mean meditation is not practiced or is secondary in premodern and modern monastic education. Meditation was most likely part of a student's training in the premodern period. Depictions of fictional and historical characters, lay and ordained, meditating can be found in narratives, murals, images, and chronicles. The general lack, but certainly not total absence, of textual material specifically guiding training in meditation leads one to believe that meditation was part of the subtle oral training that all novices, monks, nuns, and lay students receive from their teachers. This training took place in the "off-hours" and was more intimate than was textual training. Memorization of texts, which was and is very common, can also be considered a meditative practice. It is certainly how many people receive training today in monasteries. However, the large number of printed works offering *vipassanā*-type meditation guidance seen in Lao and Thai bookstores today is a relatively recent phenomenon. Furthermore, meditation training in the premodern period was often centered on preparing for rituals, developing protective powers, and developing ephemeral fetuses to ensure a favorable rebirth. The popularity of *vipassanā* meditation seen in modern Laos and Thailand has largely arisen in the twentieth century through the tutelage and popularity of Achan Sao Kantasinthera, Chaokun Phra Pannya Phitsanthera, Achan Man Phurithat, and Phra Achan Fan Acaro in Northern and Northeastern Thailand, and Phra Mahapan Anantho and Phra Ongkaeo Sitthivong in Laos.

Ritual, Abhidhamma, and even grammatical texts indicate that "esoteric" and protective meditation practices were probably more common in the past than were *vipassanā*. "Esoteric" or "*yogāvacarin*" meditation of many types was seen as important in premodern Laos and Thailand, in the preparation for protective rituals (for warriors, lay magicians, monks, and novices), for inducing trances in the service of spirit mediumship, and in the development of a range of parapsychological powers (*iddhi* and *abhiñña*). These practices have not disappeared though and are still widespread throughout Thailand and especially Laos.[9] Modern uses of meditation for "inner peace" or mental health or as a technique for reducing stress are absent from premodern literature, and there is certainly no evidence that these uses were part of monastic education.

This picture of monastic education does not depict the sectarianism that often characterizes modern Thai monastic education (although not modern Lao). Sectarianism is not as prevalent if one takes a curricular rather than an institutional approach to the history of monastic education. Since the development of the Dhammayuttika Nikāya sects (or, more properly, ordination lineages) in 1840s Bangkok, elite Thai monastic administration has been heavily affected by rivalry between the Mahānikāya and Dhammayuttika lineages.[10] Two other sects, the Santi Asok and the Dhammakāya in modern Central Thailand, have added to this sectarian rhetoric. This sectarianism seems to have been more intense in the mid-twentieth century than at any point in Lao or Thai history. Certainly, there have been different institutional sects and personal lineages that have had different emphases in practice, dress, and recitation style among Burmese, Khmer, Lao, and Thai Buddhists. Although their history is complicated, in Northern Thailand, there were two major lineages, one comprising different groups associated with a Sri Lankan or Sinhalese lineage promoted by Phra Sumana and Mahāsāmī Udumbaram and known as the *araññavāsī/pupphārāmavāsī* (forest / flower garden dwellers) and the other an older local lineage later classified broadly as *gāmavāsī/nagaravāsī* (village/city dwellers). These lineages were offered patronage by different kings over time, but precious little is known about how they distinguished themselves institutionally or ritually. These appellations are deceptive; neither lineage resided solely in the forest or in the village/city. In addition to this distinction, a traditional distinction from South Asia is found between monks across sectarian lines, known as *ganthadhura* ("those who carry the burden of [textual] study") and *vipassanādhura* ("those who carry the burden of meditation practice").[11] This distinction was never significant in Northern Thailand or Laos, and today these terms are rarely used by monks and nuns in either place. They have become relatively common in Central Thailand, but it is rare to find a nun or monk who only studies texts and never meditates or vice versa. It would be more accurate to say that any particular student "leans" toward one tendency or the other. No matter how one judges which lineage or which approach to practice is more ethical, closer to the Buddha's intentions, or more soteriologically efficacious, in terms of monastic education, in the premodern and modern period, sectarian divisions have been less prominent. In fact, the modern curricula and examination systems in Thailand were not designed along sectarian lines, although their modern impetus was born in a sectarian debate. When they do sit for examinations, which as mentioned is rare, Mahānikāya, Dhammayuttika, Ganthadhurā, and Vipassanādhurā monks take the same tests on the same texts. Often, in rural areas, these sectarian divisions are ignored since many novices and monks grow up together as boys in the same village and ordain at their parents' monastery. They become more distinctly defined at the monastic university level. Oftentimes the choice of monastery or monastery school is based on location, convenience, finances, family obligations, and personal friendships rather than on sectarian concerns.

As a Dhammayuttika monk myself, I performed rituals with Mahānikāya monks, attended sermons by Mahānikāya monks, and was even trained in one method of meditation by a Mahānikāya monk. This is certainly more common in rural areas than it is in Bangkok, Khon Kaen, and Chiang Mai. When I taught elementary monastic courses as a Dhammayuttika monk, I taught at a Mahānikāya school. I chose to be a Dhammayuttika monk based on a personal friendship I had with a monk in that order. I had little knowledge, at the time, of the institutional and ideological differences. In rural areas, this crossover is quite common. Despite subtly different personal and regional emphases, the overall pedagogical methods and choice of source texts in monastic education are shared by all sects and lineages.

My use of the term *lineage* instead of *sect* is deliberate. Institutionally written histories of Buddhism in Southeast Asia have generally overlooked the way a monk's personal teacher and personal ordination lineage (or "dispensation") trumps all other associations with monasteries, sects, provinces or regions, social classes, and linguistic dialects. Stating that a monk is ordained in the "Dhammayuttika Nikāya" is sufficiently vague and reveals nothing. It is more accurate to know with which lineage of personal teachers, within or across Dhammayuttika, Mahānikāya, or other lineages, a monk self-identifies. For example, the famous Achan Cha of Northeast Thailand was a Mahānikāya monk who self-identified with one lineage within the Dhammayuttika Nikāya. This is not to suggest that sectarian identity is not important, but it is not the only marker of a monk's (and certainly not a nun's) education.

The institutional approach has tended to remove agency from individual teachers. This is one area in which a lineage-based curricular approach could help. The intimate relationship developed between a teacher and a student and the tradition in passing down that relationship (through ordination and training) are the most important relationship and tradition most monks I know have. "My teacher" is a common refrain in conversations with monks, whereas "my sect," "my monastery," "my school," and "my hometown" are always secondary. Future work on the history of Buddhism in Southeast Asia will be fruitful if these lineages are traced in detail. Recent work by Penny Edwards and Anne Hansen in Cambodia, Patrice Ladwig in Laos, Thanissaro Bhikkhu and Hayashi Yukio in Thailand, and Patrick Pranke and Erik Braun in Burma offer new insights by taking this personal lineage–based approach.

One cannot ignore self-education. Many monks design their own curriculum, gather a diverse range of texts for their personal libraries, and seek out different teachers who are experts in different subjects. Kesarapañño's education described in chapter 2 is a perfect example, as was that of the eighth patriarch of Siamese Buddhism, Somdet Phra Mahāsamaṇachao Khrom Phrayā Pavaresuariyālongkon (Phra Ongchaorik) (1810–1891), who read widely and systematically attempted to train himself as a historian, grammarian, astrologer, and even biologist, performing experiments, drawing star and planet charts, composing Pali poems, and reading a wide range of chronicles.[12] This self-education in conjunction with exam-based modern monastic curricula is quite normal, especially among monks who have access to the Internet and to large libraries.

Finally, this has been a study of the robed. Although I interviewed a number of lay students and teachers, I was concerned with those who had ordained. Certainly, as mentioned, lay students study at all levels of monastic schooling; however, study of lay religious education is needed. I was struck by the fact that a number of laypeople I met in Northern and Central Thailand showed me their personal manuscripts, and these were mostly astrological, medical, and ritual texts (*horasat*, *tamra ya*, and *anisong*).

On the vernacular ground, changes have been organic and subtle—text by text, teacher by teacher. One change that has occurred despite curricular continuity is the rise of a modern self-reflexivity and ecumenicalism in lectures and sermons. This emphasis is largely unseen in pedagogical manuscripts and historical descriptions. Modern preachers and teachers often mention themselves as self-consciously "Buddhist" and "Thai" or "Lao." Some emphasize that the self-acknowledged state of being makes them different from Muslims, Christians, Cambodians, *Farang* (umbrella term for Caucasians), Burmese, *Khaek* (umbrella term for Hindus, Sikhs, and Jains of South Asian descent), or Japanese. Some Thai emphasize that Buddhism is universal and that all religions and ethnicities follow the same philosophy: *Tham di dai di tham cheua dai cheua* (Do good, get good; do bad, get bad). This can be seen is the rise of "World Religions" courses in monastic universities and the rise in participation of Thai monks in worldwide Buddhist fellowship conferences. There are also regular exchanges of professors and students between Christian universities like Assumption and Payab Universities and their Buddhist counterparts. There is a newly refurbished International Tipiṭaka Hall at Chulalongkorn University, which beautifully displays every major edition of the Thai canon and main commentaries since the late nineteenth century. Here, international scholars of Buddhism meet and scholarly talks in English and Thai are held. Regardless, a teacher talking about himself or referring to his "own views" was rare before the twentieth century.[13]

There are two obvious reasons that I have noticed this change. First, I, a white, "Christian-looking" person, was in the audience at many of the sermons/lectures discussed in this book, and the preacher or teacher acknowledged my presence. In some cases this was explicitly stated, and I was asked to introduce myself to the class or audience. If I regularly attended a class or listened to a preacher every week at the same time, then my presence was slowly ignored. Second, the rise in communications technology, cosmopolitanism, and the myriad changes that have come with colonialism and globalization certainly can be associated with these subtle changes in content and approach to monastic education. This change has greatly accelerated in the past ten years. When I first visited a Thai monastery in Bangkok in 1993, there were no computers and, of course, no Internet. Today, some urban monasteries in Vientiane and Bangkok have dedicated computer rooms with Internet access. High-ranking urban monks often produce CD-ROMs or construct Web sites to teach their own students as well as students who have access to the Internet globally. Buddhism is packaged as an export product. A new transnational Buddhist class is emerging. New phrases and new rhetoric have been developed to serve new audiences. These audiences are not merely non-Buddhist or new-Buddhist Westerners but other Buddhists in Asia. High-ranking Thai monks (although the same cannot be said of Lao monks) have begun traveling intensely and now can be seen in universities in India and Japan; at Buddhist tourist sites in Sri Lanka, China, Indonesia, and Taiwan; and at international ecumenical Buddhist meetings in Korea, Nepal, and Australia. There are new Buddhist universities with an ecumenical focus like the World Buddhist University in Bangkok (started in Australia) and the International Buddhist College located in Songkhla (Southern Thailand) and its parent organization, Than Hsiang Temple, Penang, Malaysia. The default language at these universities, tourist sites, and conferences is English. Joint Buddhist publications and Web sites that encourage Japanese Buddhist students to speak to Tibetan Buddhists and to Thai Buddhists are being developed. A wealthy class of international Buddhist patrons from Bangkok, Singapore, Hong Kong, and other places is subsidizing publications, conferences, and temple construction throughout Asia. New electronic Tipiṭaka editions in multiple scripts with English translations are being launched. There is a Pali dictionary "e-reader," a remote "e-learning" program through Mahachulalongkorn Monastic University, and zip-drive downloads available of the major monastic university examinations, curricula, and texts in Thai. There are Buddhist blogs and podcasts run by Thai monks and international consumers alike. English-language instruction has increased dramatically at Thai and Lao monasteries. There are Pali chanting ring tones available for cell phones. Thai and Lao monks have established monastic schools in Australia, Japan, the United States, France, Italy, Great Britain, Canada, Brazil, and New Zealand.[14] Of course, there have been Buddhist pilgrims, traveling students, ecumenical meetings, and cultural mixing for over two thousand years throughout the Buddhist world. However, the frequency, speed, and ease of this exchange changed dramatically in the last century and especially in the past ten years.

I noted this change most closely at the 2005 meeting of the International Association of Buddhist Studies in London, where I had the pleasure of organizing a panel on Theravada Buddhism. Phra Sugandha (Anil Sakya) and Phra Khammai Dhammasami, both colleagues of mine, were two of the speakers. The former, a Nepali scholar monk with a Ph.D., has been working in the office of the supreme patriarch of Thailand for fifteen years and occasionally teaches at Santa Clara College in California. The latter is a Shan monk who has studied in Thailand and Burma and recently received his doctorate from Oxford University on the subject of Burmese politics and religion. Phra Sugandha gave a talk on Newari Vernacular Buddhist literature and referred to his childhood and to his mother. Phra Khammai discussed the importance of the Shan vernacular tradition, of which he is the international expert. Both Phra Khammai and Phra Sugandha write in English as well as in their mother tongues. In 2007 they initiated the creation of the international Association of Theravada Buddhist Universities, with instruction in English and Pali.[15] They both wear traditional robes and maintain a strict adherence to the monastic disciplinary code. Despite this dependence on the "traditional," they easily operate and excel in the pedagogical realms of the Western academy. In fact, at this particular meeting, they helped the other speakers from the United States and Great Britain fix their computers when there were problems with their PowerPoint presentations. Certainly, things are changing in monastic education.

Colophon

Sradeccha laeo culasakrād dai 1369 wan 8 deuan mesā dai kae khā lae 1 gon bhariyā jeu wā christine diane lūk jai jeu wā henry thomrongsak lae lūk thī song jeu jane saifon // tua pō ngām sak noi cōng phiccaraṇā theu theua // suan wā desanā an nī mī prayojanā kae mahājjhan gō gon an māk nak nan lae // nibbana paccayo hontu Tī lī dae doe

Notes

Introduction

1 Vat Sok Paluang in Vientiane is quickly growing and may soon become the largest monastic high school in the country. Founded in 1915 and presently led by Phra Phramma Visanandho, this school is crowded with over seventy students per classroom at any one time. The new bridge connecting Mukdahan, Thailand, and Savannakhet, Laos, completed in 2006, will surely bring changes to this region. Only time will tell how this affects monastic education in the region.

2 Alton Becker, *Beyond Translation: Essays towards a Modern Philology* (Ann Arbor: University of Michigan Press, 1995), 8–9. I thank Hendrick Maier for his conversations on this issue.

3 William Johnson, "Toward a Sociology of Reading," *American Journal of Philology* 121 (2000): 601–3.

4 J. B. Jackson, *Discovering the Vernacular Landscape* (New Haven, Conn.: Yale University Press, 1986); David Biggs, personal communication, February 2006.

5 Michel de Certeau, *The Practice of Everyday Life*, trans. Steven F. Rendall (Berkeley: University of California Press, 1994), 174.

6 Roger Chartier, *The Order of Books*, trans. Lydia Cochrane (Stanford, Calif.: Stanford University Press, 1994), 2.

7 Similarly, in Cambodia, only in the past fifty years has the distinction between religious (*gambhir*) and secular (*lpaeng*) been "meaningfully applied" by Cambodians. Ian Harris, *Cambodian Buddhism* (Honolulu: University of Hawaii Press, 2005), 81.

8 Jeffrey Samuels, "Toward an Action-Oriented Pedagogy," *Journal of the American Academy of Religion* 72, no. 4 (2004): 965–66.

9 John Strong, preface to *The Legend and Cult of Upagupta* (Princeton, N.J.: Princeton University Press, 1992).

10 Bernard Faure, *Chan Insights and Oversights* (Princeton, N.J.: Princeton University Press, 1993), 269, citing Michel Foucault, *The Archaeology of Knowledge* (New York: Pantheon Books, 1972). I thank Faure for discussions on this issue.

11 Biggs, personal communication, February 2006; Denis Cosgrove, *Social Forma-*

tion and Symbolic Landscape (Totowa, N.J.: Barnes and Noble Imports, 1984; repr., Madison: University of Wisconsin Press, 1998).

12 Venerable Khammai Dhammasami's dissertation, "Between Idealism and Pragmatism" (Oxford University, 2005), is a clear exception to this trend.

13 Lorand Matory, introduction to *Black Atlantic Religion* (Princeton, N.J.: Princeton University Press, 2005).

14 The only work on *nissaya* texts from other parts of South and Southeast Asia is William Pruitt's *Étude linguistique de nissaya Birmans* (Paris: École française d'Extrême-Orient, 1994). He focuses on one major Burmese *nissaya* text, the *Bhikkhu-paṭimokkha nissaya.* See also Pruitt's three previous articles in *Cahiers de l'Asie du Sud-Est*: "Un nissaya Birman de la Bibliothèque nationale, le patimokkha: Étude linguistique; Première partie," 19 (1986): 84–119; "Un nissaya Birman de la Bibliothèque nationale, le patimokkha: Étude linguistique; Deuxième partie," 21 (1987): 7–45; and "Un nissaya Birman de la Bibliothèque nationale, le patimokkha: Étude linguistique; Troisième partie," 22 (1987): 35–57. See also Tin Lwin, "A Study of Pali-Burmese Nissaya" (master's thesis, University of London, 1961); and excerpts in Thaw Khaung's "Survey of the History of Education in Burma," *Journal of the Royal Institute of Burmese Studies* 46, no. 2 (1963): 36–64. Also useful for comparison are Charles Duroiselle, "Talaing Nissaya," *Journal of the Burma Research Society* 3 (1913): 21–38; and John Okell, "Nissaya Burmese," *Journal of the Burma Research Society* 50 (1967): 95–123 (expanded from *Lingua* 15 [1965]).

15 I thank Thomas Roach for rich conversations on this issue.

Chapter 1 From the Sala Vat to the Institut Bouddhique

Several paragraphs in this chapter appear in similar form in Justin McDaniel, "Questioning Orientalist Power: The French and Buddhism in Laos," in *Collected Papers of the International Conference on Lao Studies*, ed. John Hartmann and Carol Compton (De Kalb: Northern Illinois University Press, 2007).

1 Emile Lefèvre, *Travels in Laos*, trans. Walter E. J. Tips (Bangkok: White Lotus, 1995), 115–20 (italics mine).

2 See Marthe Bassenne, *In Laos and Siam* (1912; repr., Bangkok: White Lotus, 1995), 60–103, esp. 61, 63, 64, 69, 74.

3 Martin Stuart-Fox, *A History of Laos* (Cambridge: Cambridge University Press, 1997), 30.

4 Ibid., 31.

5 Bassenne, *In Laos and Siam*, 64.

6 Grant Evans offers a good introduction to the variety of Lao reactions to French (and Thai) ideas of civilization and modernity in his *A Short History of Laos* (Chiang Mai, Thailand: Silkworm, 2002), 62–82.

7 See especially Ronald B. Inden, *Imagining India* (Oxford: Blackwell, 1990).

8 I discuss the problems with defining Laos as a geographic space in McDaniel,

"Questioning Orientalist Power"; and McDaniel, "Notes on the Lao Influence on Northern Thai Literature," in *The Literary Heritage of Laos*, ed. Kongdeuane Nettavong, Harald Hundius, David Wharton, Dara Kanlaya, and Khanthamali Yangnuvong (Vientiane: National University of Laos, 2005), 373–96.

9 Punroeng Puasiisaengpasoet, *Pravat silapa lae sathapattayakam Lao lem 2: Meuang Luang Phrabang* (Vientiane, Laos: Toyota Foundation, 1995), 40–41. See also Sila Viravong, *Pavat Lao tae buhan theung 1946* (Vientiane: National Library of Laos and Toyota Foundation, 2001), 61–63.

10 I discuss the political uses of relic and Buddha-image chronicles in Northern Thailand extensively in Justin McDaniel, "Transformative History," *Journal of the International Association of Buddhist Studies* 25, no. 1 (2002): 151–207.

11 See Chirasak Dechawongya, *Khwam saphan rawang Lan Na Lan Xang: Kan seuksa silapakam nai Muang Chiang Mai lae Luang Phrabang* (Chiang Mai, Thailand: Social Research Institute, 2544 [2001]). The *vihāra* was burned during a Siamese attack in 1887, but it was rebuilt. The original was first described by Doudart de Lagrée in 1866, in *Voyage d'exploration en Indochine* (Paris: Collection Quentin, Bibliothèque des Beaux-Arts, 1984). See also Francis Garnier, *Further Travels in Laos and Yunnan*, composed between 1839 and 1873 and published as *Voyage d'exploration en Indo-Chine* (Bangkok: White Lotus, 1996); and Albert De Pouvourville, *L'art Indo-Chinois* (Paris: Librairies-Imprimeries Réunies, 1894). Henri Parmentier includes a description in *L'art du Laos*, the edition revised by Madeleine Giteau (Paris: École française d'Extrême-Orient, 1988), 1:76, and plates in vol. 2.

12 This date is unclear and may have been as late as 1515.

13 Souneth Photisane, "The Nidān Khun Borom" (Ph.D. diss., University of Queensland, 1996), 245.

14 Martin Stuart-Fox, *The Lao Kingdom of Lan Xang* (Bangkok: White Lotus, 1998), 74.

15 Other texts seem to have been taken or moved to Burma. Before 1558 intellectual monks, artisans, and scribes were moving to Luang Phrabang. There was a direct political connection between the royal houses of Chiang Mai and Luang Phrabang at this time. For a summary of these chronicles, see McDaniel, "Transformative History," 59–68. I also provide a bibliography of historical chronicles (in Pali, Thai, and Yuan and in French and English translations) by Camille Notton, Saraswati Ongsakun, Hans Penth, A. B. Griswold, Prasert na Nagara, George Coedès, Rattanapañña, and so on for Northern Thailand here. See also Kaxuang thalaeng khao lae wattanatham (Ministry of Information and Culture), *Pavasat Lao* (Vientiane, Laos: Rongphim haeng lat, 2000), 271–74; Douangxai Luangpasi, *Chao Maha Uparat Bunrong* (Vientiane, Laos: Sangon Likhasit, 2003); Douangxai Luangpasi, *Somdet Phra Chao Sethathirat* (Vientiane, Laos: Sangon Likhasit, 1999); (Phra Maha) Mani Rattanapathimakone and (Phra) Rattanaphimpheuang, *Thamnan Phra Kaeo Morakot* (Vientiane, Laos: Sangon Likhasit, 1999); Saengthong Photipuppha, *Pavat Muang Xieng Kaeng*

(Vientiane: Khong kan botbat raksa nangseu bailan Lao, 1998); Bunroeng Buasisaengbasoet, *Pavatsat Silapa lae sathabatthayakamsin Lao* (Vientiane, Laos: n.p., 1995); and Bunroeng Buasisaengbasoet, *Muang Luang Phrabang* (Vientiane, Laos: Toyota Foundation, 1991). This information is drawn from a local history by Luang Pho Kambhirasan (no date) and an inscription from 1812 on the monastic library of Wat Phra Singh (Hans Penth, Phanphen Khrüathai, and Silao Kesaprohm, *Chareuk nai Phiphitaphan Lamphun*, Corpus of Lanna Inscriptions [Chiang Mai, Thailand: Social Research Institute, 2542 (1999)], 3:177). The Burmese were not solely to blame for the decline in Pali literature in Northern Thailand. I discuss this extensively in Justin McDaniel, "Two Bullets in a Balustrade: How the Burmese Have Been Removed from Northern Thai History," *Journal of Burma Studies* 11 (2007).

16 The veracity of this story has been seriously questioned by Michel Lorrillard, "The Earliest Lao Buddhist Monasteries according to Philological and Epigraphical Sources," in *The Buddhist Monastery*, ed. Pierre Pichard and François Lagirarde (Paris: École française d'Extrême-Orient, 2003), 187–98. Lorrillard also provides a plethora of epigraphical evidence linking Chiang Mai and Vientiane in "Les inscriptions du That Luang de Vientiane," *Bulletin de l'École française d'Extrême-Orient* 90–91 (2003–4): 299.

17 Many of these manuscripts may be held in the National Library of Thailand.

18 Tham Sayasithsena, *Pavat Vat Inpeng Mahavihan* (Vientiane, Laos: Vat Inpeng, 1993), 35–50.

19 Stuart-Fox, *Lao Kingdom of Lan Xang*, 94. Grant Evans correctly pointed out (personal communication, October 2006) that van Wuysthoff's observation that Siamese and Cambodian monks were studying in Vientiane at that time is not corroborated. The diversity of the manuscripts and inscriptions produced at this time might suggest mobile and diverse translocal populations in the city though.

20 For reports written by Leria between 1642 and 1648, see Giovani Filippo de Marini, *Delle missioni de' Petri della Compagnia di Giesu mella provincia del Giappone e particolarmente de quella di Tumkino* (Rome: Nicolo Angelo Tinassi, 1663). See also the French translation, *Histoire nouvelle et curieuse des royaumes de Tunquin et de Lao* (Paris: Gervais Clouzier, 1666); and the English, *A New and Interesting Description of the Lao Kingdom*, trans. Walter E. J. Tips and Claudio Bertuccio (Bangkok: White Lotus, 1998). The quotation is taken from the English translation (51).

21 Jacques Leider notes in a personal communication (July 2006) that scholars need to look "at a missionary's account, through his own eyes. Missionaries had to defend themselves in Rome. They had to stress the hostility of the environment where they toiled in Southeast Asia to defend themselves against accusations they were having a jolly good time in the East. They also had innermonastic enemies (Jesuits fought against Augustinians and Dominicans; Italians against Portuguese, and the like). We are wrong to assume that their accounts

reflect their personal feelings and inoculated dogmatic stances." See also Leider's "Tilling the Lord's Vineyard and Defending Portuguese Interests: Towards a Critical Reading of Father Manrique's Account of Arakan," *Journal of the Siam Society* 90, nos. 1–2 (2002): 39–58. I thank Jacques Leider for his many helpful comments.

22 See Marini, *Description of the Lao Kingdom*, 35.

23 See Peter Koret, "'Whispered so softly it resounds through the forest, spoken so loudly it can hardly be heard': The Art of Parallelism in Traditional Lao Literature" (Ph.D. diss., School of Oriental and African Studies, London, 1994); and Anatole-Roger Peltier, "Les litteratures Lao du Lan Na, du Lan Xang, de Keng Tung et des Sip Song Panna," *Péninsule* 2 (1990): 29–44.

24 For historical overviews of nineteenth-century Lao history before the arrival of the French, see Nou Saiyasittiwong, Volker Grabowsky, Bualy Paphaphanh, and Khamrung Saenmani, *Pheun Viang Samay Chou Anu* (Vientiane: National University of Laos, 2004).

25 Administratively, Laos was included in the Vicariate Apostolic of Siam until the French made Laos an official colony. After 1899, Monsignor Marie-Joseph Cuaz was named the "Bishop of Hermopolis Minor" and was placed in charge of the Lao territory, although, he probably never set foot in the country. The Catholic Church reports that as of 1910 there were 10,682 Catholics in Laos and 33 priests (29 of whom were European). There was only one seminary with eight students, 54 churches and chapels, 35 schools with 797 pupils, and 22 orphanages with 304 "inmates." *The Catholic Encyclopedia* (1910 ed.), s.v. "Indo-China," http://www.newadvent.org/cathen/07765a.htm (accessed fall 2003); *Bibliotheca Sinica: Essai d'une Bibliographie des ouvrages relatifs à la presqu'île indo-chinoise in T'oung P'ao Archifs pour servir à l'étude de l'Aise Orientale*, 2nd ser. (Leiden, 1903), vol. 4; Emile Reclus, *Nouvelle géographie universelle* (Paris: Hachette, 1883), vol. 8; Jean Marie Antoine de Lanessan, *La colonisation française en Indo-Chine* (Paris: F. Alcan, 1895), which furthermore gives an excellent account of the state of the French possessions toward the close of the nineteenth century; Henri d'Orléans, *Autor du Tonkin* (Paris, 1894); Charles Lemire, *Le Laos annamite* (Paris, 1894); Marie Auguste Armand Tournier, *Notice sur la Laos français* (Paris, 1900); Claudius Madrolle, *Indo-Chine* (guidebook) (Paris, 1902); Emile Le Blant, *Les martyrs de Extrême-Orient et les persécutions antiques* (Arras, France, 1877); Louis Eugene Louvet, *La Cochinchine religieuse*, 2 vols. (Paris, 1885); and Jean Dépierre, *Situation de catholicisme en Cochinchine à la fin du XIX siècle* (Saigon, 1900). I thank Mme. Vachier at the Centre des archives d'Outre-Mer in Aix-en-Provence for advice on this section.

26 Stuart-Fox, *Lao Kingdom of Lan Xang*, 35. There was a school to educate Lao administrators in 1928.

27 Sila Viravong, *Pavat Lao tae buhan theung 1946*, 248–50. Of course, ethnic groups that did not traditionally go to Buddhist monastic rituals and family events (Hmong, Khamti, and Akha, among others) were not part of monastic

or French education. See also Volker Grabowsky, "Forced Resettlement Campaigns in Northern Thailand during the Early Bangkok Period," *Orient Extremus* 37, no. 1 (1994): 45–107 (reprinted in *Journal of the Siam Society* 87, no. 1 [1999]: 45–86); and Grabowsky, "Origins of Lao and Khmer National Identity: The Legacy of the Early Nineteenth Century," in *Nationalism and Cultural Revival in Southeast Asia: Perspectives from the Centre and the Region*, ed. Sri Kuhnt-Saptodewo, Volker Grabowsky, and M. Großheim (Wiesbaden: Harrassowitz Verlag, 1997).

28 See Charles Keyes, *The Golden Peninsula* (New York: Macmillan, 1977), 101.

29 See especially Catherine Clémentin-Ojha and Pierre-Yves Manguin, *Un siècle pour l'Asie: École française d'Extrême-Orient, 1898–2000* (Paris: Les editions du pacifique and l'École française d'Extrême-Orient, 2001). See also Louis Malleret, *Le cinquantenaire de l'École française d'Extrême-Orient: Compte rendu des fêtes et cérémonies* (Hanoi: École française d'Extrême-Orient, 1953). The EFEO started in Hanoi, where it replaced the Mission archéologique d'Indochine. For a brief history of the EFEO in Indochina, see Michel Lorrillard, "100 ans de recherche de l'EFEO au Laos" (talk given at the French embassy, Vientiane, Laos, June 15, 2001), http://laos.efeo.fr/spip.php?article85Svar-recherche=lorrillard (accessed October 2007).

30 Louis Finot, "Recherches sur la littèrature Laotienne," *Bulletin de l'École française d'Extrême-Orient* 17, no. 5 (1917): 1–219. In 1918 he also surveyed the royal library in Luang Phrabang.

31 In 1901, one EFEO-affiliated scholar, Alfred Lavallée, did visit the rural region of Boloven (which soon became a great center for coffee production, and so there may have been an ulterior motive for his trip), where he documented the languages and wrote a basic ethnography of eleven different ethnic groups. Most early archaeological work was by Charles Batteur, Jean-Louis Claeys, and Madeleine Colani, in restoration, pottery, and architecture.

32 *The Catholic Encyclopedia*, s.v. "Indo-China," http://www.newadvent.org/cathen/07765a.htm (accessed fall 2003).

33 Clémentin-Ojha and Manguin, *Un siècle pour l'Asie*, 164.

34 Ibid., 166.

35 EFEO, "Annual Report," *Bulletin de l'École française d'Extrême-Orient* 30 (1931): 623. Penny Edwards provides a concise history of French scholars' Indology background in "Taj Angkor: Enshrining *l'Inde in le Cambodge*," in *France and "Indochina": Cultural Representations*, ed. Kathryn Robson and Jennifer Yee (Lanham, Md.: Lexington Books, 2005), 13–27. An example of the French penchant for colonial display is seen in a 1906 advertisement for the "L'Exposition coloniale de Marseille," in which a scantily clad young Lao woman is pictured on the front page.

36 In brief, the Preservation of Lao Manuscripts Program (PLMP), with the financial and scholarly assistance of Harald Hundius (director of the Joint Preservation Program), the German Academic Exchange Service (DAAD), and the

Toyota Foundation, has surveyed almost six hundred monasteries in Laos. When I was reading manuscripts in the archive in 2000–2002, a total of over 270,000 fascicles had been surveyed and over 30,000 fascicles had been microfilmed onto five hundred rolls of 35 mm film. The majority of the manuscripts have been found in Vientiane, Luang Phrabang, and Champasak provinces (54,130, 64,809, and 48,536, respectively), while smaller remote provinces like Attapeu, Phongsali, and Udomxai have considerably fewer (4,806, 4,125, and 6,497 fascicles, respectively). In addition to the survey and microfilming, which continues at present (e.g., the PLMP recently released photos and a field report of its survey efforts in the far north of the country), the PLMP regularly produces a newsletter in Lao (fifteen volumes to date) and has published a pamphlet in English and Lao outlining its activities and goals. It also trains local monks, nuns, and laypeople in basic preservation techniques. The program finished its work in 2005 after fifteen years, but it has spawned a number of smaller programs. Recent conversations with Kongdeuane Nettavong, Harald Hundius, and David Wharton have indicated that these manuscripts will be digitized over the next four years. I thank them for their help.

37 Even though Karpelès wanted to draw Lao students away from Bangkok, she and the teachers at the Pali schools in Phnom Penh and Champasak were not anti-Siamese in their choice of source texts for the Pali examinations. In fact, the examinations designed by King Mongkut in Bangkok and those in Cambodia were nearly identical. They both emphasized commentarial over canonical texts like the *Maṅgaladīpanī*, the Visuddhimagga, the *Abhidhammasaṅgaha*, and the *Samantapāsādikā*. However, the late texts like the *Paññāsa jātaka* and the *Pathamasaṃbodhi* composed in Northern Thailand were part of the Cambodian and Lao examinations and were not part of the early Siamese examinations. In recent years many Lao students have been crossing the Mekong to study in Thailand in monastic schools in Ubon Ratchathani, Nong Khai, Nakhon Phanom, and Nan. I met several students in Savannakhet who had purchased monastic schoolbooks in Mukdahan (Thailand). At my monastery in Ubon Ratchathani there were two visiting monks from Laos. Photographs of Lao monks and royalty visiting Cambodia are found in Chheat Sreang, Yin Sombo, Seng Hokmeng, Pong Pheakdeyboramy, and Saom Sokreasey. *The Buddhist Institute in Cambodia: A History*, trans. Penny Edwards (Phnom Penh, Cambodia: Buddhist Institute, 2005). I thank Anne Hansen for sending old photographic evidence of these trips.

38 See the 1932 reports of the EFEO, *Bulletin de l'École française d'Extrême-Orient* 31, nos. 1–2 (1932): 334.

39 Ibid. If the text was in Lao, it may have been an early copy of *suphasit*, or pithy moral maxims still common today, or *phu son lan*, a collection of Lao moral maxims common in manuscript and printed form.

40 EFEO, "Annual Report," *Bulletin de l'École française d'Extrême-Orient* 31, nos. 1–2 (1932): 334.

41 Ibid., 335.

42 Søren Ivarsson is writing on this period. See his "Bringing Laos into Existence: Laos between Indochina and Siam, 1860–1945" (Ph.D. diss., University of Copenhagen, 1999).

43 Karpelès was taken out of her post because of anti-Semitic laws instituted by the Nazis in France in 1941. Anne Hansen (personal communication, August 2006) believes that Karpelès's personal correspondence reflects a scholar who was truly invested in making Pali texts available to her Khmer interlocutors, but who was, like many scholars, short on funding and needed to convince her French colonial bosses that they needed to fund humanities projects for practical economic and military reasons. I thank David Chandler for his valuable comments on the lives of Karpelès and Paul Mus.

44 Penny Edwards's comments on this section of the chapter were extremely valuable. She kindly supplied me with several handwritten telegrams, colonial administrative records, and photographs of Lao royal tours in Cambodia, which enriched this chapter considerably. Edwards correctly emphasizes that one of the most common tendencies of scholarship on the French colonial period is for scholars to underestimate the agency of Lao scholars and policy makers. See also Jean-Pierre Drège, *L'École française d'Extrême-Orient et le Cambodge*, 1898–2003 (Paris: École française d'Extrême-Orient, 2003), 41–42.

45 See EFEO, "Annual Report," *Bulletin de l'École française d'Extrême-Orient* 29 (1930): 519–21.

46 EFEO, "Annual Report," *Bulletin de l'École française d'Extrême-Orient* 31, nos. 1–2 (1932): 335 (italics mine).

47 EFEO, *Bulletin de l'École française d'Extrême-Orient* 29 (1930): 522–29. The French officially organized the monks, placing all monasteries in a district under the monastic district head. The only exception to these rules was for Luang Phrabang, where monks in the city were instructed to follow, based on the approval of the French governor, the traditional rules of the king of Laos.

48 Ibid., 526.

49 Bizot ties the modernization of monastic education in Cambodia to two forces: (1) the Siamese/Thai Thammayut (Dhammayuttika Nikāya) sect's influence and (2) French privileging of Pali canonical texts and Vinaya orthodoxy over protective rites and vernacular texts. He notes that many of the Pali texts translated into Khmer in the colonial period were based on Pali Text Society editions from Britain. François Bizot, introduction to *Le figuier à cinq branches* (Paris: École française d'Extrême-Orient, 1976); Chheat Sreang et al., *Buddhist Institute*, 13–32.

50 The talent of Thong Di is attested in the rest of the letter, which reads: "Mais d'après les articles 12 et 14 de l'Ordonnance Royale du 13 Aout 1922, concernant l'organization de l'Ecole de Pâli, il n'est permis de suivre les cours de cette école que ceux qui ont réçus au concours d'admission. Cependant cette Ordonnance Royale ne prévoit cela que pour les Cambodgiens. Or le bonze Thong Di

est un laotien, et de plus il fait preuve de bonne volonté en venant de si loin nous demander à s'inspirer. Il a entendu dire qu'on peut faire de bonnes études de pali dans cette école dont s'occupe l'Administration et c'est pourquoi il est venu demander a y entrer, dans but de pouvoir plus tard enseigner aux éleves du Laos d'après la méthode d'enseignement qu'il y aura appris. Je trouve que le bonze Thong Di pourrait etre permis à suivre le Cours Moyen de l'Ecole de Pâi parce qu'il possède déjà assez de connaisssances en cette langue, et si vous n'y voyez pas d'inconvenient, je demandera a ce qu'un arrêté soit pris à ce sujet."

51 Gregory Kourilsky recently forwarded to me a draft of his compelling article "L'Institut bouddhique ou la promotion d'une aire bouddhique 'Lao-Khmère,'" forthcoming in *Siksacakr*. He provides a list of "about 20" books that were largely produced in Cambodia and were translated into Lao for the Buddhist Institute in Vientiane between 1931 and 1932. These include the "Kalamasutta, the Traybranam, Gihivinaya, Sārādesnā" compiled/composed by the Cambodia monastic scholar Phra Maha Vimaladhamma, among others, and translated into Lao by Mahapan Phra Phichit Pricha.

52 Penny Edwards (personal communication, May 2006) notes that the Khmer text is slightly different from the French translation of this letter. The French translated "preah trey" (short for "preah treybeidak," or Tipiṭaka) and "vicchie pseing pseing" (various subjects) as simply "Pali." Perhaps "vicchie pseing pseing" meant commentarial texts as opposed to canonical/tipiṭaka texts, or it might have referred to vernacular literature, meditation and ritual, or other non-Buddhist subjects.

53 The second half of this letter consists of a complaint by the king of Luang Phrabang that the Institut bouddhique had yet to receive a promised budget allocation of fourteen hundred piastres.

54 The Bibliothèque royale du Cambodge published a periodic Khmer language report on the activity of Buddhist textual work called the *Kampuchea suriya* [Cambodian Sun]. Nothing of this kind was produced in Laos.

55 Sila Viravong's family, especially his daughter, has been building a library in his honor for the past decade. Dara Kanlaya and Douangdeuane Bounyavong presently head this project.

56 Finot, Karpelès, Coedès, and others frequently attended large Buddhist and royal ceremonies in Laos. In fact, there are reports that they, like EFEO scholars today, participated in the Lao *baxi* ceremony, an imminently local Lao protective rite not documented in translocal classical Buddhism.

57 Martin Stuart-Fox, *Buddhist Kingdom, Marxist State* (Bangkok: White Lotus, 1996), 105.

58 Evans, *Short History of Laos*, 178.

59 There was very little critical scholarship on Lao Buddhism between 1955 and 1975. The *Bulletin des Amis du Royaume Lao* special issue on Buddhism (1973) and Marcello Zago's *Rites et cérémonies en milieu bouddhiste Lao* (Rome: Univer-

sitá Gregoriana Editrice, 1972) offer little in the way of textual analysis, interviews, or in-depth analysis.

60 I thank Bualy Paphaphanh, Bounteum Sibounheuang, and Thong Xeuy, as well as the directors of the Sangha College, for all of their assistance. Achan Seng at Wat Lao Riverside was also helpful in explaining Sangha education before 1975. The students and teachers at Vat Naxai, Vat Nom Lam Chan, Vat Don Khong, Vat Mai, Vat Ban Nam Chan, Vat Paluang, and many other monasteries were extremely generous with their time and in sharing stories about their experiences from the 1940s to the present in Lao monastic schools.

61 Geoffrey Gunn, *Rebellion in Laos: Peasant and Politics in a Colonial Backwater* (Boulder, Colo.: Westview, 1990); Gunn, *Political Struggles in Laos, 1930–1954: Vietnamese Communist Power and the Lao Struggle for National Independence* (Bangkok: Duang Kamol, 1988), 76–99; and Gunn, *Theravadins, Colonialists, and Commissars in Laos* (Bangkok: White Lotus, 1998), 118. See also Joel Halpern, *Government, Politics, and Social Structure in Laos: A Study of Tradition and Innovation* (New Haven, Conn.: Yale University Press, 1964), 58–60.

62 Halpern, *Government, Politics, and Social Structure*, 60.

63 See *Phra Buddha Sasana kap kan bokkong Pathet* [Buddhism and Governing the Nation], composed in 1916 by Prince Wachirayan of Thailand, which was popular and translated into English. The English version was the basis of a Lao translation by Bunthip Chanthamontri under the sponsorship of the Asia Foundation and Lao royal patronage in 1967.

64 Many monks in Laos claim that Phra Maha Vichit Viranano, the abbot of Wat Phra That Lampang Luang, also graduated *prayok* 9 (the highest Pali degree in the modern Thai system). Although he studied at Wat Anongkaram in Bangkok, he has been vague about how his Pali 9 ranking was determined.

65 These books, many of which were published posthumously, include (Phra) Mahapan Anantho, *Prabeni Lao* (Vientiane, Laos: Vat Mikhathaya, 2517 [1973]) and his *Thang ha sai* (Vientiane, Laos: Vat Buddhavong Paluang, 1969). Phra Mahapan Anantho's legacy was promoted by a number of his students in the early 1970s and in a recent revival in the past ten years. For example, his work is mentioned in a book on the biographies of five great monks (Ongkan Buddhasāsanā Sampan Lao, *Xivit lae phon ngan khong phramahathera ha ong* (Vientiane: Ongkan Buddhasāsanā Sampan Lao, 2001), and his teachings inspired monks and lay scholars like Phra Maha Khamphuey, Phiak Chunlamontri, and Phra Philawong and the highly influential monk in contemporary Laos, Phra Sali Kanthasilo. His life is also briefly summarized in his funeral festschrift, edited by Phaya Khamnai Chantabanya, Khamha Sithiratvong, and many others.

66 (Phra) Mahapan Anantho, *Samakhom Buddhavong Lao lae Buddhayaovason Lao* (Vientiane, Laos: Vat Buddhavong Paluang, 1971).

67 Ibid., 16–17.

68 I have been able to acquire seventeen volumes of this magazine. An adequate

description deserves a separate publication, which I am in the process of completing. Subjects range widely from meditation practice to short ethical sermons to vernacular summaries of Pali texts. There are even short historical accounts of different religious sites in Laos (mostly in Vientiane) and the origins of local rituals (like the *pithi pun phra that luang*). Each issue emphasizes the importance of education.

69 I thank Patrice Ladwig for providing a number of important sources for the life of Phra Mahapan Anantho. In particular, see the report of his funeral in *Lao Samay Daily News* 288 (1968).

70 (Phra) Mahapan Anantho, *Sing thi dai phop hen nai Langka thavip* (Vientiane, Laos: Khana Pha Song Lao pai paxum Lanka, Vat Buddhavong Paluang, 1966).

71 Leuam Thamxot, trans., *Dhammabanyai bang suan*, by Phra Sunntthamrangsi Khamphiramethachan (Vientiane, Laos: n.p., 1969).

72 (Phra Maha) Sikham Vorachit, *Banha Vinai phak 1* (Vientiane, Laos: Siaonasit, 1973).

73 Several other Lao publications that emerged in the late 1950s and throughout the 1960s speak to the changing dynamics and "progressive" ideas of Lao monastic education in this period. For example, in 1958 Phra Maha Vandi Silachanthani published a book (in his own handwriting) promoting vegetarianism in Laos (a largely unpopular lifestyle in Laos' past or present), *Phommatham mangsavirat* (Vientiane, Laos, 1958).

74 Alongside secular subjects like mathematics and biology, Lao folktales are a major part of monastic education. See Justin McDaniel, "Creative Engagement," *Journal of the Siam Society* 88 (2000): 156–77. See also Anatole-Roger Peltier, *Le roman classique Lao* (Paris: École française d'Extrême-Orient, 1988); Louis Gabaude, *Les cetiya de sable au Laos et en Thaïlande*, EFEO Monograph no. 118 (Paris: École française d'Extrême-Orient, 1979); and Georges Condominas, *Le bouddhisme au village* (Vientiane, Laos: Édition des cahiers de France, 1998), 44–45.

75 Many school buildings built by the French are still standing, but often they have been abandoned or converted into farmhouses, clinics, or even garages.

76 Pierre-Bernard Lafont, "Buddhism in Contemporary Laos," in *Contemporary Laos*, ed. Martin Stuart-Fox (St. Lucia: University of Queensland Press, 1982), 149, 152.

77 Stuart-Fox, *Buddhist Kingdom*, 102.

78 Lafont, "Buddhism in Contemporary Laos," 153.

79 Ibid., 155.

80 Ibid. I recently edited a new translation of Father Marcello Zago's "Un bonze accuse!" *Pôle et tropiques*, June 1978, 131–42. In this article Zago describes the harsh conditions for monks in Laos in 1976 and 1977. He reports on suicides by monks and on the closing of "Abhidhamma schools" in Vientiane.

81 See Stuart-Fox, *Buddhist Kingdom*, 105. He notes that in 1979 "there were only 1,700 monks in the country, down from 20,000 when the PL took power" (105).

82 See (Maha) Khampheuy Vannasopha, *Religious Affairs* (Vientiane, Laos: Ministry of Information and Culture, 2003), 6.

83 See especially Chatthip Nartsupa, "The Ideology of Holy Men in North East Thailand," *Ethnological Study* 13 (1983): 111–34; and Steven Collins, *Nirvana and Other Buddhist Felicities* (Cambridge: Cambridge University Press, 1998), 405–13.

84 Many Lao monks did express their political dissatisfaction by leaving the country.

85 The term *taeng* can also mean "speak" in connection to sermons.

86 Khana khamakan bunbap kan seuksa [Ministry of Education, Research Committee], *Khong hang lak sut khong Vithayalai Song* (Vientiane, Laos: Ministry of Education, 1996).

87 Peter Koret, "Books of Search," in *Laos: Culture and Society*, ed. Grant Evans (Chiang Mai, Thailand: Silkworm, 1999), 226–57.

88 Recently I met two Lao men from California who were ordaining at Wat Boworniwet in Bangkok. I asked them why they did not ordain in Laos. They claimed that only in Bangkok could they get a "good education." See also Bungon Piyabhan, *Lao in Early Bangkok* (Bangkok: Chulalongkorn University Press, 1998); Chawalee Na Thalang, *Prathetracha khong Siam nai samai Phrabatsomdet Phra Chulachom Klao Chao Yu Hua* (Bangkok: Chulalongkorn University Press, 2541 [1998]); and Grabowsky, "Forced Resettlement Campaigns."

89 Sila Viravong's *My Life* (Vientiane, Laos: Dokbuakaeo, 2005) offers a personal account of the mobility of many Lao students.

90 See Wachirayan, *Phra Buddha Sasana kap kan bokkong Pathet*, 3–16.

91 See Justin McDaniel, "History of the National Library of Laos," *Newsletter of the Fragile Palm-Leaves Preservation Project* 5 (2002): 2–3. Thousands of Russian-language books (mostly science textbooks and engineering manuals) were given by the Soviet government to Laos in the 1970s and 1980s. Most of these books now sit in large piles in the second-floor hallway of the National Library of Laos.

92 The catalogs, curricula, and college histories are available in situ. They were compiled by the directors of the college under the auspices of the Ministry of Education (Kasuang Seuksathika). One change to monastic education in recent years has been its growing internationalism. For example, the first major international conference on Lao literary heritage was held in Vientiane in January 2004. Lao monks occasionally travel to ceremonies in Thailand, and the royal family of Thailand has made donations and public overtures to the Lao Sangha. Lao people have established monasteries in the United States, France, and Australia. While this international activity is certainly not commensurate with that of Thai monks, the Lao Sangha is growing and becoming more actively involved in its own education and past. English and World Religions are now taught as courses. Central Thai books, VCDs, and audiocassettes produced mostly in Bangkok monasteries are slowly seeping into the curriculum of Lao monasteries.

Chapter 2 Wandering Librarians

Approximately three pages from this chapter appear in similar form in McDaniel, "Notes on Lao Influence on Northern Thai Literature."

1 Patrick Jory, "Thai and Western Scholarship in the Age of Colonialism," *Journal of Asian Studies* 61, no. 3 (2002): 899.

2 See Volker Grabowsky, "Population and State in Lan Na prior to the Mid-sixteenth Century," *Journal of the Siam Society* 93 (2005): 1–68.

3 Camille Notton, *Annales du Siam* (Paris: Limoges, 1930), vol. 2; Donald Swearer, *Wat Haripuñjaya* (Missoula, Mont.: Scholars Press, 1974). See also Kham Champakaeomani, *Phra That Chedi-Wat samkhan lae Phra Khru Yot Kaeo Pun Samek* (Chiang Mai, Thailand: Social Research Institute, 2537 [1995]).

4 McDaniel, "Two Bullets in a Balustrade." Volker Grabowsky has produced the best study of this period (1558–1782) to date. See his *Bevölkerung und Staat in Lan Na* (Wiesbaden: Otto Harrassowitz, 2004), 149–76. This work focuses not only on the independence resistance movement (Antibirmanischer Unabhängigkeitskampf) in the 1760s through the 1780s and suppression of local power in the 1550s to the 1570s but also on ways in which the Burmese rule differently in different locations, like Chiang Saen and Chiang Rai. In general, he correctly notes that "die Rolle der Birmanen in Lan Na war nicht allein durch Unterdrückung und Widerstand gekennzeichnet" (149), and in many cases "der Respeckt vor den Gepflogenheiten erstreckte sich auch auf die materiellen Lebensbedingungen des Volkes" (151).

5 See *Saranukhrom wattanatham Thai phak neua* [Encyclopedia of Northern Thai Culture] (Bangkok: Thanakhan Thai Phanich 2542 [1999]), s.v. "Chedi Luang," by Ratana Phrahmphichai, 1599–1606; and Ratanapañña, *Jinakālamālīpakaraṇam*, transcribed and edited by A. P. Buddhadatta (London: Pali Text Society, 1962), xxiv, xxvi, xxvii, n128, n135.

6 The use of the word *Tai* for the peoples in Northern Thailand, the Shan States, Sipsongpanna, and Laos is a point of contention among linguists, historians, and ethnographers. Much work has been done on defining what exactly "Lan Na," or "Northern Thailand," comprises geographically, politically, and so forth. I use *Northern Thailand* as a common designation, even though the region did not have defined political borders until 1929 under the Kingdom of Siam and was not part of "Thailand" until 1939. Linguistically, ethnically, economically, and historically, of course, the region has never been bound by political borders and is a crossroads of people from what are now called the Shan States, Lao PDR, Yunnan (China), and Assam (India). Many other scholars have chosen to use the terms *Lan Na* and *Lan Xang* when referring to these regions before the modern period. *Lan Na* (One Million [*Lān*] [Rice] Fields [*Nā*]), centered in Chiang Mai, and *Lan Xang* (One Million [*Lān*] Elephants [*Xāng*]), centered alternately in Luang Phrabang and Vientiane, were terms used for royal polities (mandalas, or galatic polities or city-states). The name Lan Na is found in inscriptions dat-

ing to as early as the sixteenth century and referring to the region from which the Chiang Mai royalty could exact tribute. Lan Xang (Pali: *sata-naga-nahuta*) is attested in sixteenth-century inscriptions from Luang Phrabang and is referred to as "Dasalakkhakñjara" in the *Jinakālamālīpakaraṇam* chronicle of Chiang Mai in 1516–23. King Fa Ngum, the supposed founder of Lan Xang, called his kingdom Lān Xāng Hom Khao (One Million Elephants under a White Parasol). No information is available about how commoners self-identified in the region before the late nineteenth century. *Lan Na* and *Lan Xang* are equally obfuscating terms because they are often seen as being prenational entities with distinct peoples, literatures, religious practices, languages, and so forth. These two kingdoms had much commerce, especially intellectual commerce, as seen in any study of manuscripts before the twentieth century. Furthermore, they were rarely, if ever, intact kingdoms with stable political rule. The local princes of many cities and towns in the region paid tribute to multiple regional kings. See Evans, *Short History of Laos*, 34–36; Thongchai Winichakul, *Siam Mapped* (Honolulu: University of Hawaii Press, 1994), 97–99; and Mayoury Ngaosyvathn and Pheuiphanh Ngaosyvathn, *Kith and Kin Politics: The Relationship between Laos and Thailand* (Manila, Philippines: Journal of Contemporary Asia Publishers, 1994). Many princes, like those of Nan, Kengtung, and Luang Phrabang, considered themselves largely independent for long stretches of time. For over two hundred years the Burmese military occupied much of present-day Northern Thailand and sacked Luang Phrabang twice between 1550 and 1763. Lan Xang itself was divided into three kingdoms in 1695. The British employed hundreds of Shan forestry workers in the region. Much of Northern Laos was effectively ruled by the Vietnamese for decades.

7 David Wyatt and Aroonrut Wichienkeeo, *The Chiang Mai Chronicle*, 2nd ed. (Chiang Mai, Thailand: Silkworm, 1998), 207.

8 Saraswati Ongsakun, *Prawatsat Lan Na* (Bangkok: Amarin, 2539 [1996]), 138; Prasert na Nagara, *Tamnan munlasatsana Wat Suan Dok* (Bangkok: Ekasanwichakan Samakhom Prawatisat, 2537 [1994]), 59–65; *Saranukhrom wattanatham Thai phak neua*, 6651–58. More information is also found in (Phraya) Prachakitopachak, ed., *Phongsawadan Yonok* (Bangkok: Chabap Hosamut haeng chat, 2504 [1961]); and Wyatt and Aroonrut, *Chiang Mai Chronicle*.

9 Inscriptions at the monastery show that there were many monks with Burmese names (or monastic names [*chaya*] given in Burma). Laddawan Saesiao writes, "Many monks had names associated with Burma. For example, Phra Buddhabukam, the monk who composed the *Mūlasāsanā* [*History of Buddhism*] at Wat Suan Dok. Furthermore, there is evidence from the year 1392 [Buddhist era, or 1935] monks from Lan Na had gone to the Chawesikong Pagoda in Burma to pay homage." Laddawan Saesiao, *200 pi Bama nai Lanna* (Bangkok: Tenmay, 2545 [2002]), 126. Wat Chiang Man, the oldest monastery in Chiang Mai, was a common stop for royalty to pay homage to Buddhist relics (Wyatt and

Aroonrut, *Chiang Mai Chronicle*, 208). The school and manuscript library at this monastery were supported by the Burmese, especially the high-ranking monk Somdet Phra Mahādhammikarājādhirāt. In 1568 he oversaw the construction of a *chedi*, *vihāra*, *uposatha* hall, library, and surrounding wall (*Saranukhrom wattanatham Thai phak neua*, 1964). A Burmese abbot, Maha Hindādiccavaṃsa, was given charge of the monastery in 1682.

10 Saraswati Ongsakun, *Prawatsat Lan Na*, 148.

11 Ibid., 149; and Sommai Premchit, "Palm Leaf Manuscripts and the Traditional Sermon," in *Collected Papers of the World Fellowship of Buddhists*, ed. Saeng Chandrangaam (Chiang Mai: International Conference of Thai Studies, 1980), 74–86. Other information comes from an early draft of Daniel Veidlinger's *Spreading the Dhamma* (Honolulu: University of Hawaii Press 2006), cited with permission of the author. This early history has also been well documented in several local relic and monastery histories. For a summary of these chronicles, see McDaniel, "Transformative History," 159–75.

12 Saraswati Ongsakun, *Prawatsat Lan Na*, 138. See also Laddawan, *200 pi*, 128; and Thienchai Aksorndit, Koroknok Ratanawarabhan, and Wandi Santiwudiwedhi, *Lanna* (Bangkok: Mahamakut Monastic University Press, 2545 [2002]), 122–25.

13 *Saranukhrom wattanatham Thai phak neua*, s.v. "Wat Suan Dok," by Pupapha Kunyosaying, 6655.

14 Wyatt and Aroonrut, *Chiang Mai Chronicle*, 16, 208.

15 Laddawan, *200 pi*, 130.

16 Victor Lieberman, *Burmese Administrative Cycles: Anarchy and Conquest c. 1580–1760* (Princeton, N.J.: Princeton University Press, 1984), 41; and Laddawan, *200 pi*, 130–31. For background, see also Frank Trager and William Koenig, *Burmese Sit-tans, 1769–1826: Rural Life and Administration* (Tucson: University of Arizona Press, 1979); and Than Tun, ed., *The Royal Orders of Burma, AD 1598–1885* (Kyoto: Center for South East Asian Studies, Kyoto University, 1988).

17 *Saranukhrom wattanatham Thai phak neua*, s.v. "Wat Suan Dok," 6658.

18 Donald Swearer discusses the importance of local temple chronicles in "Signs of the Buddha in Northern Thai Chronicles," in *Wannakam Buddhasasana nai Lan Na*, ed. Phanphen Krüathai (Chiang Mai, Thailand: Silkworm, 1997). For a general introduction to Northern Thai historical material as it relates to Buddhism, see Balee Buddharaksa, introduction to *Mahāvaṃsamālinīvilāsinī* (Chiang Mai, Thailand: Social Research Institute, 2545 [2002]); and, Hans Penth, "Buddhist Literature of Lān Nā on the History of Lān Nā's Buddhism," *Journal of the Pali Text Society* 23 (1997): 43–81.

19 *Saranukhrom wattanatham Thai phak neua*, 1966; Wyatt and Aroonrut, *Chiang Mai Chronicle*, 123.

20 Wyatt and Aroonrut, *Chiang Mai Chronicle*, 186.

21 Hans Penth, Phanphen Khrüathai, and Silao Kesaprohm, *Chareuk Phra Chao*

Kawila: 2334–2357, Corpus of Lanna Inscriptions (Chiang Mai, Thailand: Social Research Institute, 2541 [1998]), 2:177–94.

22 Chirasak Dechawongya, Woralan Bunyasurat, and Yuwanat Woramit, *Ho trai Wat Phra Singh* (Chiang Mai, Thailand: Social Research Institute, 2539 [1996]), 3–6. See also Hans Penth, Phanphen Krüathai, and Silao Kesaprohm, *Chareuk nai Phiphitaphan Chiang Saen*, Corpus of Lanna Inscriptions (Chiang Mai, Thailand: Social Research Institute, 2540 [1997]), 1:69–70.

23 Quoted in Nicholas Basbanes, *Patience and Fortitude* (San Francisco: HarperCollins, 2001), 102.

24 Ibid.

25 The move to Laos may have been made easier because of the direct political connection between the royal houses of Chiang Mai and Luang Phrabang at this time. See Lorrillard, "Earliest Lao Buddhist Monasteries"; and McDaniel, "Notes on Lao Influence on Northern Thai Literature."

26 Saengthong Photipuppha, *Pavat Meuang Xieng Kouang* (Vientiane: Preservation of Lao Manuscripts Program, 1998), 27–28.

27 Hans Penth, Phanphen Krüathai, and Silao Kesaprohm, *Chareuk nai Phiphitaphan Lampitun*, Corpus of Lanna Inscriptions (Chiang Mai, Thailand: Social Research Institute, 2542 [1999]), 3:177; and Phanphen Krüathai, *Khlong pheun Wat Phra Sing* (Chiang Mai, Thailand: Social Research Institute, 2539 [1996]).

28 Harald Hundius, "Colophons from Thirty Pāli Manuscripts from Northern Thailand," *Journal of the Pali Text Society* 14 (1990): 34–35. Hundius offers the intriguing suggestion that there might have been a political reason behind Krupa Kañcana's arranging a project to which both the royal leaders of Luang Phrabang and Phrae could contribute. An inscription and a manuscript colophon reveal that the king of Luang Phrabang directly supported Kañcana in 1836. This demonstrates clearly that the provinces of Nan and Phrae in Northern Thailand were often intellectually influenced more by Luang Phrabang than by Chiang Mai. See also Wyatt and Aroonrut, *Chiang Mai Chronicle*, 71–77.

29 For sources on Phrae history in 1836, see Justin McDaniel, "Invoking the Source" (Ph.D. diss., Harvard University, 2003); and Dhawat Rotphrom, *Prawatmahatthai suan phumiphak changwat Phrae* (Phrae, Laos: Krasuang Mahatthai, 2541 [1998]), 20–27, 65–73, 146–55. Worapon Bambat gave me a funeral memorial book self-published by Seri Chomphuming called *Meuang paepin haeng haeng Gosai* (2543 [2000]) and *Virapurut Chao Meuang Phrae* (2500 [1957]). Lao sources are also vague for 1836 in Phrae. The Lao Ministry of Education's *Phongsavadan Lao* reports on events in Luang Phrabang up to 1817 and then resumes in 1839 (Kaxuang thalaeng khao lae wattanatham, *Pavasat Lao*).

30 Duangchan Khruchayan, *Prawat khong Wat Selāratanapabbatārāma Lai Hin Luang Kaeo Chang Yeun* (locally printed and composed) (n.d., n.p.). See also Mingsan Khaosaat, *Wihan dong chumchong sakun chang Lampang* (Chiang Mai, Thailand: Chiang Mai University Press, 2525 [1982]).

31 (Phra) Mahaniyom Thanathatto, *Tamnan Phra Borom That Lampang Luang* (n.p., n.d.).

32 Ibid.

33 Ibid. At the monastery there is a sign that recounts parts of the story, as well as a statue of a coconut. The abbot and his two students were very helpful in relating this history of the monastery. There are confusing accounts in some of their stories, however.

34 Kañcana's collection is not only the largest of its kind, but it contains mostly vernacular and bilingual genres that are also common in Laos. I compared passages from similar manuscripts in Luang Phrabang, Phrae, Chiang Mai, and Vientiane. I do not go into the philological and codicological details at this time but just note here that, not only do the titles of the texts overlap closely, but the contents of the texts are similar. This indicates that the "revival" of Northern Thailand's literary tradition in the early to mid-nineteenth century, which is largely attributed to Kañcana, is directly connected to the Buddhist literary tradition that had been nurtured in Luang Phrabang in the seventeenth and eighteenth centuries. David Wharton has started cataloging and analyzing ninety-nine manuscripts from Northern Thailand found in Laos. This effort will greatly improve the understanding of manuscript transfer in the region.

35 See also the major study by Thomas Borchert, "Educating Monks: Buddhism, Politics, and Freedom of Religion on China's Southwest Border" (Ph.D. diss., University of Chicago, 2006).

36 High-quality Pali manuscripts were produced, however, even after the "golden age" of Pali literature in the seventeenth and eighteenth centuries. If one just looks at Dhammapada manuscripts, one sees this activity. For example, there is a manuscript from 1583 from Wat Lai Hin and two others composed in 1647, from Wat Doi Kaeo in Chiang Mai (99 folios) and from Wat Kasa in Chiang Rai (109 folios). There are also three rare manuscripts that contain only Pali verses. These were used by Oskar von Hinüber and K. R. Norman for their Pali Text Society edition (*The Dhammapada* [London: Pali Text Society, 1994]). One, dating from 1786 (57 folios), was found at Wat Lai Hin and is missing verses 319–43. Another from 1611 is almost complete.

37 Veidlinger, in *Spreading the Dhamma* (chap. 2), convincingly argues that writing, although not as important in early Northern Thai history, grew significantly after 1800.

38 Another inscription from Doi Tung composed in 1605 (appearing on the base of a statue of a *ṛṣi* (sage) and lauding the enshrining of Buddhist relics at Doi Tung) uses three different scripts and two languages. A mixture of Northern Thai (Yuan) and Fakkham was employed for the dating and main text of the inscription that describes the history of the *ṛṣi* and the relic. This text is in Thai. The Shan script is used for Pali. It shows a population of mixed ethnicity. It also shows that there was no standard rule on the use of certain scripts for vernacular or classical languages.

39 See A. B. Griswold and Prasert na Nagara, "No. 12, Inscription 9," *Journal of the Siam Society* 62, no. 1 (1974): 95, 110–11; and Prasert na Nagara, *Tamnan munlasatsana Wat Suan Dok*, 22–32.

40 These are vernacular and Pali narratives. *Nipāta* refers most likely to chapters of the *jātaka*, and *niyai* are folktales or stories drawn from *jātaka*. *Nikāya* refers most likely to Suttanta, Abhidhamma, and Vinaya works. The list of these manuscripts (532 fascicles) can be seen as an appendix in David Wyatt's *The Nan Chronicle* (Ithaca, N.Y.: Cornell Studies on Southeast Asia, 1994).

41 See Center for the Promotion of Art and Culture (CPAC), Chiang Mai University, manuscript LP 0470008100.

42 For background, see Oskar von Hinüber, "Chips from Buddhist Workshops," *Journal of the Pali Text Society* 22 (1996): 35–57; Hundius, "Colophons from Thirty Pāli Manuscripts"; and Veidlinger, *Spreading the Dhamma*.

43 There is no evidence that women ever composed manuscripts or worked as scribes, although there were women who patronized monastic education. However, in a grammatical manuscript, used to train novices and monks as well as interested laypeople (including women) in Pali grammar, there is a simple, one-line colophon on a separate folio that suggests it was composed by a woman. It appears to have been added later and written by a scribe in a different hand. For more details and a translation of the colophon, see McDaniel, "Invoking the Source," chap. 2.

44 Clear spelling anomalies (e.g., *sradejjha*, the long *ū* in *bhikkhūno*, and *arant* for *āratta*) and several ambiguous statements are found in this colophon. I am unsure whether *kab*, which usually means "with" in Northern Thai, is actually part of Phinarassa's name, since it precedes it both times; it could also indicate the dative, like the Northern Thai word *kae*. The dative possibility is indicated by the use of the dative/genitive singular form of *bhikkhu* the second time the word is mentioned. It does not state here whether the scribe was a monk.

45 A survey of dates on colophons, in chronicles, and on inscriptions, confirms this characteristic. See J. C. Eade, *The Thai Historical Record: A Computer Analysis* (Ithaca, N.Y.: Cornell Southeast Asian Studies Publications, 1996).

46 The *Udenavatthu* is one of the longest stories in the entire *Dhammapada-atthakathā*, and parts of it are also found in the *Divyāvadāna* and in the Sanskrit *Kathāsaritsāgara* and the Tibetan *Kandjur*.

47 A record indicates that a scribe named Abhiyai was at Wat Sung Men in 1860, and since this text was written in 1831, this could be the same person, because Abbhiya was the name found on the last folio of this fascicle and Abhiñña is a version of that name; "ññ" in Northern Thai is pronounced "y," and a Northern Thai person can transliterate his or her names into other scripts following Pali spelling conventions or local pronunciation. The doubling of consonants and the dropping of consonants are also extremely common. Northern Thai and Lao monks, nuns, and novices have birth names, vocational names given by their preceptors, and nicknames. To these names a wide array of titles are added. It is

not uncommon for a person to spell his or her name two to three different ways in Northern Thailand.

Chapter 3 Kings and Universities

1 For a study of these economic, cultural, and other connections, see McDaniel, "Notes on the Lao Influence on Northern Thai Literature." See also Andrew Walker, *Legend of the Golden Boat* (Honolulu: University of Hawaii Press, 1999); Akiko Iijima, "The Nyuan in Xayabury and Cross-Border Links to Nan," in *Contesting Visions of the Lao Past*, ed. Christopher Goscha and Søren Ivarsson (Copenhagen: Nordic Institute of Asian Studies, 2002); Grabowsky, "Forced Resettlement Campaigns"; João de Barros, *Ásia de João de Barros: Dos feitos que os Portugueses fizeram no descobrimento e conquista dos mares e terras do Oriente; Terceira Década* [Asia, by João de Barros: The Deeds of the Portuguese in the Discovery and Conquest of the Seas and Lands of the East, Third Decade], ed. Hernaní Cidade and Manuel Múrias. (1563; repr., Lisbon: Agência Geral das Colónias, 1946); François Bizot and François LaGirarde, *La pureté par les mots* (Vientiane, Laos: École française d'Extrême-Orient, 1996); Katherine Bowie, "Ethnic Heterogeneity and Elephants in Nineteenth-Century Lanna Statecraft," in *Civility and Savagery: Social Identity in Tai States*, ed. Andrew Turton (Richmond, U.K.: Curzon, 2000); Bunroeng Buasisaengbasoet, *Pavatsat Silapa lae sathabatthayakamsin Lao*; Luiz de Camões, *The Lusiads of Luiz de Camões*, trans. from the 1572 Portuguese edition, ed. L. Bacon (New York: Hispanic Society of America, 1950); Douangxai Luangpasi, *Somdet Phra Chao Sethathirat*; Grant Evans, "Tai-ization: Ethnic Change in Northern Indo-China," in Turton, *Civility and Savagery*, 263–90; Evans, *Short History of Laos*, chaps. 1–2; Garnier, *Further Travels in Laos and Yunnan*; G. E. Gerini, *Researches on Ptolemy's Geography of Eastern Asia* (London: Royal Geographical Society, 1909); Volker Grabowsky and Andrew Turton, eds., *The Gold and Silver Road of Trade and Friendship: The McLeod and Richardson Diplomatic Missions to Tai States in 1837* (Chiang Mai, Thailand: Silkworm, 2003); François-Jules Harmand, *Laos and the Hilltribes of Indochina* (Bangkok: White Lotus, 1997) (composed between 1845 and 1921 and published as *Laos et les populations sauvages de l'Indochine*); Johann Mathias Hase, "Asia Secundum Legitimas," in *Maps from Ancient Times to the Mid-nineteenth Century* (1744; repr., Leipzig: Acta Humaniora, 1989); Chirasak Dechawongya, *Khwam saphan rawang Lan Na Lan Xang*; Chirasak Dechawongya, Woralan Bunyasurat, and Yuwanat Woramit, *Ho trai Wat Phra Singh*; Charuwan Chaonuan, *Nithan peun meuang Lao* (Bangkok: Chulalongkorn University Press, 2545 [2002]); Lorrillard, "The Earliest Lao Buddhist Monasteries," 187–98; Daniel McGilvary, *A Half Century among the Siamese and the Lao* (New York: Revell, 1912); Henri Mouhot, *Travels in the Central Parts of Indochina (Siam), Cambodia, and Laos, during the Years 1858, 1859, and 1860* (repr., New York: Oxford University Press, 1989); Pavie, *Recherches sur l'histoire de Cambodge, du Laos et du Siam*; Hans Penth, "On the

History of Chiang Rai," *Journal of the Siam Society* 77, no. 1 (1989): 11–30; Nicolas Sanson, "L'Asie," in *Maps from Ancient Times to the Mid-nineteenth Century*; Savaeng Phinith, *Contribution à l'histoire du royaume de Luang Prabang* (Paris: École française d'Extrême-Orient, 1990).

2 Victor Mair, *Anthologizing and Anthropologizing* (Durham, N.C.: Duke University Press, 1992), 24; Sara Davis, *Song and Silence* (New York: Columbia University Press, 2005), 13.

3 See Charles Keyes, "National Heroine or Local Spirit? The Struggle over Memory in the Case of Thao Suranari in Nakhon Ratchasima," in *Cultural Crisis and Social Memory*, ed. Shigeharu Tanabe and Charles Keyes (Honolulu: University of Hawaii Press, 2003), 120.

4 Ibid., 123. Prince Damrong also wrote the book *Thai rop pama* (1917; repr., Bangkok: Rung Watana, 2514 [1971]), in which the Burmese played no role in Siamese/Thai culture, art, language, etc.

5 Keyes, "National Heroine or Local Spirit," 123.

6 McGilvary, *Half Century among the Siamese and the Lao*, 192.

7 Ibid., 79.

8 Jessie MacKinnon Hartzell, *Mission to Siam* (1919; repr., Honolulu: University of Hawaii Press, 2001), 21.

9 See, e.g., excerpts from Block, Younghusband, and Le May's travel reports in Michel Smithies, ed., *Descriptions of Old Siam* (Singapore: Oxford Asia, 1995), 217–22, 228–32, 274–79.

10 Hartzell, *Mission to Siam*, 49.

11 Mary Backus, *Siam and Laos* (Philadelphia: Presbyterian Board of Publication, 1884); McGilvary, *Half Century among the Siamese and the Lao*; Mouhot, *Travels in the Central Parts of Indochina*; Hartzell, *Mission to Siam*; Mayoury Ngaosrivathana and Kennon Breazeale, eds., *Breaking New Ground in Lao History* (Chiang Mai, Thailand: Silkworm, 2002); Etienne Aymonier, *Notes sur le Laos* (Saigon: Imprimerie coloniale, 1885); Lillian Johnson Curtis, *The Laos of North Siam* (1903; repr., Bangkok: White Lotus, 1998).

12 Krishna Charoenwong, "Western Influence on Education in Northern Thailand" (n.p., n.d).

13 Recently, the Central Thai government has allowed Yuan script to be taught in schools as a separate subject in the North. Primary instruction still has to be in modern Thai/Siamese script.

14 Charoenwong, "Western Influence on Education," 8.

15 Thongchai Winichakul, *Siam Mapped: History of the Geo-body of a Nation* (Honolulu: University of Hawaii Press, 1994).

16 Chawalee Na Thalang, *Prathetracha khong Siam*, 68.

17 Ratanaporn Sethakul, "Political Relations between Chiang Mai and Kongtung in the Nineteenth Century," in *Changes in Northern Thailand and the Shan States, 1886–1940*, ed. Prakai Nontawasee (Singapore: Institute of Southeast Asian Studies, 1988), 311.

18 Ibid., 313.

19 Khaimuk Uthayawali states that there was no "formal" monastic education system in Northern Thailand until the Siamese took over the region. Khaimuk Uthayawali, "Rongrian Wat," in *Saranukhrom wattanatham Thai phak neua* (Bangkok: Thanakhan Thai, 2542 [1999]), 5910–12. Thongchai Winichakul, *Siam Mapped*, 18–19.

20 Even as late as 1965, Michael Moerman comments that "the comparative unintelligibility of Siamese results from its Cambodian and Sanskrit borrowings rather than from differences of tonal structure which might be of greater genetic significance." Michael Moerman, "Who Are the Lue?" *American Anthropologist* 67, no. 5 (1965): 1218.

21 Evans, *Short History of Laos*, 34–36; and Thongchai Winichakul, *Siam Mapped*, 97–99.

22 Thongchai Winichakul, *Siam Mapped*, 102–3.

23 Siamese, French, and British designs not only led to the end of Northern Thailand's "independence," the drawing of borders, and the rise of the modern nation of Thailand, but they also worked to create Laos as a discernable geopolitical entity.

24 Benedict Anderson theorizes that there was a rupture about two hundred years ago between previous dynastic, divinely ruled kingdoms and the very "modes of apprehending the world." Benedict Anderson, *Imagined Communities*, rev. ed. (London: Verso, 1991), 28. The medieval Christian mind, like the Siamese or Filipino mind, had "no conception of history as an endless chain of cause and effect or of radical separateness between past and present" (29). Classical languages like Pali, Arabic, and Chinese created a translocal community of "signs" and were seen as sacred. The eighteenth century saw the "dawn" of nationalism and the "dusk" of religious "modes of thought" (19–20). Anderson believes that there is a radical separation between the religious past and the national present. B. J. Terwiel, working specifically on Thai history, also thinks in terms of ruptures between the premodern (pre-Fourth Reign/mid-nineteenth century) and the modern. He notes that fundamental social changes were the result of the creation of civilian ranks of administration under King Mongkut; the ability of commoners to own more than ten thousand *rai* of land; the rise of prominent, nonroyal families (like the Bunnags) into court positions; and the pro-Western, reform-minded Siamese royalty. B. J. Terwiel, *A History of Modern Thailand* (Lucia: University of Queensland Press, 1983). Anthony Reid notes that the "early modern period" was a "watershed" because it marked a period of commercial expansion, the dominance of "universalist faiths" (Islam, Buddhism, Catholicism, and Confucianism) based on sacred scripture in classical languages, new technology in weapons and later in printing, and the first contacts with the West. Reid, *Charting the Shape of Early Modern Southeast Asia* (Chiang Mai, Thailand: Silkworm, 1999), 6.

25 Collins, *Nirvana*, 54–55.

26 There have been two major original Pali compositions in the past three hundred years in Central Thailand, one in 1788 and another in 2005. The first is the *Sangityavaṃsa*, a history of Buddhism; the second is the most recent history of the office of the Sangharāja in Bangkok, the *Sāsanadīpanī*, composed by Banyen Limsawat and published in honor of the present Sangahrāja of Thailand, Somdet Phra Ñāṇasaṃvara. Phra Sugandha edited the new edition of this text. See (Somdet Phra Sangharat Somdet Phra) Ñāṇasaṃvara, *Sāsanadīpanī* (Bangkok: Mahamakut Monastic University Press, 2548 [2005]).

27 Nidhi Aeusrivongse, especially, argues that the Siamese elite were not victims to these "foreign" forces, but that they actively incorporated Western notions of religiosity into their systematic reform of Buddhism. See Nidhi Aeusrivongse, "Buddha wibat," in *Kan patirūp Phra Buddha Sasana nai Prathet Thai*, ed. Nidhi Aeusrivongse and Pramuan Phengchan (Bangkok: Kongtung Raktham, 2542 [1999]), 1–28.

28 Yoneo Ishii, *Sangha, State, and Society* (Honolulu: University of Hawaii Press, 1986); Craig Reynolds, "The Buddhist Monkhood in Nineteenth Century Thailand" (Ph.D. diss., Cornell University, 1973); Jory, "Thai and Western Scholarship"; David Wyatt, *The Politics of Reform* (New Haven, Conn.: Yale University Press, 1969); Phra Khammai Dhammasami, "Between Idealism and Pragmatism" (Ph.D. diss., Oxford University, 2005). Although Reynolds's dissertation focuses on elite reform in nineteenth-century Thai Buddhism, his life's work in general has been focused on the history of the "nonelite." See also Tamara Loos's thorough and provocative study of gender and family and the rise of modernity in Thailand, in *Subject Siam: Family, Law, and Colonial Modernity in Thailand* (Ithaca, N.Y.: Cornell University Press, 2006). Wyatt also wrote several essays on the rise of secular education in Siam around 1902; see Wyatt, "Samuel MacFarland and Early Educational Modernization in Thailand, 1877–1895," "Almost Forgotten: Ban Phraya Nana School," and "Education and the Modernization," all three reprinted in his *Studies in Thai History* (Chiang Mai, Thailand: Silkworm, 1994), 219–66.

29 Ishii, *Sangha, State, and Society*, 70; see further Ishii's detailed study of the history of this act, 60–80. One can see many of the details of these reforms being either embraced or rejected in the *Thaleang kan khana Song*, a six-volume compendium of Sangha activity (especially in Bangkok), published by *Rong phim Krung Thep Daily Mail* and edited by Phraya Mathāthibodi and Phraya Phakdinrubet, printed between 2456 (1913) and 2461 (1918). These volumes drew their information from the Sangharāja's reports, reports of the Mathātherasamakhom, the Chao Khana of the monthon, district and village levels, as well as oral reports of monks and novices.

30 Wyatt associates the rise of religious educational reform in Siam partly with King Chulalongkorn's European tour of 1897 and Wachirayan's push for religious educational reform with the ascendance of Western-inspired secular education in Siam. However, the Japanese, along with the West, played a major

part in nineteenth-century religious reform in Siam. In fact, in 1902, when the Sangha Act was announced, the Japanese example was explicitly stated as its inspiration. Wutichai Mulasilpa, *Kan patirup kanseuksa nai samai Phrapatsomdet Phra Chulachom Klao Khao Yu Hua* (Bangkok: Thai Wattana Panich, 2539 [1996]), 62.

31 Jory, "Thai and Western Scholarship," 899.

32 Ibid., 912; and Siriwat Khamwansa, *Song Thai nai 200 pi* (Bangkok: Mahachulalongkorn Monastic University Press, 1981), 333–34. It should be noted, Peter Skilling (personal communication, June 2005) emphasizes, that King Chulalongkorn was a dynamic thinker in regard to the *jātaka* and Buddhist textual scholarship in general. He composed a study of the *jātaka* (based primarily on Caroline Rhys-Davids's study in 1903) that called for local folktales, histories, and religious texts to be collected and preserved. He presented this study in an address to the Boranakhadi Samoson in 1907. Therefore, without further corroboration, the claim that he had *jātaka* burned is dubious.

33 Reports by Simon De La Loubère and Jeremias van Vliet are some of the only sources for the period. The former mentioned oral translations of Pali passages in front of the king. Then there were three tiers of exams supposedly based on exams used in the late Ayutthayan period. A few haphazard efforts to reform Siamese Buddhist education had been made by King Boromatrailokanat in 1466 and King Narai in 1688. The former awarded small areas of tenable rice paddy to monks and novices who had "knowledge of the Dhamma." The latter instituted exams based on the ability to read (i.e., to sound out, not necessarily know the semantic meaning of) "a certain Bali book" (as reported by Nicolas Gervaise, a visitor to the Ayutthayan court from France in 1687). De La Loubère reported that monks outside the city refused to submit to these exams unless they were given by their own abbot. King Rama II expanded the three-tier system to nine levels of Pali examinations in 1818. See Ishii, *Sangha, State, and Society*, 82–83.

34 Ishii, *Sangha, State, and Society*, 76–77, 93–95.

35 For a summary of these mostly noncanonical exams, see ibid., chap. 3.

36 Maurizio Peleggi's *Lords of Things* (Honolulu: University of Hawaii Press, 2002) is illuminating here. Further is Alexandra Denes's work on the royal interest in "tourism" and the consumption of exotica and Orientalia (forthcoming).

37 A new branch of Mahachulalongkorn Monastic University, the Buddhaghosa College in Nakhon Pathom near Bangkok, has grown significantly over the past three years. It is a campus focused on Paliseuksa and is quickly becoming, along with "Section 25" of the central Bangkok campus, the center of Pali grammatical study.

38 For more detailed information on the content and implementation of the curricula in these different categories and with an emphasis on lower-level monastic education, see Chamroen Sekdhira, *Laksut Phra Pariyatidham phanaek saman seuksa* (Bangkok: Krasuang Seaksathikan, 2534 [1993]).

39 That the Sangha Act of 1902 and the promotion of Pali education by the reformers of the nineteenth century have not been well implemented is pointed out in Buratin Khampirat's master's thesis at the School of Education at Chulalongkorn University, "Chabhap lae banha khong kan seuksa Phra Pariyatidham phanaek Pali nai Samnak Rian Suan Klang" (Withyaniphon Phak Wicha Sarat Seuksa Mahawithyalai Chulalongkorn, 2539 [1996]), and by Thipawan Khwanon's study, "Chabhap lae banha chai laksut Phra Buddhasasana tam laksut prathomseuksa Buddhasasana nai rongrian sangkat samnakngan khana kammakan kan seuksa ekachon Krungthep Mahanakhon" (Withyaniphon Phak Wicha Prathom Seuksa Chulalongkorn, 2541 [1998]). Buratin attributes the poor implementation to budgetary problems and the fact that Pali education focuses too much on memorization and not enough on how Pali texts can offer perspectives on global problems (147–66). Thipawan, by comparison, identifies the problems with lack of adequate facilities (ventilated classrooms, proper desks, etc.) and the fact that the teachers are not well trained in method or content (166–89). See also Sukanya Nitungkorn, "Higher Education Reform in Thailand," *Southeast Asian Studies* 38, no. 4 (2001): 461–80.

40 I again thank Peter Skilling for discussions on this issue.

41 Wyatt, *Politics of Reform*, 219.

42 Ibid.

43 Damrong had been administering educational reform in the North since 1880.

44 Ishii, *Sangha, State, and Society*, 72.

45 Ibid., 85–92. There are certainly exceptions. In fact, the present head of the Abhidhamma institute at Mahachulalongkorn University is from rural Ubon Ratchathani Province, on the Lao and Cambodian border. One of the highest-ranking Pali professors is from a small village in Lampang Province in the North. Many of the monks at the famous royal monastery, Wat Benchamophit, are from the North. These changes have been slow in coming.

46 The Sociology Department at the secular Chiang Mai University recently started a Lan Na–language radio program (CMU FM 93.2).

47 *Prawat Mahamakut Rachawithyalai nai Phra Borom Rachupatham* (Bangkok: Mahamakut Monastic University Press, 2521 [1977]), 73–74. The curricula of the various faculties of Mahachulalongkorn Monastic University (education, Buddhism, humanities, and social sciences) and information about the graduate programs and the various campuses (Nakhon Sri Thammarat, Nakhon Ratchasima, Khon Kaen, Ubon Ratchathani, Phrae, Surin, Phayao, and the Paliseuksa Buddhaghosa Campus in Nakhon Pathom) are now available online, at http://www.mcu.ac.th/.

48 Originally, in 1898, the Pariyatidhamma secondary curriculum of Mahamakut had nine levels of instruction in Thai using Thai texts or Thai translations of Pali texts, followed by four levels of Pali textual studies. The nine Thai (or *fai* Thai) levels are the study of the *Dhammapada-atthakathā* (three levels), *Maṅgaladīpanī*, *Sāratthasaṅgaha*, samāṇera *Pathamasamantapāsādikā*, Visuddhimagga,

and *Sāratthadīpanī*. The Pali (or *fai rāmaṇa*) levels are *Vinaya vibhanga*, *Vinaya mahāvagga*, *Muttaka Vinaya vinicchaya*, and *Pathamasamantapāsādikā*. See *Prawat Mahamakut Rachawithyalai nai Phra Borom Rachupatham*, 26–27. This curriculum was designed to assist students in preparing for examinations. The secondary system has been expanded in recent years, and students not sitting for examinations use other texts, which are shared by both sects.

49 Wyatt, *Politics of Reform*, 235.

50 I thank Balee Buddharaksa and the vice presidents of educational policy at both Wat Chedi Luang and Wat Suan Dok for their help and permission to observe classes and interview students at these campuses in January 2001.

51 The source for these statistics is Rung Kaendaeng, ed., *Raingan sathitidansasana khong Prathet Thai*, CD-ROM (Bangkok: Samnakngan khana kammakan kan seuksa haeng chat, 2542 [1999]).

52 Besides these three divisions of primary and secondary religious education in Thailand, there are also Buddhist Sunday schools (Rongrian kanseuksa Buddhasāsanā wan athit). In 1958 they were introduced formally to Thailand at Wat Yuwanajaransristi in Bangkok. They are usually funded by private donors who are dissatisfied with the purely secular education provided by government schools. These local and independent Sunday schools design their own curricula and schedules, hire their own teachers (usually monks or lay volunteers), and produce or purchase their own materials. There are 1,239 registered Sunday schools in Thailand. Of these, 82 percent are in the North and Northeast. Sunday schools continue to grow as government schools become less accessible, less funded, and more overcrowded. There are 59,000 students in monastic Sunday schools. Most of these students are not novices or monks. In fact, female lay students (31,434) under eighteen years of age make up the largest percentage of students in monasteries. These students are served by 1,787 teachers (about 3 teachers for every 100 students). Of these teachers, 1,329 are laypeople. Only 2,233 go on for high school–level monastic education (about 4 percent).

53 The only study of monastic education in Northern Thai is by Swearer. His book *Wat Haripuñjaya* looks at one very large monastery in Lamphun Province (63–79).

54 A number of new "secular" subjects are being taught, and now the results of the examinations and the curriculum for those examinations are produced in CD-ROM. I thank the staff at the "Sanam Luang," examination office for all of their help in acquiring the CD-ROM editions of the curricula, the examination guidebooks for the past ten years, and the statistics of the results. See also Phot Saphianchai (the former secretary of the National Ministry of Education), *Chabhap chatkan seuksa khong khana Song Thai* (Bangkok: Samnakngan khana kammakan kan seuksa haeng chat, 2523 [1979]); Sawana Phonphatkun, *Kan seuksa lae kan damrong samanaphet Song Thai* (Bangkok: Mahamakut Monastic University Press, 2524 [1980]); and Phra Mahasuk Suwiro, "Khwam sonchai to kan seuksa Phra Pariyatidham khong Phra Song seuksa karani Phra Nisit

Mahachulalongkorn Rachawithyalai" (Ph.D. diss., Withyaniphon Khana Sangkhomwithyalai lae Manusyawithaya Mahawithyalai Thammasat, 2539 [1996]).

55 I thank the participants at the Buddhism and Law workshop at the Rockefeller Center in Bellagio, Italy (March 2006), for comments on this section of the book. The direct comments of Peter Skilling, Frank Reynolds, Ryuji Okudaira, Richard Whitecross, Bernard Faure, Vesna Wallace, Petra Keifer-Pülz, Leslie Gunawardana, and Mark Tamthai were especially helpful. Tamthai informed me of two new programs at Payap University. First, there is a "team-taught" World Religions course offered at Mahachulalongkorn Monastic University (and occasionally at Mahamakut Monastic University), in which monastic students study with students at Payap University and are taught by professors at both institutions. The location of the class even changes week by week, with students visiting each other's campuses. A projected program will expand joint study by students at the Islamic University in Pattani (Southern Thailand) and Payap University, which also may include monastic university students. In a new program at Mahidol University (a famous secular institution near Bangkok) monks are studying religious studies. Its students are mostly lay, undergraduate women and some senior monks. The former are primarily interested in the secular study of comparative religion (I thank a number of students there for the time spent answering my questions), and the latter are in a special program that allows monks who have passed *prayok* 9 Pali examinations to write a thesis and obtain their Ph.D. in Buddhist studies in less than four years. Certainly, monks study often in modern Thailand at secular universities throughout the country (especially in Chulalongkorn, Thammasat, and Kasetsart), and lay teachers advise dissertations at monastic universities. An increase is seen in Indian professors of Sanskrit at Thai monastic university campuses, and a growing number of Thai monks are seeking a range of degrees in India and Australia. Also, new Buddhist universities are opening in Thailand, like that initiated by the Dhammakāya sect in Pathum Thani and a branch of the ecumenical Australian World Buddhist University that was started in 2000 in Bangkok.

56 I thank Phra Sillapa, a professor of Pali and Dhammaseuksa at Mahamakut, for providing me with photocopies of these curricula and for his humorous stories of trying to fit a lifetime of dhamma studies into fifteen-day curricula. These curricula are not published for distribution and can be obtained only at the university. Their details are beyond the scope of this study.

57 Shawn McHale, *Print and Power* (Honolulu: University of Hawaii Press, 2004), 60.

Chapter 4 Genres, Modes, and Idiosyncratic Articulations

1 William Johnson, "Toward a Sociology of Reading in Classical Antiquity," *American Journal of Philology* 121, no. 4 (2000): 593–627; Veidlinger, *Spreading*

the Dhamma; and Steven Collins, "Notes on Some Oral Aspects of Pāli Literature," *Indo-Iranian Journal* 35, nos. 2/3 (1992): 121–35.

2 Hayden White, *Metahistory: The Historical Imagination in Nineteenth Century Europe* (Baltimore: Johns Hopkins University Press, 1973).

3 Mikhail Bakhtin, *The Dialogic Imagination: Four Essays by Mikhail Bakhtin*, ed. Michael Holquist (Austin: University of Texas Press, 1982), quoted in Allon White, *Carnival, Hysteria, and Writing: Collected Essays and Autobiography* (Oxford: Oxford University Press, 1993), 136–39.

4 Ernst Gombrich, "The Necessity of Tradition," in *The Essential Gombrich*, ed. Richard Woodfield (London: Phaidon Press, 1996), 172–73. I thank Michael Feener for giving me this essay.

5 George Bond, *The Word of the Buddha* (Colombo, Sri Lanka: Gunasena, 1975), 402–13.

6 Pali is often called a prestige language. See Reid, *Charting the Shape of Early Modern Southeast Asia*, 11; Victor Lieberman, "Was the Seventeenth Century a Watershed?" in *Southeast Asia in the Early Modern Era*, ed. Anthony Reid (Chiang Mai, Thailand: Silkworm, 1993), 242; Collins, *Nirvana and Other Buddhist Felicities*, 47; and Oskar von Hinüber, *Untersuchungen zur Mündlichkeit früher mittelindischer Texte der Buddhisten* (Mainz: Akademie der Wissenschaften und der Literatur, 1994), 198–232. The importance of the exact pronunciation of Pali in ordination ceremonies is well known. See François Bizot, *Les traditions de la pabbajjā en Asie du Sud-est* (Paris: École française d'Extrême-Orient, 1988).

7 Dominic LaCapra, *Rethinking Intellectual History* (Ithaca, N.Y.: Cornell University Press, 1983); Tristan Todorov, *Les genres du discours* (Paris: Éditions du Seuil, 1978); Cesare Segre, *Introduction to the Analysis of the Literary Text*, trans. John Meddemmen (Bloomington: Indiana University Press, 1988); Thomas Beebee, *The Ideology of Genre* (University Park: Pennsylvania State University Press, 1994); David Duff, *Modern Genre Theory* (London: Pearson Education, 2000).

8 While some *nissaya* and *nāmasadda*, especially narrative *nissaya*, were for a general audience specific triggers to general topics, they were most often the basic texts of the serious monastic students' curriculum. However, *vohāra* were, and are, used as sermon notes on more general topics for both lay and monastic audiences. Audiences for *vohāra* would have been (and are today) mostly serious lay audiences sitting at public sermons. *Nissaya* and *nāmasadda* audiences were more likely to be monks and novices in private classes. *The Dictionary of Monastic Terms* [Prochananukrom pheua kan seuksa Buddhasat chut kham wat], ed. (Phra) Thammakittiwong Thongdi Suratecho (Bangkok: Choraka, 2548 [2005]), provides definitions of several homiletic terms. For example, the definition for "thet chaeng" (clarifying sermon) notes that the sermon giver "khayai khwam" (expands the meaning) of the Buddha's words when giving a sermon.

9 George Steiner describes each translator as having his own "private thesaurus . . . part of his subconscious, of his memories so far as they may be verbalized, and of

the singular irreducibly specific ensemble of his somatic and psychological identity." George Steiner, *After Babel* (Oxford: Oxford University Press, 1992), 47.

10 See Justin McDaniel, "A Lao Homily," Études thématiques Lao (Paris: École française de Extrême-Orient, forthcoming).

11 Umberto Eco, *Serendipities* (New York: Harvest Books, 2002), 30–31.

12 Ibid., 39.

13 Bakhtin, cited in White, *Carnival, Hysteria, and Writing*, 145.

14 From the title *Madhurāsajambū*, this manuscript should be based on the first section (the *Jambūdīpuppattivatthu*) of the thirteenth-century Pali text *Madhurasavāhinī*. However, this manuscript shows little connection to the Pali source.

15 Historians Anthony Reid, Victor Lieberman, and Keith Taylor have all noted the shift from textual production based largely in externally validated (i.e., texts written in classical languages like Arabic, Latin, Pali, Chinese, and Sanskrit) sources of authority over local traditions to the rise of vernacular textual production in the late seventeenth century. While this general trend is certainly true, there had been great efforts to compose or at least translate texts in and into the vernacular before this period. *Nissaya, vohāra*, and *nāmasadda* are the first stages of this transformation. These scholars overlook the existence of vernacular literature in Southeast Asia prior to the seventeenth century, for example, epic poems from Java, like the *Sutasoma* and *Arjuna Wiwaha*. Moreover, the *Mahājāti Kham Luang* was composed in sixteenth-century Thailand. Authors of texts like the *Ratanabimbavaṃsa* and the *Sihiṅganidāna* state that they are translated from Deyyavbhāsā (vernacular/lit.: language of the giver).

16 Donald Swearer, *The Legend of Queen Cāma* (Albany: State University of New York Press, 1998); Steven Collins, *Selfless Persons* (Cambridge: Cambridge University Press, 1982); and Ranjini Obeyesekere, *Jewels of the Doctrine* (Albany: State University of New York Press, 1991).

17 On the lasting popularity of the *jātaka* in Thailand and Laos, see Jory, "Thai and Western Scholarship," 892–96, 911–13. There are dozens of studies on the use of *jātaka* in art and drama. For an overview, see McDaniel, "Invoking the Source," 128–43. The most "substantial published account of Thai literature," by John Leydon in 1808, notes that some of the most popular texts in Thailand were "cheritas" or "chinok" (*jātaka*). He calls *jātaka* "romantic fictions" and "historical mythological fables." See David Smyth, "James Low on Siamese Literature (1839)," *Journal of the Siam Society* 95 (2007): 159–200, 159. Prince Damrong in 1904 wrote that "King Chulalongkorn, Rama V, proclaimed that these volumes containing all this deep Buddhist philosophy were not very enjoyable for most people to read. He requested that people begin to publish fables, *jakata* tales, and fiction." Cited in Grant Olson, "Thai Cremation Volumes: A Brief History of a Unique Genre of Literature," *Asian Folklore Studies* 51 (1992): 279–94, 285.

18 Bosaengkham Vongthala, *Vannakhadi Lao* (Vientiane, Laos: Kaxuang Seuksa,

1987), 208. Vernacular epic poems, which do not have any particular religious themes, such as the *Thao Hung Thao Chuang* and *Xin Sai*, are also often chanted at Buddhist ceremonies in Laos. See Douangdeuane Bounyavong, *Thao Hung Thao Chuang* (Vientiane: National Library of Laos, 2000).

19 The last two are drawn from the non-Buddhist Sanskrit *Pañcatantra*.

20 Daniel Veidlinger gladly found a colophon on a *nāmasadda* for me that offers a clue as to how *nāmasadda* worked. It is titled *Niruttisadda* and *Uccaaraṇadīpanī* (CS 1160 [1798]), from Wat Duang Di, archive 19–04–035–00 (one fascicle) His translation reads as follows: "The sponsor Rājaguru the forest dweller got me, Mahāyassa Bhikkhu, to write it for the benefit of good people who know about the function and origin of the syllables, namely: long (*dīgha*), short (*rassa*), heavy (*guru*), light (*lahu*), soft (*sithila*), sounded (*dhanita*), connected (*saṃbandha*), vocalized/turned round(?) (*vattita*) . . . to analyze it according to the Pali."

21 *Mahāvagga* I.32, 1; I.54, 4; I.1, 36; V.1, 5; V.4, 2.

22 The term *nissaya* may be derived from the fact that *nissaya* "lean on" Pali texts.

23 I thank Michel Lorrillard for a particularly stimulating discussion of this issue.

24 On the history of writing in Northern Thailand, see Daniel Veidlinger, "Spreading the Dhamma" (Ph.D. diss., University of Chicago, 2002), 273.

25 This manuscript is SRI 7902401E068, of the Social Research Institute.

26 These lists are similar to those found in the *Petavatthu-atthakathāa* (PvA 144) and *Vimānavatthu-atthakathā* (VvA 100).

27 See Peter Skilling, "The Rakṣā Literature of the Śravakayāna," *Journal of the Pali Text Society* 27 (1992): 109–82; and Skilling, "Sources for the Study of the Maṅgala and Mora Suttas," *Journal of the Pali Text Society* 24 (1998): 185–93.

28 To do so, however, is strictly against Indic *mīmāṃsā* rules.

29 It should be noted that no manuscript with the title *Dhammasaṅgaṇī-mūlaṭīkā* or -anuṭīkā has been found in Laos. After a long search, I could find no sustained parallels between the *ṭīkā* and this manuscript.

30 See Justin McDaniel, "Notes on the Study of Pali in Thailand," in *Embedded Religions: Essays in Honour of W. S. Karunatillake*, ed. Suzanne Mrozick, Carol Anderson, and W. Rajapakse (Colombo, Sri Lanka: S. Godage and Brothers, 2007).

31 See, e.g., f.v.53–f.v.55.

32 The *Padarūpasiddhi* and its *ṭīkā* are of particular importance to modern Pali grammatical resources in Thailand and Laos. In his introduction to the Thai script edition (2000), Phra Dhammānanda states that the *Padarūpasiddhi* is needed by modern students of Pali grammar because Kaccāyana does not employ enough examples. (Phra) Dhammānanda Mahāthera, ed., *Padarūpasiddhi khong Buddhappiya-Mahāthera* (Bangkok: Thammasapha, 2000). I thank Phra Maha Sompong Mudito for allowing me to sit in on his advanced Pali grammar classes.

33 The "()" indicates a missing, damaged, or unreadable part of the manuscript. There is no direct object that ends the phrase "[this] is called." I imagine that

the scribe naturally wrote "wā" after "mai jeu," taking it as a verb (as is common in Northern Thai) instead of a noun, which in this case it should mean "appellation." Therefore, the author may have meant "*si* is the appellation for the vocative case." This shows how texts and translations through the natural process of accretion resulting from human error can change a source text in strange, confusing, expansive, and significant ways.

34 *Nissaya* on grammatical texts are found scattered in many monastic libraries in the region, but never as a complete set (e.g., all eight sections of Kaccāyana). Wat Lai Hin, for example, possesses two *Nissaya tatthadhita*, two *Nissaya samāsa*, one *Nissaya kitaka* and two *Nissaya kāraka*, one *Nissaya nāma*, and one *Nāmasabda* (*Nāmasadda*), but no *Nissaya ākhyāta* or *Nissaya sandhi*. Although the incompleteness of collections could mean that some texts were lost, it could also indicate that they were not kept or bound together as were many other texts.

35 Arthid Sheravanichkul, personal communication, July 2006.

36 Chonlada Reuangraklikhit, *Wannakhadi Ayutthya ton ton* (Bangkok: Chulalongkorn University Press, 2544 [2001]).

37 I thank Amara Prasithrathsint for providing me with a copy of her essay. See her "Reduplication as a Device for Forming Adjectives and Adverbs in Thai" (paper delivered at the Thai Language and Literature conference, Chulalongkorn University, Bangkok, November 11, 2006).

38 Chonlada Reuangraklikhit, *Wannakhadi Ayutthya ton ton*, 292–329.

39 Of course, many popular "secular" Thai stories are adaptations for oral performance of *jātaka* and other Buddhist and Hindu narratives. See Pomarin Charuwon's "Suat Phra Malai: Botbat khong khatikam lang khwam tai to wannakam lae sangkhom," in *Phithikam tamnan nithan phleng: Botbat khong khatichon kap sangkhom thai*, ed. Sukanya Succhaya (Bangkok: Chulalongkorn University Press, 2548 [2005]), 113–62.

40 The title on the manuscript is *Wohan Thammapot* [*Vohāra Dhammapada*], Chiang Mai University Center for the Promotion of Art and Culture, Phrae Province, Thailand, CPAC PHR 010207600, 15 fascicles, CS 1193 (1831). For a detailed discussion of the problems with this colophon and the authorship of this text, see McDaniel, "Invoking the Source," 302–15. The distinction between the rounded script (*mul*) used for Pali words and the slanted script (*crieng*) used for vernacular words in Khmer manuscripts is not found in Lao or Thai manuscripts. For Cambodian manuscripts, see Olivier de Bernon, "L'état des bibliothèques dans les monastères du Cambodge," *Sorn Samnang* 2 (1998): 872–82; see also Harris, *Cambodian Buddhism*, 82–84.

41 Jacques Leider (personal communication, October 2004) directed me toward royal orders (dated May 7, 1635; July 3, 1783; and December 14, 1785) in which different kings emphasized the importance of correct spelling. These efforts at consistent spelling in Pali texts are not unknown for Pali texts in Northern Thailand and Laos, but the authors of *nissaya*, *vohāra*, and *nāmasadda* were generally not concerned with precise spelling. Orthophonic spelling led to much

variation. However, the correct spelling in *yantra* (Thai: *phra yan*) is essential, because they are incantations.

42 See Harald Hundius, *Phonologie und Schrift des Nordthai*, Abhandlungen für die Kunde des Morgenlandes 48.3 (Stuttgart: Franz Steiner Verlag, 1990); and Richard Davis, *A Northern Thai Reader* (Bangkok: Siam Society, 1970). See also several script charts and Northern Thai readers and practice books published in Thai (and two in Lao). In 2004 the National Library of Thailand published a comprehensive set of script charts covering every major script used in the Thai-speaking regions (although not showing the numerous exceptions to all charts found in many manuscripts); see Arak Sanghitkun, *Baep akson boran chabap nak rian nak seuksa* (Bangkok: Hong samut haeng chat, 2547 [2004]). See also Kesem Siriratphiriya, *Tua Meuang: Kan rian phasa Lanna phan khrong srang kham* (Chiang Mai, Thailand: Sukhothai University Press, 2548 [2005]). Still very useful for Tham script is (Phay Luang Maha) Sena Phouy's handwritten *Méthode d'enseignment élémentaire du Laotien* (Vientiane, Laos: Institut bouddhique, 1934).

43 Johnson, "Toward a Sociology of Reading," 607.

44 Susan Cherniack, "Book Culture in Sung China," *Harvard Journal of Asiatic Studies* 54, no. 1 (1994): 7.

45 Ibid., 15. See also G. Thomas Tanselle, "The Varieties of Scholarly Editing," in *Scholarly Editing: A Guide to Research*, ed. D. C. Greetham (New York: Modern Language Association of America, 1995), 11–31.

46 Fred Robinson, *The Editing of Old English* (London: Blackwell, 1982), chap. 1.

47 Katherine O'Brien O'Keeffe, "Editing and the Material Text," in *The Editing of Old English: Papers from the 1990 Manchester Conference*, ed. D. G. Scragg and Paul E. Szarmach (Cambridge, U.K.: D. S. Brewer, 1994), 148–151.

48 John Dagenais, introduction to *The Ethics of Reading in Manuscript Culture* (Princeton, N.J.: Princeton University Press, 1994).

49 Panel at the 2002 American Academy of Religion Annual Meeting, "Buddhist Manuscript Cultures," Toronto.

50 Beautifully illustrated palm-leaf manuscripts are found throughout the region. Many are from Central Thailand, but they are not *nissaya*, *vohāra*, or *nāmasadda*. Most Northern Thai and Lao manuscripts do have gilded edges and red- and gold-lacquered wooden covers, long and eloquent colophons, silk binding ribbons, and straight and glossy sepia-colored palm leaves. Although the blue, black, gold, and scarlet palm and mulberry paper manuscripts of Central Siam (especially in the nineteenth century), the red- and gold-lacquered Burmese manuscripts, and the ivory and squid-ink Mon manuscripts are evidence of better-funded scriptoria, the Lao and Northern Thai scriptoria appear to be the product of a stable and well-funded educational and artistic atmosphere. Recently in Laos, I had two opportunities to learn how to cut leaves from trees, hang and dry the leaves on bamboo racks, and etch the leaves using a wooden stylus with a sharp metal tip. After the leaves were cut and dried and the text

inscribed, ash was rubbed over the leaves so that the ash became embedded in the grooves made by the stylus. The dark ash makes the inscribed letters stand out in contrast to the sepia-colored leaves. Then we applied an oil (*nam man yang purisut*, a type of "pure rubbery" oil) to the leaves to make the ash stick in the grooves. These were produced through direct copying—text to text. This was and is accomplished with a lightweight bamboo rack, whereby the original leaf and the leaf to be copied are held in the rack by the scribe (see photos). I thank Donna Strahan at the Asian Art Museum in San Francisco for helping me chemically analyze this oil. I also thank Thong Xeuy and Phra Prasoet.

51 For manuscript production, economy, time span, and patronage, see von Hinüber, "Chips from Buddhist Workshops." For manuscript production in Southeast Asia, see Noel Singer, "Kammavaca Texts: Their Covers and Binding Ribbons," *Arts of Asia* 23, no. 1 (1993): 91–105; *Kan tam sammutthai lae kan triam bai lan* (Bangkok: National Museum, 2530 [1988]); and *Baeprian nangseu phasa boran* (Bangkok: Ho samut haeng chat, 2543 [1999]). The Northern Thai encyclopedia, *Saranukhrom watthanatham Thai phak neua*, has several sections on the production and use of palm leaf; see, especially, vol. 7 (2542 [1999]), 3541–46. For a study on the storage of manuscripts in Northern Thailand, see Na Baknam, *Tu Phra Traipidok* (Bangkok: Silapakorn University, 2543 [1999]).

52 These hybrid Sanskrit and Pali lexemes are very common in Thai, Northern Thai, and Lao. *Nissaya* texts often give both the Pali and Sanskrit spelling or a hybrid.

53 Chinese translators often inserted their own interpretations and additions into the original Sanskrit text. Lewis Lancaster, "An Analysis of the Aṣṭasahāśrikaprajñāpāramitāsūtra from Chinese Translations" (Ph.D. diss., University of Wisconsin–Madison, 1968).

54 See Oskar von Hinüber, "Pali und Lanna in den Kolophonen alter Palmblatthandschriften aus Nord-Thailand," in *Indogermanica et Italica*, ed. G. Meiser (Innsbruck: Universität Innsbruck, 1993); von Hinüber, "Pāli Manuscripts of Canonical Texts from Northern Thailand," *Journal of the Siam Society* 71 (1983): 75–88; and von Hinüber, "Die Sprachgeshichte des Pali im Spiegel der südostasiatischen Handschriftenüberlieferung," in *Untersuchungen zur Sprachgeschichte und Handschriftenkunde des Pāli I* (Mainz: Abhandlungen der Akademie der Wissenschaften und der Literatur, 1988), 46–49.

55 Suzanne Reynolds, *Medieval Reading* (Cambridge: Cambridge University Press, 1996), 8; Vivien Law, *The Insular Latin Grammarians* (Totowa, N.J.: Biblio Distribution Services, 1982); and Law, *The History of Linguistics in Europe* (Cambridge: Cambridge University Press, 2003), 94–109, 230–43.

56 Reynolds, *Medieval Reading*, 8.

57 Prapod Assavavirulhakarn, "From the Vessantara Jātaka to the Mahājāti Kham Luang" (paper presented at the Thai Language and Literature conference, Chulalongkorn University, Bangkok, November 11, 2006).

58 The *Aṭṭhakathāmātikā nissaya* instructs the reader/listener how to understand

sandhi (euphonic combination) rules in Pali. Folio *ghā*, line four, explicitly mentions the reason the long *a* is found in a compound. Even though the *Madhurāsajampū* is a known Pali text, this local manuscript has little relation to the Pali source. Instead, the folktale contained herein is native to Northern Thailand and seems to exist only in the vernacular. It is related to the Lao story of *Om lom daeng khiao*, which has no known and extant *nissaya*.

59 Fascicle f.*kā*.v.3–f.*kā*.v.5: this passage is unclear as a result of damage to the manuscript.

60 F.6.3–f.7v.1.

61 This story reveals close parallels with the Lao version of the Sanskrit story *Nandukapakaraṇam*. The Lao version was most likely drawn from the Tamil version of the original Sanskrit. Often in Laos, Buddhist narratives are conflated with "secular" Sanskrit stories. See Henry Ginsburg, "Thai Literary Tales Derived from the Sanskrit Tantropākhyāna" (master's thesis, University of Hawaii, 1967); and Jean Brengues, "Une version laotienne du Pañcatantra," *Journal Asiatique* 10 (1908): 357–95.

62 In the ninth and tenth folios of the *Sutmon nissaya* from Chiang Mai, the terms *maṅgala* (auspicious) and *uttamaṃ* are translated five times in exactly the same way. The repetitive definition teaches that *maṅgala* is cognate with Northern Thai (*monkon*) and that *uttamaṃ* and *udom* are cognate, even if spelled differently. The definition also employs alliteration. Depending on how the ligature is written and on the status of the final consonant in Northern Thai or Lao, two words spelled in identical ways can be pronounced differently. These differences can often be emphasized when reading a text out loud, but they would be difficult to discern if read silently without the aid of a teacher familiar with the phonetic parameters of both Pali/Sanskrit and Northern Thai / Lao. While modern Thai/Siamese script retains the spellings of words that are derived from Pali/Sanskrit (even though their vocalization does not follow the orthography), the different Lao governments have changed the Lao script three times in the past century. These changes have effectively dropped all letters from the alphabet that exist for the purpose of transliterating Pali and Sanskrit. So whereas the Thai alphabet has three different letters for the palatal, lingual, and dental sibilants, in order to be able to write the three sibilants in Sanskrit, the Lao alphabet has dropped all but the dental sibilant. Where the Thai alphabet had two letters for the retroflexed and non-retroflexed *l* in Pali, Lao has dropped to just one, since there is no phonetic equivalent to a retroflexed *l* in spoken Lao.

63 Mark Allon has done the most extensive study on repetition in Pali texts, in *Style and Function*, Studia Philologica Buddhica 12 (Tokyo: International Institute for Buddhist Studies, 1997). Allon sees Pali texts as using repetition to ensure exact repetition of the texts and as signs that the texts were orally composed and conveyed, and in so doing he departs from the theses of Albert Lord (*The Singer of Tales* [1965, in German; New York: Atheneum, 1968]); Jan Gonda, (*Stylistic Repetitions in the Veda* [Amsterdam: Royal Netherlands Academy of

Arts and Sciences, 1959]); Hermann Oldenberg (*Zur Geschichte der altindischen Prosa: Mit besonderer Berücksichtigung der prosaisch-poetischen Erzählung* [Berlin, Weidmannsche Buchhandlung, 1917]); and Klaus Bruhn ("Repetition in Jaina Narrative Literature," *Indologica Taurinensia* 11 [1983]: 27–75). The type of repetition found in *nissaya, nāmasadda,* and *vohāra* is very different. *Nissaya* rarely employ verbatim repetition but use instead a relatively loose type of repetition based on lexical association and grammatical sequencing. *Nissaya*-style repetition is similar to that of the *ākhyaṇa* theory. On repetition, see Rupert Gethin, "The Mātikās, Memorization, Mindfulness, and the List," in *The Mirror of Memory*, ed. Janet Gyatso (Albany: State University of New York Press, 1992); Richard Gombrich, "How the Mahāyana Began," in *The Buddhist Forum*, vol. 1, ed. Tadeusz Skorupski (London: School of Oriental and African Studies, 1990); and Lance Cousins, "Pali Oral Literature," in *Buddhist Studies: Ancient and Modern*, ed. P. Denwood and A. Piatigorsky, 71–90 (London: Curzon Press, 1983).

64 Wirawat Intaraporn shows a similar use of repetition in early Bangkok poetry. See his "The Dynamics of Khlong in Thai Literature" (paper presented at the Thai Language and Literature conference, Chulalongkorn University, Bangkok, November 12, 2006).

65 This commentarial practice was not limited to post-canonical texts in either the Sanskrit or Pali tradition. The *Mahākammavibhaṅga sutta, Koṭṭhika sutta, Sīvaka sutta, Aggivacchagotta sutta,* and *Sallekha sutta,* as well as sections of the *Cullavaga* and *Mahāvagga,* the *Atthuddhāro* (of the *Dhammasaṅgaṇī*), and the *Niddesa* of the *Khuddaka nikāya,* are classed as canonical but employ many of the commentarial services discussed earlier.

66 From the introduction to Buddhaghosa's commentary of *Samantapāsādikā,* in E. W. Adikaram, *Early History of Buddhism in Ceylon* (Colombo, Sri Lanka: Gunasena, 1946), 2.

Chapter 5 The Culture of Translation

1 See Khana thamngan prawat kanphim nai Prathet Thai [Committee of the History of Printing in Thailand], *Siam phimopakan prawatsat kan phim nai Prathet Thai* (Bangkok: Matichon, 2006). I thank Peter Skilling for calling it to my attention. See also a short introduction in Pirasri Powathong, "Transformation of Bangkok in the Press during the Reign of Rāma V," *Manusya: Journal of Humanities* 6, no. 1 (2003): 47–53.

2 For a study of literacy in the region, see Anthony Reid, *Southeast Asia in the Age of Commerce,* 1450–1680 (New Haven, Conn.: Yale University Press, 1990), 1:215–35.

3 In the 1960s and early 1970s scribes worked at the palace in Luang Phrabang. They copied by hand old texts on palm leaf onto new palm leaf instead of producing printed texts. This activity continued until the Pathet Lao takeover in

1975. For mention of this process, see, e.g., the introduction to Sachchidanand Sahai, *Rāmāyana in Laos* (Delhi: B. R. Publications, 1973), xiii.

4 *Plae* (often transcribed as *blae*) means "translation" in Thai. It is a word that I have found only once in Northern Thai manuscripts and seems to have been uncommon among Northern Thai speakers.

5 Pali dictionaries did not become available in Central Thai until the mid-twentieth century, and only in 1996 was the first Northern Thai dictionary printed. These dictionaries are not widely available in the North. There is not a Pali-Lao dictionary, although numerous Lao dictionaries do mention if a word "originated" from Pali/Sanskrit. One rare example of a modern Lao *nāmasadda* is *Kham son lao buat*, composed at Vat Phonphranao in Vientiane in 1969. It provides a Pali to Lao gloss of the terms used in the ordination ritual.

6 Paitun Sinlarat, "Influence of Western Education and Adjustment of Thai Education," in *Proceedings of the Fourth International Conference of Thai Studies* (Kunming: China Institute of Southeast Asian Studies, 1990), vol. 1. There are many *nissaya* in the National Library (Bangkok). Most were taken from Laos in the nineteenth century.

7 Segre, *Analysis of a Literary Text*, 199–200.

8 Burt Roest, ed., *Aspects of Genre and Type in Pre-modern Literary Cultures* (Groningen, Netherlands: Styx, 1999), 57.

9 Todorov, *Les genres du discours*, 45–46.

10 Alastair Fowler, "Transformations of Genre," in *Modern Genre Theory*, ed. David Duff (London: Harlow Press, 2000), 234.

11 According to Thomas Beebee, "Generic differences are grounded in the 'use-value' of a discourse rather than its content, formal features, or its rules of production." Beebee, *Ideology of Genre*, 7.

12 No author is listed, and there is no introduction. It seems to be a transcription of a Northern Thai *nissaya* manuscript of the *Maṅgalatthadīpanī* (a Pali commentary composed around 1525 in Chiang Mai). The history of the Tha Phra Chan Press is described well in Peter Skilling, *Manuscripts Transmitted in Central Siam, Materials for the Study of the Tripiṭaka*, vol. 1 (Bangkok: Fragile Palm Leaves Project, 2002).

13 Pricha Changkhwanyeun, introduction to *Thammawacana wohan Thai* (Bangkok: Chulalongkorn University Press, 2540 [1997]).

14 Ibid., 1–3.

15 Ibid. Udom Rungreuangsri's new *Wohan Lan Na* (Chiang Mai, Thailand: Chiang Mai University Press, 2549 [2006]) provides further evidence of the link between premodern *vohāra* and modern didactic prose.

16 Skilling (personal communication, September 2002) notes that even the term *source text* is problematic, because the *buddhavacaṇa* should more properly be understood as a "pool of concepts" from which to draw the "holy water" of the sermon. In early Buddhism there was no exact literary concept of a "source text."

17 Pricha Changkhwanyeun, *Thammawacana wohan Thai*, 2.

18 (Phaya) Upakit Silapasan, *Lak phasa Thai*, 10th ed. (1918; Bangkok: Watthana Panich, 2544 [2002]), 3.

19 Ibid., 338–47. See also Chaleomchai Chaichomphu "Wacana wikrao khaeng phra dhammadesanā Lanna" (master's thesis, Mahidol University, 2001). He analyzes four recorded Northern Thai sermons that referred to manuscripts composed in Northern Thai script. Here he found the use of Pali "exhortative points" (*rop khong prayok kham phut*) used repetitively to reinforce certain ethical lessons. He writes that "exhortative points are mostly highlighted by repetition as seen in parallel structure, exact repetition, and partial repetition" (iii). See also Chaleomchai Chaichomphu, "Na thi khong phasa Pali nai phra dhammadesanā Lanna," *Phasa lae phasasat* 19 (2000): 1–8.

20 There is one manuscript titled *vohāradesanā* from nineteenth-century Chiang Mai, but it is badly damaged. The parts that I eventually could read looked very much like a standard *vohāra*. Peter Skilling and Prapod Assavavirulhakarn show the importance of sermons in teaching about Buddhist texts to (often illiterate) lay audiences in Thailand in the late nineteenth and early twentieth centuries. Skilling and Prapod, "Tripiṭaka in Practice in the Fourth and Fifth Reigns" (60–72), and Skilling, "Ārādhanā Tham: Invitation to Teach the Dhamma" (84–92), both in a special issue of *Manusya: Journal of the Humanities*, vol. 4 (2002).

21 See the *nisai-itipiso-desanā* (MS 0601850500306) from the Luang Phrabang Museum (HPLP) in Laos, composed in CS 1199 (1837). The early date of this *desanā* and its rare title in comparison with other *desanā* could suggest evidence of a transition of texts titled *nissaya* and texts titled *desanā* since composition of texts called *nissaya* dropped off significantly after the 1840s and the production of *desanā* increased.

22 It is worth noting that, as in Laos, the Burmese, according to John Okell's report in 1965, occasionally composed new *nissaya* in the twentieth century. Okell, "Nissaya Burmese," n187.

23 These cassettes can be purchased at many temples and at any religious bookstore in Thailand.

24 For examples, see the sermons of Amos Jones, *As You Go Preach: Dynamics of Sermon Building and Preaching in the Black Church* (Bathgate, N.D.: Bethlehem Book Publishers, 1996); see also Robert Lischer, ed., *Theories of Preaching: Selected Readings in the Homiletical Tradition* (Durham, N.C.: Duke University Press, 1987). Although the lifting and repetitive explanation of terms is a significant part of African-American homiletics, modern *nissaya* and *vohāra* methodology in Laos and Thailand does not include the "call and response" that is characteristic of many African-American sermons.

25 Sirichando Chandra (Phra Upālīguṇūpamācāriya), *Bandeuk dhamma desanā 4* (Bangkok: Liang Chiang, 2505 [1962]). Phra Upālīguṇūpamācāriya was one of the most important monks in the Thammayut lineage and trained with Phra Achan Man and Phra Achan Sao. His sermons are a good example of the mod-

ern *nissaya* method. First, in the transcript to a sermon given by Phra Upālīguṇūpamācāriya (Sirichando Chandra) in 1962, one sees a style similar to premodern *vohāra*. First a Pali passage of more than twenty-five words from an unidentified source text is cited, and then the sermon progresses by defining selected words from the passage, dividing compounds, offering creative derivations/etymologies, and synonyms in both Pali and Thai. In the process of defining, glossing, and explaining the words from this passage, other Pali words are cited and explained as well through word association. Another example would be Somdet Phra Ñāṇasangwon's sermon titled "Chittagon," which is closer to *nissaya* style than is Phra Upālīguṇūpamācāriya's. The former structures his sermon around the definition of individual Pali terms, rather than the citation of a longer Pali passage. For example, he introduces his sermon by defining the term *jarā* (old age) by providing vernacular glosses, metaphors, short narratives, and folk etymologies. The progression of his sermon is unplanned and unfocused since there seems to be no unifying factor or purpose; however, on the level of individual words, a close reading reveals that alliteration, word association, repetition, and progressive or associative glossing drive the prose.

26 The well-known royal intellectual and important builder of the constitutional monarchy in Thailand in the 1930s was Prince Wan. He is famous for coining new Thai words from Pali terms. For example, since modern Thai had no word for "revolution," he coined the term *abhiwat* (Pali: *abhivati*) over another popular Pali-derived Thai word for *revolution, patiwat* (*paṭivati*).

27 See especially Phra Achan Cha Sugatto, *Nok het neua phon* (Bangkok: Hanghun Suan, 2524 [1980]).

28 For a good, general introduction to this sermon style, see Hartmann's Web site, at http://www.seasite.niu.edu/hartmann/.

29 A few examples would be *Nangseu rian klum wichaphrapariwattham* (Bangkok: Mahachulalongkorn Monastic University Press, 2534 [1991]), vols. 1–6; another six-volume series, *Pali waiyakon* (Bangkok: Rongphimsāsanā, 1985); and, under the same title, a series published by Krombhrayā Wachirayānworarot in Bangkok (2538 [1995]). There are also Pali handbooks in English to help Thai students learn both English and Pali. These use the same *nissaya* methods. One handbook, Phradit Punyabhakdi Bhirin's *Khu meu rian phasa Pali duai ton eng* (Bangkok: Liang Chiang, 2538 [1995]), does provide more formal grammatical explanation than do most Pali handbooks, but it still relies mostly on example rather than on explanations of syntax, morphology, and phonology.

30 I thank Achan Supatra and Achan Worapon for inviting me to their classes and explaining their pedagogical methods to me. For the daily schedule of a monastic university student in the twentieth century, see Khana Kamakān Mahāmakut Rāchawithyālai, *Prawat Mahamakut Rachawithyalai nai Borom Rachapatham* (Bangkok: Mahamakut Monastic University Press, 2518 [1975]), chap. 3. Modern nonformal study at urban monastic schools is well described in (Somdet Phra Buddhachan) Buddhasaramahathen na Meruwatthepasirintharawat,

Prawat kan sasana seuksa kan seuksa nangseu Thai (originally published in Thai in 1916 and translated into Lao from the English translation) (Vientiane, Laos: Yaova Buddhikasamakhom, 1967), 2–6.

31 *Buddhasasana subhasit chabap matrathan* (Bangkok: Mahamakut Monastic University Press, 2536 [1993]), 3. For a particularly good example of repetitiveness as a rhetorical and pedagogical tool in this text, see 61.

32 *Khu meu triam sop bot thong sop ban sanam luang* (Bangkok: Mahamakut Monastic University Press, 2537 [1994]), 57–59. This text also provides simple lists of Pali terms followed by their glosses.

33 In the entire country, there is effectively only one bookstore for books specifically written and published in Lao. The state, in theory, controls the publication of all books. There are four major used-book dealers in the country, but they charge extremely high prices and are generally not patronized by monks or even lay Lao citizens; they are patronized by foreign scholars, librarians, and tourists.

34 (Phra) Mahavichit Singchalat, *Baeb hian taeng thesana san mathayom seuksa Song* (Vientiane, Laos: n.p., 1993), 17–20; and (Phra Achan) Mahasali Anucaro, *Nangseu thesana xalong tang 50 kap* (Vientiane, Laos: n.p., 1990). The latter book provides the Pali text for a number of Lao Buddhist rituals and then explains them in the vernacular. Certain terms from the sources are cited, but there is not the level of repetition as seen in *nissaya.*

35 (Phra) Thavon Bumpasoet, *Dhamma panyai* (Vientiane, Laos: n.p., 2000), 4. A collection of sermons by Phra Achan Mahapan Anantho, *Nangseu desanā thang ha sai* (Vientiane, Laos: Vat Buddhavong Pāluang, 2000), is one clear example of the lifting, repetition, and reinforcement of Pali terms. Although much has changed in Laos Buddhist education since the 1960s, from his base at Vat Pāluang in the 1990s he was giving sermons on Pali terms like *dosa* and *kāya,* which closely follows the methods of older *nissaya.*

36 As a side note, over the past few years I have attended a number of Pali grammar classes at the major monastic universities of Thailand and Laos to inquire about which texts they used to instruct Pali. At Vat Ong Teu in Laos they do not use a standard Pali grammar textbook, but instead the instructor reads Pali passages and translates them into Lao for his students orally. Translation is more at the level of memorization than are detailed explanations of grammar or linguistic issues. Etymology was also not a significant part of any Pali class I attended between 1999 and 2003. Pali passages are often drawn from *jātaka* and the *Dhammapada-atthakathā.* At Mahamakut Monastic University instruction generally takes the form of memorization of passages as well; however, there is a series of short paperback Pali grammars for novices. These textbooks are used more by some instructors than by others. Although the *yok sab nissaya*-like method was common, some professors like Phra Sugandha did use grammatical terms in advanced courses. At Mahachulalongkorn Monastic University there are several different sections in which Pali is taught. One can study (lay and

monk) under Phra Sompong and his assistants in Section 25 or receive more basic instruction at the Abhidhamma Jotika College or the undergraduate college on the same campus. The most common source for these Thai-Pali liturgy books is (Phra Khru) Run Thamrangsi, *Suat mon chabap luang plae*, 2534 (1991) (and many other editions since the late nineteenth century). I interviewed students at the monastic high school at Wat Sung Men, and students there showed me the textbook their teacher used (which was the same textbook commonly used at Wat Boworniwet in Bangkok). One student told me that the teacher read out the Pali and Thai translation and the students repeated him. One student told me that the teacher would occasionally ask the students to identify the subject and the verb of the Pali sentences, but the students did not know the differences between cases, gender, and number in Pali. They could translate roughly by knowing the meanings of the words and some basic grammar. I observed similar patterns and methods in many monastic high schools and universities.

37 (Maha) Sila Viravong, *Payok khong vannakhadi* (Vientiane: National Library of Laos, 1995), 4–5. The reason modern Thai speakers use *roi kaeo* for "prose" is most likely connected to the fact that the earliest non-verse vernacular literature, of which *nissaya* are evidence, was distinct from Pali texts and early vernacular verse poetry/drama.

38 Chonlada Reuangraklikhit, *Wannakhadi Ayutthya ton ton* (Bangkok: Chulalongkorn University Press, 2544 [2001]), 292–329.

39 Inscriptions of land grants, votive inscriptions, and edicts are the oldest examples of the vernacular in Thailand and Laos. However, the practice of composing *nissaya* is found in the oldest palm-leaf manuscripts in the region.

40 Anuson Bhuribhiwatanakhun, *Abhidhammatthasaṅgahādipakaraṇa lem thī 3* (Bangkok: Abhidhamma Jotika College, 2544 [2001]), 343.

41 Anuson pointed out that one book still used by monastic students has *nissaya* as part of its title—*Mātikājotika Dhammasaṅgaṇī Rūpattha nissaya*, composed by Phra Saddadhammajotika Dhammācāriya and published by the Abhidhamma Jotika College at Mahachulalongkorn Monastic University (2003). This textbook is used to teach the important terms from the *mātikā* of the *Dhammasaṅgaṇī*. It presents a full page of Pali text and then offers expanded glosses and short commentaries on each passage. This text's translation and commentary are much more comprehensive than are the Northern Thai and Lao palm-leaf *nissaya* versions of the *mātikā*.

42 Phra Sompong Mudito follows a method whereby he reads example Pali sentences out loud and then reads their translations. Grammatical explanations are rare and often consisted in providing no more than the Thai gloss for individual Pali words contained in the example sentences (*yok sab*). Certain Pali compounds were split and each part was given its Thai gloss. No specific grammatical terms were used except for the Thai word for "subject of the sentence."

Occasionally, the nuns, monks, and novices (and a couple female lay students) would ask questions about the meanings of the words, but rarely did they ask about the grammatical endings. One day, a monk asked a question regarding a *sandhi* rule, and the teacher answered, "That is the way it happens, *a* changes to *u*." I asked a question regarding the modern Thai use of Sanskrit spellings for certain Thai words, like *śālā*, instead of Pali spellings. The answer was, "It is because Hinduism was in Thailand before Buddhism." At the end of every lesson the Pali example sentences and Thai translations were read out loud again. This means that each sentence and its Thai translation were read out loud by everyone three times in the two-hour class.

43 Becker, *Beyond Translation*, 9.

44 Judith Jacob shows how Khmer, from pre-Angkorian times to the present, incorporated foreign terms not because of "a lack of appropriate vocabulary in Khmer; the foreign vocabulary is deliberately chosen." Other terms are "absorbed into the language unconsciously, and over time, being gradually naturalized to fit as far as possible the native phonological system . . . referred to as 'established loans.'" She shows that Khmer used "reduplication, repetition, and assonance" to incorporate Pali into Khmer. The most common texts that employed these loans words were vernacular, often noncanonical, *jātaka*, which "elevated" the vernacular through "deliberate inclusion of Pali." Judith Jacob, "The Deliberate Use of Foreign Vocabulary by the Khmer," in *Context, Meaning, and Power in Southeast Asia*, ed. Mark Hobart and Robert H. Taylor (Ithaca, N.Y.: Cornell University Press, 1986), 115–25.

45 No major study has been done on this hyper-Sanskrit lexicon in Thai. However, a good introduction is provided in Anant Laoloetsuankun, "Kham Thai kham Pali-Sanskrit," *Wanasan phasa lae phasasat* 21 (2002): 185–96. More generally, see Sunant Anchalinukun, "Kan seuksa phasa thai samai rachakan thi 5," *Wanasan phasa lae phasasat* 19 (2002): 157–78.

46 Jit Bhumisak employs a method of citing terms in Thai, giving their etymology through Khmer, Sanskrit, or Pali and explaining their political, cultural, or social import. Jit Bhumisak, *Khwam pen ma khong kham Siam, Thai, Lao, lae Khom lae laksana thang sangkhom khong cheu chon chat chabap som pen boem toem kho thae ching wa duai chon chat Khom* (Bangkok: Khet Thai, 2540 [1976]), 1–14, 236–302.

47 In 2001, in a large student protest at Bangkok's Mahidol University, graduate students refused to continue the practice of writing their theses in English. A compromise was reached whereby only abstracts in English were required; however, that decision was later reversed, and English theses are still required.

Chapter 6 Canons and Curricula

Approximately four pages of this chapter appeared in similar form in McDaniel, "The Curricular Canon in Northern Thailand and Laos," special issue, *Manusya: Journal of Thai Language and Literature*, 2002, 20–59.

1 Brian Axel, ed., *From the Margins* (Durham, N.C.: Duke University Press, 2002), 12–15.

2 Charles Keyes, "Meta-transference in the Kammic Theory of Popular Theravada Buddhism," in *Karma: An Anthropological Inquiry*, ed. Charles Keyes and E. Valentine Daniel (Berkeley: University of California Press, 1983), 272.

3 Steven Collins, "On the Very Idea of the Pali Canon," *Journal of the Pali Text Society* 15 (1990): 103–4.

4 See Blackburn's important distinction between "apprentice" and "curricular" education here. Anne Blackburn, introduction to *Buddhist Learning and Textual Practice in Eighteenth-Century Lankan Monastic Culture* (Princeton, N.J.: Princeton University Press, 2001).

5 For *paritta* literature in Southeast Asia, see Skilling, "Rakṣā Literature of the Śravakayāna"; for *tamnan*, see McDaniel, "Transformative History."

6 For example, I recently made a trip to the rural temple in Ban Nong Lam Chan of Savannakhet Province in Southern Laos. In this temple's rather large collection of manuscripts I found only one text in Pali—the commentarial *Dhammapada-atthakathā*. By its placement in the closet (*tu*) and the dust on its cover, it had not been untied or read in years (probably since the National Library's survey in 1993, since the label had been tied to the binding cord and neither seemed as if they had been tampered with). Furthermore, the abbot, Luang Phu Phomma, was unaware that he had a Pali *Dhammapada-atthakathā* manuscript in the collection, but he did call my attention to several manuscripts of Lao folktales. Oliver Freiberger offers a criticism of the anti-canonical thrust in modern Buddhist studies; see his "The Buddhist Canon and the Canon of Buddhist Studies," *Journal of the International Association of Buddhist Studies* 27, no. 2 (2004): 261–83. Jory notes that King Chulalongkorn followed Spence Hardy and other early Western scholars of Pali Buddhism when commissioning the Siamese edition of the Tipiṭaka instead of following local notions of what texts were canonical. King Chulalongkorn funded the first printed Siamese edition of the canon in 1893 and sent 230 copies to institutions all over the world, mostly to the West. He did not send one to Laos, "which is in the kingdom of Siam," because "the princes and people there profess a distorted form of the faith. . . . Hence it is only in Siam that Buddhism stands inviolate." Jory, "Thai and Western Scholarship," 908.

7 See K. R. Norman "Pali Literature," in *A History of Indian Literature*, ed. Jan Gonda (Wiesbaden: Otto Harrassowitz, 1983), vol. 4, pt. 2, 140. Even the canon was considered closed before the common era; there are texts like the *Milindapaṇhā*, *Peṭakopadesa*, and the *Nettipakaraṇa* that have been included in some canon collections and not in others. Many commentaries and anthologies offer a wide description of what the Buddha taught, referring to the "Dhamma" and "Vinaya" instead of the three *piṭaka* or nine *aṇga* of the canon. Comparatively, Origen used the term *canon* as an adjective in the phrase *scriptuae canonicae*, but the first nominative use was not until the fourth century. Brevard Childs,

Introduction to the Old Testament as Scripture (Philadelphia: Fortress Press, 1979), 50. In the Jewish tradition, the definition of *canon* was simply "sacred writings" that would not "defile the hands." Marvin Pope elucidates the difficulty in defining canonical and noncanonical works. Marvin Pope, *The Anchor Bible: Song of Songs* (Garden City, N.Y.: Doubleday, 1977), 29–33. See also John Cort, "Śvetāmbara Murtipujak Jain Scripture in a Performative Context," in *Texts in Context*, ed. Jeffrey Timm (Albany: State University of New York Press, 1991), 175.

8 Skilling and Prapod, "Tripiṭaka," 1–3. Phra Sughanda recently explained to me the sermon training a monk receives at Mahamakut Monastic University. A monk in sermon training must be ordained for five years and have completed some Pali-language training (mostly memorization). Then he is given the time of 9:00 A.M., 1:00 P.M., or 3:00 P.M. to deliver his sermon. He is judged on the quality of his voice and his rhythm. The 1:00 P.M. slot is for the least trained and poorly evaluated monks; 3:00 P.M. is reserved for the rank of *maha* and *phra kru*; and 9:00 A.M. is for senior monks and the abbot (rank of *chao khun* or higher). Venerable Sughanda stated that a monk's level of Pali education, based on the number of examinations he passed (nine total), primarily determined his sermon time slots and ranks (given by the king). Strangely, even though a monk could pass these examinations without knowing much Pali grammar, etymology, or philology or without the ability to compose in Pali (since the examinations are based on memorization), the passing of these examinations is considered the primary mark of the ability to give sermons. This indicates, on the one hand, the prestige of Pali education and, on the other hand, the intimate connection between one's perceived knowledge of Pali and one's recognized ability to give a good sermon. Phra Sughanda, personal communication, Wat Boworniwet, January 2005. For a list of these royal ranks for monks and for a list of recipients in Thailand, see *Paṭidin sāsanā 2546* (Bangkok: Mahamakut Monastic University, 2546 [2003]).

9 Anna Allott, "Continuity and Change in the Burmese Literary Canon," and Yury Osipov, "Buddhist Hagiography in Forming the Canon in the Classical Literatures of Indochina," both in *The Canon in Southeast Asian Literatures*, ed. David Smyth (London: Curzon, 2000). Allott, studying Burmese literary history and canon formation, assumes that the Tipiṭaka was widely known, standardized, and studied in pre-nineteenth-century Burma (Allott, 21). However, she discusses the *pyo*, or indigenous vernacular *jātaka* stories, in Burma and how they offered a "simpler" introduction to Buddhist ethics and conceptions of time and selfhood than did Pali texts, and she notes that they were often abbreviated and probably expanded on in performance (21–22). Osipov shows that vernacular stories often were not translations of Pali and Sanskrit classics, but that they merely retained some words and plot structure, and expanded on this matrix.

10 *The Royal Orders of Burma* report that on April 4, 1638, the king ordered the

copying of "new sets" of the canon. He had thirty Shan guards to protect the more than fifty monks, novices, scribes, and clerks working on the sets. Later that month, he ordered the production of 10,008 ivory plaques, 10,008 gold plaques, and 10,008 silver plaques from the ministry of the interior and food from the office of granaries to support these monks and scribes. There is little way of knowing exactly what texts these "new sets" included or whether they contained vernacular and commentarial material. Than, *Royal Orders of Burma.*

11 Amnuay Sukhumanan and [Prince] Damrong Rachanuphap, *Tamnan Ho Phra Samut* (Bangkok: Sobhanaphiphan Thanākon, 2456 [1913]). I thank Andrew Huxley for pointing out a short article by Robert Chalmers called "The King of Siam's Edition of the Pāli Tipiṭaka" (*Journal of the Royal Asiatic Society* 1 [1898]: 1–10). Herein he describes the thirty-nine-volume 1894 King Chulalongkorn edition and offers a loose translation of the preface of the edition in which the king writes, "Cambodia came under French domination, so that people there could not maintain the faith in full vigour. As regards to the country of Laos, *which is in the kingdom of Siam*, the princes and people there professed a distorted form of the faith, which included such errors as the worship of angels and demons, and therefore cannot be regarded as having authority. . . . Hence it is only in Siam that Buddhism stands inviolate" (2–3; italics mine). This preface also declares that, for the first time, the Khmer script was not used, and instead Siamese script was employed. Chalmers calls this choice a "triumph for rationalism. To the Siamese there is nothing sacred in the Siamese character, and accordingly he can view the new volumes printed in the Siamese character without any superstition which gathered around the old MSS. in the Cambodian character" (7). He states that the use of Khmer script formerly "was to give to the latter [Khmer script] a sacrosanct significance in the eyes not only of the unlettered but even of the cultured Siamese" (7). The King did struggle, it is said, over the use of palm-leaf versus wood-pulp paper. He saw the European paper as "less durable" but as easier to use to reproduce multiple copies. Most of the *Khuddaka nikāya* in this edition remained unedited and were not included (including the *jātaka*, *Thera/Therīgāthā*, and *Cariyāpiṭaka*, among others). The *Buddhavaṃsa pathamasaṃ* is listed as canonical, but was not edited or included. Chalmers notes that the Siamese editors knew of Sinhalese and Burmese editions, but these were largely ignored, and basically the Siamese editions produced in the 1780s were consulted. Therefore, he concludes that "it appears the learned editors did not feel themselves at liberty to prepare what we would call a critical edition . . . they restricted themselves, very naturally and intelligibly, to restoring the *national* redaction" (8; italics mine). Prince Damrong also wrote a description about the troubles in collecting lost manuscripts in Thailand and Europe and in building the national library. See his "Palace Library Manuscripts," *Occasional Papers of the Santi Pracha Dhamma Institute* 10 (1929): 1–28; reprinted with an English translation in 1969. See also Craig Reynolds's study of Prince Damrong, the building a national library, and King Chula-

longkorn's concern over historical inaccuracies, in "Mr. Kulap and Purloined Documents," in *Seditious Histories* (Seattle: University of Washington Press, 2006), 55–79; originally published in *Journal of the Siam Society* 61, no. 1 (1973): 63–90.

12 Skilling also gave me a quick description of the Chiang Mai *Piṭakamāla* manuscript, which is a long list (sixty folios) of texts in the Tipiṭaka. This text, although as yet unedited and unscrutinized, seems to change the order of many texts and to expand the parameters of the Sri Lankan Mahāvihāra canon.

13 In 2006 the class schedule had changed slightly, but the content was the same.

14 Many faux manuscripts are also printed on yellow paper with red edges, mimicking the color and form of palm-leaf manuscripts. Anne Hansen notes that in "1918, the culmination of four years of work by a clandestine 'cell' of young Khmer monks to produce and publish the first printed translation of a Buddhist scripture in Cambodia was brought to a halt by higher religious authorities who viewed their efforts as seditious if not downright heretical. In response to their careful attempt to print a portion of the Vinaya, the Khmer Sangha head wrote: 'Permission will be granted only for study of *Vinay* written on palm-leaf; *Vinay* written on paper in the manner of a book is considered to be "new *Vinay*," which is not in accord with the traditions established during the [previous century].'" Anne Hansen, *How to Behave* (Honolulu: University of Hawaii Press, 2007), 104–7.

15 The most common ones would certainly be (Phra Khru) Run Thamrangsi, *Monpithi plae samrap Phra Phiksusamanen lae Buddhasasanikachon tua bai* (Bangkok: Mahamakut Monastic University Press, 2534 [1991]), and (Phra) Ariyamuni [Chaem], *Suat mon blae* (Bangkok: Rongphim phisalapanani, 2456 [1913]), as well as subsequent reprints (some with additions).

16 See also Jonathan Z. Smith, *Imagining Religion: From Babylon to Jonestown* (Chicago: University of Chicago Press, 1982), 299–300; and Smith, *Map Is Not Territory: Studies in the History of Religions* (Chicago: University of Chicago Press, 1978), 45.

17 Paul Griffiths, *Religious Reading* (Oxford: Oxford University Press, 1999), 54.

18 Ibid., 74.

19 Michael Fishbane, *Biblical Interpretation in Ancient Israel* (Oxford: Oxford University Press, 1985), 285–91.

20 See also John Henderson, *Scripture, Canon, and Commentary* (Princeton, N.J.: Princeton University Press, 1991), chap. 5; and Laurie Patton, *Myth as Argument* (Berlin: Walter de Gruyter, 1996), chap. 2.

21 Richard Freeman, "Genre and Society: The Literary Culture of Pre-modern Kerala," in *Literary Cultures in History*, ed. Sheldon Pollock (Berkeley: University of California Press, 2003), 439.

22 Collins, *Nirvana*, 112–14.

23 Steven Collins, in talk delivered in January 2006 at the University of California, Riverside. A good example of the movement between "systematic" and

"narrative" knowledge in Buddhist textual history is seen in the study of Buddhist law codes by Ryuji Okudaira. He shows that Burmese Buddhist lawmakers in the eighteenth century, like Maung Hmaing of the Yezagyo judicial court, would cite evidence for cases from both *jātaka* and Vinaya texts. Moreover, both canonical and extra-canonical texts would be cited for evidence equally. Ryuji Okudaira, "Theft Cases in Eighteenth-Century Burma with Special Reference to the Atula Hsayadaw Hpyathton," unpublished paper (2006).

24 *Atthasālinī* 290; see also *Atthasālinī* 293.

Chapter 7 From Manuscript to Television

Parts of this chapter appeared in Justin McDaniel, "The Art of Reading and Teaching Dhammapadas," *Journal of the International Association of Buddhist Studies* 28, no. 2 (2005): 299–338.

1 Kevin Trainor is undertaking a larger study of the Dhammapada.

2 See the summary in Stephen Prothero, "Henry Steel Olcott and 'Protestant Buddhism,'" *Journal of the American Academy of Religion* 63, no. 2 (1995): 281–303.

3 Jory, "Thai and Western Scholarship," 893.

4 For background, see Blackburn, introduction to *Buddhist Learning and Textual Practice*.

5 For good introductions to this text, see von Hinüber and Norman, *Dhammapada* (London: Pali Text Society, 1994); and J. R. Carter and M. Palihawadana, *The Dhammapada* (Oxford: Oxford University Press, 1987). Dozens of translations of the Dhammapada have been published in European and Asian languages, and many are available on the Internet.

6 Hellmuth Hecker, *Dhammapada: Ein bibliographischer Führer durch Übersetzungen der berühmtesten buddhistischenn Spruchsammlung* (Constance: Universität Konstanz, 1993); and the "Dhammapada" entry in Oskar von Hinüber, *A Handbook of Pali Literature* (Berlin: Walter de Gruyter, 1996).

7 Harlan indicts the field of history and its allegiance to "context" in his *The Degradation of American History* (Chicago: University of Chicago Press, 1997), xxxii–xxxiii, quoted in Elizabeth Clark, *History, Theory, Text: Historians and the Linguistic Turn* (Cambridge, Mass.: Harvard University Press, 2004), 20.

8 For a longer discussion on this topic and a bibliography on Buddhist narrative transformations in Thailand and Laos, see McDaniel, "Creative Engagement." For a good model on how stories in India become intertwined, see Stanley Insler, "The Shattered Head Split and the Epic Tale of Śakuntalā," *Bulletin d'études indiennes* 7–8 (1991): 97–139.

9 The diversity of Dhammapada and *Dhammapada-atthakathā* manuscripts in the region can be seen from the most cursory of surveys. For example, in Balee Buddharaksa's catalog of eighty-nine Pali manuscripts from Northern Thailand, there is a manuscript from 1583 from Wat Lai Hin that has one *phuk* (fascicle)

and forty-two folios, which is not complete, and contains two stories (*Velatthis-īsattithera* and another unidentified narrative). Another manuscript titled simply "Dhammapada" was composed in 1511 by a Lao monk from Xaiyaburi, but it was found in Northern Thailand with twenty-three verses. Other Dhammapada manuscripts include one from Wat Doi Kaeo in Chiang Mai with one *phuk* and 99 folios and one from Wat Kasa in Chiang Rai with one *phuk* and 109 folios composed in 1647. These are all commentarial narratives. There are also three rare manuscripts that contain only Pali verses. These were used by von Hinüber and Norman for their Pali Text Society edition. One, from 1786, has one *phuk* and fifty-seven folios and was found at Wat Lai Hin. It is missing verses 319–43. Another is from 1611 (Wat Lai Hin) and is almost complete. The last, from 1827, is from Wat Kasa and has 109 folios. In the catalogs from the Center for the Promotion of Art and Culture at Chiang Mai University, over twenty Dhammapada manuscripts were found in Phrae province alone, many from Wat Sung Men (although many were probably composed in Luang Phrabang). Most are vernacular *nissaya* stories and not verses. I examined many of these manuscripts myself at the monastery, but a whole study is needed. In the library of Wat Boworniwet in Bangkok is a printed edition of the Dhammapada in Ariyaka script. I thank Phra Mahasillapa Dhammasippo (Hinchaisri) for his assistance and guidance.

10 In their introduction, Carter and Palihawadana note that little is known about the "original" Dhammapada. There are several early versions in a *Gāndhārī prakrit* and the *Patna dharmapada*, as well as the *Udānavarga* of the Sarvāstivādins in hybrid Sanskrit.

11 McDaniel, "Invoking the Source," 247–73. The manuscript's catalog number from the Chiang Mai University Center for the Promotion of Art and Culture, Phrae Province, is CPAC PHR 010200800.

12 This was a common practice in Southeast Asia, as I. B. Horner and Padmanabh Jaini note similar practices in Burma, where Buddhist authors have a "penchant . . . to embellish old canonical tales with new elements drawn from the indigenous cultures of their own native regions." *Nissaya* "vernacularize" the Pali source or at least the genre of texts. They mimic the genre and therefore "domesticate" it. I. B. Horner and Padmanabh Jaini, "The Apocryphal Jātakas," in *Apocryphal Birth Stories* (Oxford: Pali Text Society, 1985), 1:31.

13 This, of course, is not the only published edition of the text, but it is the most frequently used by students. See, e.g., (Sāmanera) Udit Sirivanna Prian, *Dhammapot phak 1–6 Plae doi byanjana* (Bangkok: Liang Chiang, 2530 BE [1987]); and Prince Wachirayan's often reprinted *Dhammapada-atthakathā*, published by Mahamakut Monastic University Press in multiple editions.

14 A small "pocket edition" (*chabap krapao*) of this book is very popular. See the most recent edition: (Sāmanera) Udit Sirivanna Prian, *Khu meu kan plae Dhammapot* [Handbook for Translating the Dhammapada] (Bangkok: Liang Chiang, 2531 BE [1988]).

15 See the Mahidol University Buddhist study group's Web site, at http://www.mahidol.ac.th/budsir/buddhism.htm.

16 *Phra Buddha Sasana kap kan bokkong Pathet*, composed in 1916 by Prince Wachirayan of Thailand with verses from the Dhammapada, was popular and was translated into English.

17 Homiletic style is by no means rigid, proscribed, and/or universal. Even though the *nissaya/vohāra* mode is popular and pervasive, some sermon givers like the nun Maechi Sansanee Sathirasut, Luang Pho Khun, and Phra Phayom Kalyano are famous for their own unique styles of giving sermons that incorporate jokes and dramatic analogies and allusions to contemporary news events.

18 George Coedès noticed that the *Dhammapada-atthakathā*, not the verses, alongside the *Maṅgala-atthadīpanī* and the Sāratthasaṅgaha, served as the basis for Thai monastic education. Coedès, "Notes sur les ouvrages Pālis composés en pays Thäi," *Bulletin de l'École française d'Extrême-Orient* 13, no. 1 (1915): 23–26; Harris, *Cambodian Buddhism*, 83.

19 These Pali terms are part of a string of terms from a common formula in the Vinaya and Suttanta.

20 Translated from the Thai.

21 Jeffrey Samuels, "Learning to Attract the Heart: The Aesthetics of Ritual Performance in Contemporary Sri Lanka" (paper presented at the annual meeting of the American Academy of Religion, San Antonio, Tex., 2004).

22 Being attentive to the needs of audiences is also apparent in a 1969 textbook published by Vat Phonphranao in Vientiane. This short "History of the Buddha for Students" (which is a loose translation of the strangely worded title "Buddha Phavat Thasana Seuksa") emphasizes that the teacher use simple and short stories to illuminate the life of the Buddha for students so that they behave correctly. Because of the separation of state and religion in Lao public education, local monasteries, in seeking to take part in the public revival of Buddhism in present-day Laos while also avoiding scrutiny by the state, have published a wide array of short handbooks for students. These handbooks, like the *Malayat thang sangkhom* [Social Etiquette] by Douangxai Luangpasi, mix pseudo-moral pithy maxims (in Lao and English)—for example, "Idleness is the root of all evil"; "Don't get married with the one you love, but with the one who loves you"; "Knowledge is a treasure, but practice is the key to it"; and "Your dress and handwriting show your character"—and write short commentary on them in the same manner as *nissaya* manuscripts. The format is in the tradition of Buddhist monastic pedagogy, but the content has become secular.

23 The format of printing texts was also a significant change. The simple fact that students can each have their own copy of a book and study on their own changes their relationship to the teacher and weakens their power to deviate from the text. However, despite mass printing, most students in rural Thailand (and especially Laos) cannot afford or do not have access to books in school, and teachers' handwritten notebooks still are widely used.

Chapter 8 Philosophical Embryology

1 A lively debate ensued in the first few decades of Buddhist studies over the classification of Abhidhamma as "philosophy." Many scholars refer to it as "psychology" or "applied philosophy" as opposed to "speculative philosophy." However, this debate over terms is not my concern here.

2 Rita Langer and Rupert Gethin pointed out a story in the *Dhammapada-atthakathā* III.223 in which bats die while listening to the Abhidhamma being recited. Even though, as bats, they did not understand a word of what they heard, they were reborn among the gods. This story further supports the idea that a lack of understanding of the semantic import of the Abhidhamma does not elide the text's transformative and salvific power. Langer and Gethin, personal communication, October 2006. I thank them and Eisel Mazard and Alexander von Rospatt for valuable comments.

3 The following is archival information given on the *Nissaya atthakathā mātikā*. Title on manuscript: *Nisai mātikāṭṭhakathā*; archive number: Social Research Institute Chiang Mai University 81.146.11F.006–006; size: 1 fascicle, 24 folios; date: CS 931 (1569); location: National Museum (Chiang Mai branch); script: Tai Yuan; material: palm-leaf. Its condition is very good, few corrections, clear and uniform handwriting for first 14 folios and then a different scribe completes the fascicle, few cracked leaves, minor mold accretion, complete single *phuk* (fascicle). The colophon provides little information except for the date and the name of the patron: Mahāmaṅgalapaño Cao, 1569.

4 Shwe Zan Aung, "Abhidhamma Literature in Burma," *Journal of the Pali Text Society* 6 (1908): 106–23; reprinted in journal, 1978. The *mātikā* of the *Dhammasaṅgaṇī* is also central to Burmese monastic examinations designed in the eighteenth century. For example, on June 16, 1785, a royal order in Burma proclaimed that passing examinations of the *mātikā* was required before a novice could ordain as a monk. The *Abhidhammasaṅgaha*, the *Atthasālinī*, and Shin Aruruddha's *Abhidhammattha saṅgruih* were part of the first examinations. See Than Tun, *Royal Orders of Burma*, 4:111–16.

5 Norman, "Pāli Literature," 99.

6 Aung, "Abhidhamma Literature of Burma," 115. The first *akauk* was written in 1629 and the second, by Myauk-nangyaung Sadaw, in 1648. The last was composed in 1819. There were also numerous subcommentaries of the *mātikā* composed in Burma, like the *Mātikāganṭhi*. For more information on the relationship between *akauk* and *nissaya* in Burma, see Mabel Bode, *The Pāli Literature of Burma* (London: Royal Asiatic Society, 1966), 127–30.

7 The *Atthasālinī* contains quotations from later texts such as the Visuddhimagga and the *Samantapāsādikā*, but Dhammakitti suggests that Buddhaghosa simply revised the *Atthasālinī* in Sri Lanka, although it was composed in India. Caroline Rhys-Davids, *A Buddhist Manual of Psychological Ethics*, 3rd ed. (London: Pali Text Society, 1974), xxvi–xxvii.

8 Including the *Atthasālinī*, *Atthasālinī-muṭlaṭīkā Atthasālinā-anuṭīkā*, *Atthasālinī-atthayojanā*, *Madhurāsa-atthadīpanī*, and the *Mohavicchedanī*. In Thailand editions of the *Atthasālinī* and the *Atthasālinī-atthayojanā* are spelled *Aṭṭhasālinī* and *Aṭṭhasālinī-aṭṭhayojanā*, respectively. For a good introduction (in Thai), see Buddhaghosa Ācariya, *Atthasālinī-atthayojanā* (Bangkok: Munithi Phumiphalo-bhikkhu, 1982), 21–24.

9 Von Hinüber demonstrates that the practice of composing Abhidhamma handbooks has persisted over time in the Theravada. The *Abhidhammāvatāra*, *Rūpārūpavibhāga*, *Abhidhammatthavibhāvinī*, *Abhidhammāvatāraporāṇaṭīkā*, *Abhidhammmatthavikāsinī*, *Abhidhammatthasaṅgaha*, and *Paramatthavinicchaya* are just a few of the texts composed in Sri Lanka and Burma on the Abhidhamma. See von Hinüber, *Handbook of Pali Literature*, 160–64; and Bode, *Pāli Literature of Burma*, 81–101, 120–23, as well as her section on *lethan*, or "little finger manuals." See also A. K. Warder, ed., introduction to *Mohavicchedanī* (London: Pali Text Society, 1961).

10 Von Hinüber, *Handbook of Pali Literature*, 66–68. See also Rhys-Davids, introduction to *Buddhist Manual of Psychological Ethics*. Leo Pruden, in the introduction to his English translation of Louis de la Vallée Poussin's *Abhidharmakoṣa*, provides a good summary of the *mātikā* of the *Dhammasaṅgaṇī* by indicating how it is connected to the origin of the Abhidhamma itself. The *mātikā* is the "itemized dharmas in the sūtras and the vinaya, and identification is made between it and the Abhidharma." Louis de la Vallèe Poussin, *Abhidharmakosā bhāsyam*, trans. and with introduction by Leo Pruden (Berkeley, Calif.: Asian Humanities Press, 1988), xxxix. The *mātikā* is the "bare-bones list of dharmas which underwent later elaboration, and the eventual codification of this elaboration developed into various books of the Pali Abhidhamma-piṭaka" (Pruden, xxxviii).

11 Commentary on the *Kathāvatthu* as cited by Aung, "Abhidhamma Literature of Burma," 118.

12 Ibid. John Okell, in "Nissaya Burmese," sees the explanation of Pali grammar as the primary function of Burmese *nissaya*. The influence of Burmese *nissaya* on later Burmese grammar is significant and is studied extensively by Pruitt, *Étude linguistique de nissaya Birmans*.

13 Pe Maung Tin, preface to Rhys-Davids, *Buddhist Manual of Psychological Ethics*, xlii.

14 Rupert Gethin, "The Mātikās: Memorization, Mindfulness, and the List," in *The Mirror of Memory*, ed. Janet Gyatso (Albany: State University of New York Press, 1992), 161.

15 Ibid., 163.

16 The *Abhidhamma chet kamphi*, excerpts from the *Abhidhammasaṅgaha*, and the *mātikā* are not the only texts chanted at funerals. Funerals, like most Thai and Lao rituals, also include the recitation of texts like the *Nāmo tassa*, *Itipiso*, *Tisaraṇa*, and *Bahum* and other standard liturgical texts. Additional texts can be chanted upon request of the family of the deceased. When I performed funerals,

my abbot instructed the other monks and me (a quorum of four is standard) to chant Abhidhamma texts, standard liturgical texts, and often a text of his choosing. These extra texts, which we had to commit to memory, were based on my abbot's preference rather than on a standard liturgical prescription or tradition. See especially François Lagirarde, "Une interprétation bouddhique des rites funéraires du Lanna et du Laos: Le sutta apocryphe de Mahā Kāla," *Aséanie* 2 (1998): 47–77.

17 In 1968 Charles Keyes noted that there was a close connection between the Abhidhamma's use at funerary rites in Central Thailand and that in the far rural North. Charles Keyes and (Phrakhru) Anusaranasasanakiarti, "Funerary Rites and the Buddhist Meaning of Death: An Interpretive Text from Northern Thailand," *Journal of the Siam Society* 68, no. 1 (1980): 8, 13.

18 I thank Donald Swearer for providing me with a copy of this manuscript from his personal library. The manuscript's colophon does not provide a date, but it was most likely copied in the mid-nineteenth century. Although my translation is different at points, Swearer translated this manuscript in 1996.

19 Donald Swearer, "A Summary of the Seven Books of the Abhidhamma," in *Buddhism in Practice*, ed. Donald Lopez (Princeton, N.J.: Princeton University Press, 1996), 340. See also *Saranukhrom wattananatham Thai phak neua*, s.v. "Apitham," by Anant Chandprasat, 7793–94.

20 K. E. Wells, *Thai Buddhism*, 3rd ed. (Bangkok: AMS Press, 1974): 214–16; Terwiel, *Monks and Magic*, 3rd rev. ed. (1975; Bangkok: White Lotus, 1994); and Phya Anuman Rajadhon, *Life and Ritual in Old Siam*, trans. and ed. William Gedney (New Haven, Conn.: Yale University Press, 1961). Very useful is Charles Keyes, "The Cremation of a Senior Monk," in *The Life of Buddhism*, ed. Frank Reynolds and Jacob Carbine (Berkeley: University of California Press, 2000), 123–36. There are too many Thai sources to list. They range from close descriptions of funerals in different regions to cremation volumes published at the time of important monks and laypersons. A study of cremation volumes and funeral liturgies in Thai is needed.

21 They are easily found at most monasteries and bookstands in the central markets of Vientiane, Paksé, and Luang Phrabang. Good examples are (Phra Achan) Ongkaeo Sitthivong's *Khu meu Pasong-Samanen Vat Sisaket* (Vientiane, Laos: Vat Sisaket, 2003), 77–79, and his *Sut xayamungkhun lae bot desanā mungkhun heuan* (Vientiane, Laos: Vat Sisaket, 1990), 42–43. The latter was produced by a committee of monks in Vientiane. Condominas's *Le bouddhisme au village* also describes funerals briefly. François Lagirarde has written on the esoteric use of the Abhidhamma in Northern Thailand and Cambodia. Lagirarde also notes that a Lao manuscript of the *Pvārabandh* [The Noble Garland] was found in the Siam Society archive in Bangkok, dated to 1835. Several of these manuscripts also are still held in Lao archives. These manuscripts connect the chanting of the syllables of the seven texts of the Abhidhamma to magical protection. See François Lagirarde, "Textes bouddhiques du pays khmer et du

Lanna," *Recherches nouvelles sur le Cambodge*, *Études thematiques* 1 (1994): 63–77. Earlier and still useful studies include Pierre Macey, "Une cérémonie funébre au Laos," *Bulletin de la Société de géographie de l'Est*, 1899, 222–34; Didier Brengues, "Les cérémonies funéraires à Ubon" *Bulletin de l'École française d'Extrême-Orient* 8 (1904): 730–36: Ange Gouin, *Les idées superstitieuses des Laotiens* (Paris: École française d'Extrême-Orient, 1902), 94–99; Henri Deydier, *Introduction à la connaissance du Laos* (Saigon: Imprimerie française d'Outre-Mer, 1952), esp. 57–62; Abhay Nhouy, "Rites de la mort et des funérailles," in *Présence du Royaume Lao*, ed. René de Berval (Saigon: Numéro spécial de France-Asie, 1956), 831–35; Charles Archaimbault, "Contribution à l'étude de Rituel funéraire lao," *Journal of the Siam Society* 51 (1963): 1–58. Somchine Pierre Nginn, *Les fêtes profanes et religieuses au Laos* (Vientiane, Laos: Éditions du Comité littèraire, 1967); Nginn, "Les funérailles au Laos," *Sud-Est* 22 (1951–53): 25; and Zago's comprehensive book, *Rites et cérémonies en milieu bouddhiste Lao*. The famous Lao scholar-monk Phra Khampun Philavong also describes Lao funerals in his *Wattanatham Lao* (Vientiane, Laos: Buddhavong Vat Paluang, 1967), 185–200. Recently, Patrice Ladwig has undertaken extensive ethnographic studies of Lao funerary rites.

22 François Bizot and François Lagirarde, *La pureté par les mots* (Paris: École française d'Extrême-Orient, 1996), 44.

23 François Bizot, *Le figuier à cinq branches*, EFEO Monograph no. 107 (Paris: École française d'Extrême-Orient, 1976), 45–49, 120–42. In Cambodia one ritual designed to create a new fetus is based on a genre of texts known as the "Mūl Kammaṭṭhāna."

24 François Bizot, "La grotte de la naissance," *Recherches sur le bouddhisme khmer II*, *Bulletin de l'École français d'Extrême-Orient* 67 (1980): 240–73.

25 The world's leading expert on these illuminated Siamese *jātaka* manuscripts is Henry Ginsburg of the British Library. On understanding the relationship between the Abhidhamma and the illuminated *dāsajātaka*, he was very helpful to me, as were Pattaratorn Chirapravati and Forest McGill. See particularly Henry Ginsburg, *Thai Art and Culture* (Honolulu: University of Hawaii Press, 2000). Ginsburg provides plates and descriptions of numerous manuscripts from collections in Ireland, the United States, Britain, and Thailand. For good examples, see pages 55, 63, 79, 84. I also thank the late Dr. Ginsburg for taking the time to show me rare manuscripts in the archives of the British Library.

26 (Phra) Platawisut Kuttachayo, *Khu meu kanseuksa Phra Abhidhamma chan chulabhidhammikatri* (Bangkok: Mahachulalongkorn Monastic University Press, 2545 [2001]).

27 Chanting the *si na* is common in Northern Thailand, while sections of the *Abhidhammatthasaŋgaha* are common in Central Thailand.

28 Somanassasahagataṃ diṭṭhigatasampayuttaṃ asankhārikaṃ, somanassasahagataṃ diṭṭhigatasampayuttaṃ sankhārikaṃ, somanassasahagataṃ diṭṭhigatavippayuttaṃ asankhārikaṃ, somanassasahagataṃ diṭṭhigatavippayuttaṃ

sankhārikaṃ, upekkhāsahagataṃ diṭṭhigatasampayuttaṃ asankhārikaṃ, upekkhāsahagataṃ diṭṭhigatasampayuttaṃ sankhārikaṃ, upekkhāsahagataṃ diṭṭhigatavippayuttaṃ asankhārikaṃ, upekkhāsahagataṃ diṭṭhigatavippayuttaṃ sankhārikaṃ.

29 Little documentation has been done on the rise of Abhidhamma schools in modern Laos and Thailand. There seems to have been much influence from Burmese Buddhist missionary teachers in the early 1950s in Bangkok and later in the late 1950s in Laos through the efforts of Sayadaw Saddhammajotika Dhammaācāriya. Sayadaw Saddhamajotika (known in Thailand as Phra Saddhammajotika) took up residence in Wat Rakhang Khositaram (Dhonburi/Bangkok) on the river directly across from the Grand Palace in 1951. He started an Abhidhamma school, which was later named after him in 1966. He composed many textbooks. The *Abhidhammasaṅgaha* guidebook examined here was not composed by Phra Saddhammajotika and seemingly not a subject of his expertise, which was primarily on, but not limited to, canonical Abhidhamma texts. In Laos, Phra Mahapan, whose work is discussed in chapter 1, was the motivator behind the rise of five Abhidhamma schools in Vientiane, Luang Phrabang, Paksé, and Savannakhet. These schools opened in 1959 and disappeared after the rise of the Pathet Lao in 1975. Their primary textbook for advanced students was the *Abhidhammasaṅgaha* in Pali (with Tham script), printed through the assistance of the Institut bouddhique. It was first printed in 1959. I have found little evidence in Lao of textbooks used by students who could not read Pali (in either Tham or Lao script). I value the assistance of Phra Ongkaeo Sitthivong and Patrice Ladwig here.

Conclusion

1 Blackburn, *Buddhist Learning and Textual Practice*, 45–47.

2 Talal Asad, "Interview: Modern Power," *Stanford Electronic Humanities Review* (*SEHR*) 5, no. 1 (1996): 3.

3 Ibid.

4 Malcolm Miles, *Urban Avant-Garde: Art, Architecture, and Change* (London: Routledge, 2004), 24–25, quoted in Wolfgang Welsch, *Undoing Aesthetics* (London: Sage, 1997), 104.

5 Mikhail Bakhtin, "Discourse in the Novel," in his *Dialogic Imagination*, 259–421.

6 Donald Swearer, *Becoming the Buddha* (Princeton, N.J.: Princeton University Press, 2004), 3–4.

7 Arjun Appadurai, "Grassroots Globalization and the Research Imagination," *Public Culture* 12, no. 1 (2000): 1–19.

8 Alternatively, see Victor Lieberman, *Strange Parallels* (Cambridge: Cambridge University Press, 2003).

9 See Mettanando Bhikkhu, "Meditation and Healing in the Theravada Buddhist Order of Thailand and Laos" (Ph.D. diss., University of Hamburg, 1999); Lance Cousins, "Aspects of Southern Esoteric Buddhism," in *Indian Insights*, ed. Peter

Connolly and Sue Hamilton (London: Luzac Oriental, 1990), 185–207; Catherine Becchetti, *Le mystere dans les lettres* (Bangkok: Éditions des cahiers de France, 1991); Kate Crosby, "Tantric Theravada: A Bibliographic Essay on the Writings of François Bizot and Other Literature on the Yogāvacara Tradition," *Journal of Contemporary Buddhism* 1, no. 2 (2000): 141–98; and Swearer, *Becoming the Buddha*. Catherine Newell, a Ph.D. candidate at the School of Oriental and African Studies in London, is writing a dissertation on the history of Thammakai meditation that touches on a number of these subjects.

10 See chapter 3, note 48. See also McDaniel, "Modern Buddhism in Thailand," in *Buddhism in World Cultures: Comparative Perspectives*, ed. Steven Berkwitz (Santa Barbara, Calif.: ABC-CLIO, 2006), 101–28.

11 Jeffrey Samuels (draft in progress) notes that in an early Pali commentary on the Aṅguttara Nikāya, the *Manorathapūraṇī*, there is a rarer distinction between the *paṃsukūlikathera* (rag-clothed ascetic monks) and the *dhammakathikāthera* (dhamma-preaching monks). See *Aṅguttara-nikāya* I.93, *Dhammapada-atthakathā* III.898, and *Manorathapūraṇī* IV.115.

12 Suchao Ploichum, *Somdet Phra Mahāsamaṇachao* (Bangkok: Mahamakut Monastic University Press, 2541 [1998]).

13 Newspaper articles in Thailand have begun to promote innovative Buddhist pedagogical methods. For example, Pakorn Tancharoen has developed a computer-aided "ethics game" that, with animated monks, helps children ask and answer simple dhamma questions (Chatrarat Kaewmorakhot, "A Buddhist Game to Help Teach Ethics," *Nation*, March 12, 2007). Phra Maha Krieng Krai teaches dhamma and science at Wat Bun Yuan School in Nan Province, he states, because "science and Buddhism are based on the same logical principles" (Pongpen Sutharoj, "Mixing Dharma with Science," *Nation*, December 19, 2006).

14 These changes have been discussed extensively in two recent sets of collected essays: Steven Dovert, ed., *Thaïlande contemporaine* (Paris: L'Harmattan, 2001), especially Louis Gabaude's contribution, "Approche du bouddhisme," 3–38; and Steven Berkwitz, ed., introduction to *Buddhism in World Cultures* (Santa Barbara, Calif.: ABC-CLIO, 2006).

15 Association of Theravada Buddhist Universities, at http://atbu.org/.

Note on Manuscripts, Archives, Monastic Libraries, and Catalogs

*Many manuscripts I consulted for this book were read in situ at various monas*tic libraries in Laos and Thailand. I visited individual manuscript libraries in Nan, Phrae, Lampang, Chiang Mai, Phayao, Uttaradit, Ubon, Mukdahan, Savannakhet, Champasak, Attapeu, Luang Phrabang, Vientiane, and other places. I also researched at archives in Chiang Mai, Vientiane, Ubon Ratchathani, Bangkok, Luang Phrabang, London, Paris, and Washington, D.C., and at the National University of Singapore, the University of Michigan, Cornell University, and the University of California, Berkeley. No comprehensive catalog for these manuscripts has been done. The National Library of Laos is attempting to combine catalogs of Lao manuscripts from throughout the world in order to make a master list, a project that is in its nascent stages. Excluding the catalogs of inscriptions and reference works that are useful for studying local manuscripts, a partial list of catalogs of the major manuscripts in Laos and Thailand includes Louis Finot, "Recherches sur la littèrature laotienne," *Bulletin de l'École française d'Extrême-Orient* 17, no. 5 (1917); George Coedès, "Documents sur l'histoire politique et religieuse du Laos occidental," *Bulletin de l'École française d'Extrême-Orient* 25, nos. 1–2 (1925); and *Inventaire des manuscripts Bibliothèque royal de Copenhagen: Catalogue des manuscripts en pali, laotien et siamois provenant de la Thailande* (manuscripts collected between 1911 and 1935 by the Royal Library of Copenhagen in 1966 and part of the Catalogue of Oriental Manuscripts, Xylographs, and so forth in the Danish Collections [vol. 2, pt. 2]). Together with Henri Parmentier, Coedès also compiled several "Listes générales des inscriptions et des monuments," which make reference to loose connections between inscriptions and manuscripts. See also Pierre-Bernard Lafont, "Inventaire des manuscrits des pagodes du Laos," *Bulletin de l'École française d'Extrême-Orient* 52, no. 2 (1965): 429–546; *Raicheunangseu boran Lan Na ekasan maikrofilm khong Sathapan Wichai Mahawithyalai Chiang Mai 2521–2533* [1978–90] (Chiang Mai, Thailand: Social Research Institute, 1990); *Banchi maikrofilm khwang Luang Phrabang lae ho phaphitaphan khwang Luang Phrabang lae Hongsamut haeng xat Lao* (printed at the National Library of Laos in 1999 and updated periodically [the German Foreign Office, Chiang Mai University, and Chulalongkorn University also have copies of this catalog]). Catalogs for the Center for the Promotion of Art and Culture are produced and updated periodically for each of the seven Northern Thai provinces. They are available at the center and have not been published or distributed. For a relatively complete list of catalogs (in the "abbreviations and references" section) in which Central and Northern Thai manuscripts appear, see the first two volumes of the *Materials for the Study of the Tripiṭaka* (vol. 1, *Pāli Literature Transmitted in Central Siam* [Bangkok: Fragile Palm Leaves Foundation, 2002]; and vol. 2, *Pāli and Vernacular Literature Transmitted in Central and Northern Siam* [Bangkok: Fragile Palm Leaves Foundation, 2004]), compiled, translated, and edited by Peter Skilling and Santi Pakdeekham. Skilling and Santi reproduce, with commentary and an introduction, a list of Pali texts that Prince Damrong believed were composed in Thailand. This list was included in the introduction to Prince Damrong's edition of the *Saṅgītyavaṃsa phongsawadan ruang sanggayana Phra Dhammawinai Somdet Phra Wanaratana Wat Phra Chetuphon nai Ratchakan thi 1 thang phasa Magadha* (Bangkok: Hang hun suan camkatsivaphon, 2421 [1923]). I have found Antoine Cabaton's *Catalogue sommaire des manuscrits sanscrits et pālis, 2e fascicule-manuscrits pālis* (Paris: Bibliothèque nationale, 1908) particularly useful, especially for *nissaya* manuscripts. He produced several other smaller catalogs, including *Catalogue sommaire des manuscrits indiends, indo-chinois et malayo-poly-nesians* (Paris: E. Leroux, 1912); "Fonds indochinois de la Bibliothèque nationale," in *Un supplement manuscrit donne les notices des manuscrits Indochinois* (Paris: E. Leroux, 1912); "Manuscrits laotiens," in *Un supplement manuscrit donne les notices des manuscrits Indochinois* (Paris: E. Leroux, 1912); and "Manuscrits siamois," in *Un supplement manuscrit donne les notices des manuscrits Indochinois* (Paris: E. Leroux, 1912). In January 2003, Monique

Cohen at the Bibliothèque nationale in Paris (Division orientale) was working to update this catalog and was extremely helpful to me in my research in Paris. Klaus Wenk's *Laotische Handschriften* (Wiesbaden: Franz Steiner Verlag, 1975) lists some interesting manuscripts held in Berlin. Other useful catalogs include Au Chieng, *Catalogue du fonds khmer* (Paris: Imprimerie nationale, 1953); Au Chieng, *Catalogue descriptif des manuscrits du fonds pali de la Bibliothèque nationale* (Paris: Bibliothèque nationale, 1956 [updated]); Balee Buddharaksa, *Pali Literature in Lan Na: Catalogue of 89 Manuscripts with Summaries* (in Thai) (Chiang Mai, Thailand: Social Research Institute, 2543 [2000]); L. Barnett and D. Barnett, A *Supplementary Catalogue of Sanskrit, Pali, and Prakrit Books in the Library of the British Museum Acquired during the Years 1906–1928* (London: British Museum, 1988); Heinz Bechert, *Abkürzungsvorzeichnis zur Buddhistischen Literatur in Indein und Südostasien* (Göttingen: Vandenhoeck and Ruprecht, 1990); Heinz Bechert, Daw Khin Khin Su, and Saw Tin Tin Myint, *Burmese Manuscripts* (Wiesbaden: Franz Steiner Verlag, 1979); Cecil Bendall, *Catalogue of Sanskrit, Pali, and Prakrit Books in the Library of the British Museum Acquired during the Years 1876–1892* (London: British Museum, 1893); Annie Berthier, *Manuscrits, xylographes, estampages: Les collections orientales du départments des manuscrits* (Paris: Bibliothèque nationale, 2000); (Phra Maha) Athison Thirasilo, *Prawat kamphi Pali* (Bangkok: Mahamakut Monastic University Press, 2541 [1998]); Henri Chambert-Loir, "Les manuscrits malais a Bale, Singapour et Paris," *Archipel* 20 (1980); and Leon Feer, "Manuscrits du Laos," in *Indochinois*, sec. 508 (Paris: Bibliothèque nationale, 1879). Jacqueline Filliozat has produced a number of useful catalogs: "Catalogue of the Pali Manuscript Collection in Burmese and Siamese Characters Kept in the Library of Vijayasundararamaya Asgiriya," *Journal of the Pali Text Society* 21 (1995); and "Survey of the Burmese and Siamese Pāli Manuscript Collections in the Wellcome Institute," *Journal of the Pali Text Society* 19 (1993). Filliozat has also provided a helpful guide: "Documents Useful for the Identification of Pāli Manuscripts of Cambodia, Laos, and Thailand," *Journal of the Pali Text Society* 26 (1992): 13–55. Additional useful catalogs include Ernst Haas, *Catalogue of Sanskrit and Pali Books in the British Museum* (London: Trübner and Co., 1876); François Lagirarde, "Les manuscrits en Thai du Nord de la Siam Society," *Journal of the Siam Society* 84, no. 1 (1996); J. Liyanratne, "Pāli Manuscripts from Sri Lanka in the Cambridge University Library," *Journal of the Pali Text Society* 28 (1992); Otani University Library, *Catalogue of Palm Leaf Manuscripts Kept in the Otani University Library* (Kyoto: Otani University, 1995); Sommai Premchit, *Lan Na Literature: Catalogue of Palm Leaf Texts in Wat Libraries in Chiang Mai* (Chiang Ma, Thailand: Social Research Institute, 1986) (updated from Sommai Premchit and Puangkham Thuikaeo's catalog of 1975 in Thai); Francis Xavier Tessier, "Catalogue des manuscrits siamois de la bibliothèque Impériale," [compiled in 1858 with comments from Mgr. Pallegoix and Hermann Zotenberg] in *Indochinois*, sec. 512 (Paris: Bibliothèque nationale, 1912); and Petrus Voorhoeve, "Additions et corrections au catalogue de Cabaton" (an insertion placed in Cabaton, *Catalogue sommaire des manuscrits sanscrits et pālis*, in 1952 in the Bibliothèque nationale). The Siam Society in Bangkok produces several short catalogs of its manuscript holdings (*Banchi ekasan boran*), which can be read at the library. There are several texts by Supaphanh na Bangchang useful for the study of Thai manuscript traditions (especially Northern Thai) listed in the bibliography. For research in Thailand, permission of the National Research Council of Thailand is often necessary to consult these Thai collections. Finally, the sixty-three-volume *Saranukhrom watthanatham Thai* (Encyclopedia of Thai Culture) (especially the thirty volumes dedicated to Northern and Northeastern Thailand), published by Thanakhan Thai Panich beginning in 1999, is useful for some background on individual manuscripts and texts. Several other Thai encyclopedias were also consulted.

Bibliography

Abbi, Anvita. *Reduplication in South Asian Languages*. New Delhi: Allied Publishers, 1992.

Abhay Nhouy. *Aspects du pays Lao*. Vientiane: Comité littèraire lao, 1956.

———. "Rites de la mort et des funérailles." In *Présence du Royaume Lao*, edited by René de Berval, 831–35. Saigon: Numéro spécial de France-Asie, 1956.

Abhidhamma chet kamphi. Bangkok: Liang Chiang, n.d.

Adikaram, E. W. *Early History of Buddhism in Ceylon*. Colombo, Sri Lanka: Gunasena, 1946.

Akiko Iijima. "The Nyuan in Xayabury and Cross-Border Links to Nan." In *Contesting Visions of the Lao Past*, edited by Christopher Goscha and Søren Ivarsson, 165–80. Copenhagen: Nordic Institute of Asian Studies, 2002.

Allon, Mark. *Style and Function: A Study of the Dominant Stylistic Features of the Prose Portions of Pali Canonical Sutta Texts and Their Mnemonic Function*. Studia Philologica Buddhica 12. Tokyo: International Institute for Buddhist Studies, 1997.

Allott, Anna. "Continuity and Change in the Burmese Literary Canon." In *The Canon in Southeast Asian Literatures*, edited by David Smyth, 21–40. London: Curzon, 2000.

Alsdorf, Ludwig. "The Akhyana Theory Reconsidered." In *Kleine Schriften Herausgegeben von Albrecht Wezler*. Wiesbaden: Franz Steiner Verlag, 1974.

Amnuay Sukhumanan and [Prince] Damrong Rachanuphap. *Tamnan Ho Phra Samut*. Bangkok: Sobhanaphiphan Thanākon, 2456 (1913).

Anant Laoloetsuankun. "Kham Thai kham Pali-Sanskrit." *Wanasan phasa lae phasasat* 21 (2002): 185–96.

Anderson, Benedict. *Imagined Communities: Reflections on the Origins and Spread of Nationalism*. Rev. ed. London: Verso, 1991.

(Phya) Anuman Rajadhon. *Life and Ritual in Old Siam: Three Studies of Thai Life and Customs*. Translated and edited by William Gedney. New Haven, Conn.: Yale University Press, 1961.

Anuson Bhuribhiwatanakhun. *Abhidhammatthasaṅgahādipakaraṇa lem thī* 3. Bangkok: Abhidhamma Jotika College, 2544 (2001).

(Phra) Anuthera. *Bantheuk phra dhamma desanā ruang paticcasamupat*. Funeral volume. Bangkok: Wat Pathumwanaram, 2499 (1956).

Appadurai, Arjun. "Grassroots Globalization and the Research Imagination." *Public Culture* 12, no. 1 (2000): 1–19.

Arak Sanghitkun. *Baep akson boran chabap nak rian nak seuksa.* Bangkok: Hong samut haeng chat, 2547 (2004).

Archaimbault, Charles. "La cérémonie du Khun cieng khun ni à Basak-Campasak (Sud-Laos)." *Aséanie* 8 (2001): 149–58. Originally published in J. Thomas and L. Bernot, eds. *Langues et techniques*, 13–19. Paris: Klincksieck, 1972.

———. "Contribution à l'étude de Rituel funéraire lao." *Journal of the Siam Society* 51 (1963): 1–58.

———. "L'histoire de Champasak." *Journal Asiatique* 249, no. 1 (1961): 519–95.

———. "Religious Structures in Laos." *Journal of the Siam Society* 52 (1964): 57–74.

(Phra) Ariyamuni [Chaem]. *Suat mon blae.* Bangkok: Rongphim phisalapanani, 2456 (1913).

Asad, Talal. "Interview: Modern Power." *Stanford Electronic Humanities Review (SEHR)* 5, no. 1 (1996): 1–8.

Axel, Brian, ed. *From the Margins: Historical Anthropology and Its Futures.* Durham, N.C.: Duke University Press, 2002.

Aymonier, Etienne. *Notes sur le Laos.* Saigon: Imprimerie coloniale, 1885.

———. *Voyage dans le Laos.* Paris: Leroux, 1897.

Backus, Mary. *Siam and Laos: As Seen by Our American Missionaries.* Philadelphia: Presbyterian Board of Publication, 1884.

Baeprian nangseu phasa boran. Bangkok: Ho samut haeng chat, 2543 (1999).

Bakhtin, Mikhail. *The Dialogic Imagination: Four Essays by Mikhail Bakhtin.* Edited by Michael Holquist. Austin: University of Texas Press, 1982.

———. "Discourse in the Novel." In Bakhtin, *The Dialogic Imagination.*

Balee Buddharaksa. *Mahāvaṃsamālinīvilāsinī: Kan sob chamra choeng wikro wannakam Buddhasāsanā phasa Pali chak ekasan tua khian blae ton chabap ben phasa Thai.* Chiang Mai, Thailand: Social Research Institute, 2545 (2002).

Bampen Rawin. *Mūlasāsanā samnuan Lanna.* Chiang Mai: Social Research Institute, 2538 (1995).

———. *Tamnan Wat Pa Daeng.* Chiang Mai, Thailand: Social Research Institute, 2538 (1995).

Bandeuk dhammadesanā 4. Bangkok: Liang Chiang, 2505 (1962).

Banyen Limsawat. *Sāsanadīpanī.* Bangkok: Mahamakut Monastic University Press, 2548 (2005).

Barros, João de. *Ásia de João de Barros: Dos feitos que os Portugueses fizeram no descobrimento e conquista dos mares e terras do Oriente; Terceira Década* [Asia, by João de Barros: The Deeds of the Portuguese in the Discovery and Conquest of the Seas and Lands of the East, Third Decade]. Reprinted from the 1563 edition and edited by Hernaní Cidade and Manuel Múrias. Lisbon: Agência Geral das Colónias, 1946.

Basbanes, Nicholas. *Patience and Fortitude.* San Francisco: HarperCollins, 2001.

Bassenne, Marthe. *In Laos and Siam.* 1912. Reprint, Bangkok: White Lotus, 1995.

Bastian, Adolf. "On Some Siamese Inscriptions." *Journal of the Asiatic Society of Bengal* 34 (1865): 27–38.

Becchetti, Catherine. *Le mystere dans les lettres*. Bangkok: Éditions des cahiers de France, 1991.

Becker, Alton. *Beyond Translation: Essays Toward a Modern Philology*. Ann Arbor: University of Michigan Press, 1995.

Beebee, Thomas. *The Ideology of Genre*. University Park: Pennsylvania State University Press, 1994.

Berger, Victor. "Pagodes du Laos: La République démocratique populaire lao." *Tour du monde* 225 (1978): 45–53.

Berkwitz, Steven, ed. Introduction to *Buddhism in World Cultures: Comparative Perspectives*. Santa Barbara, Calif.: ABC-CLIO, 2006.

Berliner, Paul. *Thinking in Jazz*. Chicago: University of Chicago Press, 1994.

Bernon, Olivier de. "L'état des bibliothèques dans les monastères du Cambodge." *Sorn Samnang* 2 (1998): 872–82.

———. "Le manuel des maîtres de kammaṭṭhān." Ph.D. diss., Institut nationale des langues et civilisations orientales, Paris, 2000.

Bésème, Marianne. "Pagodes, centres de vie des communautés originaires d'Asie du Sud-Est." *Les bulletins du Mékong* 5 (2002): 16–17.

Bhikkhu Bodhi, ed. *A Comprehensive Manual of Abhidhamma: The Abhidammattha Sangaha of Ācāriya Anuraddha*. Kandy, Sri Lanka: Buddhist Publication Society, 1993.

Bibliotheca Sinica: Essai d'une Bibliographie des ouvrages relatifs à la presqu'ïte indo-chinoise in T'oung P'ao Archifs pour servir à l'étude de l'Aise Orientale. 2nd ser. Leiden, 1903.

Bizot, François. *Le chemin de Lankâ*. Paris: École française d'Extrême-Orient, 1992.

———. "La consecration des statues et le culte des morts." In *Recherches nouvelles sur le Cambodge*. Paris: École française d'Extrême-Orient, 1994.

———. *Le don de soi-même*. EFEO Monography no. 130. Paris: École française d'Extrême-Orient, 1981.

———. *Le figuier à cinq branches*. EFEO Monograph no. 107. Paris: École française d'Extrême-Orient 1976.

———. "La grotte de la naissance." *Recherches sur le bouddhisme khmer II, Bulletin de l' École française d'Extrême-Orient* 67 (1980): 240–73.

———. "Notes sur les yantra bouddhiques d'Indochine." In *Tantric and Taoist Studies in Honour of R. A. Stein: Melanges chinois et bouddhiques XX*, edited by Michael Strickmann. Vol. 1. Brussels, 1981.

———. "La place des communautés du Nord-Laos dans l'histoire du bouddhisme d'Asie du Sud-Est." *Bulletin de l'École française d'Extrême-Orient, mélanges du centenaire* 87, no. 2 (2001): 511–28.

———. *Les traditions de la pabbajjā en Asie du Sud-Est*. Paris: École française d'Extrême-Orient 1988.

Bizot, François, and François LaGirarde. *La pureté par les mots*. Paris: École française d'Extrême-Orient, 1996.

Blackburn, Anne. *Buddhist Learning and Textual Practice in Eighteenth-Century Lankan Monastic Culture*. Princeton, N.J.: Princeton University Press, 2001.

Bode, Mabel. *The Pali Literature of Burma*. London: Royal Asiatic Society, 1966.

Bond, George. *The Word of the Buddha*. Colombo, Sri Lanka: Gunasena, 1975.

Borchert, Thomas. "Educating Monks: Buddhism, Politics, and Freedom of Religion on China's Southwest Border." Ph.D. diss., University of Chicago, 2006.

Bosaengkham Vongthala. *Vannakhati Lao*. Vientiane, Laos: Kaxuang Seuksa, 1987.

Bouasysavath Samlith. "Sakkaraj." *Lanxang Heritage Journal* 3 (1997): 41–65.

Bounpheng Naovarang. *Baep hian sin tham*. Vientiane, Laos: n.p., 1966.

Bourlet, Alan. "Superstitions laotiennes, la vie ordinaire d'un Thay." *Missions Catholiques* 38 (1906): 202–15.

Bowie, Katherine. "Ethnic Herterogeneity and Elephants in Nineteenth-Century Lanna Statecraft." In Turton, *Civility and Savagery*, 330–48.

Brengues, Didier. "Les cérémonies funéraires à Ubon." *Bulletin de l'École française d'Extrême-Orient* 8 (1904): 730–36.

Brengues, Jean. "Une version laotienne du Pañcatantra." *Journal Asiatique* 10 (1908): 357–95.

Brocheux, Pierre. *Indochine: La colonisation ambiguë, 1858–1954*. Paris: La Découverte, 1995.

Bruhn, Klaus. "Repetition in Jaina Narrative Literature." *Indologica Taurinensia* 11 (1983): 27–75.

Buddhaghosa Ācāriya. *Atthasālinī-atthayojanā*. Bangkok: Munithi phumiphalobhikkhu, 1982.

(Somdet Phra Buddhachan) Buddhasaramahathen na Meruwatthepasirintharawat. *Prawat kan sasana seuksa kan seuksa nangseu Thai.*Vientiane, Laos: Yaova Buddhikasamakhom, 1967.

Buddhasasana subhasit chabap matrathan. Bangkok: Mahamakut Monastic University Press, 2536 (1993).

Bung-on Piyabhan. *Lao in Early Bangkok*. Bangkok: Chulalongkorn University Press, 1998.

Bunroeng Buasisaengbasoet. *Muang Luang Phrabang*. Vientiane, Laos: Toyota Foundation, 1991.

———. *Pavatsat Silapa lae sathabatthayakamsin Lao*. Vientiane, Laos: n.p., 1995.

Buratin Khampirat. "Chabhap lae banha khong kan seuksa Phra Pariyatidham phanaek Pali nai Samnak Rian Suan Klang." Master's thesis, Withyaniphon Phak Wicha Sarat Seuksa Mahawithyalai Chulalongkorn, 2539 (1996).

Butler, Lucius. *Laos Educational Documents*. Honolulu: University of Hawaii, Educational Communications, College of Education, 1971.

Butler-Diaz, Jacqueline. "In Search of the Life History of an Object: An Amulet from Laos." Ph.D. diss., Arizona State University, 1995.

Butt, John. "Thai Kingship and Religious Reform (Eighteenth to Nineteenth Centuries)." In *Religion and Legitimation of Power in Thailand, Laos, and Burma*, edited by Bardwell Smith, 34–51. Chambersburg, Pa.: Anima Books, 1978.

Camões, Luiz de. *The Lusiads of Luiz de Camões*. Translated from the 1572 Portuguese edition, edited by L. Bacon. New York: Hispanic Society of America, 1950.

Carter, J. R., and M. Palihawadana. *The Dhammapada*. Oxford: Oxford University Press, 1987.

Cha Prian. *Anisong 108 kan chabap poem toem mai*. Bangkok: Amnuisasana, 2510 (1966).

(Phra Achan) Cha Sugatto. *Nok het neua phon*. Bangkok: Hanghun Suan, 2524 (1980).

Chaleomchai Chaichomphu. "Na thi khong phasa Pali nai phra dhammadesanā Lanna," *Phasa lae phasasat* 19 (2000): 1–8.

———. "Wacana wikrao khaeng phra dhammadesanā Lanna. Bangkok." Master's thesis, Mahidol University, 2001.

Chalmers, Robert. "The King of Siam's Edition of the Pāli Tipiṭaka." *Journal of the Royal Asiatic Society* 1 (1898): 1–10.

Chalong Soontravanich. "Thai-Lao choeng prawatsat kon khristasatawat 20." *Silapawattanatham* 6, no. 1 (2529 [1986]): 142–50.

Chamroen Sekdhira. *Laksut Phra Pariyatidham phanaek saman seuksa*. Bangkok: Krasuang Seaksathikan, 2534 (1993).

(Phra) Chanthasusat. *Katha Thammabot*. Vientiane, Laos: n.p., 1966.

Chartier, Roger. *The Order of Books*. Translated by Lydia Cochrane. Stanford, Calif.: Stanford University Press, 1994.

Charuwan Chaonuan. *Nithan peun muang Lao*. Bangkok: Chulalongkorn University Press, 2545 (2002).

Chatthip Nartsupa. "The Ideology of Holy Men in North East Thailand." *Ethnological Study* 13 (1983): 111–34.

Chawalee Na Thalang. *Prathetracha khong Siam nai samai Phrabatsomdet Phra Chula-chom Klao Chao Yu Hua*. Bangkok: Chulalongkorn University Press, 2541 (1998).

Cherniack, Susan. "Book Culture in Sung China." *Harvard Journal of Asiatic Studies* 54, no. 1 (1994): 5–125.

Chheat Sreang, Yin Sombo, Seng Hokmeng, Pong Pheakdeyboramy, and Saom Sokreasey. *The Buddhist Institute in Cambodia: A History*, translated by Penny Edwards. Phnom Penh, Cambodia: Buddhist Institute, 2005.

Childs, Brevard. *Introduction to the Old Testament as Scripture*. Philadelphia: Fortress Press, 1979.

Chirasak Dechawongya. *Khwam saphan rawang Lan Na Lan Xang: Kan seuksa silapakam nai Muang Chiang Mai lae Luang Phrabang*. Chiang Mai, Thailand: Social Research Institute, 2544 (2001).

Chirasak Dechawongya, Woralan Bunyasurat, and Yuwanat Woramit. *Ho trai Wat Phra Singh: Prawat laksana silapakam lae naeo thang kan anurak*. Chiang Mai, Thailand: Social Research Institute, 2539 (1996).

Chonlada Reuangraklikhit. *Wannakhadi Ayutthya ton ton*. Bangkok: Chulalongkorn University Press, 2544 (2001).

Choron-Baix, Catherine. "La pratique du bouddhisme par les Lao." *Accueillir* 182 (1992): 9–20.

Clark, Elizabeth. *History, Theory, Text: Historians and the Linguistic Turn*. Cambridge, Mass.: Harvard University Press, 2004.

Clémentin-Ojha, Catherine, and Pierre-Yves Manguin. *Un siècle pour l'Asie: École française d'Extrême-Orient, 1898–2000*. Paris: Les éditions du pacifique and l'École française d'Extrême-Orient, 2001.

Coedès, George. "Documents sur l'histoire politique et religieuse du Laos occidental." *Bulletin de l'École française d'Extrême-Orient* 25, nos. 1–2 (1925).

———. "Notes sur les ouvrages Pālis composés en pays Thäi." *Bulletin de l'École française d'Extrême-Orient* 13, no. 1 (1915): 2–37.

———. *Recueil des inscriptions du Siam*. Bangkok: Siam Society, 1961.

Collins, Steven. *Nirvana and Other Buddhist Felicities*. Cambridge: Cambridge University Press, 1998.

———. "Notes on Some Oral Aspects of Pāli Literature." *Indo-Iranian Journal* 35, nos. 2–3 (1992): 121–35.

———. "On the Very Idea of the Pali Canon." *Journal of the Pali Text Society* 15 (1990): 89–126.

———. *Selfless Persons*. Cambridge: Cambridge University Press, 1982.

Condominas, Georges. *Le bouddhisme au village*. Vientiane, Laos: Édition des cahiers de France, 1998.

Copeland, Rita. *Rhetoric, Hermeneutics, and Translation in the Middle Ages: Academic Traditions and Vernacular Texts*. Cambridge: Cambridge University Press, 1991.

Cort, John. "The Intellectual Formation of a Jain Monk: A Śvetāmbara Monastic Curriculum." *Journal of Indian Philosophy* 29, no. 3 (2001): 327–49.

———. "Śvetāmbara Murtipujak Jain Scripture in a Performative Context." In *Texts in Context: Traditional Hermeneutics in South Asia*, edited by Jeffrey Timm, 151–78. Albany: State University of New York Press, 1991.

Cortembert, E., and Léon de Rosny. *Tableau de la Cochinchine*. Paris: Armand le chevalier, 1862.

Cosgrove, Denis. *Social Formation and Symbolic Landscape*. Totowa, N.J.: Barnes and Noble Imports, 1984; reprint, Madison: University of Wisconsin Press, 1998.

Cousins, Lance. "Aspects of Southern Esoteric Buddhism." In *Indian Insights*, edited by Peter Connolly and Sue Hamilton, 185–207. London: Luzac Oriental, 1990.

———. "Pali Oral Literature." In *Buddhist Studies: Ancient and Modern*, edited by P. Denwood and A. Piatigorsky, 71–90. London: Curzon Press, 1983.

Crosby, Kate. "Tantric Theravada: A Bibliographic Essay on the Writings of François Bizot and Other Literature on the Yogāvacara Tradition." *Journal of Contemporary Buddhism* 1, no. 2 (2000): 141–98.

Cunningham, Mary. *Preacher and Audience: Studies in Early Christian and Byzantine Homiletics*. Leiden: Brill 1998.

Curtis, Lillian Johnson. *The Laos of North Siam: Seen through the Eyes of a Missionary*. 1903. Reprint, Bangkok: White Lotus, 1998.

Dagenais, John. *The Ethics of Reading in Manuscript Culture*. Princeton, N.J.: Princeton University Press, 1994.

Damrong (Somdet Krom Phraya Damrong Rachanubhap). *Nithan borankhadi*. Bangkok: Khurusapha, 2509 (1966).
———. "Palace Library Manuscripts." *Occasional Papers of the Santi Pracha Dhamma Institute* 10 (1929): 1–28. Reprinted with an English translation in 1969.
———. *San Somdet*. 23 vols. Bangkok: Khurusapha, 2509 (1966).
———. *Tamnan Phra Parit*. Funeral volume. Bangkok: Wat Somanat, 2511 (1968).
———. *Thai rop pama*. 1917. Reprint, Bangkok: Rung watana, 2514 (1971).
Davis, Richard. *A Northern Thai Reader*. Bangkok: Siam Society, 1970.
Davis, Sara. *Song and Silence*. New York: Columbia University Press, 2005.
de Certeau, Michel. *The Practice of Everyday Life* [*L'invention du quotidien*]. Translated by Steven F. Rendall. Berkeley: University of California Press, 1994.
de la Vallèe Poussin, Louis. *Abhidharmakosā bhāsyam*. Translated and with introduction by Leo Pruden. Berkeley, Calif.: Asian Humanities Press, 1988.
Dépierre, Jean. *Situation de catholicisme en Cochinchine à la fin du XIX siècle*. Saigon, 1900.
De Pouvourville, Albert. *L'art Indo-Chinois*. Paris: Librairies-imprimeries Réunies, 1894.
Deydier, Henri. *Introduction à la connaissance du Laos*. Saigon: Imprimerie française d'Outre-Mer, 1952.
(Phra) Dhammānanda Mahāthera, ed. *Padarūpasiddhi khong Buddhappiya-Mahāthera*. Bangkok: Thammasapha, 2000.
Dhawat Rotphrom. *Prawatmahatthai suan phumiphak changwat Phrae*. Phrae, Laos: Krasuang mahatthai, 2541 (1998).
The Dictionary of Monastic Terms [Prochananukrom pheua kan seuksa Buddhasat chut kham wat]. Edited by (Phra) Thammakittiwong Thongdi Suratecho. Bangkok: Choraka, 2548 (2005).
d'Orléans, Henri. *Autor du Tonkin*. Paris, 1894.
Douangdeuane Bounyavong. *Thao Hung Thao Chuang*. Vientiane: National Library of Laos, 2000.
———. *Watchananukhrom*. Vientiane, Laos: Toyota Foundation, 1995.
Douangxai Luangpasi. *Chao Maha Uparat Bunrong*. Vientiane, Laos: Sangon likhasit, 2003.
———. *Malayat thang sangkhom* [Social Etiquette]. Vientiane, Laos: Sangon likhasit, 1997.
———. *Somdet Phra Chao Sethathirat*. Vientiane, Laos: Sangon likhasit, 1999.
Dovert, Steven, ed. *Thaïlande contemporaine*. Paris: L'Harmattan, 2001.
Drège, Jean-Pierre. *L'École française d'Extrême-Orient et le Cambodge, 1898–2003*. Paris: École française d'Extrême-Orient, 2003.
Duangchan Khruchayan. *Prawat khong Wat Selāratanapabbatārāma Lai Hin Luang Kaeo Chang Yeun*. N.p., n.d.
Duara, Prasenjit. *Rescuing History from the Nation*. Chicago: University of Chicago Press, 1995.
Duff, David. *Modern Genre Theory*. London: Pearson, 2000.

Duroiselle, Charles. "Talaing Nissaya." *Journal of the Burma Research Society* 3 (1913): 21–38.

Eade, J. C. *The Thai Historical Record: A Computer Analysis*. Ithaca, N.Y.: Cornell Southeast Asian Studies Publications, 1996.

Eckel, David. *To See the Buddha*. San Francisco: HarperCollins, 1992.

Eco, Umberto. *Serendipities: Language and Lunacy*. New York: Harvest, 2002.

École française d'Extrême-Orient [EFEO]. "Annual Reports." *Bulletin de l'École française d'Extrême-Orient* 30–34 (1929–33).

Edwards, Penny. "Taj Angkor: Enshrining *l'Inde in le Cambodge*." In *France and "Indochina": Cultural Representations*, edited by Kathryn Robson and Jennifer Yee, 13–27. Lanham, Md.: Lexington Books, 2005.

Ehrhard, Albert. *Überlieferung und Bestand des hagiographischen und homiletischen Literatur der grieschischen Kirche von den Anfangen bis zum Ebde des 16.Jahrhunderts*. 3 vols. Leipzig: J. C. Hinrichs, 1937–39.

Evans, Fred. "Bakhtin, Communication, and the Politics of Multiculturalism." In *Mikhail Bakhtin: Sage Masters of Modern Social Thought*, vol. 4, edited by Michael E. Gardiner, 271–93. London: SAGE Publications, 2003.

Evans, Grant, ed. *Laos: Culture and Society*. Chiang Mai: Silkworm, 1999.

———. "Millennial Rebels in Colonial Laos." *Peasant Studies* 18, no. 1 (1990): 53–57.

———. *The Politics of Ritual and Remembrance: Laos since 1975*. Honolulu: University of Hawaii, 1998.

———. *A Short History of Laos*. Chiang Mai, Thailand: Silkworm, 2002.

———. "Tai-ization: Ethnic Change in Northern Indo-China." In Turton, *Civility and Savagery*, 263–90.

———. "What Is Lao Culture and Society?" In Evans, *Laos: Culture and Society*.

Faure, Bernard. *Chan Insights and Oversights*. Princeton, N.J.: Princeton University Press, 1993.

Fernquist, John. "The Flight of Lao War Captives from Burma Back to Laos in 1596." *School of Oriental and African Studies Bulletin of Burma Research* 3, no. 1 (2005): 41–68.

Finot, Louis. "Recherches sur la littèrature laotienne," *Bulletin de l'École française d'Extrême-Orient* 17, no. 5 (1917): 1–219.

Fishbane, Michael. *Biblical Interpretation in Ancient Israel*. Oxford: Oxford University Press, 1985.

Foucault, Michel. *The Archaeology of Knowledge*. New York: Pantheon, 1972.

Fowler, Alastair. "Transformations of Genre." In *Modern Genre Theory*, edited by David Duff, 232–49. London: Harlow Press, 2000.

Frauwallner, Erich. *The Earliest Vinaya and the Beginnings of Buddhist Literature*. Translated by L. Petech. Rome: Italian Institute for Middle and Far East, 1956.

———. *Studies in Abhidharma Literature and the Origins of Buddhist Philosophical Systems*. Translated from the German by Sophie Francis Kidd under the supervision of Ernst Steinkellner. Albany: State University of New York Press, 1995.

Freeman, Richard. "Genre and Society: The Literary Culture of Pre-modern Kerala."

In *Literary Cultures in History*, edited by Sheldon Pollock (Berkeley: University of California Press, 2003).

Freiberger, Oliver. "The Buddhist Canon and the Canon of Buddhist Studies." *Journal of the International Association of Buddhist Studies* 27, no. 2 (2004): 261–83.

Gabaude, Louis. "Approche du bouddhisme." In *Thaïlande contemporaine*, edited by Steven Dovert, 3–38. Paris: L'Harmattan, 2001.

———. *Les cetiya de sable au Laos et en Thaïlande: Les textes*. EFEO Monograph no. 118. Paris: École française d'Extrême-Orient, 1979.

Gagneux, Pierre-Marie. "Note sur un mode particulier d'acquisition de mérites dans le Laos ancien: L'inscription des images du Bouddha." *Asie du Sud-Est et du monde Insulindien* 8, no. 1 (1977): 93–102.

Galvano, Antonio. *The Discoveries of the World from Their First Original unto the Year of Our Lord 1555*. London: Hakluyt Society, 1862. In Portuguese, from a 1563 original.

Garnier, François. *Further Travels in Laos and Yunnan*. Bangkok: White Lotus, 1996. Composed between 1839 and 1873, and published as *Voyage d'exploration en Indo-Chine*.

———. *A Pictorial Journey on the Old Mekong: Cambodia, Laos, and Yunnan; The Mekong Exploration Commission Report (1866–1868)*. Vol. 3. Bangkok: White Lotus, 1998.

———. *Travels in Cambodia and Part of Laos: The Mekong Exploration Commission Report (1866–1868)*. Vol. 1, translated by Walter Tips. Bangkok: White Lotus, 1996.

Gelder, Geert Jan van. "Some Brave Attempts at Generic Classification in Pre-modern Arabic Literature." In *Aspects of Genre and Type in Pre-modern Literary Cultures*, edited by Bert Roest, 64–89. Groningen, Netherlands: Styx, 1999.

Gerini, G. E. *Researches on Ptolemy's Geography of Eastern Asia*. London: Royal Geographical Society, 1909.

Gethin, Rupert. "The Mātikās: Memorization, Mindfulness, and the List." In *The Mirror of Memory: Reflections on Mindfulness and Remembrance in Indian and Tibetan Buddhism*, edited by Janet Gyatso. Albany: State University of New York Press, 1992.

Ginsburg, Henry. *Thai Art and Culture*. Honolulu: University of Hawaii Press, 2000.

———. "Thai Literary Tales Derived from the Sanskrit Tantropākhyāna." Master's thesis, University of Hawaii, 1967.

Giteau, Madeleine. "Vat Phu: Histoire et légende du monastère de la montagne." *Connaissance des arts* 519 (1995): 56–63.

Gombrich, Ernst. "The Necessity of Tradition: An Interpretation of the Poetics of I. A. Richards." In *The Essential Gombrich*, edited by Richard Woodfield, 97–116. London: Phaidon Press, 1996.

Gombrich, Richard. "How the Mahāyāna Began." In *The Buddhist Forum*, vol. 1, edited by Tadeusz Skorupski. London: School of Oriental and African Studies, 1990.

Gonda, Jan. *Stylistic Repetitions in the Veda*. Leiden: Royal Netherlands Academy of Arts and Sciences, 1959.

Gouin, Ange. *Les idées superstitieuses des Laotiens*. Paris: École française d'Extrême-Orient, 1902.

Grabowsky, Volker. *Bevölkerung und Staat in Lan Na*. Wiesbaden: Harrassowitz, 2004.

———. "Comprehensive List of Monasteries in Luang Prabang, and Residences of the Nagao Queens and Kings of Luang Prabang," In *Het bun dai bun: Sacred Rituals of Luang Prabang*, edited by Hans Georg Berger. London: Westzone, 2000.

———. "Forced Resettlement Campaigns in Northern Thailand during the Early Bangkok Period." *Orient Extremus* 37, no. 1 (1994): 45–107. Reprinted in *Journal of the Siam Society* 87, no. 1 (1999): 45–86.

———. "The Isan Up to Its Integration into the Siamese State." In *Regions and National Integration in Thailand, 1892–1992*, edited by Volker Grabowsky, 107–29. Wiesbaden: Harrassowitz, 1994.

———. "Origins of Lao and Khmer National Identity: The Legacy of the Early Nineteenth Century." In *Nationalism and Cultural Revival in Southeast Asia: Perspectives from the Centre and the Region*, edited by Sri Kuhnt-Saptodewo, Volker Grabowsky, and M. Großheim, 145–65. Wiesbaden: Harrassowitz, 1997.

———. "Population and State in Lan Na prior to the Mid-sixteenth Century." *Journal of the Siam Society* 93 (2005): 1–68.

———. "The Thai and Lao Ethnic Minorities in Cambodia: Their History and Their Fate after Decades of Warfare and Genocide." In *Ethnic Minorities and Politics in Southeast Asia*, edited by Thomas Engelbert and Hans Dieter Kubitscheck, 197–224. Frankfurt: Peter Lang, 2004.

———. "Traditional Lao Literature in the Late Lan Xang Period: A Case Study of 'Kap Müang Phuan.'" *Tai Culture* 7, no. 1 (2002): 68–105.

Grabowsky, Volker, and Andrew Turton, eds. *The Gold and Silver Road of Trade and Friendship: The McLeod and Richardson Diplomatic Missions to Tai States in 1837*. Chiang Mai, Thailand: Silkworm, 2003.

Grabowsky, Volker, Khamhung Sengmany, Bounleuth Sengsoulin, and Nou Xayasithiwong. *Pheun viang samai Chao Anu*. Vientiane: National University of Laos, 2004.

Green, D. H. *Medieval Listening and Reading: The Primary Reception of German Literature, 800–1300*. Cambridge: Cambridge University Press, 1994.

Griffiths, Paul. *Religious Reading: The Place of Reading in the Practice of Religion*. Oxford: Oxford University Press, 1999.

Griswold, A. B., and Prasert na Nagara. "No. 12, Inscription 9." *Journal of the Siam Society* 62, no. 1 (1974): 95, 110–11.

Gunn, Geoffrey. *Political Struggles in Laos, 1930–1954: Vietnamese Communist Power and the Lao Struggle for National Independence*. Bangkok: Duang Kamol, 1988.

———. *Rebellion in Laos: Peasant and Politics in a Colonial Backwater*. Boulder, Colo.: Westview, 1990.

———. *Theravadins, Colonialists, and Commissars in Laos*. Bangkok: White Lotus, 1998.

Halpern, Joel. *Government, Politics, and Social Structure in Laos: A Study of Tradition and Innovation*. New Haven, Conn.: Yale University Press, 1964.

Hamasse, Jean, and X. Hermand, eds. "De l'homélie au sermon, histoire de la préducation médiévale." In *Actes du colloque international de Louvain-la-Neuve (9–11 juillet 1992)*. Publications de l'Institut d'études médiévales, textes, études, congrès, 14. Louvain-la-Neuve, 1993.

Hansen, Anne. *How to Behave: Buddhism and Modernity in Colonial Cambodia, 1860–1930*. Honolulu: University of Hawaii Press, 2007.

Harlan, David. *The Degradation of American History*. Chicago: University of Chicago Press, 1997.

Harmand, François-Jules. *Laos and the Hilltribes of Indochina*. Bangkok: White Lotus, 1997 Composed between 1845 and 1921, and published as *Laos et les populations sauvages de l'Indochine*.

Harris, Ian. *Cambodian Buddhism: History and Practice*. Honolulu: University of Hawaii Press, 2005.

Hartzell, Jessie MacKinnon. 1919. *Mission to Siam*. Honolulu: University of Hawaii Press, 2001.

Hase, Johann Mathias. "Asia Secundum Legitimas [Map]." In *Maps from Ancient Times to the Mid-nineteenth Century*. 1744. Reprint, Leipzig: Acta Humaniora, 1989.

Hasegawa, Kiyoshi. "Buddhism and Spirit Cults among the Tai Lüü in Yunnan." *Tai Culture* 4, no. 1 (1999): 53–76.

Hayashi, Yukio. *Practical Buddhism among the Thai-Lao*. Melbourne: Trans Pacific; Abingdon: Marston, 2003.

Hecker, Hellmuth. *Dhammapada: Ein bibliographischer Führer durch Übersetzungen der berühmtesten buddhistischenn Spruchsammlung*. Constance: Universität Konstanz, 1993.

Henderson, John. *Scripture, Canon, and Commentary*. Princeton, N.J.: Princeton University Press, 1991.

Hinüber, Oskar von. "Chips from Buddhist Workshops: Scribes and Manuscripts from Northern Thailand." *Journal of the Pali Text Society* 22 (1996): 35–57.

———. *A Handbook of Pali Literature*. Berlin: Walter de Gruyter, 1996.

———. "Pāli Manuscripts of Canonical Texts from Northern Thailand." *Journal of the Siam Society* 71 (1983): 75–88.

———. "Pali und Lanna in den Kolophonen alter Palmblatthandschriften aus Nord-Thailand." In *Indogermanica et Italica*, edited by G. Meiser. Innsbruck: Universität Innsbruck, 1993.

———. "Die Sprachgeshichte des Pali im Spiegel der südostasiatischen Handschriftenüberlieferung." In *Untersuchungen zur Sprachgeschichte und Handschriftenkunde des Pāli 1*. Mainz: Abhandlungen der Akademie der Wissenschaften und der Literatur, 1988.

———. *Untersuchungen zur Mündlichkeit früher mittelindischer Texte der Buddhisten*. Mainz: Akademie der Wissenschaften und der Literatur, 1994.

Hinüber, Oskar von, and K. R. Norman. *The Dhammapada*. London: Pali Text Society, 1994.

Horner, I. B., and Padmanabh Jaini. "The Apocryphal Jātakas." In *Apocryphal Birth Stories*. Oxford: Pali Text Society, 1985.

Hudak, Thomas. *The Indigenization of Pali Meters in Thai.* Athens: Ohio University Press, 1990.

———. *The Tale of Prince Samuttakote: A Buddhist Epic from Thailand.* Athens: Ohio University Press, 1993.

Hundius, Harald. "Colophons from Thirty Pāli Manuscripts from Northern Thailand." *Journal of the Pali Text Society* 14 (1990): 1–179.

———. "Lao Manuscripts and Traditional Literature: The Struggle for Their Survival." In *The Literary Heritage of Laos*, edited by Kongdeuane Nettavong, Harald Hundius, David Wharton, Dara Kanlaya, and Khanthamali Yangnuvong, 1–11. Vientiane: National Library of Laos, 2005.

———. *Phonologie und Schrift des Nordthai.* Abhandlungen für die Kunde des Morgenlandes, 48.3. Stuttgart: Franz Steiner Verlag, 1990.

Hurch, Berhard. *Studies on Reduplication.* Berlin: Mouton de Gruyter, 2005.

Inden, Ronald B. *Imagining India.* Oxford: Blackwell, 1990.

Insler, Stanley. "The Shattered Head Split and the Epic Tale of Śakuntalā." *Bulletin d'études indiennes* 7–8 (1991): 97–139.

Ishii, Yoneo. *Sangha, State, and Society: Thai Buddhism in History.* Honolulu: University of Hawaii Press, 1986.

Ivarsson, Søren. "Bringing Laos into Existence: Laos between Indochina and Siam, 1860–1945." Ph.D. diss., University of Copenhagen, 1999.

———. "Towards a New Laos: Lao Nhay and the Campaign for National 'Reawakening' in Laos, 1941–45." In Evans, *Laos: Culture and Society*, 61–78.

Jackson, J. B. *Discovering the Vernacular Landscape.* New Haven, Conn.: Yale University Press, 1986.

Jacob, Judith. "The Deliberate Use of Foreign Vocabulary by the Khmer." In *Context, Meaning, and Power in Southeast Asia*, edited by Mark Hobart and Robert H. Taylor, 115–30. Ithaca, N.Y.: Cornell University Press, 1986.

Jayawickrama, N. A. *The Sheaf of Garlands of the Epochs of the Conquerer.* London: Pali Text Society, 1978.

Jit Bhumisak. *Khwam pen ma khong kham Siam, Thai, Lao, lae Khom lae laksana thang sangkhom khong cheu chon chat chabap som pen boem toem kho thae ching wa duai chon chat Khom.* Bangkok: Khet Thai, 2519 (1976).

Johnson, William. "Toward a Sociology of Reading in Classical Antiquity." *American Journal of Philology* 121, no. 4 (2000): 593–627.

Jones, Amos. *As You Go Preach: Dynamics of Sermon Building and Preaching in the Black Church.* Bathgate, N.D.: Bethlehem Book Publishers, 1996.

Jones, Robert. *Thai Titles and Ranks.* Data Paper 81. Ithaca, N.Y.: Cornell University Press, 1971.

Jory, Patrick. "Thai and Western Scholarship in the Age of Colonialism: King Chulalongkorn Redefines the Jatakas." *Journal of Asian Studies* 61, no. 3 (2002): 891–918.

Kan tam sammutthai lae kan triam bai lan. Bangkok: National Museum, 2530 (1988).

Kaxuang thalaeng khao lae wattanatham [Ministry of Information and Culture]. *Pavasat Lao.* Vientiane, Laos: Rongphim haeng lat, 2000.

Kesem Siriratphiriya. *Tua Meuang: Kan rian phasa Lanna phan khrong srang kham.* Chiang Mai, Thailand: Sukhothai University Press, 2548 (2005).

Keyes, Charles. "The Cremation of a Senior Monk." In *The Life of Buddhism* edited by Frank Reynolds and Jacob Carbine, 123–36. Berkeley: University of California Press, 2000.

———. *The Golden Peninsula.* New York: Macmillan, 1977.

———. "Meta-transference in the Kammic Theory of Popular Theravada Buddhism." In *Karma: An Anthropological Inquiry*, edited by Charles Keyes and E. Valentine Daniel, 261–86. Berkeley: University of California Press, 1983.

———. "Millennialism, Theravāda Buddhism, and Thai society." *Journal of Asian Studies* 36, no. 2 (1977): 283–302.

———. "National Heroine or Local Spirit? The Struggle over Memory in the Case of Thao Suranari in Nakhon Ratchasima." In *Cultural Crisis and Social Memory*, edited by Shigeharu Tanabe and Charles Keyes, 113–36. Honolulu: University of Hawaii Press, 2003.

Keyes, Charles, and (Phrakhru) Anusaranasasanakiarti. "Funerary Rites and the Buddhist Meaning of Death: An Interpretative Text from Northern Thailand." *Journal of the Siam Society* 68, no. 1 (1980): 1–28.

Kham Champakaeomani. *Buddha phra sek kham.* Vientiane, Laos: n.p., 1980.

———. *Pavatsat khong Phrabang.* Vientiane, Laos: n.p., 1980.

———. *Phra That Chedi-Wat samkhan lae Phra Khru Yot Kaeo Pun Samek.* Chiang Mai, Thailand: Social Research Institute, 2537 (1995).

(Phra) Khammai Dhammasami. "Between Idealism and Pragmatism: A Study of Monastic Education in Burma and Thailand from the Seventh Century to the Present." Ph.D. diss., Oxford University, 2005.

Khamman Vongkitratana. *Tamnan Vat Muang Luang Phrabang.* Vientiane, Laos: Hongphim Viangkung, 1964.

(Maha) Khampheuy Vannasopha. *Religious Affairs in Lao PDR: Policies and Tasks.* Vientiane, Laos: Ministry of Information and Culture, 2003.

(Phra) Khampun Philavong. *Vattanatham Lao.* Vientiane, Laos: Buddhavong Vat Paluang, 1967.

Khana khamakan bunbap kan seuksa [Ministry of Education, Research Committee]. *Khong hang lak sut khong Vithayalai Song.* Vientiane, Laos: Ministry of Education, 1996.

Khana khamakan Mahāmakut Rāchawithyālai. *Prawat Mahamakut Rachawithyalai nai Borom Rachapatham.* Bangkok: Mahamakut Monastic University Press, 2518 (1975).

Khanasit [Student Committee]. *Kan pokkrong khanasong lae ruang khong pak.* Bangkok: n.p., 2468 (1925).

Khana thamngan prawat kanphim nai Prathet Thai [Committee of the History of Printing in Thailand]. *Siam phimopakan prawatsat kan phim nai Prathet Thai.* Bangkok: Matichon, 2006.

Khu meu triam sop bot thong sop ban sanam luang. Bangkok: Mahamakut Monastic University Press, 2537 (1994).

Kieffer-Pülz, Petra. *Die Sim: Vorschriften zur Regelung der Buddhistischen Gemeindegrenze in älteren Buddhistischen Texten.* Berlin: D. Reimer, 1992.

Kirsch, Thomas. "Modernizing Implications of Nineteenth Century Reforms in the Thai Sangha." In *Religion and Legitimation of Power in Thailand, Laos, and Burma,* edited by Bardwell Smith, 20–33. Chambersburg, Pa.: Anima Books, 1978.

Koret, Peter. "Books of Search: The Invention of Traditional Lao Literature as a Subject of Study." In Evans, *Laos: Culture and Society,* 226–57.

———. "'Whispered so softly it resounds through the forest, spoken so loudly it can hardly be heard': The Art of Parallelism in Traditional Lao Literature." Ph.D. diss., School of Oriental and African Studies, London, 1994.

Kourilsky, Gregory. "L'Institut bouddhique ou la promotion d'une aire bouddhique 'Lao-Khmère.'" *Siksacakr* (forthcoming).

Krishna Charoenwong. "Western Influence on Education in Northern Thailand." N.p., n.d.

LaCapra, Dominic. *History and Reading: Tocqueville, Foucault, French Studies.* Toronto: University of Toronto Press, 2000.

———. *Rethinking Intellectual History.* Ithaca, N.Y.: Cornell University Press, 1983.

Laddawan Saesiang. *200 pi Bama nai Lanna.* Bangkok: Tenmay, 2545 (2002).

Lafont, Pierre-Bernard. *Bibliographie du Laos II.* Paris: École française d'Extrême-Orient, 1978.

———. "Buddhism in Contemporary Laos." In *Contemporary Laos,* edited by Martin Stuart-Fox, 148–62. St. Lucia: University of Queensland Press, 1982.

———. "Inventaire des manuscrits des pagodes du Laos." *Bulletin de l'École française d'Extrême-Orient* 52, no. 2 (1965): 429–546.

———. "Transformations politique et évolution du bouddhisme au Lao depuis 1960." In *Bouddhismes et sociétés asiatiques: Clerges, sociétés et pouvoir,* edited by Alain Forest, Eiichi Kato, and Léon Vandermeersch, 155–62. Paris: Éditions l'Harmattan, 1990.

Lafort, Remy, and John Cardinal Farley, eds. *The Catholic Encyclopedia.* Vol. 7. New York: Robert Appleton Company, 1910. http://www.newadvent.org/cathen/08794b.htm.

Lagirarde, François. "Gavampati-Kaccayana: Le culte et la legende du disciple ventripotent dans le bouddhisme des Thais." Vols. 1–2. These de doctorat en histoire des religions et des systemes de pensee, Sorbonne, École pratique des hautes etudes, Section des sciences religieuses, 2001.

———. "Textes bouddhiques du pays khmer et du Lanna." *Recherches nouvelles sur le Cambodge, Études thematiques* 1 (1994): 63–77.

———. "Une interprétation bouddhique des rites funéraires du Lanna et du Laos: Le sutta apocryphe de Mahā Kāla." *Aséanie* 2 (1998): 47–77.

Lagrée, Doudart de. *Voyage d'Exploration en Indochine effectué pendant les années 1866, 1867, 1868, par une Commision française présidée par M. le Capitaine de frégate Doudart de Lagrée et publié par ordre du Ministre de la Marine sous la direction de M. le Lieutenant de vaisseau Francis Garnier.* Paris: Collection Quentin, Bibliothèque des Beaux-Arts, 1984.

Lamun Canhom. *Wannakam thong thin Lanna*. Chiang Mai, Thailand: Suriwong Book Center, 2538 (1995).

Lancaster, Lewis. "An Analysis of the Aṣṭasahāṣrikaprajñāpāramitāsūtra from Chinese Translations." Ph.D. diss., University of Wisconsin–Madison, 1968.

Lanessan, Jean Marie Antoine de. *La colonisation française en Indo-Chine*. Paris: F. Alcan, 1895.

Law, Vivien. *The History of Linguistics in Europe*. Cambridge: Cambridge University Press, 2003.

———. *The Insular Latin Grammarians*. Totowa, N.J.: Biblio Distribution Services, 1982.

Le Blant, Emile. *Les martyrs de Extrême-Orient et les persécutions antiques*. Arras, France, 1877.

Le Boulanger, Paul. *Histoire du Laos française*. Paris: P. Plon, 1930.

Leclercq, Jean. *The Love of Learning and the Desire for God: A Study of Monastic Culture*. New York: Oxford University Press, 1961.

Lefèvre, Emile. *Travels in Laos: The Fate of Sip Song Panna and Muong Sing (1894–1986)*. Bangkok: White Lotus, 1995.

Lefèvre-Pontalis, Pierre. "Les Laotiens du Royaume de Lan Chang." *T'ouang Pao*, 1900, 149–67.

Leider, Jacques. "Tilling the Lord's Vineyard and Defending Portuguese Interests: Towards a Critical Reading of Father Manrique's Account of Arakan." *Journal of the Siam Society* 90, nos. 1–2 (2002): 39–58

Lemire, Charles. *Le Laos annamite*. Paris: A. Challamel, 1894.

Leuam Thamxot, trans. *Dhammabanyai bang suan*, by Phra Sunntthamrangsi Khamphiramethachan. Vientiane, Laos: n.p., 1969.

Lieberman, Victor. *Burmese Administrative Cycles: Anarchy and Conquest c. 1580–1760*. Princeton, N.J.: Princeton University Press, 1984.

———. *Strange Parallels*. Cambridge: Cambridge University Press, 2003.

———. "Was the Seventeenth Century a Watershed in Burmese History?" In *Southeast Asia in the Early Modern Era*, edited by Anthony Reid, 214–49. Chiang Mai, Thailand: Silkworm, 1993.

Lischer, Robert, ed. *Theories of Preaching: Selected Readings in the Homiletical Tradition*. Durham, N.C.: Duke University Press, 1987.

Loos, Tamara. *Subject Siam: Family, Law, and Colonial Modernity in Thailand*. Ithaca, N.Y.: Cornell University Press, 2006.

Lord, Albert. *The Singer of Tales*. New York: Atheneum, 1968. Originally published in German in 1965.

Lorrillard, Michel. "100 ans de recherche de l'EFEO au Laos." Talk given at the French embassy, Vientiane, Laos, June 15, 2001. http://laos.efeo.fr/spip.php?article85Svar-recherche=lorrillard (accessed October 2007).

———. "The Earliest Lao Buddhist Monasteries according to Philological and Epigraphical Sources." In *The Buddhist Monastery*, edited by Pierre Pichard and François Lagirarde, 187–98. Paris: École française d'Extrême-Orient, 2003.

———. "Les inscriptions du That Luang de Vientiane: Données nouvelles sur l'histoire d'un stūpa lao." *Bulletin de l'École française d'Extrême-Orient* 90–91 (2003–4): 289–348.

———. "La succession de Setthāthirāt: réappréciation d'une période de l'histoire du Lān Xāng." *Aséanie* 4 (1999): 45–64.

Louvet, Louis Eugene. *La Cochinchine religieuse*. 2 vols. Paris, 1885.

Lunet de Lajonquiere, Etienne. "Le Laos siamois." *Asie française* 7 (1907): 268–94.

———. "Vieng-Chan." *Bulletin de l'École française d'Extrême-Orient*, 1901, 99–118.

Macey, Pierre. "Une cérémonie funébre au Laos." *Bulletin de la Société de géographie de l'Est*, 1899, 222–34.

Madrolle, Claudius. *Indo-Chine*. Guidebook. Paris, 1902.

(Phra) Mahaniyom Thanathatto. *Tamnan Phra Borom That Lampang Luang*. N.p., n.d.

(Phra) Mahapan Anantho. *Nangseu desanā thang ha sai*. Vientiane, Laos: Vat Buddhavong Pāluang, 2000.

———. *Prabeni Lao*. Vientiane, Laos: Vat Mikhathaya, 2517 (1973).

———. *Samakhom Buddhavong Lao lae Buddhayaovason Lao*. Vientiane, Laos: Vat Buddhavong Paluang, 1971.

———. *Sing thi dai phop hen nai Langka thavip*. Vientiane: Khana Pha Song Lao pai paxum Lanka, Vat Buddhavong Paluang, 1966.

———. *Thang ha sai*. Vientiane, Laos: Vat Buddhavong Paluang, 1969.

(Phra) Mahasali Anucaro. *Nangseu thesana xalong tang 50 kap*. Vientiane, Laos: n.p., 1990.

(Phra) Mahasitthikan. *Laksut naktham lae thammaseuksa chan tri ruam thuk wicha*. Bangkok: Liang Chiang, 2544 (2001).

(Phra) Mahasuk Suwiro. "Khwam sonchai to kan seuksa Phra Pariyatidham khong Phra Song seuksa karani Phra Nisit Mahachulalongkorn Rachawithyalai." Ph.D. diss., Withyaniphon Khana Sangkhomwithyalai lae Manusyawithaya Mahawithyalai Thammasat, 2539 (1996).

(Phra) Mahavichit Singchalat. *Baep hian taeng thesana san mathayom seuksa Song*. Vientiane, Laos: n.p., 1993.

Malasekara, G. P. *The Pali Literature of Ceylon, Compiled by U Ko Lay*. Rangoon: Burma Pitaka Association, 1986.

Malleret, Louis. *Le cinquantenaire de l'École française d'Extrême-Orient: Compte rendu des fêtes et cérémonies*. Hanoi: École française d'Extrême-Orient, 1953.

Mallaret, Louis, and Georges Taboulet. *Groupes ethniques de l'Indochine française*. Saigon: Societe des études Indochinois, 1937.

Maṅgalatthadīpanī yoksap plae. Bangkok: Rongphim Tha Phrachan, 2475 (1932).

Mani Phayomyong. *Saraphochananukhrom Lanna*. Chiang Mai, Thailand: Dao computgraphik, 2546 (2003).

(Phra Maha) Mani Rattanapathimakone and (Phra) Rattanaphimpheuang. *Tamnan Phra Kaeo Morakot*. Vientiane, Laos: Sangon likhasit, 1999.

Marini, Giovani Filippo de. *Delle missioni de' Petri della Compagnia di Giesu mella provincia del Giappone e particolarmente de quella di Tumkino*. Rome: Nicolo Angelo Tinassi, 1663. Reports written between 1642 and 1648. Translated into French as *Histoire nouvelle et curieuse des royaumes de Tunquin et de Lao* (Paris: Gervais Clouzier, 1666); and into English as *A New and Interesting Description of the Lao Kingdom*, by Walter E. J. Tips and Claudio Bertuccio (Bangkok: White Lotus, 1998).

Martini, Martino. *Novus Atlas Sinensis*. Amsterdam: Joan Bleau, 1655.

Maspero, Henri. *Les coutumes funéraires chez les Tai-Noirs du Haut Tonkin*. Paris: Gallimard, 1950.

Matory, Lorand. *Black Atlantic Religion*. Princeton, N.J.: Princeton University Press, 2005.

Mayoury Ngaosrivathana and Kennon Breazeale, eds. *Breaking New Ground in Lao History*. Chiang Mai, Thailand: Silkworm, 2002.

Mayoury Ngaosyvathn and Pheuiphanh Ngaosyvathn. *Kith and Kin Politics: The Relationship between Laos and Thailand*. Manila, Philippines: Journal of Contemporary Asia Publishers, 1994.

———. *Paths to Conflagration: Fifty Years of Diplomacy and Warfare in Laos, Thailand, and Vietnam, 1778–1828*. Ithaca, N.Y.: Southeast Asia Program Publications, Cornell University, 1998.

McDaniel, Justin. "The Art of Reading and Teaching Dhammapadas: Reform, Texts, Contexts in Thai Buddhist History." *Journal of the International Association of Buddhist Studies* 28, no. 2 (2005): 299–338.

———. "Creative Engagement: The Sujavanna Wua Luang and its Contribution to Buddhist Literature." *Journal of the Siam Society* 88 (2000): 156–77.

———. "The Curricular Canon in Northern Thailand and Laos." Special issue, *Manusya: Journal of Thai Language and Literature*, 2002, 20–59.

———. "History of Lao Buddhism." In *Encyclopedia of Buddhism*, edited by Robert Buswell. New York: Macmillan Reference, 2004.

———. "History of the National Library of Laos." *Newsletter of the Fragile Palm-Leaves Preservation Project* 5 (2002): 2–3.

———. "Invoking the Source: Nissaya Manuscripts, Pedagogy, and Sermon-Making in Northern Thailand and Laos." Ph.D. diss., Harvard University, 2003.

———. "A Lao Homily: The *Kammavācā nissaya sadda*." Études thématiques Laos. Paris: École française de Extrême-Orient, forthcoming.

———. "Modern Buddhism in Thailand." In *Buddhism in World Cultures: Comparative Perspectives*, edited by Steven Berkwitz, 101–28. Santa Barbara, Calif.: ABC-CLIO, 2006.

———. "Notes on the Lao Influence on Northern Thai Literature." In *The Literary Heritage of Laos*, edited by Kongdeuane Nettavong, Harald Hundius, David Wharton, Dara Kanlaya, and Khanthamali Yangnuvong, 373–96. Vientiane: National University of Laos, 2005.

———. "Notes on the Study of Pali Grammar in Thailand." In *Embedded Religions: Essays in Honour of W. S. Karunatillake*, edited by Suzanne Mrozick, Carol Anderson, and W. Rajapakse. Colombo, Sri Lanka: S. Godage and Brothers, 2007.

———. "Paritta and Rakṣā." In *Kith and Kin Politics: The Relationship between Laos and Thailand*, edited by Robert Buswell. New York: Macmillan Reference, 2004.

———. "Questioning Orientalist Power: The French and Buddhism in Laos." In *Collected Papers of the International Conference on Lao Studies*, edited by John Hartmann and Carol Compton. De Kalb: Northern Illinois University Press, 2007.

———. "Transformative History: The *Nihon Ryoiki* and the *Jinakālamālīpakaraṇam*." *Journal of the International Association of Buddhist Studies* 25, no. 1 (2002): 151–207.

———. "Two Bullets in a Balustrade: How the Burmese Have Been Removed from Northern Thai History." *Journal of Burma Studies* 11 (2007).

McGilvary, Daniel. *A Half Century among the Siamese and the Lao*. New York: Revell, 1912.

McHale, Shawn. *Print and Power: Confucianism, Communism, and Buddhism in the Making of Modern Vietnam*. Honolulu: University of Hawaii Press, 2004.

Mettanando Bhikkhu. "Meditation and Healing in the Theravada Buddhist Order of Thailand and Laos." Ph.D. diss., University of Hamburg, 1999.

Miles, Malcolm. *Urban Avant-Garde: Art, Architecture, and Change*. London: Routledge, 2004.

Mingsan Khaosaat. *Wihan dong chumchong sakun chang Lampang*. Chiang Mai, Thailand: Chiang Mai University Press, 2525 (1982).

Mouhot, Henri. *Travels in the Central Parts of Indochina (Siam), Cambodia, and Laos, during the Years 1858, 1859, and 1860*. Edited by C. Pym. Reprint, New York: Oxford University Press, 1989.

Murdoch, J. B. "The 1901–1902 'Holy Man's Rebellion.'" *Journal of the Siam Society* 62 (1974): 47–66.

Na Baknam. *Tu Phra Traipitok*. Bangkok: Silapakorn University, 2543 (1999).

(Somdet Phra Sangharat Somdet Phra) Ñāṇasaṃvara. *Prawatsat khong Wat Suan Dok*. Chiang Mai, Thailand: Wat Suan Dok, 1932.

———. *Sāsanadīpanī*. Bangkok: Mahamakut Monastic University Press, 2548 (2005).

Nangseu rian klum wichaphraparivatitham. 6 vols. Bangkok: Mahachulalongkorn Monastic University Press, 2534 (1991).

Narada Thera, trans. *A Manual of Abhidhamma: Being Abhidhammattha-Sangaha of Anuruddhācāriya*. Colombo, Sri Lanka: Buddhist Publication Society, 1956.

Nginn, Somchine Pierre. "La coutume des funérailles au pays Lao." *Kinnary* 4 (1946): 17–22.

———. *Les fêtes profanes et religieuses au Laos*. Vientiane, Laos: Éditions du Comité littèraire, 1967.

———. "Les funérailles au Laos." *Sud-Est* 22 (1951–53).

Nidhi Aeusrivongse. "Buddha wibat." In *Kan patirup Phra Buddha Sasana nai Prathet Thai*, edited by Nidhi Aeusrivongse and Pramuan Phengchan, 1–28. Bangkok: Kongtung Raktham, 2542 (1999).

———. *Kan meuang Thai samai Phrachao Khrung Thonburi*. 4th ed. Bangkok: Matichon, 1996.

Nithan Thammabot. Bangkok: Liang Chiang, n.d.

Norman, K. R. "Pali Literature." In *A History of Indian Literature*, vol. 7, pt. 2, edited by Jan Gonda. Wiesbaden: Harrassowitz, 1983.

Notton, Camille. *Annales du Siam*. Vol. 2. Paris: Limoges, 1930.
Nou Saiyasittiwong, Volker Grabowsky, Bualy Paphaphanh, and Khamrung Saenmani. *Pheun viang samay Chou Anu*. Vientiane: National University of Laos, 2004.
Obeyesekere, Ranjini. *Jewels of the Doctrine*. Albany: State University of New York, 1991.
O'Brien O'Keeffe, Katherine. "Editing and the Material Text." In *The Editing of Old English: Papers from the 1990 Manchester Conference*, edited by D. G. Scragg and Paul E. Szarmach, 147–54. Cambridge, U.K.: D. S. Brewer, 1994.
Okell, John. "Nissaya Burmese." *Journal of the Burma Research Society* 50 (1967): 95–123. Expanded from *Lingua* 15 (1965).
Okudaira, Ryuji. "Theft Cases in Eighteenth-Century Burma with Special Reference to the Atula Hsayadaw Hpyathton." Unpublished paper, 2006.
Oldenberg, Hermann. *Zur Geschichte der altindischen Prosa: Mit besonderer Berücksichtigung der prosaisch-poetischen Erzählung*. Berlin: Weidmannsche Buchhandlung, 1917.
Olson, Grant. "Thai Cremation Volumes: A Brief History of a Unique Genre of Literature." *Asian Folklore Studies* 51 (1992): 279–94.
(Phra Achan) Ongkaeo Sitthivong. *Khu meu Pasong-Samanen Vat Sisaket*. Vientiane, Laos: Vat Sisaket, 2003.
———. *Sut xayamungkhun lae bot desanā mungkhun heuan*. Vientiane, Laos: Vat Sisaket, 1990.
Ongkan Buddhasāsanā Sampan Lao. *Xivit lae phon ngan khong phramahathera ha ong*. Vientiane: Ongkan Buddhasāsanā Sampan Lao, 2001.
Osipov, Yury. "Buddhist Hagiography in Forming the Canon in the Classical Literatures of Indochina." In *The Canon in Southeast Asian Literatures*, edited by David Smyth, 1–7. London: Curzon, 2000.
Paitun Brahmawichit. *Chandasat Thai*. Bangkok: Ton O, 2541 (1998).
Paitun Dokbuakaeo. *Horasat Lan Na*. Chiang Mai, Thailand: Social Research Institute, 2547 (2004).
Paitun Sinlarat. "Influence of Western Education and Adjustment of Thai Education." In *Proceedings of the Fourth International Conference of Thai Studies*, vol. 1. Kunming: China Institute of Southeast Asian Studies, 1990.
Pali waiyakon. Bangkok: Krombhrayā Wachirayān-worarot, 2538 (1995).
Pallegoix, Jean-Baptiste. *Description du Royaume Thai ou Siam comprenant la topographie, histoire naturelle, moeurs et coutumes, léagislation, commerce, industrie, langue, littérature, religion, Annales des Thai et précis historique de la mission*. Paris: Ligny, 1854.
Pamaree Surakiat. "Thai-Burmese Warfare during the Sixteenth Century and the Growth of the First Tounggoo Empire." *Journal of the Siam Society* 93 (2005): 69–100.
Parmentier, Henri. *L'art du Laos*. Paris: École française d'Extrême-Orient, 1988. Edition revised by Madeleine Giteau.
Paṭidin sāsanā 2546. Bangkok: Mahamakut Monastic University Press, 2546 (2003).
Patton, Laurie. *Myth as Argument*. Berlin: Walter de Gruyter, 1996.

Pavie, Auguste. *Recherches sur l'histoire de Cambodge, du Laos et du Siam: Mission Pavie en Indochine* [Études Diverse, expose des travaux de la Mission geographie et voyages, passage du Mekhong au Tonkin, 1887 et 1888, journal de marche, 1888–1889, evenements du Siam, 1891–1893] contenant la transcription et la traduction des inscriptions par M. Schmitt, 1879–95. Vols. 1–11. Paris: E. Leroux, 1898–1919.

Pe Maung Tin. Preface to *Buddhist Manual of Psychological Ethics: Being a Translation, Now Made for the First Time, from the Original Pali, of the First Book in the Abhidhamma Pitaka Entitled Dhammasangani, Compendium of States or Phenomena*, edited by Caroline Rhys-Davids. 3rd ed. London: Pali Text Society, 1974.

Peleggi, Maurizio. *Lord of Things: The Fashioning of the Siamese Monarchy's Modern Image*. Honolulu: University of Hawaii Press, 2002.

Peltier, Anatole-Roger, ed. *Chao Bun Hlong*. Chiang Mai, Thailand: École française d'Extrême-Orient, 1992.

———. *La littèrature Tai Khoen*. Chiang Mai, Thailand: École française d'Extrême-Orient, 1989.

———. "Les litteratures Lao du Lan Na, du Lan Xang, de Keng Tung et des Sip Song Panna." *Péninsule* 2 (1990): 29–44.

———. *Le roman classique lao*. Paris: École française d'Extrême-Orient, 1988.

———, ed. *Sujavaṇṇa wua luang*. Chiang Tung, Burma: Publié á l'occasion de l'offrande du Cullakaṭhina Monastère du Wat Tha Kradas, 1993.

Penth, Hans. *A Brief History of Lanna*. Chiang Mai, Thailand: Silkworm, 1994.

———. "Buddhist Literature of Lān Nā on the History of Lān Nā's Buddhism." *Journal of the Pali Text Society* 23 (1997): 43–81.

———. "King Kawila of Chiang Mai 1742–1816: Attempt at a Bibliography." *Bulletin of the Archive of Lan Na Inscriptions* 5 (1993): 109–32.

———. "A Note on Old Tak." *Journal of the Siam Society* 61 (1973): 183–86.

———. "On the History of Chiang Rai." *Journal of the Siam Society* 77, no. 1 (1989): 11–30.

———. "Reflections on the Saddhamma-Saṅgaha." *Journal of the Siam Society* 65, no. 1 (1977): 259–80.

———. "Der Wiederaufbau des Lan Na Thai nach den Birmanenkriegen." *Nachrichten der Akademie der Wissenschaften in Göttingen, Philologisch-Historische Klasse* 1 (1974): 207–51.

Penth, Hans, Phanphen Krüathai, and Silao Kesaprohm. *Chareuk nai Phiphitaphan Chiang Saen*. Corpus of Lanna Inscriptions, vol. 1. Chiang Mai, Thailand: Social Research Institute, 2540 (1997).

———. *Chareuk nai Phiphitaphan Lamphun*. Corpus of Lanna Inscriptions, vol. 3. Chiang Mai, Thailand: Social Research Institute, 2542 (1999).

———. *Chareuk Phra Chao Kawila: 2334–2357*. Corpus of Lanna Inscriptions, vol. 2. Chiang Mai, Thailand: Social Research Institute, 2541 (1998).

Phanphen Krüathai. *Khlong pheun Wat Phra Sing*. Chiang Mai, Thailand: Social Research Institute, 2539 (1996).

Phimmasone Pouvong. "L'Institut bouddhique et l'enseignement religieux." In *Présence du Royaume Lao*, edited by René de Berval, 1107–9. Saigon: Numéro spécial de France-Asie, 1956.

Phongsavadan Muang Luang Phrabang. Vientiane, Laos: n.p., 1969.

Phot Saphianchai. *Chabap chatkan seuksa khong khana Song Thai*. Bangkok: Samnakngan khana kammakan kan seuksa haeng chat, 2523 (1979).

Phunphisamai Disakul. *Sasanakhun: Nangseu son Phra Buddhasāsanā kae dek*. Bangkok: Sobhanaphiphantanakon, 2472 (1929).

Pirasri Powathong. "Transformation of Bangkok in the Press during the Reign of Rāma V." *Manusya: Journal of Humanities* 6, no. 1 (2003): 47–53.

(Phra) Platawisut Kuttachayo. *Khu meu kanseuksa Phra Abhidhamma chan chulabhidhammikatri*. Bangkok: Mahachulalongkorn Monastic University Press, 2545 (2001).

Polecritti, Cynthia. *Preaching Peace in Renaissance Italy*. Washington, D.C.: Catholic University Press, 2000.

Pollock, Sheldon. "The Cosmopolitan Vernacular." *Journal of Asian Studies* 57, no. 1 (1998): 6–37.

———, ed. *Literary Cultures in History*. Berkeley: University of California Press, 2003.

Pomarin Charuwon. "Suat Phra Malai: Botbat khong khatikam lang khwam tai to wannakam lae sangkhom." In *Phithikam tamnan nithan phleng: Botbat khong khatichon kap sangkhom Thai*, edited by Sukanya Succhaya, 113–62. Bangkok: Chulalongkorn University Press, 2548 (2005).

Pope, Marvin. *The Anchor Bible: Song of Songs*. Garden City, N.Y.: Doubleday, 1977.

(Phraya) Prachakitopachak, ed. *Phongsawadan Yonok*. Bangkok: Chabap hosamut haeng chat, 2504 (1961).

Prakai Nontawasee, ed. *Changes in Northern Thailand and the Shan States, 1886–1940*. Singapore: Institute of Southeast Asian Studies, 1988.

Prapod Assavavirulhakarn. "From the Vessantara Jātaka to the Mahājāti Kham Luang." Paper presented at the Thai Language and Literature conference, Chulalongkorn University, Bangkok, November 11, 2006.

Prasert na Nagara. *Tamnan munlasatsana Wat Suan Dok*. Bangkok: Ekasanwichakan Samakhom Prawatisat, 2537 (1994).

Prasithrathsint, Amara. "Reduplication as a Device for Forming Adjectives and Adverbs in Thai." Paper delivered at the Thai Language and Literature conference, Chulalongkorn University, Bangkok, November 11, 2006.

Prawat Mahamakut Rachawithyalai nai Phra Borom Rachupatham. Bangkok: Mahamakut Monastic University Press, 2521 (1977).

Pricha Changkhwanyeun. *Thammawacana wohan Thai*. Bangkok: Chulalongkorn University Press, 2540 (1997).

Prothero, Stephen. "Henry Steel Olcott and 'Protestant Buddhism.'" *Journal of the American Academy of Religion* 63, no. 2 (1995): 281–303.

Pruitt, William. *Étude linguistique de nissaya Birmans: Traduction commentée de textes bouddhiques*. Paris: École française d'Extrême-Orient, 1994.

———. "Un nissaya Birman de la Bibliothèque nationale, le patimokkha: Étude linguistique; Deuxième partie." *Cahiers de l'Asie du Sud-Est* 21 (1987): 7–45.

———. "Un nissaya Birman de la Bibliothèque nationale, le patimokkha: Étude linguistique; Première partie." *Cahiers de l'Asie du Sud-Est* 19 (1986): 84–119.

———. "Un nissaya Birman de la Bibliothèque nationale, le patimokkha: Étude linguistique; Troisième partie." *Cahiers de l'Asie du Sud-Est* 22 (1987): 35–57.

Punroeng Puasiisaengpasoet. *Pravat silapa lae sathapattayakam Lao lem 2: Meuang Luang Phrabang*. Vientiane, Laos: Toyota Foundation, 1995.

(Phradit) Punyabhakdi Bhirin. *Khu meu rian phasa Pali duai ton eng*. Bangkok: Liang Chiang, 2538 (1995).

Raenchen, Oliver, ed. "Special Issue: Muang." *Tai Culture: International Review on Tai Cultural Studies* 3, no. 1 (1998).

Ratanapañña. *Jinakālamālīpakaraṇam*. Transcribed and edited by A. P. Buddhadatta. London: Pali Text Society, 1962.

Ratanaporn Sethakul. "Political Relations between Chiang Mai and Kongtung in the Nineteenth Century." In *Changes in Northern Thailand and the Shan States, 1886–1940*, edited by Prakai Nontawasee, 296–327. Singapore: Institute of Southeast Asian Studies, 1988.

Reclus, Emile. *Nouvelle géographie universelle*. Vol. 8. Paris: Hachette, 1883.

Reid, Anthony. *Charting the Shape of Early Modern Southeast Asia*. Chiang Mai, Thailand: Silkworm, 1999.

———. *Southeast Asia in the Age of Commerce, 1450–1680*. 2 vols. New Haven, Conn.: Yale University Press, 1988–93.

———, ed. *Southeast Asia in the Early Modern Era: Trade, Power, and Belief*. Ithaca, N.Y.: Cornell University Press, 1993.

Reynolds, Craig. "The Buddhist Monkhood in Nineteenth Century Thailand." Ph.D. diss., Cornell University, 1973.

———. "Monastery Lands and Labour Endowments in Thailand: Some Effects of Social and Economic Change, 1868–1910." *Journal of the Economic and Social History of the Orient* 22 (1979): 190–227.

———. "Mr. Kulap and Purloined Documents" In *Seditious Histories: Contesting Thai and Southeast Asian Pasts*. Seattle: University of Washington Press, 2006. Originally published in *Journal of the Siam Society* 61, no. 1 (1973): 63–90.

———. "The Plot of Thai History: Theory and Practice." In *Patterns and Illusions: Thai History and Thought in Memory of Richard B. Davis*, edited by Gehan Wijeyewardene and E. C. Chapman. 313–32. Melbourne: Australian National University, 1992.

Reynolds, Suzanne. *Medieval Reading: Grammar, Rhetoric, and the Classical Text*. Cambridge: Cambridge University Press, 1996.

Rhys-Davids, Caroline, ed. *A Buddhist Manual of Psychological Ethics: Being a Translation, Now Made for the First Time, from the Original Pali, of the First Book in the Abhidhamma Pitaka Entitled Dhammasangani, Compendium of States or Phenomena*. 3rd ed. London: Pali Text Society, 1974.

Rhys-Davids, Caroline, and Shwe Zan Aung. *Compendium of philosophy: being a translation now made for the first time from the original Pali of the Abhidhammatthasangaha*. London: Published for the Pali Text Society by Luzac, 1972.

Robinson, Fred. *The Editing of Old English*. London: Blackwell, 1982.

(Phra) Roengsuk Natthammo. "Kan seuksa choeng wikhro wannakam Lan Na yut lang rueang wohan mahapatthana sangkhep." Ph.D. diss., Mahachulalongkorn Monastic University, Bangkok, 2542 (2000).

Roest, Burt, ed. *Aspects of Genre and Type in Pre-modern Literary Cultures*. Groningen, Netherlands: Styx, 1999.

Rujaya Abhakorn. *Changes in the Administrative System of the Northern Thai States, 1884–1908*. Chiang Mai, Thailand: Chiang Mai University, 1984.

Rung Kaendaeng, ed. *Raingan sathitidansasana khong Prathet Thai*. CD-ROM. Bangkok: Samnakngan khana kammakan kan seuksa haeng chat, 2542 (1999).

(Phra Khru) Run Thamrangsi. *Monpithi plae samrap Phra Phiksusamanen lae Buddhasasanikachon tua bai*. Bangkok: Mahamakut Monastic University Press, 2534 (1991).

———. *Suat mon chabap luang plae*. Bangkok: Mahamakut Monastic University Press, 2534 (1991).

Sachchidanand, Sahai. *Rāmāyana in Laos*. Delhi: B. R. Publications, 1973.

(Phra) Saddadhammajotika Dhammācāriya. *Mātikājotika Dhammasaṅgaṇī Rūpattha nissaya*. Bangkok: Abhidhamma Jotika College at Mahachulalongkorn Monastic University, 2546 (2003).

Saengthong Photipuppha. *Pavat Muang Xieng Kouang*. Vientiane: Khong kan botbat raksa nangseu bailan Lao, 1998.

Saksi Yaemnadda. *Wannakhadi Buddhasāsanā phak Thai*. Bangkok: Chulalongkorn University Press, 2543 (2000).

Saksiri Mirsomseub. *Khon soi tao*. Bangkok: DK Books, 2542 (1999).

Samuels, Jeffrey. "Learning to Attract the Heart: The Aesthetics of Ritual Performance in Contemporary Sri Lanka." Paper presented at the annual meeting of the American Academy of Religion, San Antonio, Tex., 2004.

———. "Toward an Action-Oriented Pedagogy: Buddhist Texts and Monastic Education in Contemporary Sri Lanka." *Journal of the American Academy of Religion* 72, no. 4 (2004): 955–71.

Sanson, Nicolas. "L'Asie." In *Maps from Ancient Times to the Mid-nineteenth Century*. 1669. Reprint, Leipzig: Acta Humaniora, 1989.

Saranukhrom watthanatham Thai phak neua. Bangkok: Thanakhan Thai Panich, 2542 (1999).

Saraswati Ongsakun. *Chumchon boran nai aeng Chiang Mai–Lamphun*. Chiang Mai, Thailand: Toyota Foundation and Amarin, 2543 (2000).

———. *Prawatsat Lan Na*. Bangkok: Amarin, 2539 (1996).

(Phra) Sasanasobhon. *Suatmon chapab Luang*. Bangkok: Mahamakut Monastic University Press, 2518 (1975).

Savaeng Phinith. *Contribution à l'histoire du royaume de Luang Prabang*. Paris: École française d'Extrême-Orient, 1990.

Sawana Phonphatkun. *Kan seuksa lae kan damrong samanaphet Song Thai*. Bangkok: Mahamakut Monastic University Press, 2524 (1980).

Schwab, Raymond. *La renaissance orientale*. Paris: Payot, 1950.
Segre, Cesare. *Introduction to the Analysis of the Literary Text*. Translated by John Meddemmen. Bloomington: Indiana University Press, 1988.
Seligman, Edwin. "The French Colonial Fiscal System." *Publications of the American Economic Association* 1, no. 3 (1900): 21–39.
(Phay Luang Maha) Sena Phouy. *Méthode d'enseignment élémentaire du Laotien pour apprendre a lire les caractères Tham dans les textes Palis*. Vientiane, Laos: Institut bouddhique, 1934.
Shibasaki, Reijirou. "On the Grammatization of Verbal Reduplication in Japanese." *Studies on Reduplication*, edited by Berhard Hurch, 283–314. Berlin: Mouton de Gruyter, 2005.
Shigeharu, Tanabe. "Autochthony and the Inthakhin Cult of Chiang Mai." In Turton, *Civility and Savagery*, 294–318.
———. *Religious Traditions among Tai Ethnic Groups*. Ayutthya, Thailand: Historical Study Center, 1991.
Shigeharu Tanabe and Charles Keyes, eds. *Cultural Crisis and Social Memory: Modernity and Identity in Thailand and Laos*. London: RoutledgeCurzon, 2002.
Shwe Zan Aung. "Abhidhamma Literature in Burma." *Journal of the Pali Text Society* 6 (1908): 106–23. Reprinted in journal, 1978.
(Phra Maha) Sikham Vorachit. *Banha Vinai phak 1* [Problems in the Vinaya, vol. 1]. Vientiane, Laos: Siaonasit, 1973.
(Maha) Sila Viravong. *My Life*. Vientiane, Laos: Dokbuakaeo, 2005
———. *Pavat Lao tae buhan theung 1946*. Vientiane: National Library of Laos and Toyota Foundation, 2001.
———. *Pavat nangseu Lao*. Vientiane: National Library of Laos, 1995.
———. *Payok khong vannakhadi*. Vientiane: National Library of Laos, 1995.
Singer, Noel. "Kammavaca Texts: Their Covers and Binding Ribbons." *Arts of Asia* 23, no. 1 (1993): 91–105.
———. "Palm Leaf Manuscripts of Myanmar." *Arts of Asia* 21, no. 1 (1991): 133–43.
Sirichando Chandra. *Bandeuk dhamma desanā 4*. Bangkok: Liang Chiang, 2505 (1962).
Siriwat Khamwansa. *Song Thai nai 200 pi*. Bangkok: Mahachulalongkorn Monastic University Press, 1981.
Skilling, Peter. "Ārādhanā Tham: Invitation to Teach the Dhamma." Special issue, *Manusya: Journal of Humanities* 4 (2002): 84–92.
———. "The Rakṣā Literature of the Śravakayāna." *Journal of the Pali Text Society* 27 (1992): 109–82.
———. "Sources for the Study of the Maṅgala and Mora Suttas." *Journal of the Pali Text Society* 24 (1998): 185–93.
Skilling, Peter, and Prapod Assavavirulhakarn. "Tripiṭaka in Practice in the Fourth and Fifth Reigns." Special issue, *Manusya: Journal of Humanities* 4 (2002): 60–72.
Skilling, Peter, and Santi Pakdeekham, comps., trans, and eds. *Materials for the Study of the Tripiṭaka*. Vol. 1, *Pāli Literature Transmitted in Central Siam*. Bangkok: Fragile Palm Leaves Foundation, 2002.

———. *Materials for the Study of the Tripiṭaka*. Vol. 2, *Pāli and Vernacular Literature Transmitted in Central and Northern Siam*. Bangkok: Fragile Palm Leaves Foundation, 2004.

Smith, John D. "The Singer or the Song? A Reassessment of Lord's 'Oral Theory.'" *Man* 12, no. 1 (1977): 141–53.

Smith, Jonathan Z. *Imagining Religion: From Babylon to Jonestown*. Chicago: University of Chicago Press, 1982.

———. *Map Is Not Territory: Studies in the History of Religions*. Chicago: University of Chicago Press, 1978.

Smithies, Michael, ed. *Descriptions of Old Siam*. Singapore: Oxford Asia, 1995.

Smyth, David. "James Low on Siamese Literature (1839)." *Journal of the Siam Society* 95 (2007): 159–200.

Sommai Premchit. "Palm Leaf Manuscripts and the Traditional Sermon." In *Collected Papers of the World Fellowship of Buddhists*, edited by Saeng Chandrangaam, 74–86. Chiang Mai: International Conference of Thai Studies, 1980.

Souneth Photisane. "The Importance of the Khoun Bourom Chronicle and Lao History." *Lanxang Heritage Journal* 1 (1996): 48–62.

———. "Khwam sampan rawang Lanna lae Lanxang." *In Khwam sampan rawang Chiang Mai lae Luang Phrabang thang silapa*, edited by Thirasak Dedvongna, 1–15. Chiang Mai, Thailand: Nopburi, 2545 (2001).

———. "The Nidān Khun Borom: Annotated Translation and Analysis." Ph.D. diss., University of Queensland, 1996.

Steiner, George. *After Babel*. Oxford: Oxford University Press, 1992.

Strong, John. *The Legend and Cult of Upagupta: Sanskrit Buddhism in North India and Southeast Asia*. Princeton, N.J.: Princeton University Press, 1992.

Stuart-Fox, Martin. *Buddhist Kingdom, Marxist State: The Making of Modern Laos*. Bangkok: White Lotus, 1996.

———. "The French in Laos: 1887–1945." *Modern Asian Studies* 29, no. 1 (1995): 111–39.

———. *A History of Laos*. Cambridge: Cambridge University Press, 1997.

———. *The Lao Kingdom of Lan Xang: Rise and Decline*. Bangkok: White Lotus, 1998.

———. "On the Writing of Lao History: Continuities and Discontinuities." *Journal of Southeast Asian Studies* 24 (1993): 106–21.

Stuart-Fox, Martin, and Mary Kooyman, eds. *Historical Dictionary of Laos*. London: Scarecrow, 1992.

Suchao Ploichum. *Somdet Phra Mahāsamaṇachao*. Bangkok: Mahamakut Monastic University Press, 2541 (1998).

Suchip Bunnanuphap. *Phra Traibidok chabap samrap prachachon*. Bangkok: Mahamakut Monastic University Press, 1996.

(Phra) Sugandha (Anil Sakya). *Suatmon tua Ariyaka*. Bangkok: Mahamakut Monastic University Press, 2547 (2004).

Sukanya Nitungkorn. "Higher Education Reform in Thailand." *Southeast Asian Studies* 38, no. 4 (2001): 461–80.

Sunant Anchalinukun. "Kan seuksa phasa Thai samai rachakan thi 5." *Wanasan Phasa lae Phasasat* 19 (2002): 157–78.

Suni Hanyawong. *Kan samruat chum chon boran nai changwat Lampang nai prawasat lae borankhadi nakon Lampang*. Lampang, Thailand: Lampang Teacher's College Press, 2534 (1991).

Supaphanh na Bangchang. *Waiyakon Pali*. Bangkok: Mahamakut Monastic University Press, 1998.

———. *Wiwathanakan ngan khian phasa Pali nai Prathet Thai: Chareuk tamnan phongsawadan san prakat*. Bangkok: Mahamakut Monastic University Press, 2529 (1986).

———. *Wiwathanakan Pali sai Phra Suttantabidok thi taeng nai Prathet Thai*. Bangkok: Chulalongkorn University Press, 2533 (1990).

Sutthiphong Tontyaphisalasut. *Pramuan dhamma nai Phra Traibidok*. Bangkok: Rongphim Kan Sasana, n.d.

Swanson, Herbert. "Using Missionary Records for the Study of Northern Thai History: An Introduction and Appraisal." In *Change in Northern Thailand and the Shan States (1886–1910)*. Seminar Papers, Department of History, Chiang Mai University, Thailand, 1992.

Swearer, Donald. *Becoming the Buddha*. Princeton, N.J.: Princeton University Press, 2004.

———. *The Legend of Queen Cāma*. Albany: State University of New York Press, 1998.

———. "Signs of the Buddha in Northern Thai Chronicles." *Wannakam Buddhasasana nai Lan Na*, edited by Phanphen Krüathai. Chiang Mai, Thailand: Silkworm, 1997.

———. "A Summary of the Seven Books of the Abhidhamma." In *Buddhism in Practice*, edited by Donald Lopez, 336–42. Princeton, N.J.: Princeton University Press, 1996.

———. *Wat Haripuñjaya*. Missoula, Mont.: Scholars Press, 1974.

Swearer, Donald, and Sommai Premchit. "A Translation of Tamnan Mulasasana Wat Pa Daeng." *Journal of the Siam Society* 65, no. 2 (1977): 73–110.

Tanselle, G. Thomas. "The Varieties of Scholarly Editing." In *Scholarly Editing: A Guide to Research*, edited by D. C. Greetham, 11–31. New York: Modern Language Association of America, 1995.

Taupin, G., ed. *Bulletin des Amis du Laos*. Vols. 1–3. Hanoi: École française d'Extrême-Orient, 1937–39.

Taylor, Keith. "Surface Orientations in Vietnam: Beyond Histories of Nation and Region." *Journal of Asian Studies* 57, no. 4 (1998): 949–78.

Tej Bunnag. *The Provincial Adminstration of Siam, 1892–1915*. Kuala Lumpur: University of Malaysia Press, 1983.

Terwiel, B. J. *A History of Modern Thailand, 1767–1942*. Lucia: University of Queensland Press, 1983.

———. *Monks and Magic: An Analysis of Religious Ceremonies in Central Thailand*. 3rd rev. ed. Bangkok: White Lotus, 1994.

Tham Sayasithsena. *Pavat Vat Inpeng Mahavihan*. Vientiane, Laos: Vat Inpeng, 1993.

(Somdet Phraphoutthajinorot) Thammayana Mahathera with M. Demaratray, Narada

Mahathera, and K. Viphakone. *Les Gāthās Dhammapada.* [Verses in Lao, Pali, English, and French]. Vientiane, Laos: Young Buddhists Association, 1993.
Than Tun, ed. *The Royal Orders of Burma, AD 1598–1885.* Kyoto: Center for South East Asian Studies, Kyoto University, 1988.
(Phra) Thavon Bumpasoet. *Dhamma panyai.* Vientiane, Laos: n.p., 2000.
Thaw Khaung. "Survey of the History of Education in Burma." *Journal of the Royal Institute of Burmese Studies* 46, no. 2 (1963): 36–64.
Thienchai Aksorndit, Koroknok Ratanawarabhan, and Wandi Santiwudiwedhi. *Lanna: Chakrawat tuaton amnat.* Bangkok: Mahamakut Monastic University Press, 2545 (2002).
Thipawan Khwanon. "Chabhap lae banha chai laksut Phra Buddhasasana tam laksut prathomseuksa Buddhasasana nai rongrian sangkat samnakngan khana kammakan kan seuksa ekachon Krungthep Mahanakhon." Withyaniphon Phak Wicha Prathom Seuksa Chulalongkorn, Bangkok, 2541 (1998).
Thongchai Winichakul. "The Quest for 'Siwilai': A Geographical Discourse of Civilizational Thinking in Late Nineteenth and Early Twentieth Century Siam." *Journal of Asian Studies* 59, no. 3 (2000): 528–49.
———. *Siam Mapped: History of the Geo-body of a Nation.* Honolulu: University of Hawaii Press, 1994.
Tin Lwin. "Monastic Education and the Beginning of Western Education in Myanmar." Paper presented at the Historical Research Center conference, Yangon, Myanmar, December 2003.
———. "A Study of Pali-Burmese Nissaya." Master's thesis, University of London, 1961.
Todorov, Tzvetan. *Les genres du discours.* Paris: Éditions du Seuil, 1978.
Tournier, Marie Auguste Armand. *Notice sur la Laos français.* Paris, 1900.
Trager, Frank, and William Koenig. *Burmese Sit-tans, 1769–1826: Rural Life and Administration.* Tucson: University of Arizona Press, 1979.
Trankell, Ing-Britt. "Royal Relics: Ritual and Social Memory in Louang Prabang." In Evans, *Laos: Culture and Society,* 191–213.
Tun Aung Chain. "Chiang Mai in Bayinnaung's Polity." In *Proceedings of the Sixth International Conference of Thai Studies.* Chiang Mai: International Conference of Thai Studies, 1996.
Turton, Andrew, ed. *Civility and Savagery: Social Identity in Tai States.* Richmond, U.K.: Curzon, 2000.
(Sāmanera) Udit Sirivanna Prian. *Dhammabot phak 1–6 Plae doi byanjana.* Bangkok: Liang Chiang, 2530 (1987).
———. *Khu meu kan plae Dhammabot* (chabap krapao). Bangkok: Liang Chiang, 2531 (1988).
Udom Rungreuangsri. *Wohan Lan Na.* Chiang Mai, Thailand: Chiang Mai University Press, 2549 (2006).
(Phaya) Upakit Silapasan. *Lak pasa Thai.* 10th ed. Bangkok: Watthana Panich, 2544 (2002).

(Phra) Upālīguṇūpamācāriya (Sirichando Chandra). *Bandeuk dhamma desanā 4*. Bangkok: Liang Chiang, 2505 (1962).
(Phra Maha) Vandi Silachanthani. *Phommatham mangsavirat*. Vientiane, Laos, 1958.
Vatthana Pholsena. "Changing Historiographies of the Lao Past." *Journal of Southeast Asian Studies* 35, no. 2 (2004): 235–59.
———. *Post-war Laos: The Politics of Culture, History, and Identity*. Ithaca, N.Y.: Cornell University Press, 2006.
Veidlinger, Daniel. "Spreading the Dhamma." Ph.D. diss., University of Chicago, 2002.
———. *Spreading the Dhamma*. Honolulu: University of Hawaii Press, 2006.
(Phra maha) Vichit Sangharat. *Pali vaiyakon: Phak thi neung akkharawithi*. Vientiane: Khata sun kan seuksa song and the Lao-German Cooperative Manuscript Preservation Project, 2000.
Wachirayan [Somdet Phra Mahāsamanachao Krom Phra Vajirayāṇa Wororot]. *Phra Buddha Sasana kap kan bokkong Pathet*. Vientiane: Yaova Buddikasamākhom haeng Rāxānāchak Lao, 1967. Originally published in Thai in 1916 and translated into Lao from the English translation.
Walker, Andrew. *Legend of the Golden Boat*. Honolulu: University of Hawaii Press, 1999.
Warder, A. K., ed. *Mohavicchedani*. London: Pali Text Society, 1961.
Wells, K. E. *Thai Buddhism: Its Rites and Activities*. 3rd ed. Bangkok: AMS Press, 1974.
Welsch, Wolfgang. *Undoing Aesthetics*. London: Sage, 1997.
White, Allon. *Carnival, Hysteria, and Writing: Collected Essays and Autobiography*. Oxford: Oxford University Press, 1993.
White, Hayden. *Metahistory: The Historical Imagination in Nineteenth Century Europe*. Baltimore: Johns Hopkins University Press, 1973.
White, Richard. *Middleground*. Cambridge: Cambridge University Press, 1991.
Wilson, Constance M. "State and Society in the Reign of Mongkut, 1851–1868: Thailand on the Eve of Modernization." Ph.D. diss., Cornell University, 1970.
Wirawat Intaraporn. "The Dynamics of Khlong in Thai Literature." Paper presented at the Thai Language and Literature conference, Chulalongkorn University, Bangkok, November 12, 2006.
Wutichai Mulasilpa. *Kan patirup kanseuksa nai samai Phrapatsomdet Phra Chulachom Klao Khao Yu Hua*. Bangkok: Thai Wattana Panich, 2539 (1996).
Wuysthof, Geebard van. *Le Journal de voyage de G. van Wuysthoff et de ses assistants au Laos, 1641–1642* [The Journal of Geebard van Wusthof and His Assistants in Laos, 1641–1642]. Translated by Claude Lejosne. Brussels: Éditions Thanh-Long, 1986.
Wyatt, David. *The Nan Chronicle*. Ithaca, N.Y.: Cornell Studies on Southeast Asia, 1994.
———. *The Politics of Reform in Thailand: Education in the Reign of King Chulalongkorn*. New Haven, Conn.: Yale University Press, 1969.
———. *Siam in Mind*. Chiang Mai, Thailand: Silkworm, 2002.
———. *Studies in Thai History*. Chiang Mai, Thailand: Silkworm, 1994.

———. *Thailand: A Short History*. New Haven, Conn.: Yale University Press, 1984.

Wyatt, David, and Aroonrut Wichienkeeo. *The Chiang Mai Chronicle*. 2nd ed. Chiang Mai, Thailand: Silkworm, 1998.

Wynne, Alexander. "The Oral Transmission of Early Buddhist Literature." *Journal of the International Association of Buddhist Studies* 27, no. 1 (2004): 99–127.

Xaiyaphet Champhon. *Abhidhammatthasaṅgaha pae*. Vientiane, Laos: Institut bouddhique, 1968.

"Xivit lae phon ngan khong Than Achan Mahapan Ananto." *Lao Samay* 277 (1969): 1–4.

Zack, Stephen. "The Reform of Monastic Education under Prince Wachirayan Wororot." Ph.D. diss., Cornell University, 1977.

Zago, Marcello. *Rites et cérémonies en milieu bouddhiste Lao*. Rome: Universitá Gregoriana Editrice, 1972.

———. "Un bonze accuse!" *Pôle et tropiques*, June 1978, 131–42.

Index

Abhidhamma, the, 31, 135, 185, 248, 252; Abhidhamma Jotika handbook and, 241–45; applied, 228; Buddhist courses on, 11; and Buddhist philosophy, 11, 228–32, 236–38, 245; and funerary rites, 233, 236–43; in Laos, 238–39; the *mātikā* of, 230–31; drawn from, 37, 129–30; seven books of, 229–30; as spiritual "mother," 241. See also *Abhidhamma chet kamphi; Handbook for the Study of the Abhidhamma;* Tipiṭaka, the

Abhidhamma chet kamphi, 7; and funerary rites, 233, 235–41, 242–43, 244; and rebirth, 228; versions of, 233–34, 235–38, 240–41, 245. See also *Abhidhamma*, the

Abhidhamma Jotika. See *Handbook for the Study of the Abhidhamma*

Abhidhamma schools, 54, 56

Abhidhammatthasaṅgaha, the; as commentary on the Abihidhamma, 228, 229; and funerary rites, 236, 238, 242–43; in *Handbook for the Study of the Abhidhamma*, 241–42. *See also* Abhidhamma, the

Agyachulathera, Phra Maha, 75

ānisamsa (blessings), 7, 36, 187, 192

Anuson Bhuribhiwatanakhun, 185, 186

Appadurai, Arjun, 250

Association of Theravada Buddhist Universities, 258

Atthakathamātikā nissaya, 129–30, 153. See also *nissaya* manuscripts; pedagogical manuscripts; ritual texts

Atthasālinī, the, 135, 203, 229, 231–32

Atthasālinī-atthayojanā, the, 135, 203

Aung, Shwe Zan, 231

Aymonier, Etienne, 94

Ayutthaya, 13, 29, 72, 93, 139

Backus, Mary, 94

Bakhtin, Mikhail, 121, 127, 249. *See also* heteroglossia

Bang Chao, Phra, 29, 30, 32, 74

Bangkok, 44, 50, 188; as center of Buddhism, 80, 100, 107, 112, 218, 234; as center of Thai government, 92, 94, 95, 96, 108–9, 110, 113; monastic education in, 43, 65, 66, 67–68, 71, 106, 200, 238, 253, 254. *See also* Mahachulalongkorn Monastic University

Bassac, 43, 45. *See also* Champasak

Bassenne, Marthe, 26, 27, 46

Biggs, David, 9–10

Bizot, François, 47, 239–40

Blackburn, Anne, 192, 209

Block, Carl, 94

Bualy Paphaphanh, 65, 182

Buddha, the, 21, 29, 44; and the Abhidamma, 229, 231, 232, 233–34, 237, 238, 242; in images and relics, 32–33, 70–71, 74–75, 79, 81, 83, 124, 149;

Buddha *(continued)*
and the *jātaka*, 3–4, 36, 192, 215–16, 240–41; in manuscripts and source texts, 122–23, 128, 133, 140, 159, 167, 187, 188, 201; in modern Laos and Thailand, 219; in monastic education, 11, 13, 14, 35, 59, 60, 61, 180, 182, 254; monks as representative of, 180; Pali as language of, 126, 196, 200. *See also* Abhidhamma, the; Buddhism
Buddhadasa, 187
Buddhaghosa: descriptions of Buddhist literature, 186; Pali commentaries of, 158, 160, 201, 231; and *Three Baskets*, 14
Buddhasāsanāsubhāsit, 103, 248
Buddhasasana subhasit chabap matrathan, 174–75
Buddha Sihing, Phra, 74, 75. *See also* Wat Phra Singh
buddhavacaṇa, 196
Buddhavaṃsa, 72, 212, 215
Buddha Vipassī , 212, 213–14
Buddhavong Association (Samakhom Buddhavong): and Lao monastic education reform, 53–54; magazine, 54–55, 56
Buddhism: Bangkok and Chiang Mai as centers of, 69–76, 80, 100, 107, 111–12, 218, 234; as an "export product," 257–58; lack of unified study of, 85; in modern Thailand, 100; Mon tradition of, 40, 70, 72; struggle to define, 17; teaching, 120–21, 211–17. *See also* canon, Buddhist; Dhammapada, the; Lao Buddhism; monastic education; Siamese Buddhism; Thai Buddhism; Theravada Buddhism
Buddhist Youth School of Laos, 53, 54–55

calendrical rituals, 62, 199
canon, Buddhist, 6, 72, 106, 162, 180; defined, 197–98, 204; as fluid, 193–97; and interpretative communities, 9, 14–15; in Laos, 51–52, 163; in monastic education, 38, 105, 193–96, 214; and notion of "ritual canon," 191–92; in pedagogical texts, 21, 185, 187, 191–94, 198–99, 201–02, 249; "practical canon" and 14–15, 192; and royal reforms, 100, 102–3, 107; in sermons, 25, 192–93; Theravada, 194, 228, 230–31; Western influence on, 102, 194, 208. *See also* Buddhism; Lao Buddhism; Thai Buddhism; Tipiṭaka, the
Cariyapiṭaka, the, 215
chalong manuscripts, 37–38
Champasak, 39, 43, 60, 66
Chan Souk, Phra, 48–49, 50, 51
chanting: and the Abhidhamma, 233, 234–40, 242–43, 244; in monastic education, 11, 12, 29, 35, 47, 73, 84, 182; *nissaya* as guides in, 129, 132, 133–34; Pali in, 177, 181, 185; *roi kaeo*, 179; and the Royal Chanting Book, 234–35. *See also* orality
Cha, Phra Achan, 171, 173, 255
Chartier, Roger, 10–11
Cherniack, Susan, 146
C*het tamnan paritta* collection, 134. See also *paritta*
Chiang Mai, 30, 78, 128, 130, 188, 193, 254; as center of Buddhist education, 69–72, 73–76, 111, 112; monastic education in, 11, 18, 112, 195; and Siamese colonization, 93, 94, 95–96. *See also* Wat Chedi Luang; Wat Phra Singh; Wat Suan Dok
Chiang Mai University, 81, 114
Chiang Rai, 112, 173, 195
Chirapa, Maechi, 185
Chulalongkorn, King (Rama V): 96, 103, 137; and missionary support in Northern Thailand, 94; and monastic education reform, 100–2, 107,

108–9; and 1902 Sangha Act, 69, 99–100
Chulalongkorn University, 58, 171, 193, 256
Collins, Steven, 97–98, 201, 251, 252
colonialism, French: and effort to unite Indochine culture, 45, 48, 50; and historiography, 18, 25–27; and Lao Buddhism, 27, 40–51; Laos under, 26–27, 28–29, 38–51, 52–57, 63, 65, 67, 97, 108, 115, 221; monastic education during, 39–40, 46–47, 50–51. *See also* École française l'Extrême-Orient (EFEO); Institute Bouddhique
colophons, manuscript, 28, 33, 85, 211, 219; monastic history revealed in, 28, 33, 76–77, 84, 89–90, 148–49, 170, 224, 251; scribes of, 86–88, 90; orthography revealed in, 143–44; in Wat Sung Men collection, 79. *See also* pedagogical manuscripts
commentarial services, 150–53. *See also* commentaries; glossing; pedagogical methods; source texts
commentaries, 70, 72; and the Abhidhamma, 228, 229–31, 233; and the Dhammapada, 208–9, 210, 211–12, 217, 219, 223; intertextual nature of, 203–4; in modern texts, 173–76; and monastic education, 85, 103, 104; and Pali source texts, 37, 125, 129, 130, 133, 159, 175, 177, 200, 203, 214–15; in pedagogical manuscripts, 164, 197–98, 199–201, 204; and pedagogical methods, 150–54, 178–79; vernacular, 108, 160, 198, 208; and the vohāra genre, 131, 167–70, 182–83, 185–86; sermons as, 170–72. See also *nāmasadda*, *nissaya*, and *vohāra* genres; pedagogical manuscripts; sermons
Condominas, Georges, 57
curricular history, study of, 11–15, 20–21, 116, 119, 121–22, 202; and the canon, 192–93; interpretative communities in, 7–9, 97; and premodern v. modern perceptions of religious study, 18–19; "process geographies" in, 250–51; as study of "proximate mechanisms," 19, 58. *See also* heteroglossia; monastic education; *nāmasadda, nissaya*, and *vohāra* genres; pedagogical methods
Curtis, Lillian Johnson, 93

Dagenais, John, 147–48
Damrong, Prince, of Siam, 92–93, 101, 102, 108, 109–10
de Certeau, Michel, 10, 18
Dep, Luang Chao Phra Maha (Dhamma Sena Chao), 30
desanā. See sermons
Dhamma, the, 44, 82, 83, 103, 232
dhamma desanā (dhamma sermon), 88, 170
Dhammadesanā Biyakarakathā, Phra, 170
Dhammadesanā Dhammacārīkathā, Phra, 170
Dhammapada, the, 66, 133, 140, 161, 228; as the "Buddhist Bible," 220; and continuity in pedagogy, 226–27; modern v. premodern versions of, 221–23; in *nissaya* form, 210–11, 216, 221, 224; in sociohistorical context, 207–9, 217–20
Dhammapada-atthakathā, the, 36, 128, 143, 147, 161, 162; as commentary, 7, 103, 140; and pedagogy, 150, 152, 157; and textual vicissitudes, 208, 210, 215–18, 221–22
Dhammapada nāmasadda manuscripts, 216
Dhammapada nissaya manuscripts, 143, 211, 213; and orthography, 143; and pedagogy, 123, 147, 152, 153, 155–56, 216
Dhammapada vohāra manuscripts, 87, 130, 139, 216

Dhammapala, 158, 180, 201
Dhamma panyai, 177
Dhammasanganī, the: mātikā of, 130, 201, 229, 230–31, 240; in rituals, 235, 236–37, 239. *See also* Abhidhamma, the
Dhammaseuksa courses, 106, 112–13
Dibbamon nissaya, 130, 150
École française l'Extrême-Orient (EFEO), 40–45, 47, 50, 66. *See also* colonialism, French
École supérieure de Pâli, 40
Edwards, Penny, 47, 255
EFEO. *See* École française l'Extrême-Orient (EFEO)
elementary monastic schools *(rongrian pathom)*, 106. *See also* monastic schools
Emerald Buddha, the, 71, 74. *See also* Buddha, the
enlightenment, 99, 133; and the Abhidhamma, 240; four fruits of, 243; pursuit of, 17, 250
examination preparation handbooks, 163, 174–75

Faure, Bernard, 15
Finot, Louis, 14–15, 40–42
Foucault, Michel, 15, 16, 18
Fowler, Alastair, 165
Freeman, Rich, 199
French colonialism. *See* colonialism, French

Gabaude, Louis, 173
genres, pedagogical, 111; and evolution into modes, 165–66, 181. See also *nāmasadda, nissaya,* and *vohāra* genres; pedagogical manuscripts
Gethin, Rupert, 232
glossing: and the Dhammapada, 208, 211–17; and *hoi kaeo*, 178–79; in Lao texts, 176–77; *nissaya* and, 141–42, 198, 208; as pedagogical method, 150–51, 157–58; repetitive, 198, 215; secular texts and, 138–39; and sermons, 170–72, 223–24; translation and teaching through, 67, 91, 125–32, 135–36, 140, 163, 173–76, 179, 232; *vohāra* and, 139–40, 142, 176, 185–86. *See also* commentaries; *nissaya* manuscripts; Pali; pedagogical manuscripts; source texts; *vohāra* manuscripts; *yok sab*
grammatical texts, 128, 129–30, 247. *See also* pedagogical manuscripts; source texts
Gunn, Geoffrey, 53

Halpern, Joel, 53
Handbook for the Study of the Abhidhamma, 241–45
Hansen, Anne, 47, 255
Harlan, David, 209
Hartmann, John, 173
Hartzell, Jessie MacKinnon, 94
heteroglossia, process of, 121–22
Hinayana Buddhism, 44, 45, 66
historiography in religious education, 18–19, 80, 96
hoi kaeo, 178–79, 180
homiletics: the Dhammapada and, 217; and epistemological links, 97; in pedagogical manuscripts, 10; *vohāra* in modern Thai, 169–70, 182–83
homilies, 123–24, 125. *See also* sermons

Institut bouddhique, 42–45, 47, 49–50, 66. *See also* colonialism, French
Internet use, 68, 114, 177, 255, 257
interpretative communities: as borderless, 97; curriculum and, 7–8; defined through manuscript genres, 9; and interpretative process, 16–17, 248, 250; and texts, 12–15, 158, 160; and textual-oral interaction, 10–11
Ishii, Yoneo, 100, 102, 107–8

Jackson, J. B., 9–10
jātaka, 11, 13, 102, 149, 182, 196, 199, 200; as birth stories of Buddha, 3–4, 36, 192, 215–16; in comic books, 174; illuminations from, 240–41; in libraries, 192; *nidāna*, 212, 213; as teaching tools, 128–29
Jātaka-atthakathā, 103
Jātaka-nidāna, 3
Jit Bhumisak, 187
Johnson, William, 9, 145–46

Kaccāyanavyākaraṇa, the, 135–36, 192, 196
Kammavācā, 36, 53, 89, 125, 133, 148, 187, 192. *See also* ritual texts
Kammavācā nissaya nāmasadda, 129, 130
Kamphira, Phra Chao, 75
Karaṇīyametta sutta, 134
Karpelès, Suzanne, 41, 42
Kawila, King, 75. *See also* Wat Phra Singh
Kesarapañño, Mahāthera, 80, 82–84, 86, 87, 255
Keyes, Charles, 93, 191, 192
Khoen: monks, 70, 71, 178; source texts, 80, 84, 119, 144
Krishna Charoenwong, 94
Krupa Kañcana, 84, 86, 87, 89, 111; as local hero, 79–80; manuscript collection, 77, 78–79; and monastic education history, 80; at Wat Phra Singh, 75–76. *See also* Wat Sung Men
Krupa Sri Wichai, 74, 101
Kupa Thammayano, 52, 60
kuṭi (monastic cell), 17, 29, 133, 214, 247

Lampang: monasteries in, 81, 87, 112, 186; monastic education in, 18, 78, 195–96; relics in, 74
languaging, process of, 5–6, 98, 162, 187–90, 248. *See also* Pali
Lan Na (Northern Thailand), 33, 69, 95; political history, 92–93,105; Siam control of, 95, 163
Lao Buddhism: and the Abhidhamma, 238–39; American anticommunism and, 53; canon, 51–52, 163; under communism, 52–53, 57–60, 63–64, 248; under French, 27, 40–51, 108; government guidelines for religion and, 60–62, 63; and modern/premodern dichotomy, 19–20, 98; and monastic education, 37, 127–28, 145, 176–78; in post-French era, 52–57; in precolonial era, 28–38; revealed in manuscripts, 28, 119; in rural Laos, 67; today, 64–68. *See also* colonialism, French; pedagogical manuscripts
Lao Front for National Construction (LFNC), 60–61, 62
Lao Ministry of Education, 5
Lao Patriotic Front. *See* Pathet Lao
Lao People's Democratic Republic, 57, 60. *See also* Pathet Lao
Lao Sangha, 30, 43, 45, 55, 134; under communism, 52–53, 57, 59, 60; under French, 46–47; government guidelines affecting, 62–63
Lefèvre, Emile, 25, 28, 34, 38
legends: significance of, 76–78, 84, 214; of rural monasteries, 78–83. *See also* Wat Lai Hin; Wat Sung Men
Le May, Reginald, 94
Leria, Giovanni-Marie, Father, 34–37, 46, 66
Leuam Thamxot, 56
Leu influences: 5, 33, 70, 84, 119, 143, 144, 178
libraries, monastic, 36, 66, 70, 77, 122, 162, 178; and collection at Vat Mai, 31; and collection at Vat Ong Teu, 66; and collection at Wat Lai Hin, 80–81; and collection at Wat Sung Men, 79, 80; description of, 149; historiography revealed in, 84–85, 191–93; secular manuscripts at, 85–86

"lifting words." See *yok sab*
Lokabhāsā nissaya, 130, 152
Luang Pho Krupa Kamphirasan, 78
Luang Phrabang, 32, 47, 48, 73, 177, 188; French in, 38–39, 51; as Lan Xang center, 71, 72; manuscripts from, 89, 90, 147, 150, 152, 155, 170; monastic education in, 18, 25, 29, 31, 62, 66, 78
Luang Phu Sompun, 172
Luang Ta Mahabua, 170–71

Madhurāsajambu nissaya, the, 130, 150, 153, 157
Mahābharata, 16, 215–16
Mahābuddhaguna, 241
Mahachulalongkorn Monastic University, 53, 74, 100, 104, 112, 161, 183, 257; Abhidhamma Jotika College at, 185, 241; curriculum, 66, 111, 189; Pali Grammar Research Institute, 186; and royal reforms, 113
Mahamakut Monastic University, 71, 100, 104, 111–13, 115
Mahanikaya monasteries, 107, 112
Mahapan Anantho, Phra, 53, 55, 63, 252
Maha Sichantho, 30, 31
Mahayana Buddhism, 44
Maṇḍapakaraṇa nissaya, 130
Maṅgala sutta, the, 134, 157, 196
Mangalatthadīpanī yok sab plae, 166
mātikā, the, 130–31, 135, 201, 237, 241–42; in funerary rites, 241–42; as "mother," 232–33, 239–40; significance of, 230–31, 237. *See also* Abhidhamma, the; *Dhammasanganī*, the
Matory, Lorand, 19
Matthakundalīvatthu, the, 140
McGilvary, Daniel, 93
McHale, Shawn, 115
meditation, 7, 11, 14, 28, 54, 55, 107, 222, 240, 252–53, 254
Meṇḍaka, 156
Miles, Malcolm, 249
Ministry of Education, 109
Mission Pavie, 26, 79
modernity, 19–20, 65, 97–99, 100, 241, 248–49
Mohavicchedanī, the, 135, 203, 229, 231, 232
monasteries: 107, 112; number of, 106; as ritual centers through possession of images and relics, 74–75; royal, 110; rural, 76–77, 82–83, 105, 109–10. *See also* individual monastery *entries*; libraries, monastic; monastic education
monastic education: in Bangkok, 43, 65, 66, 67–68, 71, 106, 200, 238, 253, 254; the Buddha in, 11, 13, 14, 35, 59, 60, 61, 180, 182, 254; canon in, 193–97; career choices, 114; in Chiang Mai, 11, 18, 112, 195; curricular approach to study of, 20, 21, 116, 119, 121–22, 248, 250–51; Dhammapada in, 210–11, 217, 221, 224; epistemology in study of, 10, 27–28, 96–97, 122, 166, 241, 245, 250; examination systems, 247–48, 254; under French, 28–29, 38–51, 115; and Internet usage, 68, 114, 177, 255, 257; meditation in, 252–53; modern curricula, 182–86, 256–58; modern texts in, 173–78, 180–81; and nation building, 18; oral tradition in, 12–13, 36, 162–64, 179, 202, 222, 252; Pali language classes, 91; and pedagogical historiography, 17–19, 27–28, 52, 108, 120–21; premodern, 31, 32, 34–36, 127–29, 140; recent scholarship in, 15–16; and royal reform, 99–101, 108–9, 110–11, 113; and sectarianism, 253–54; textual production in, 84–85; women in, 251. *See also* monastic schools;

monastic universities; pedagogical methods
monastic schools: defined, 28; elementary (*rongrian pathom)*, 106; Pariyatidhamma (secondary), 11, 18, 106, 111, 113; premodern, 84; statistics on, 106. *See also* monastic universities
monastic universities: contemporary, 114, 256, 257; curricula at, 115, 249; and ritual legitimacy, 74; and royal reforms, 103, 104, 110, 111–12; statistics on, 105–6, 113
Mongkut, King (Rama IV), 100
monks, as teachers, 134, 181–82
Mon sect, 40, 70, 72, 121, 138, 144, 207
mulberry-leaf manuscripts, 38

nak dham examinations, 103, 107, 111, 113
Nāma nissaya, 130, 152
nāmasadda manuscripts: characteristics of, 131, 135–37, 142; physical features of, 146, 148–49; repetition and reinforcement in, 154–58; as "sermons," 170; as source texts, 127–31, 135–37; storage of, 149; syntactical structures of, 154–55; translation/commentary in, 169. See also *nissaya* manuscripts; pedagogical manuscripts; pedagogical methods; *vohāra* manuscripts
nāmasadda, *nissaya*, and *vohāra* genres: contemporary knowledge of, 181–87; as curricular canon, 190, 192–93, 199; disappearance of, 162–64, 166; pedagogical function of, 120, 122–27, 150–60, 167, 178–79; as record of instruction, 119–20; and rural monastic education, 80; and textual-oral interaction, 6, 8, 10–11, 19, 21, 29, 155, 158, 162, 192–93, 204, 222–27, 244–45; in the vernacular landscape, 9–10, 19–20, 199–200; *yok sab* method in, 131, 166. *See also* commentaries
Ñānakitti, Phra, 72, 201, 204
nangseu plae (translations), 163
Nantha, Phra Chao, 75
National Monastic College of Laos, 64, 65–66. *See also* Vat Ong Teu
nation building: and monastic education, 18; and religious reform, 100, 116
nidāna, the, 4, 135, 215
Nisai sūtra manta, 133–34. See also *nissaya* manuscripts
Nissaya atthakathā mātikā, 228, 230–32. *See also* Abhidhamma, the
nissaya, defined, 132–33
nissaya manuscripts: and chanting, 129, 132, 133–34; characteristics of, 131, 132, 135, 139–40, 141–42, 146–49, 161–62, 164, 249; and commentary, 169, 198–99, 200; and the Dhammapada, 123, 143, 147, 152, 153, 155–56, 210–11, 213, 216, 221, 224; as guides to oral homilies, 125; and *hoi kaeo* poetry, 179; as pedagogical texts, 131–33; repetition and reinforcement in, 134, 154–58; as "sermons," 170, 181; and source texts, 131–34, 157, 185–87, 200–201, 224; storage of, 149; syntactical structures of, 154–55. *See also* commentaries; *nāmasadda* manuscripts; pedagogical manuscripts; *vohāra* manuscripts
Nissaya mātikātthakathā, 90
nissaya mode, 173, 181
nissaya nāma, 153
nissaya-sampanno, 132
Nithan Khun Borom, the, 30, 36
Nithan Thammabot, the 7, 196, 223–24
Norman, K. R., 231
nuns, in Laos, 62

O'Brien O'Keeffe, Katherine, 147, 148
Ong Teu, Phra, 74
orality: in Laos, 66, 145; as monastic tradition, 12–13, 36, 37, 162–64, 179–

orality *(continued)*
80, 202, 231–32, 252; and textual-oral interaction, 6, 8, 10–11, 19, 21, 29, 155, 158, 162, 192–93, 204, 216–17, 222–27, 244–45; and translation, 213–17. *See also* chanting; glossing; pedagogical manuscripts, premodern; pedagogical methods; sermons
ordination, 47, 115–16, 129; lineages, 253–55
orientalism, 27, 41, 42, 45, 50, 97
orthography, 143–46. *See also* colophons, manuscript; pedagogical manuscripts, premodern
Oskar, von Hinüber, 231

Paksé Province, 38–39, 43, 62
Pali, 138; in Buddhist education, 120–21, 248; canonical texts, 192, 196, 248; in chanting, 177, 181, 185; and glossing, 67, 91, 129–32, 163, 173–76, 179; grammar texts, 173–74; in historical manuscripts, 119, 126–27; and *hoi kaeo*, 178–79, 180; as the language of the Buddha, 126, 196, 200; languaging of, 5–6, 187–90, 248; language study, 50, 91, 176; and modern monastic education, 97–98; and orthography, 143–45; and *roi kaeo*, 179–80; schools, 41, 42, 47–48. See also *nāmasadda* manuscripts; *nissaya* manuscripts; pedagogical manuscripts, premodern; source texts; *vohāra* manuscripts; *yok sab*
Pali Grammar Research Institute, 186
Paliseuksa, 113. *See also* Pali
Pali Text Society, 41, 42, 196
palm-leaf manuscripts, 66, 70, 82, 119, 135, 144, 197, 225; dimensions of, 161; efforts to preserve, 62–63; in Laos, 38, 40; in teaching Pali, 29; in textual and philological research, 122–23, 203, 222–23. *See also* pedagogical manuscripts, premodern
Paññāsa jātaka nissaya, the, 37, 129, 157, 196
parian examinations, 103, 107, 111, 113
paritta (protective mantras), 134, 248
Pariyatidhamma secondary schools, 106, 111, 113
Pathet Lao, 52, 57–59, 60
Paṭimokkha (monastic disciplinary code), 30, 124, 187
pedagogical manuscripts, premodern, 28, 87, 146, 191; the Buddha in, 122–23, 128, 133, 140, 159, 167, 180, 188; and canon, 21, 185, 187, 191–94, 198–99, 201–2, 249; commentaries in, 164, 197–198, 199, 204; and glossing, 124–28, 150–51, 157–58; as grammatical texts, 128, 129–30, 247; homiletics in, 10, 169–70, 182–83; intertextual nature of, 199–200, 204; and oral tradition, 6, 8, 10–11, 19, 21, 29, 154–56, 162, 163–64, 192–93, 204, 217, 222–27, 244–45; orthography of, 143–46; rhetorical style of, 154–58, 164; ritual texts as, 31–32, 36, 42, 125, 127–30; and source texts, 131–46, 152, 157, 166–67, 185–87, 200–201, 224; tracing social history of, 120–21; and transition to modern handbooks, 162, 163, 166. See also *nāmasadda* manuscripts; *nissaya* manuscripts; pedagogical methods; *vohāra* manuscripts
pedagogical methods, 13–14; and the Abhidhamma, 245; commentarial services as, 120, 151–54; continuity over time, 241, 248; and the Dhammapada, 150, 152, 157, 210–11, 216, 221, 224; and discourse on tradition and modernity, 248–49; examination systems, 247–48; *hoi kaeo*, 178–79, 180; and institutional

reform, 63; and narratives as teaching tools, 128–29; *yok sab* as, 7–8, 166, 202–3, 226, 247. *See also* commentarial services; commentaries; glossing
Pe Maung Tin, 231–32
Petavatthu-atthakathā, the, 140
Phan Tao, Phra, 75
Phaya Kaeo, 72
Phaya Keu Anasong, 71–72. *See also* Wat Suan Dok
Phayom, Phra, 171, 173
Phnom Penh, 26, 42, 43, 44, 45, 47–48, 49–50
phochananukhrom (dictionaries), 163
Phongsavadan Muang Luang Phrabang, 28
Phothisarat, King, 30, 31, 62, 66. *See also* Vat Vixun
Phrae, 113, 148, 174; manuscripts from, 216, 235–36; monasteries in, 78, 79, 112, 139, 182, 183; relics in, 74; Shan Rebellion in, 95
Phra Lak Phra Ram, 37
Phraya Upakit Silapasan, 169, 170
Phu Si Hill (Luang Phrabang), 29
"practical canon," 14–15, 192
prayer, 6, 7, 15, 47, 53, 88, 129, 133, 174, 176, 181, 199
prayok examinations, 54, 103
Pricha Changkhwanyeun, 167–69
"proximate mechanisms," 19, 158

Rama VI, King, 187
Rama IX, King, 187
Rāmayāna, 37, 149
Ratanapañña, Phra, 72
Ratana sutta, 134
rhetorical style, 154–58, 164
"ritual canon," notion of, 191–92
ritual texts: in Laos, 42; in premodern monastic education, 31, 32, 36, 127–28; as source texts, 125, 127–29. *See also* pedagogical manuscripts, premodern; source texts
Robinson, Fred, 146, 148
roi kaeo, 179–80
rongrian pathom (primary schools), 106. *See also* monastic schools
Royal Chanting Book, 234

Saccasaṅkhepa nissaya, the, 157–58
Sakuṇa nissaya, 130
Sangha Act (1902), 69, 99–103, 105–7, 110–11
San kuo chi (Three Kingdoms), 16
Sansanee Sathirasut, Maechi, 171
Sanskrit: 41, 66, 121; in glosses, 138–39; and interplay between classical and vernacular, 160, 187–88, 215–16; language classes today, 64, 65; and translation culture, 189, 190; and *vohāra*, 137. *See also* Pali
Saraswati Ongsakun, 72
Satharana Pasason Pathet Lao. *See* Pathet Lao
Sathouk, 25–26, 28. *See also* Vat Mai
Sattaparitta, the, 127, 128, 130, 133
Savannakhet, 39, 53, 251; Buddhist education in, 13, 18, 62, 66, 78, 209, 221
scribes, 180, 203; and colophons, 84, 88–91, 131, 149; creativity of, 15, 80; and *nissaya* manuscripts, 131; and orthography, 143–45, 146; training and background of, 86–87; and *vohāra* manuscripts, 137, 139–40
Seng Ngonevongsa, 182
sermons (*desanā*), 216; canon in, 25, 192–93; and glossing, 170–72, 223–24; and homilies, 123–24, 125; modern, 256; and premodern pedagogical texts, 128, 169–71, 181
Seven Books of the Abhidhamma. See *Abhidhamma chet kamphi*
Shan: language, 119, 144, 258; manuscripts, 134, 145; monks, 70, 71, 178; region, 33, 40, 92. *See also* Theravada Buddhism

Siam: colonization by, 92–96; monastic education reforms, 69, 97–104. *See also* Chulalongkorn, King; Sangha Act (1902); Thai Buddhism
Siamese Buddhism, 102, 255
Siao Savat, 37
Sila Viravong, 5, 50, 65, 66
Sinhala language, 160
Sirimaṅgala, 187, 201
Sirimaṅgala, Phra, 72
Somdet Phra Buddhachinorot Sakonmahasanghapamokkha, 51
source texts: the Abhidhamma volumes as, 229; and canon, 193–95; and handbooks and guides, 174–76; *nāmasadda* manuscripts and, 135–37; *nissaya* manuscripts and, 131–34, 157, 185–87, 200–201, 224; and pedagogy, 152, 193; in premodern curricula, 127–31, 152, 193, 202–3; ritual texts as, 125, 127–29; and sermons, 223–24; sociohistoric revelations in, 13–14, 17; vernacular texts as 127–29, 140; *vohāra* manuscripts and, 137–46, 166–67, 185–86, 224. See also *nāmasadda*, *nissaya*, and *vohāra* genres; pedagogical manuscripts, premodern
Stuart-Fox, Martin, 58, 60
Sudodhamma, King, 73
Sumana, Phra, 70, 71–72, 73, 79, 81, 253
Surinyavong, King, 33. *See also* Vat Ong Teu
Sutmon nissaya, 128, 129, 130, 157. *See also* ritual texts
Sutthithamrangsi Khamphiramethachan, Phra, 56
Swearer, Donald, 250

Taillard, Christian, 57
Tamnan Phra Bang, 28
textbooks, modern monastic, 173–78. *See also* pedagogical methods
textual-oral interaction, 6, 8, 10–11, 19, 21, 29, 155, 158, 162, 192–93, 204, 222–27, 244–45. *See also* orality; pedagogical manuscripts, premodern; *vohāra* manuscripts
Thai Buddhism, 18, 119, 128, 158, 173, 208–9, 241, 256; under Burmese, 70; centralized structure, 100; and government reforms, 103–7, 115–16, 221; in Internet age, 257–58; and Lao translations, 55–56; and modern monastic education, 105–16, 253; and modern/premodern dichotomy, 19–20, 97–98, and rural monasteries, 76–77; and the Sangha Act of 1902, 69, 99–101, 105–6; sectarianism in, 253–54; and Siam rule, 92–96, 97–104; and translation culture, 187; Western influence on, 101–2
Thai Buddhist Sangha, 101
Thammayut monasteries, 105, 107, 111, 112
Tham script, 35, 50, 59, 63, 245; in contemporary monastic education, 161, 181, 182; in Laos, 45, 46, 53; and orthography, 143; reading, 146
tham vat xao, 47
tham vat yen, 47, 124
Thao Hung Thao Chuang, 37, 192
Tha Phra Chan Press, 166
Thavat Buddhasāsanā latthi Hinayan (The Foundations of Hinayana Buddhism), 66
Theravada Buddhism, 29, 50, 63, 138, 195, 237–38, 258; canon, 228, 229–30; Mon-influenced, 40
Thong Di (Phra Thammapanya), 47–48, 51
Thongchai Winichakul, 95, 96
Tilokarat, King, 70, 72
Tipiṭaka, the, 15, 30–31, 32, 72, 111; in the Abhidhamma, 229; in Cambodia, 44–45, 50; and communication

technology, 257; defined, 193–95, 197; in Laos, 48–49, 51–52; in Siam, 75–76; *Three Baskets*, 14, 193. *See also* canon, Buddhist
Todorov, Tzvetan, 165
translation culture, 187–90. *See also* Pali
Tripidok sabap Lao, Phra, 51

van Wuysthoff, Gerrit, 33–34
Vat Chan, 45
Vat Chanthabuli, 54
Vat Don Khong, 66–67
Vat Inpeng, 31–34, 37
Vat Mai, 25–26, 28–29, 31, 48, 51, 86, 193
Vat Manoram, 30, 31
Vat Mixai, 37
Vat Nakon Noi, 56
Vat Na Son, 62–63
Vat Naxai, 37, 91, 181
Vat Nom Lam Chan, 66, 67
Vat Ong Teu, 50, 86, 91, 176, 193, 220; as Buddhist educational center, 64–68; under communism, 59–60; history of, 32–35; library at, 66; manuscript collection at, 37–38; National Monastic College of Laos at, 64, 65–66; Sangha Monastic College at, 50
Vat Paluang, 55, 56
Vat Sisaket, 43, 45, 176
Vat Unnalom, 48
Vat Vixun, 29–31, 32, 86
Vat Xainyaphum, 3, 5, 6, 7, 68, 91
vernacular texts, 42, 84, 85–86; and curriculum, 16; in premodern monastic education, 32, 35, 36; as source texts, 127–29, 140. *See also* pedagogical manuscripts, premodern; source texts
Vessantara jātaka, 12, 16, 37, 82, 129, 139, 179, 240
Vientiane, 42, 62, 66; monasteries in, 31–34, 37, 54, 56, 62, 66; Siamese armies in, 31–32. *See also* Vat Inpeng; Vat Ong Teu
Vimānavatthu-atthakathā, the, 140
Vinaya, the, 31, 43, 101, 103, 130, 132
vipassanā meditation, 54, 55, 252, 254
Vipassī Buddha, 212, 213
Visuddhimagga, the, 47, 103, 130, 192, 248
Vixun, King, 29, 30. *See also* Vat Vixun
vohāra, defined, 137
vohāra manuscripts: characteristics of, 131, 136–42, 161–62, 164; and commentary, 198–99; and the Dhammapeda, 87, 130, 139, 216; and *hoi kaeo* poetry, 179; modern, 167–70; and oratory, 137–39, 166–70, 179, 181; physical features of, 146, 148–49; repetition and reinforcement in, 139, 154, 157–58; and sermons, 169–70; and source texts, 137–46, 166–67, 185–86, 224; storage of, 149; syntactical structures of, 154–55. See also *nāmasadda* manuscripts; *nāmasadda, nissaya,* and *vohāra* genres; *nissaya* manuscripts; pedagogical manuscripts, premodern
vohāra mode, 164–66, 176, 178, 181

Wachirayan, Prince, 65, 99, 101, 107, 218, 248; and Buddhist education reform, 102–4, 108; and Mahamakut Monastic University, 111; and rural monastery reforms, 109–10
Wat Boworniwet, 104, 166
Wat Chedi Luang, 69–70, 74, 91; as Buddhist education center, 111–12; as ritual and cosmic center of Chiang Mai, 71. *See also* Chiang Mai
Wat Lai Hin, 81–83
Wat Luang Pa Chang Haripunchai, 81
Wat Mahathat, 54, 91, 111

Wat Phra Singh, 70, 79, 91, 166; under Burmese, 75; and dissemination of Buddhist materials, 111; library at, 75–76; in post-Burmese period, 74–75
Wat Phra Thatchomgiri, 136
Wat Phra That Haripunchai, 166
Wat Rakhang (Khositaram), 54, 91, 161, 174
Wat Sri Chum, 79, 87, 182
Wat Suan Dok, 69–70, 75, 91, 183; under Burmese, 73; as center of Buddhist education, 71–74, 111, 112
Wat Sung Men, 77–79, 80, 140. *See also* Krupa Kañcana; legends
Welsch, Wolfgang, 249
Western influence: and modernity, 97, 98; on monastic education, 38; on Thai Buddhism, 101–2, 241
women, 251
Wyatt, David, 100, 102, 107–8

Xiang Khoang, 39, 79
Xin Sai, 36, 37, 192

yok sab (lifting words), 3, 138–39, 170–73, 181, 196, 215, 233, 237; learning Pali through, 106, 183; pedagogical manuscripts and, 130–31, 247; pedagogical method and, 7–8, 202–3, 226; and sermons, 223–24, 235; in textbooks and guides, 175–76, 177; and translation, 157, 161, 166, 188. *See also* commentaries; glossing; *nāmasadda*, *nissaya*, and *vohāra* genres; pedagogical manuscripts, premodern; pedagogical methods
Younghusband, George, 94

www.ingramcontent.com/pod-product-compliance
Lightning Source LLC
Chambersburg PA
CBHW030603230426
43661CB00053B/1830
9780295988498